Reflecting on India's Development

National Institute of Labour Economics Research
and Development (NILERD)
Editor

Reflecting on India's Development

Employment, Skill and Health

Springer

Editor
National Institute of Labour Economics
Research and Development (NILERD)
Delhi, India

ISBN 978-981-13-4630-9 ISBN 978-981-13-1414-8 (eBook)
https://doi.org/10.1007/978-981-13-1414-8

This Springer imprint is published by the registered company Springer Nature Singapore Pte Ltd.
The registered company address is: 152 Beach Road, #21-01/04 Gateway East, Singapore 189721, Singapore

Preface

National Institute of Labour Economics Research and Development (NILERD) (formerly, Institute of Applied Manpower Research) under the aegis of NITI Aayog (formerly, Planning Commission) was set up way back in 1962. In the area of labour market research, particularly in relation to human capital development and growth of the informal sector, the Institute's pioneering role has been documented significantly. At present, given the changing scenario, especially post-globalization, the Institute's focus lies on a huge spectrum of development issues, locating labour in a larger context and relating it to the dynamics of overall growth and development. The Institute has expanded its research to encompass growth and inequality issues, rural–urban development diversities and migration patterns, efficacies of industry-led growth, human capital formation and the role of manpower in the context of inclusive growth, functioning of the labour market, interlinks between the formal and informal sectors, labour reforms, employment and manpower projection, social concerns including caste and gender dimensions, and health, sanitation and water-related issues. Monitoring and evaluation of several government flagship programmes comprise a key component of research conducted by the Institute.

The other activity which is pursued very vibrantly at the Institute includes the international and national training programmes on various themes related to human capital issues and monitoring and evaluation methods and analysis. From a number of developing countries, middle- and senior-level government officers participate in these training programmes and benefit enormously from the rich experience of the Indian economy. The state government officers have also shown their keenness in the training programmes.

The Institute organized a workshop during 15–16 March 2018 in collaboration with International Labour Organization (ILO) at the India Habitat Centre, Lodhi Road, New Delhi, on a number of research questions. It primarily dealt with three important aspects: (a) growth, employment and inequality issues, (b) education and skill and (c) social concerns, health and empowerment. The first theme reflects on inclusiveness with a specific reference to growth–employment relationship, regional inequality aspect, structural transformation issues and rural–urban disparities in terms of consumption indicators. The second theme covers skill development efforts in higher education to fulfil the objective of "Make in India" programme, skill crisis in the organized sector in some of the industrialized parts of the country, frontline technologies and knowledge support for the farmers being transferred from laboratory to land, the impact of education disparity on wages and employment across space (rural and urban areas) and targets and gaps of some of the flagship programmes such as Sarva Shiksha Abhiyan. The papers under the third theme focus on gender inequality and ways of empowerment, social inequality with a special reference to the tribal population and their development, reproductive health and sanitation programmes. All these studies reflect on India's development and bring out policy implications.

Our sincere thanks are due to our knowledge partner ILO. In particular, we owe a lot to Dr. Sher Verick and Dr. Noman Majid of ILO. Chairs and discussants of the sessions who offered enormous amount of academic support and research comments on the papers presented deserve a special mention: Prof. Rajesh Chadha, Dr. Mohan Chutani, Prof. Nilabja Ghosh, Prof. B. N. Goldar, Dr. Nomaan Majid, Dr. Veena Naregal and Prof. J. B. G. Tilak; and Dr. Ankush Agrawal, Dr. Bornali Bhandari, Dr. Debkusum Das, Dr. William Joe, Dr. Seema Joshi, Dr. Debolina Kundu and Dr. Amarnath Tripathi. Without the full-fledged cooperation of NILERD faculty, this project could not have been successful. The administration extended support services at every stage. Ms. Dipika Sen's editorial help formed the backbone of this endeavour. We would like to place on record our sincere gratitude to NITI Aayog for inculcating confidence in us.

Based on the papers presented in the workshop, NILERD brings out a volume published by Springer. We express our sincere gratitude to Springer, especially Ms. Sagarika Ghosh and Ms. Nupoor Singh.

Delhi, India

Arup Mitra
DG, NILERD

About the Institution

National Institute of Labour Economics Research and Development (NILERD) which was formerly known as Institute of Applied Manpower Research is an autonomous Institute under NITI Aayog, Government of India. More than half a century old, the Institute has expanded the scope of its work in all spheres of evidence-based empirical research with a special focus on the evaluation of various flagship programmes and schemes of the union and state governments. Building synthesis of secondary information emanating from data generating/disseminating agencies, and establishing empirical linkages among skill development, growth, employment, productivity, investments and technology are some of the research priorities of the Institute. Besides, primary survey-based research is pursued to address policy issues with profoundness. NILERD also carved a niche by developing competencies and training programmes in the areas of public policy, capacity development, monitoring and evaluation, and human resource development for the officers of state governments and the middle-level officers from developing countries across the globe under ITEC (Indian Technical and Economic Cooperation) programmes.

Contents

Introduction

India's economic development since 1991 has crossed several milestones, but at the same time, it has been staggering on certain other fronts. Economic growth has been quite impressive in some of the phases though the dips consequent to some of the international phenomena, such as financial crisis, and radical policy changes in the domestic economy like demonetization, are significantly noticeable. In fact, India is now believed to grow faster than China in the next thirty years.[1] Timely corrective actions have enabled the economy to recover fast though growing global risks envisaged in terms of increasing oil prices and the possibility of capital outflows are alarming.[2] Among the four major drivers of growth—public expenditure, consumption, private investment and net exports—at least the first three have shown up.[3] However, the growth story is not sufficient to make India shine in the world map. A number of key indicators of development and the inclusive aspect of growth are still lagging behind. Though some of the states, particularly in the eastern India, have done remarkably well in terms of doing business index, the progress on human development index in these states is yet to come.[4] Even economic reforms in certain areas have been sluggish. For example, some of the states have been slow in implementing market reforms for agriculture to benefit.[5]

In the backdrop of the issues related to development in India, the National Institute of Labour Economics Research and Development (NILERD, formerly IAMR) organized a workshop in collaboration with ILO focusing primarily on three important aspects: (a) growth, employment and regional inequality issues, (b) education and skill and (c) social concerns, empowerment and health. The present

[1]https://www.financialexpress.com/economy/india-gdp-to-grow-at-9-heres-why-rajiv-kumar-thinks-it-can-become-a-reality-soon/1176918.

[2]https://www.financialexpress.com/budget/india-economic-survey-2018-arvind-subramanian-says-economic-revival-underway-4-key-takeaways/1034552/.

[3]https://qz.com/1218116/bibek-debroy-thinks-indias-economy-can-surely-grow-at-7-5-in-fiscal-2019/.

[4]https://economictimes.indiatimes.com/news/economy/policy/need-for-india-to-do-well-on-human-development-index-amitabh-kant/articleshow/63915354.cms.

[5]https://www.smartindianagriculture.com/niti-aayogs-ramesh-chand-wants-agricultural-marketing-in-concurrent-list/.

volume compiles the revised version of the papers presented in the workshop in March 2018.

Under Part I, the chapter by Kumar, Mitra and Pandey revisits the issue of elasticity of employment with respect to growth. Since employment data are not available on annual basis, the existing estimates are limited in nature. In order to generate time series data on employment, the chapter uses the cross-sectional data on organized sector employment provided by DGET (Ministry of Labour and Employment). After deducting the organized sector employment from the total employment calculated for the years for which NSS employment–unemployment surveys are available, the residual is designated as the unorganized sector employment. In the next step, the cross-sectional elasticity of unorganized sector employment with respect to various components of the organized sector employment is estimated. Based on these estimates and given the time series information on organized sector employment, the total unorganized sector employment is predicted for the in-between years for which the NSS figures are not available. The growth–employment relationship is then visited in both the time series framework and a simultaneous equation framework. With regard to the former, the impulse response function and variance decomposition exercises allow us to assess the sensitivity of employment in relation to growth shocks and vice versa. Findings tend to suggest that growth does not impact largely on employment at least in comparison with the effect of employment on growth. However, in the simultaneous equation model after correcting for endogeneity, the employment elasticity of growth turns out to be much higher than what is usually observed. Finally, the policy implications of the results are drawn.

The chapter by Kumar, Pandey Wordsworth and Chauhan looks at the regional aspects of growth, particularly in relation to the MSME sector which is indeed considered to be the key to industrial growth and employment generation across space. Historically, capital investment and employment generation were found to be positively correlated. This tendency was found in first, second and third censuses while making a comparative assessment of states in India. This meant that the states with more capital investment had more employment and those with less investment had less employment. However, in the fourth census, there was a deviation from the above trend as the states had differential patterns of growth and concentration of employment and investment per enterprise. There were states with more capital investment share but less employment share and vice versa. Variables such as employment intensity per unit, labour productivity, capital intensity measured as the ratio of capital share to working unit share, and capital–labour ratio are considered to understand the overall convergence/divergence across the states. Determinants of convergence/divergence are also looked into, and finally, policy recommendations are drawn in the light of the findings.

The chapter by Yadav, Singh and Joseph looks at the structural transformation in terms of both value-added composition and occupational structure and reflects on productivity differentials across sectors in various Indian states. How the population shift (rural–urban) is linked to the structural transformation, educational attainment and labour reforms is an important aspect of this study. It is observed from the analysis that the growth rates have been widely fluctuating on yearly basis. Further, the growth rates have been negative for four years which could be attributed to the three wars India fought with China and Pakistan and another being the draught year. This has been true for the plan-wise growth rates as well. As far as the shares of GDP are concerned, it is changing faster from agriculture to industry and also to the services sector. This is also quite similar in the case of the states as has been observed. Though the share of employment is changing in a similar manner, it is relatively at a slower pace. Indeed, it is because of this reason that the productivity relatives are keeping low in the agriculture and higher in the industry as well as the services sector. It is in fact the highest for the services sector. The correlation matrix shows that agriculture is negatively related to most of the variables, while the other two sectors are positively associated with them. As far as the story of urbanization is concerned, it seems to have been faster in those states where industrialization and literacy rates are higher. The chapter has also made an effort to relate the sectoral shift with that of labour reforms. It has been found that where the labour reforms have been accepted, the sectoral shifts are also higher. If we go further, we may also say that in those states where urbanization is higher, the shifts in state domestic product are also higher and these states also followed the labour reforms. But the argument may be taken with some caution because there arc some states where there is no labour reform but the shift in state domestic product as well as the shifts in population structure is higher. Looking at the results, one may suggest that the urbanization should be encouraged so as to achieve higher levels of development. Secondly, the labour reforms have also been found beneficial in states where it has been followed resulting in faster sectoral shifts.

The chapter by Parida and Pradhan examines the implications of structural changes in the Indian economy on the welfare of the households in both rural and urban India. While per capita household expenditure is taken as a proxy variable to measure the welfare of the households, the structural changes have been captured through the changes in some of the socio-economic and demographic variables. NSSO data of 61st round (2004–2005) and 68th round (2011–2012) are used for the analysis. The study applies OLS technique to find out the key determinants of household consumption expenditure and the Blinder–Oaxaca (B-O) decomposition method to understand the urban–rural gap. The authors noted that education, wages, occupation, household size, gender and age are important determinants of household consumption expenditure in both rural and urban India. However, the impact of these factors is found to be relatively higher in urban areas than the rural areas. The B-O test suggests the evidence of an increase in the urban–rural gap between the two data points. But, the endowment effect which explains nearly 60% of the urban–rural difference has declined southwards, suggesting the possibility of convergence of consumption expenditure between the urban and rural areas.

Part II covering skill and education comprises five chapters. It begins with the examination of skill development efforts in higher education to fulfil the objective of "Make in India" programme and reflects on the challenges with respect to skill development in India. Joshi and Bhattacharya argue that the technical education system in the country has grown into a fairly large-sized one, offering opportunities for technical education in a wide range of disciplines keeping in view the emerging need of the economy. India has the second highest population of the working age (15–59) in the world, but it is very crucial to examine further what proportion of this population should be skilled. Before the planning period, there were only about 50 technical institutions, whereas today the number is more than 10,000 in the country. Because of the high growth in the number of technical institutions, the availability of a required number of skilled manpower has contributed speed to the engines of economic growth. In the present chapter, an effort has been made to review the current status of the technical/skill education in the country. Finally, it reflects on the signals in the labour market keeping in view the concept of Make in India initiative of the government.

The chapter by Prasad, Joshi, Indrakumar, Saxena and Sarangi reflects on skill crisis in the organized sector in the western region of India. It covers the following stakeholders: on-roll trainees at establishments, ex-trainees who were employed in different establishments based on the training under NATS, establishments providing skill training under NATS, control groups of all stakeholders, professional institutions and finally policymakers. The Scope of The Apprentices Act, 1961, was broad-based in 1973 to accommodate fresh degree and diploma holders from engineering institutes in industrial establishments in order to gain practical experience and to fill the gap of skill requirement in the labour market. Popularly known as National Apprenticeship Training Scheme (NATS), it is intended to provide last mile skill development with exposure to changing technologies and new processes at the enterprise level. Ministry of HRD, Government of India, through four autonomous bodies is implementing the scheme by providing incentives to youth to encourage them to achieve skill enhancement. This study tries to find out the effectiveness and impact of the scheme on the western region, which is industrially developed and is supposed to provide intended support in skill development of youth.

The chapter by Joshi, Indrakumar and Kumra carries out an impact assessment of innovations and technology sharing on the farming community. In order to assess, refine and demonstrate the agricultural technologies in micro-farming situations of the farmers under various production systems operated under different agro-ecologies in the country, ICAR has created a network of 647 Krishi Vigyan Kendras (KVKs) in all the rural districts of the country. These KVKs are the real carriers of frontline technologies and impart knowledge and critical input support for the farmers and play a crucial role in the transfer of technology from the laboratory to land. India is a large agricultural country with around 50% of its population depending on agriculture and allied sector which contributes only 17% of GDP. Technological change has been the major driving force for the increase in agricultural productivity and promoting agriculture development. Agricultural innovations and diffusion of new technologies are important factors for all developing countries including India in their quest for food and nutritional security and improving the quality of life of people engaged in agriculture and related activities.

This necessitates that farmers have access to sustainable technology which is suitable to the micro-farming situations under various production systems and agro-ecologies in India. Moreover, technology transfer should aim at enhancing the socio-economic standards of rural farmers by upgrading their knowledge and skills. Krishi Vigyan Kendras (KVKs) are one such set of institutions which are helping farmers in this area. In view of the crucial role played by KVKs in technology transfer, this chapter aims to assess the role of KVKs in technology sharing to the farmers. As new research/innovation on agriculture and allied sectors is a continuous process in the country, the chapter analyses how these changes are known to farmers and whether these changes are accessible to farmers and helping them.

The next chapter deals with the impact of education disparity on wages and employment across space (rural and urban areas) using the NSS unit level data. Pradhan, Parida and Sarangi examine the returns to education with respect to three labour market outcomes, namely wages, employment and occupation, using the National Sample Survey Office (NSSO) 68th round (2011–2012) data. Wage equation (without selection bias) results point to the fact that returns to education increase at an increasing rate as the level of education increases and the impact of education is found relatively higher in the case of urban than rural areas. In case of employment, the study finds that compared to illiterates, the chances of higher educated people going to agriculture sector are less. This is true even in the case of rural areas, whereas the interactive variable (education with rural dummy) is found to be negatively associated with employment in the agriculture sector. Occupation related results suggest that there is a strong association between higher education (undergraduate and graduate and above) with professional occupations and less with agriculture and fishery and unskilled occupations, suggesting the need for improving education and creating quality employment opportunities in the rural areas that may help in arresting the growing urban burden.

Finally, the chapter on Sarva Shiksha Abhiyan by Yadav, Sharma and Birua in this section identifies the gap between targets and achievements, diagnoses the shortfalls in achieving the targets and suggests ways to overcome problems keeping in view the future prospects of SSA. To achieve the goal of universalization of elementary education in India, Sarva Shiksha Abhiyan (SSA) has been playing a pivotal role. SSA, a flagship programme of the Government of India, has been operational since 2000–2001 and as an intervention programme since 2010. SSA was launched to achieve universalization of elementary education in a time-bound manner, as mandated by 86th amendment of the Constitution of India, making free and compulsory education for the children in age groups of 6–14 years as a fundamental right. It is evident from the available data that quantitatively there was a minimum gap in targets and achievements under various components of SSA. In most of the years since 2001, not much gap has been observed in targets and achievements. Analyses of data and findings of research and evaluation studies conducted by different organizations revealed that SSA programme has been quite successful in achieving its goal quantitatively. But quality aspects also need to be looked into seriously. To improve the quality of the programme, the Government of India has taken many initiatives and positive results of these initiatives are visible.

In view of the 26% illiterate population in India, SSA programme should be continued as a regular programme or till an alternate regular system is evolved to achieve the goal of universalization of elementary education in the country.

Part III comprises seven chapters, reflecting on various aspects of inclusiveness, mechanisms to empower the groups lagging behind and the importance of health and sanitation in triggering development. The first deals with the scheduled tribes in India. The chapter focuses on tribal research institutes which came up as a solution to tribal community development and analyses the workings of TRIs from the perspective of the aspirations of the local community. The chapter by Wordsworth and Kumar argues that TRIs play multiple roles in bringing changes in the life of tribal communities. Despite coming into existence at different periods, these institutes have no temporal or spatial distinctions among them. As some of TRIs have outlived their existence without accomplishing their goals, they require a complete revival. While creating TRIs, the population parameters, locational advantages and geographical proximity were not taken into consideration. TRIs as evolving institutes have not included much of utility value for approach and access, as there are discrepancies in research, training, content, publication, museum, title, websites, digitization, etc. In the absence of a dedicated "Lead Research Centre", the concomitant efforts across TRIs seem to suffer. Although Planning Commission (2013) observes that the potentialities of TRIs are not being harnessed fully, MOTA observes that TRIs have weakened over a period of time and lost their direction. At the same time, MOTA cannot contravene their own observation and confer the status of COEs to select TRIs. Conclusively, this chapter suggests for creating a Lead Research Centre at NILERD with some refurbished plan for better research coordination and performance of TRIs.

The other aspect of social concern relates to gender inequality which is discussed in two chapters. While reflecting on the causes and impact of gender inequality, the chapters go into the details of the selected indicators. The chapter by Sekhar and Dhar attempts to trace the history of the debate on the relationship between men and women since the days of the overthrow of matriarchy and placing the institution of property at the centrality of this debate. Beginning with the classical debates of Morgan-Engels, the chapter looks at the current debates on gendered and gendering practices, glass ceiling hypothesis, and gender as a social structure. Indicating the inherent flaws of the existing concepts and methods, a blueprint of the possible theoretical outline has been attempted by moving from individual subjectivity to plural objectivity, by challenging the locus of research, dilemma and jeopardy of gender studies, thus giving way to a new approach of gender as a social fact. The chapter by Ved Prakash and Singh reflects on areas in which gender differences are staggering and/or narrowing down.

The social concerns include poor, particularly women. In this context, how the self-help groups can be effective in empowering women is an important consideration. The chapter by Kamla Devi, Sarangi and Lal refers to DAY-NRLM which is one of the flagship programmes of the Ministry of Rural Development. This programme is aimed at alleviating poverty and implementing a mission mode for targeted and time-bound delivery of results. The study analyses the functioning of

SHGs and the impact of the interventions taken up under DAY-NRLM on the coverage of the target households, the revival of defunct SHGs and the socio-economic changes in the lives of the SHG members. Based on fieldwork in Telangana, this article analyses the functioning of SHG institutions, including the problems faced by them and some of the ways in which these problems have been tackled by members of and other stakeholders in these institutions. There has been regular saving and borrowing from internal funds and banks. Though SHGs are stable, they lack vibrancy in their functioning. The analysis leads to a better understanding of the factors contributing towards stability, quality and sustainability of the groups and helps design appropriate policies.

The chapter by Sinha elaborates on the digital revolution which is transforming the labour market significantly, particularly in relation to the opportunities for women. Digital technology and globalization have brought in a sea change in the landscape of work with increasing access to work, information, newer production hubs, etc. In India, there had been significant strides in digital intervention through Digital India initiative, Aadhaar (unique identity number), JAM, ICT initiatives to enhance women's economic autonomy, newer production structure, digital transactions, etc. In the labour market in India, however, most of the workers are informal workers. Women are either self-employed (mostly unpaid family workers) or casual workers, working mostly at the lower rung of the occupational ladder as agricultural labourers, petty traders, manufacturing outworkers, etc. In this context, the chapter explores whether women can leverage the opportunities, be it trade or manufacturing or financial services, created by digital transformation. The study argues that differences in access along with factors like inequality in education and professional training, access to finance, asset holding lead to gender digital divide, restricting the transformational effects that digital technologies are creating. Women are typically employed at the last end of the value chains or occupational chain and bereft of any social security and in a survivalist state, rather than growing. The chapter suggests a set of policies so that women in India are a part of and benefit from the digital dividends.

The health issues, particularly the reproductive health services, need a thorough investigation as maternal mortality, illnesses and inadequacy of the support system are on the forefront. The chapter by Dhar, Kakkar and Roy evaluates the sanitation programmes with special reference to health and growth. It covers all the sanitation programmes launched by the Government of India and presents a comparison of different schemes in terms of their mandate, sanctioned and utilized budgets and targets achieved. The lack of access to improved sanitation and the associated health risks is a major issue in developing countries including India. Many national and international efforts have been made over the past few decades to improve the situation. However, the net outcome is reported to be not proportionate to the efforts made and money spent. A world mapping on access to clean water and sanitation around the world shows that a large number of India's population practise open defecation despite decades of government programmes. India has a far higher open defecation rate when compared with countries with higher poverty and lower literacy. In practice, government programmes paid little attention in understanding why so many rural Indians defecate in the open rather than use affordable pit latrines. Government programmes are focused on subsidizing the building of toilets, but research shows that the toilets that are built lie unused. An understanding of beliefs and values held by people is essential in ensuring acceptance and usage by people as is shown by states that have been able to achieve ODF status, rather than focus on subsidy alone. The non-timely release of allocated money has also been a major hindrance to the achievement of targets by many states. The chapter also finds a relationship between sanitation and various socio-economic indicators which directly impacts the overall growth and productivity of a country.

The other chapter by Sharma carries out a thorough analysis of family planning and reproductive health services. In this study, the reasons for non-use of family planning (FP) and reproductive health (RH) services in Kanpur slums, non-slums and rural areas are analysed. The study uses USAID-ITAP Kanpur Nagar Reproductive and Child Health Status in slum, non-slum and rural areas data of 2006. Percentage distribution and multinomial logistic regression analysis technique are used to study the reasons of non-use of family planning and reproductive health services in the Kanpur Nagar District of Uttar Pradesh. Across the residence category, the private sector health facility was used by the inmates for seeking FP and RH care services. For non-use of government health facility, poor quality care (56%), no nearby government facility (50%) and waiting time being too long (28%) were the most cited reasons by males, females and children. Mean distance to government health facility for delivery care is higher than the private facility. About 26% of the women wanted to have more children, the reason being they never used contraception. Urban women those never used contraception for the want of more children range from 26% in non-slum to 27% in slums, while in rural areas, this was 26%. The health-related problem was the most cited reason (40%) for women discontinuing IUCD/Copper-T. The reason for not consuming the 100+ days of IFA tablets/syrup that was received is that they either felt sick (39%) after consuming the medicine or felt (15%) that they did not need all the tablets. The main reason why mothers of children aged 0–35 months stopped breastfeeding is that they got pregnant (29%) with higher percentages saying so in rural areas (40%) compared to urban areas (23%). Twenty-five percentage of the women said they got insufficient breast milk, while another 10% told that the child refused the breast milk, with marked rural–urban variations. The government targeted conditional cash transfer schemes relating to health care such as Janani Suraksha Yojana (JSY), and benefits under Janani Shishu Suraksha Karyakram (JSSK) may be remodelled such that it builds better compliance on part of the beneficiaries.

All these studies reflect on various aspects of development in India and bring out the underlying policy implications. In the context of the development discourse, the volume may serve a better understanding as it focuses on a number of not-so-widely covered research issues.

Arup Mitra

Part 1

Revisiting Growth–Employment Relationship in India

Yogesh Kumar, Arup Mitra and Kailash Pradhan

1 Introduction

One of the ways of conceptualizing inclusive growth is to lay emphasis on the creation of productive jobs in the process of economic growth, particularly keeping in view the vast supplies of unskilled and semi-skilled variety of labour. In the face of rising inequality, growth alone is not sufficient to benefit all the sections of the society, especially those located at the lower echelons. While from supply side, the quality of labour has to improve in order to keep pace with the requirements of the changing technology and labour demand has to rise for bridging the gap between supply and demand. In a broad sense, the elasticity of employment with respect to growth is a summary index of the employment generating capacity of economic growth.

In the Indian context, several studies have tried to estimate the employment elasticity of growth keeping in view the mismatches in the changes in value-added composition and the work force structure (Mundle 1993; Bhattacharya and Mitra 1993). However, due to the lack of time series data on total employment, only point to point average elasticity could be computed at the aggregate level. For the organized manufacturing, however, more profound econometric exercises could be pursued as employment figures are available at a fairly comparable form over time. Most of the macromodels in India also exclude aggregate employment variable

Y. Kumar · A. Mitra · K. Pradhan
National Institute of Labour Economics Research and Development
(Formerly IAMR), Delhi, India
e-mail: yogesh.vaish@gmail.com

K. Pradhan
e-mail: kailasheco@gmail.com

A. Mitra (✉)
Institute of Economic Growth, New Delhi, India
e-mail: arupmitra7@gmail.com

NILERD, *Reflecting on India's Development*,
https://doi.org/10.1007/978-981-13-1414-8_1

precisely because the annual time series data are not available. In this sense, the macroanalysis is incomplete since from the point of view of inclusive and poverty reduction, employment is an important consideration.

Our contention in this paper is that the organized sector employment on which time series data are available can play a major role in generating figures on unorganized sector employment and total employment. Second, once the total employment figures are generated over time, the growth–employment relationship is studied rigorously which is attempted in two different ways. First, in the time series framework, the impulse response of employment to growth shocks and the impulse response of growth to employment shocks are discerned. Second, a small macromodel is developed to reflect on the employment elasticity of growth. The single equation model used widely to estimate the elasticity coefficients is not sufficient as different macro-variables are interdependent. The rest of the paper is organized as follows. The next section reviews some of the studies on employment elasticity of growth. In Sect. 3, we estimate the cross-sectional elasticity of informal to formal sector employment and using these estimates, the informal sector employment is predicted annually over time given the magnitude of the organized/formal sector employment. In Sect. 4, the growth–employment relationship is pursued in the time series framework. Section 5 presents results on growth–employment relationship considering a production function and an employment function at the aggregate level and suggesting simultaneity between growth and employment. Finally, Sect. 6 summarizes the findings with policy implications.

2 Evidence on Employment Elasticity from Existing Literature

We get to see two groups of studies in the Indian context on employment aspect in relation to economic growth. One of them considered both at the sectoral level and the aggregate level the proportion of employment growth rate to value added growth rate to reflect on employment generating capacity of economic growth. Different sectors unfold varied experiences. The agriculture sector to begin with had the highest employment elasticity though it has been declining over time as the employment growth in this sector is declining. Mechanization has added to value-added growth mostly coming from improvements in yield. On the other hand, disguised unemployment already existed in agriculture to a large extent with limited scope for further expansion in employment prospect. The lack of rural diversification did not allow the rural employment growth to pick up significantly (Bhattacharya and Mitra 1993).

Though in the services sector, employment elasticity has been higher than manufacturing, one would have expected it to be much greater in magnitude. Possibly because of the lack of skill, employment growth in the high productivity services did not pick up as expected. Other than skill intensity rising capital intensity also seems to have reduced the pace of labour absorption. The residual component within the services sector is overcrowded and characterized by low levels of productivity and meagre earnings. The excess-supplies-limited-demand paradigm applies to this segment of the sector, unfolding the shift of unskilled labour from agriculture seasonally and permanently both.

The second group of studies on employment elasticity is based on econometric estimation. Corresponding to the organized manufacturing sector availability of annual time series data facilitated such technical exercises. Usually, value added, wage rate, and man-days per hour are included in the equation (Mitra 2013). In the double-log specification, the coefficients are the elasticity estimates. Pooling of time series data across various industry groups is also pursued in order to enlarge the dataset. The usual criticism of such estimation is that the equation does not consider the impact of technology on employment directly which can be tackled by incorporating the capital-output ratio. In the labour demand, function which is derived from the output function value added involves endogeneity which in fact must be overcome though the existing literature has not been much responsive to this criticism. Empirically, the employment elasticity of growth in the organized manufacturing sector has not been impressive to designate industry as the engine of growth. With an increase in the man-days per worker, the scope for additional employment to be created in the process of growth can be negligible. Particularly in the face of increasing contractualization, labour utilization tending to trespass the limits of exploitation, employment growth is seen to be sluggish. Besides, the import of technology which is highly intensive in terms of capital and skill reduces the pace of labour absorption. While innovation is undertaken on a limited scale, it is also said to be highly capital and skill intensive, resulting in sluggish employment growth. However, distinction has to be made between process and product innovation. While certain phases in the production process may turn increasingly capital intensive, certain others are labour intensive, which at the aggregate may actually add to the total work force engaged by the unit (Vivarelli 2013). Besides, the scope to process byproducts without proportionate increase in capital results in employment expansion and thus, the elasticity of employment with respect to innovation is seen to be positive in a number of industries (Mitra 2015).

For the unorganized manufacturing, the lack of time series data again does not allow econometric estimation. However, cross-industry estimation is a popular method. Pooling of time series data across regions and industry groups allows a number of data points to be included and a more reliable estimate is obtained. However, for the own account manufacturing enterprises (OAMEs), earning information is not available while these enterprises account for a large majority of the employment in the unorganized manufacturing units. But the availability of the unit level data allows many data points to be used from the non-directory manufacturing enterprises and directory manufacturing enterprises even when the OAMEs are dropped. Another view very much in currency suggests that business subcontracting from the organized to the unorganized sector has been encouraging employment growth, reducing labour turn over cost and raising productivity and wages. However, empirical results refute most of these assertions (Mitra and Pandey 2013): ancillarization and subcontracting did not unravel any sizeable impact on employment generation or wage up-gradation. The practice of piece rate based payment allows the labour intermediaries to downsize the labour cost and charge a higher intermediary fee. There is a possibility that many home-based workers are not counted as full-fledged workers because household activities and remunerative work are pursued simultaneously which does not create an impression in the mind of the workers of being actually in the labour market. Given that home-based workers are being increasingly utilized by firms, there is a possibility that actual employment in the economy is somewhat underestimated.

Data analysis shows a decline in employment growth in the unorganized manufacturing without any effect on value added (Goldar et al. 2011). This could be either because of technological development or a significant part of the labour might have been redundant, for which employment loss does not necessarily cut into output growth. Based on the unit level data, we noted that the employment elasticity is almost equal to one in the unorganized manufacturing sector. This is possibly because the unorganized manufacturing enterprises constitute redundant labour to a large extent. Labour productivity witnessed a positive growth in various industry groups within the unregistered segment. Though many of the unorganized manufacturing units are surviving at the margin some of them, especially the directory manufacturing enterprises, are well connected with the formal sector, with effective supply chains and mutual benefits accruing to both the formal and the informal sector enterprises. Other than the unorganized manufacturing sector, even in the activities falling into the domain of the unorganized tertiary sector, the indirect effects of the growth in the organized sector are said to be beneficial (Das 2011), resulting in enhanced employment and incomes in the informal segments. However, Mitra and Pandey (2013) noted that the growth in petty activities in manufacturing and trade could be because of sluggish employment prospects in the high productivity sector which largely adopts capital-intensive technology. It restricts the employment growth even when rapid industrialization occurs, which in turn leads to increased residual absorption in the informal or unorganized sector. However, for the services sector, they noted a positive impact of contract dummy on employment in the unorganized sector units, indicating that large units get their work done by the small units which indirectly contributes to the overall employment. In fact, several new services have emerged in the recent years, and large firms usually contract out work to the small units in the unorganized sector.

3 Estimating Total Employment

The unorganized or informal sector employment is perceived to be a function of the organized sector employment in various activities.[1] This sort of a postulation can be rationalized in terms of inter-sectoral linkages (Papola 1981). The main drive for

---

[1]The organized sector includes all units in the public sector and non-agricultural establishments in the private sector employing at least 10 employees.

employment creation in the informal sector is seen to be provided by the formal sector. For example, rapid industrialization and/or growth in the high productivity services results in employment generation in the informal sector. On the other hand, the lack of dynamism in the organized sector can result in a residual absorption of labour in the unorganized sector. Hence, in both the situations—with and without a vibrant formal sector—the informal sector can expand.

The information on organized sector employment is taken from DGE&T yearly data. The total employment figures for specific years are derived by applying the NSS work participation rates (usual principal-cum-subsidiary status) to the projected population figures from the census data. From the total employment figures, the aggregate organized sector employment has been deducted to arrive at the unorganized sector employment for the NSS survey years. In the next step, the logarithmic transform of unorganized sector employment has been regressed on the logarithmic transform of employment in various activities within the organized sector, using the cross-sectional state level figures. Subsequently presuming that the cross-sectional estimates would also hold in the long run, the ex post forecasting of informal/unorganized sector employment has been carried out given the organized sector employment in different activities at the all-India level. Chakravarty and Mitra (2009) calculated the total employment for the years 1975 through 1998. The error margin turns out to be only 2% for the year 1983, and then it goes up to 6.5% in 1993–1994. The margin of error increases as the forecast year tends to move further away from the base year. In such situations, the cross-sectional elasticity of the informal sector employment with respect to different components of formal sector employment has to be recalculated from time to time using the data for some of the recent years. This we have done for the NSS-years 1999–2000 and 2004–05 for which the large surveys on employment and unemployment were carried out and the total employment figures are available. Forecasting is done for the years up to 2003–04 on the basis of the 1999–2000 cross-sectional regression and up to 2011–12 based on the cross-sectional regression for 2004–05.

The point which still remains valid is that in the absence of time series information on total employment, time series data on organized sector employment can be used to predict the informal sector employment, using the cross-sectional elasticity. Thus, the total employment can be derived without much bias. These figures can then be used in the macromodel for employment planning and poverty reduction strategies to be worked out.

Table 1 reports the cross-sectional regressions in which informal or unorganized sector employment is taken to be a function of various organized sector employment, using a double-log specification. After deducting the organized sector employment from the total employment figures, the unorganized sector employment has been derived across states. For the total employment first, the population figures were estimated for the corresponding NSSO survey years, using the population census data and then the work force participation rates (UPS-cum-USS) were applied to those population figures.

Table 1 presents the elasticity coefficients of unorganized sector employment with respect to various components of the organized sector employment.

Table 1 Cross-sectional elasticity coefficients

Variables	Equation 1 for 1999–2000 dep. var. Ln (unorg emp)	Equation 2 for 2004–05 dep. var. Ln (unorg emp)
Ln (org Ag etc.)	0.06 (0.87)	0.02 (0.22)
Ln (org Mfg etc.)	0.52 (4.91)[a]	0.29 (1.78)[b]
Ln (org construction)	−0.12 (−0.84)	0.09 (0.38)
Ln (org trade)	−0.12 (−1.09)	−0.33 (−1.97)[b]
Ln (orga transport)	0.07 (0.39)	0.53 (2.38)[a]
Ln (org financing)	−0.45 (−2.01)[a]	−0.34 (−1.18)
Ln (org other services)	1.29 (4.93)[a]	0.92 (3.27)[a]
Intercept	−1.27 (−0.82)	0.67 (0.37
Adj R2	0.97	0.93
N	27	25

Note [a, b]Represent significance at 5 and 10% levels respectively
Source Authors' calculation

Manufacturing and other services are the two activities which show positive and significant coefficients for both the years. It is important to note that the elasticity with respect to organized manufacturing almost halved as we move from the first cross section to the second cross section. For the category of other services, the elasticity still appears to be unity from the second cross section.

The employment figures from 1975 to 1998 are taken from an earlier study done by one of the authors, using the same methodology (Chakravarty and Mitra 2009). For the year 1999 through 2004, the equation for 1999–2000 has been used and for the rest of the years, 2005 through 2012, the equation for 2004–05 has been used. The employment estimates are provided in Table 2.

4 Growth–Employment Relationship: Time Series Analysis

In the time series framework, we have considered employment and GDP to examine the strength of association. Both the series are non-stationary in the level form though in the first difference form, (i.e., the rate of growth since the original variables are taken in log form), they are stationary (Table 3). There is also a

Table 2 Projected employment: total estimated employment (in million)

Year	Employment	Year	Employment	Year	Employment
1975	262.46	1989	333.24	2003	359.88
1976	262.36	1990	337.48	2004	390.90
1977	268.40	1991	342.28	2005	455.36
1978	275.0	1992	345.74	2006	441.03
1979	285.57	1993	347.20	2007	421.86
1980	290.17	1994	350.82	2008	453.27
1981	296.62	1995	353.15	2009	392.14
1982	303.12	1996	357.74	2010	376.95
1983	308.40	1997	361.22	2011	413.35
1984	312.16	1998	361.83	2012	470.49
1985	317.57	1999	394.17		
1986	321.84	2000	395.35		
1987	325.19	2001	393.01		
1988	329.49	2002	386.83		

Source Authors' calculation

Table 3 Unit root test

Variable	ADF test statistic	PP test statistic	Hypothesis accepted
LnEmp	−1.06	−0.67	Unit root exists
Ln GDP	3.56	3.53	Unit root exists
LnPrice	−1.001	−0.35	Unit root exists
Rog in emp	−5.97	−5.07	No unit root
Rog in GDP	−3.63	−5.87	No unit root
Rog in price	−3.80	−4.23	No unit root

The critical value at 1% level for both the tests is around −3.62

Table 4 Co-integration test

	Likelihood ratio	Hypothesis accepted
LnEMP LnGDP	28.45	At least one co-integrating vector exists
LnEMP LnPRICE	21.78	At least one co-integrating vector exists
LnGDP LnPRICE	17.77	At least one co-integrating vector exists

The critical values at 1 and 5% levels are 20.04 and 15.41, respectively

co-integrating relationship between the variables (Table 4) and hence, vector error correction model has been estimated (Table 5).

The impulse response of employment to GDP shock is very nominal to begin with (0.004 at the end of one year period) though over time it declines to 0.001 by the fifth year (Table 6). However, subsequently, it rises marginally and remains at around 0.002 from the seventh year onward. On the other hand, the response of

Table 5 Vector error correction model

Variable	Equation 1		Equation 2		Equation 3	
LnEMP (−1)	1.0		1.0			
LnGDP (−1)	−0.122 (−2.05)[a]				1.0	
LnPRICE (−1)			−0.19 (−17.32)[a]		45.31 (3648.7)	
INTER	−4.11		−5.13		−189.84	
Error correction	DLnEMP	DLnGDP	DLnEMP	DLnPRICE	DLnGDP	DLnPRICE
CointEq 1	−0.23 (−1.63)	0.20 (2.71)[a]	−0.85 (−3.51)[a]	0.08 (0.40)	0.0005 (2.88)[a]	−0.0002 (−0.86)
DLnEMP (−1)	0.08 (0.45)	−0.13 (−1.41)	0.45 (2.29)[a]	−0.001 (−0.006)		
DLnEMP (−2)	−0.43 (−2.32)[a]	−0.12 (−1.14)	−0.06 (−0.29)	−0.101 (−0.603)		
DLnGDP (−1)	0.17 (0.50)	−0.19 (−1.01)			−0.09 (−0.44)	−0.24 (−0.88)
DLnGDP (−2)	0.006 (0.02)	−0.12 (−0.69)			−0.11 (−0.61)	0.25 (1.01)
DLnPRICE (−1)			0.12 (0.55)	0.37 (2.00)[a]	0.20 (1.34)	0.31 (1.49)
DLnPRICE (−2)			−0.27 (−1.32)	−0.08 (−0.44)	−0.16 (−1.20)	0.04 (0.25)
INTER	0.009 (0.31)	0.08 (4.70)[a]	0.02 (1.16)	0.05 (3.49)[a]	0.07 (2.72)[a]	0.04 (1.39)
AdjR2	0.17	0.08	0.38	−0.02	0.21	0.09
N	36	36	36	36	36	36

[a] Represents significane at 5% level

Table 6 Impulse response function

	Response of EMP to GDP shock	Response of GDP to EMP shock	Response of EMP to price shock	Response of price to EMP shock	Response of GDP to price shock	Response of PRICE to GDP shock
Pd 2	0.004	0.007	0.009	0.006	0.006	−0.023
Pd 3	0.0037	0.009	0.005	0.005	0.004	−0.0199
Pd 5	0.001	0.019	0.006	0.007	0.004	−0.02
Pd 7	0.002	0.022	0.010	0.008	0.005	−0.0195
Pd 10	0.002	0.027	0.007	0.007	0.007	−0.0189

Table 7 Variance decomposition

	Variance decomposition of EMP (contribution of GDP)	Variance decomposition of GDP (contribution of EMP)	Variance decomposition of EMP (contribution of PRICE)	Variance decomposition of PRICE (contribution of EMP)	Variance decomposition of GDP (contribution of PRICE)	Variance decomposition of PRICE (contribution of GDP)
Pd 2	0.61	9.32	3.85	1.35	4.45	28.33
Pd 3	0.97	14.09	4.93	1.32	4.70	26.32
Pd 5	0.92	31.46	6.31	1.76	4.75	23.94
Pd 7	1.17	41.83	13.0	2.40	5.94	23.02
Pd 10	1.36	53.10	18.5	2.59	8.97	22.42

GDP to employment shock is greater in magnitude both in the short run and the long run and more importantly, the response tends to increase over time instead of dying down. The variance decomposition results also confirm that employment accounts for nearly half of the GDP variance in the long run while GDP constitutes less than 2% of the employment variance though both are indicative of an increasing tendency over time (Table 7). From all this, it may be inferred that employment has a greater impact on GDP rather than the vice versa. This is quite consistent with the literature that employment contracts can be long term in nature, and they are usually not flexible in the short run. Hence, fluctuations in the commodity market do not affect employment immediately. On the other hand, labour is indispensable as far as production is concerned and reduction in employment can have adverse effect on output (deceleration in demand hypothesis).

In the employment–price constellation, the response of employment to price shock and the response of price to employment shock are almost similar in the long run (0.007). However, the sign in both the cases is positive, implying that price rise through expansion in output by incentivizing the producers encourages employment and employment expansion can result in price rise by raising the effective demand for goods and services. In terms of variance decomposition of employment, prices are seen to play a significant role as they account for nearly one-fifth of the total variance in employment. On the other hand, employment is not able to influence the prices to any significant extent as they constitute only around 2.5% of the price variance in the long run. Employment expansion does not seem to be inflationary. On the other hand, an expansionary monetary policy may be beneficial for the economy as prices are seen to influence employment, substantiating with evidence the impact of monetary variable on the real sector of the economy.

Turning to GDP–price relationship, it is seen that the response of GDP to price shock is positive and has a tendency to increase in the long run. This would tend to indicate that price rise can provide an inducement to production. On the other hand, the response of price to GDP shock is negative and the absolute magnitude is higher in magnitude with a slight declining tendency in the long run. This implies that prices rise with respect to a decline in production and vice versa. From the variance decomposition, it may be inferred that prices account for nearly one-tenth of the production variance while GDP constitutes a little less than one-third of the price variance, meaning that production influences prices to a much greater extent than the monetary variable's impact on production. In the long run, however, the quantity effect on prices slows down as indicated by the magnitude of price variance accounted by GDP variance. For controlling inflation in the economy, it will be, therefore, quite meaningful to augment production. However, comparing the impact of prices on production and employment, both the findings are contrasting because price rise is seen to be more beneficial for employment creation rather than output expansion. This means that employers may be having provision to employment creation which they may be deliberately suppressing in order to avoid labour issues and maximize profit. The possibilities of employment creation are explored with a rise in product prices even without expanding production proportionately. This is an important finding from policy point of view which tends to corroborate Philip's curve hypothesis but without really adhering to the output expansion mechanism. With a rise in prices leading to an increase in profitability, one component of employment which seems to be secondary to the employer gets a boost.

5 Growth–Employment Relationship: Simultaneous Model

In this section, we propose to estimate a model in order to reflect on the employment elasticity of growth. Usually in econometric studies of this kind, employment is taken to be a function of value added and wage rate, (log-linear form). The coefficient of logarithmic transformation of value added in the equation is treated as the elasticity of employment with respect to growth. However, value added itself is determined by capital and labour. Hence, it will be desirable to highlight the simultaneity:

$$\ln \mathrm{GVA} = \mathrm{a0} + \mathrm{a1} \ \ln \ \mathrm{CAP} + \mathrm{a2} \ \ln \ \mathrm{LAB} + \mathrm{e1}$$
$$\ln \mathrm{EMP} = \mathrm{b0} + \mathrm{b1} \ \ln \ \mathrm{GVA} + \mathrm{b2} \ \ln \ \mathrm{EMOL} + \mathrm{e2}$$

Where GVA is gross value added, CAP is capital, LAB is labour, EMOL is emolument per employee, and e1 and e2 are random errors.

For capital, we have used the gross fixed capital stock which at the aggregate level is estimated in the following manner. The gross fixed capital formation (GFCF) and gross fixed capital stock (GFCS) are linked to each other through the standard linear specification in which gross fixed capital stock at the current year is updated taking into account gross fixed capital stock of the previous year, gross consumption of fixed capital (GCFC) and gross fixed capital formation during the current period. We assumed the gross fixed capital formation (GFCF) of 1969–70 as initial gross fixed capital stock of 1970–71 and then estimated the gross fixed capital stock from 1970–71 to 2013–14 using the following formula:

$$\mathrm{GFCS(Y)} = \mathrm{GFCS(Y-1)} + \mathrm{GFCF(Y)} - \mathrm{GCFC(Y)}$$

It has been deflated by the WPI (base 2004–05) in order to deduce it in real terms. Total GVA is taken in 2004–05 prices and the aggregate employment figures are derived as per the methodology described above. Regarding emolument per person, it may be noted that no figure is available at the aggregate level except some sectoral information from diverse sources. NSS data on sectoral wages are available but the figures are available only for the survey years. In the absence of any time series on wage data, we have taken the total salary and wage bill of all employees engaged in the organized component of the manufacturing sector and divide it by the number of persons employed. This is taken as a proxy for the emolument rate at the level of the aggregate economy.

In order to estimate the equations given above, the problem of endogeneity has to be overcome first. We have, therefore, taken the reduced form equations in the first step where each of the endogenous variables is expressed as a function of the exogenous variables in the model, i.e., gross fixed capital stock and emolument per person employed. The reduced form equations are estimated by OLS and the fitted values of the endogenous variables are generated which are then used in the right-hand side of the structural model replacing their observed values.

In the reduced form equations for GDP and employment, only capital turns out to be significant while emolument per employee is highly insignificant (Table 8).

Applying two-stage-least-square method to the structural model the GDP equation has the capital stock as the only significant variable. Predicted

Table 8 Regression results (OLS and 2SLS estimates)

Variables on RHS	Structural form (OLS est.)		Reduced form (OLS Est.)		Structural form (2SLS Est.)	
	LHS Var Ln GDP OLS	LHS Var Ln EMP OLS	LHS Var Ln GDP	LHS Var Ln EMP	LHS Var Ln GDP	LHS Var Ln EMP
Ln GDP		0.18 (3.14)[a]				0.36 (5.62)[a]
Ln EMP	0.20 (0.5)				0.18 (0.70)	
Ln CAP	0.703 (11.59)[a]		0.59 (7.0)[a]	0.21 (5.62)[a]	0.83 (3.39)[a]	
Ln EMOL		0.11 (0.85)	0.21 (0.75)	−0.18 (−1.44)		−0.25 (−1.85)[b]
INTER	5.75 (4.34)[a]	2.01 (3.17)[a]	3.21 (1.73)[b]	4.69 (5.69)[a]	8.73 (1.58)	3.55 (5.57)[a]
Adj R2	0.97	0.87	0.97	0.91	0.97	0.91
N	38	38	38	38	38	38

Note [a]Denotes significance at 5% level and [b]at 10% level. OLS is ordinary least square and 2SLS is two-stage-least-square method of estimation employment turns out to be highly insignificant. In the equation for employment, both emolument per employee and GDP are statistically significant. As expected, higher emoluments tend to reduce labour demand. On the other hand, predicted GDP raises employment—the employment elasticity of growth is 0.36 which is a little above the popularly held estimate of one-fourth. Interestingly enough, as per the OLS estimation of the employment equation in the structural model which does not consider the endogeneity issue, the employment elasticity is seen to be only 0.18. On the whole, though employment elasticity of growth is not very high from either of the two methods, particularly keeping in view the labour surplus situation in a developing country like India, it is definitely much higher when the simultaneity between value added and employment is considered compared to the single equation method which is widely applied and could be faulty.

The wage elasticity of employment as per 2SLS estimate is around one-fourth and the sign is negative as expected. However, the OLS estimate of the elasticity of employment with respect to emolument per person is only 0.10 and it is statistically insignificant. Keeping in view the difference in the OLS and 2SLS results which are statistically significant we would like to highlight that the results from the simultaneous equation model are more reliable with important policy implications. Rapid economic growth seems to have beneficial effect on labour absorption. The wage flexibility argument also shows relevance in the sense that wage reduction can encourage labour demand to some extent. However, this should not be taken to suggest that labour deregulation can have miraculous effect on employment as the emolument per person is not highly significant.

From the reduced form as well as the structural form equation for GDP, it is clear that capital stock has a very strong effect on value added as the elasticity is estimated at 0.7 and 0.83 as per OLS and 2SLS, respectively. This tends to substantiate the fact that the adoption of capital-intensive method in the production process is prevalent though output expansion policy due to scale effect will generate employment to a somewhat larger extent than usually thought. This element of optimism is due to the instrument used for overcoming the endogeneity issue; else, the employment elasticity would have been estimated at a low of less than one-fifth.

6 Conclusion

In this paper, we have addressed the issue of non-availability of time series data on employment and have deployed a mechanism to generate figures on the relevant variable. Based on the cross-sectional regressions, the elasticity of unorganized sector employment with respect to organized sector employment has been worked out for the NSSO's survey years on employment–unemployment. The total unorganized sector employment is estimated by applying the NSS work force participation rate to the absolute number of population derived from the interpolation of the census figures on population and then deducting the organized sector employment as reported by DGE&T from the total employment figures. Given the elasticity estimates and the time series information on organized sector employment, the forecasts of unorganized sector employment for the years between the NSSO's survey years have been carried out. In this manner, we have generated a long time series on employment starting from 1975 through 2012.

In the second stage, the study deploys both time series framework and simultaneous equation approach to reflect on employment–output relationship. Since there is a co-integrating relationship between employment and output, a VECM model has been estimated and subsequently the impulse response and variance decomposition exercises have been carried out. The findings are indicative of a very nominal effect of GDP on employment. Rather prices tend to encourage employment though output does not necessarily respond strongly to the monetary policy resulting in price rise. Thus, the beneficial effect of price rise occurring in employment not so much through output expansionary methods can be rationalized in terms of increased profitability due to price rise which motivates employers to create employment. This means that one component of employment is sensitive to profitability of the employers which is otherwise suppressed and substituted by mechanization. However, it is equally important to note that wage flexibility argument does not have much relevance in stimulating employment as the simultaneous model estimated thereafter is not indicative of a strong statistical significance. The price rise effect seems more meaningful than the wage reduction effect on employment creation. However, in order to control inflation output, expansionary methods will have to be employed to a significant extent.

The simultaneous equation model demonstrates the seriousness of the endogeneity issue and suggests that overcoming it by choosing an appropriate instrument enables us to witness a relatively greater impact of output expansion on employment. Hence, the employment elasticity of growth is generally underestimated in a single equation approach—rather the scale effect seems to be somewhat pertinent even when adoption of capital-intensive technology has been on the rise.

The time series analysis and simultaneous equation model are in a sense contrasting as they do not conform to similar findings, particularly in relation to the sensitivity of employment with respect to output. Besides, the effect of employment on output is negligible from the structural model though in the time series frame employment is seen to impact on output sizably.

It is also distinct from the reduced form version of the simultaneous equation model that capital alone explains the variations in output and employment both and the nature of relationship between capital and employment is positive. Though in relative terms capital and employment may be holding a negative relationship, the scale effect seems to be positive. With the greater deployment of capital, employment is also expected to rise though to a very limited extent (the elasticity being only 0.21). The emolument per person neither affects output nor employment in the reduced form version, indicating the exaggeration of labour regulation policy as far as its adverse effect on output and employment is concerned.

The policy implication of the study is quite interesting. While labour market deregulation and removal of downward wage rigidity do not have much scope for employment enhancement, raid growth can contribute to employment creation.

Hence, output expansionary policy seems to be effective in the context of employment generation. Besides, from the time series analysis, it is also distinct that price incentive can motivate employers to engage more labour even when output does not respond proportionately. Thus, the monetary policy can be effective in impacting on some of the real variables. Finally, for controlling inflation, it is pertinent to augment output as price rise is sensitive to production.

References

Bhattacharya, B. B. & Mitra, A. (1993). Employment and structural adjustment-a look at 1991 census data. *Economic and Political Weekly, 28*(38).

Chakravarty, S., & Mitra, A. (2009). Is industry still the engine of growth? An econometric study of the organized sector employment in India. *Journal of Policy Modeling, 31,* 22–35.

Das, K. (2011). *Micro and small enterprises in India: the era of reforms*. New Delhi: Routledge.

Goldar, B., Mitra, A., & Kumari, A. (2011). Performance of unorganized manufacturing in the post reforms period in micro and small enterprises in India In K. Das (Ed.), *The era of reforms*. New Delhi: Routledge.

Mitra, A. (2013, December). *Can industry be the key to pro-poor growth? An exploratory analysis for India*, ILO Asia-Pacific Working Paper Series.

Mitra, A., & Pandey, A. (2013). Unorganised sector in India: Employment elasticity and wage-productivity nexus. *Journal of Developmental Entrepreneurship, 18*(4).

Mitra, A., & Jha, A. K. (2015). *Innovation and employment: A firm level study of Indian industries* (Vol. 5, No. 1).

Mundle, S. (1993). Unemployment and financing of relief employment in a period of stabilisation India, 1992–94. *Economic and Political Weekly, 28*(5).

Papola, T. S. (1981). *Urban informal sector in a developing economy*. New Delhi: Vikas Publishing House.

Vivarelli, M. (2013). Technology, employment and skills: An interpretative framework. *Eurasian Business Review, 3,* 66–89.

Regional Imbalances in MSME Growth in India

Yogesh Kumar, Gayatri Pandey, A. P. William Wordsworth and J. S. Chauhan

1 Introduction

Over the past five decades, Micro Small and Medium Enterprises (MSME) sector has emerged as a highly vibrant and dynamic sector of the Indian economy. In addition to playing a crucial role in providing large employment opportunities at comparatively lower capital cost than large industries, SMEs also help in industrialization of rural and backward areas. Theirs is thus an invaluable contribution towards reducing regional imbalances, and assuring more equitable distribution of national income and wealth. Playing a complementary role to large industries as ancillary units, this sector is contributing enormously to the socio-economic development of the country (see https://msme.gov.in/about-us/about-us-ministry for more details). Also significant is their "contribution in domestic production, significant export earnings, low investment requirements, operational flexibility, location wise mobility, low intensive imports, capacities to develop appropriate indigenous technology, import substitution, contribution towards defence production, technology-oriented industries, and competitiveness in domestic and export markets thereby generating new entrepreneurs by providing knowledge, training and skill development" (Subina 2015, https://msme.gov.in/about-us/about-us-ministry).

Y. Kumar (✉) · G. Pandey · A. P. William Wordsworth · J. S. Chauhan
National Institute of Labour Economics, Research and Development, Delhi, India
e-mail: yogesh.vaish@gmail.com

G. Pandey
e-mail: gpandey1304@gmail.com

J. S. Chauhan
e-mail: jagbirchouhan@yahoo.com

NILERD, *Reflecting on India's Development*,
https://doi.org/10.1007/978-981-13-1414-8_2

Over the years, the share of MSMEs in total manufacturing export has risen to a healthy level of over 40%. The "sector contributes significantly to manufacturing output, employment and exports of the country. In terms of value, the sector accounts for about 45% of the manufacturing output and 40% of total exports of the country. It is estimated to employ about 60 million persons in over 26 million units throughout the country. There are over 6000 products ranging from traditional to high-tech items, which are being manufactured by the MSMEs in India. It is well known that the MSME sector provides maximum opportunities for both self-employment and wage-employment, outside agriculture sector" (Ministry of Micro, Small & Medium Enterprises 2007).

The MSME sector in India is highly ***heterogeneous*** in terms of the size of the enterprises, location, variety of products and services, people employed, coverage of social sector, and leveraging information, communication and technology (ICT) in running their enterprises (Intellectual Capital Advisory Services Private Limited 2012). "MSME sector contributes not only to higher rate of economic growth but also in building an inclusive and sustainable society in innumerable ways through creation of non-farm livelihood at low cost, balanced regional development, and gender and social balance" (Ministry of Micro, Small & Medium Enterprises 2007).

In his seminal paper on the mechanics of economic development, Lucas (1998) observed that "…the problem of economic development…" is "… simply the problem of accounting for the observed pattern across countries and across time in levels and rates of growth of per capita income". While this definition addresses explicitly the issue of comparative economic development of countries, it is equally relevant for the comparative study of development of regions within a given country, especially so far a country as large as India, which is easily viewed as a collection of interconnected sub-economies, viz, the states which comprise the country needs, so to speak, to be studied both from without as well as within (Dasgupta 2000).

Methodology in brief

The study is carried out with three objectives in mind: The first intention is to have a detailed picture of the extent of diversity in MSME spread having a glance of various salient economic attributes contributing to the spread, its growth trends and scenario emerging from one time to another. We then find the relative levels of capital and employment as two major contributing factors of MSME spread and its growth. As corollary of the capital, and employment endowments and changes therein, the inter-state differentials emerged and changed from one census of MSME Sector to another.

Secondly, an analysis of the manner change in disparity over time is carried out. In view of the fact that during the period of convergence, the value of the state relative in base year and the percentage change or growth rate, i.e., Compound Annual Growth Rate (CAGR) of the same over time will move in opposite direction (converse is true, in case of divergence), the coefficients of correlation are computed between the initial year value of the state relative and CAGR during initial and subsequent year (this way correlation is established: first census value and CAGR between first and second census value, second census value and CAGR between second and third census value and so on) are compared to have an inter-temporal changes in regional disparities.[1]

The paper also attempts to explain the changing tendencies of inter-state differentials with respect to different state values emerging. In doing so, it seems logical to consider a few infrastructure and institutional factors (including government initiatives) as possible explanatory variables.

The very first steps in the search for a clue lie in observations, i.e. in establishing whether the regions in question are truly diverse from the economic point of view. To the extent that economic development is largely concerned with per unit accumulation, this conclusion follows from the law of diminishing returns to capital. Sustainable growth rates fall as the capital stock expands relative to other factors, thereby allowing poorer regions to catch up with richer ones over time. Although the hypothesis has been questioned and subsequently modified, it has turned into an important point of departure for most investigations on inter-regional diversities.

As with most other recent studies on the subject, the investigation begins with references to the convergence hypothesis. The findings here are similar in certain respects to previous contributions. However, our convergence analysis differs from these in certain other important respects. For one thing, the data used in the paper is probably detailed/cleaner than that utilised by some of the existing papers. More importantly, the convergence analysis pursued here is more disaggregative in nature. For example, we attempt to provide a clear picture of the behaviour of the labour quotient (LQ henceforth, measured as ratio of employment share to working unit share), labour productivity (LP henceforth, measured as production turnover per unit employment), capital quotient (CQ henceforth, measured as ratio of capital share to working unit share) and Capital-labour ratios (CLR henceforth) to try to draw conclusions about the contribution to the overall convergence/divergence by each of these variables.

In the explanation to differentials and its convergence and divergence tendencies, a multi-dimensional factorial analysis in terms of relative convergence/divergence between states is attempted in terms of infrastructural development, government policy initiatives and other correlated factors (clustering of MSMEs, Technology/ Innovations levels, access to credit facility).

[1]The issue here is more controversial than one might suppose. For example, a time honoured evidence of divergence amongst regions lies in observed differences in growth rates in labour and capital employed per unit. So, the so-called convergence hypothesis raised doubts on this score (Barro and Sala-i-Martin 1995). Following the dictates of the neo-classical growth model (Solow 1956), it claims that, two regions differing mainly in the levels and growth rates of economic attributes in question may actually be approaching closer, provided that the lower growth rate region was richer than the higher growth rate regions at some initial point of time.

Objectives:

The purpose of the present paper is to offer analytical description of the manner in which the Indian states have behaved vis-a-vis one another over the different Censuses carried out since the first one in 1972–73, and second census in 1987–88, in particular. The paper also aims to find out the main factors causing differential growth of MSME in the states (Table 1).

2 Regional Differentials

We have carried out our study using data from MSME Censuses conducted by Directorate of Census-MSME (DC-MSME).[2] The second census of small scale industrial units under the purview of Small Industries Development Organisation (SIDO) was undertaken by the Office of Development Commissioner, Small Scale Industries (DCSSI) in association with State/UT Governments and National Informatics Centre (NIC), during the period 1989–1991. Data collected relate to the base year (1987–88), field work for which commenced in right earnest from April 1990. The aspects on which information was collected included employment, investment, working capital, capacity, production, exports, raw materials, energy consumption, etc. "Third All India Census of Small Scale Industries (SSI) was conducted with reference year 2001–02. The Census covered both Registered and Unregistered Sectors for the first time. The census adopted different methodology for Registered and Unregistered Sectors. While complete enumeration of enterprises was adopted in Registered Sector, Sample Survey was resorted to in Unregistered Sector. The latest census conducted on Micro, Small and Medium Enterprises (MSME) is the Fourth All India Census of MSME 2006–07. The data was collected till 2009, results of which were published in 2011–12. The census adopted different methodology for Registered and Unregistered Sectors. While complete enumeration of enterprises was adopted in Registered Sector, Sample Survey was resorted to in Unregistered Sector. However, for activities under Wholesale/Retail trade, legal, educational and social services, hotel and restaurants, transports and storage and warehousing (except cold storage), which were excluded from the coverage of Fourth All India Census of MSME 2006–07, data was extracted from Economic Census 2005 conducted by Central Statistics Office, Ministry of Statistics and Programme Implementation for finalising the report on MSME Sector" (http://www.dcmsme.gov.in/ito_msme/censuses.htm).

There are significant geographical variations in India that impact the distribution of micro, small and medium enterprises. International Finance Corporation (2012) split the states in India into three broad regions based on the availability of natural

[2]But as the first census conducted in 1972–73 was not a complete census of all organised and unorganised units, for comparison purpose, the paper uses data and statistics of second (1987–88), third (2001–02) and fourth (2006–07) censuses.

Table 1 Terms used in paper and what they signify

Sl. no.	Term	What they signify
1.	LQ—Labour quotient	Ratio of employment share to working unit share in a state
2.	CQ—Capital quotient	Ratio of capital share to working unit share in a state
3.	CLR	Capital-labour ratio
4.	LP	Labour productivity
5.	LI—Labour intensity	Employment per unit
6.	CI—Capital intensity	Capital per unit

resources and other regional characteristics as also the type of an enterprise and scale of operations. The three categories are: 1. Low-Income States (LIS[27])—Bihar, Chhattisgarh, Jharkhand, Madhya Pradesh, Orissa, Rajasthan, Uttar Pradesh, 2. North-eastern States (NES)—Assam, Arunachal Pradesh, Nagaland, Manipur, Meghalaya, Mizoram, Tripura and 3. Rest of India—All states other than Low Income States and North-eastern States (Intellectual Capital Advisory Services Private Limited 2012).

Our analysis is primarily based on MSME Censuses. There are large differentials in the spread of MSMEs across States according to the fourth Census, as the below table indicates. On the one hand the large number of states (16) have less than one percent of enterprises, six have one to three percent share of total enterprises. Bihar, Odisha, Punjab and Rajasthan have 3–5% of enterprises, while Gujarat Andhra Pradesh, Karnataka, Kerala, Madhya Pradesh have between five and seven percent of enterprises. Four states that have large number of MSME enterprises (8–12%) are Maharashtra, Tamil Nadu, Uttar Pradesh and West Bengal. Similarly, 17 states have less than 1% of employment share, as against 20 states have less than one per cent investment share. In five states, employment as well as investment lies between 1 to three percent of the total. While five states have employment between 3 and 5% of total employment in MSME sector in the country, four states have 3–5% of total investment. Only three states, namely, Gujarat, Karnataka, and Kerala have between five and seven percent of employment and state of Maharashtra provide employment to almost 8.70% of labour, three states, namely, Tamil Nadu, Uttar Pradesh and West Bengal provide employment to more than 10% people. So far as investment is concerned, UP has 8.27% share, Maharashtra 10% while Gujarat more than 24% of investment (Table 2).

In the above context of wide variation in the number of enterprises, employment and investment, for better understanding of the spread of MSMEs particularly with respect to employment and investment, the, coefficients of localisation and the coefficient of specialisation have been calculated. The various *coefficients* that have been developed to quantify degrees of *specialisation* or diversification generally involve simple manipulations of profiles of proportions (e.g. *coefficients* includes those measures that are determined for each unit of analysis e.g. for all of the regions).

Table 2 Number of units shares, employment and investment share among states as per fourth census (2006–07)

Sl. no.	States/UTs	No. of working units share	Employment share	Investment share
1.	Andaman and Nicobar Islands	0.04	0.05	0.01
2.	Andhra Pradesh	7.15	8.78	4.83
3.	Arunachal Pradesh	0.39	0.15	0.14
4.	Assam	1.82	1.77	1.02
5.	Bihar	4.05	3.51	1.24
6.	Chandigarh	0.14	0.15	0.09
7.	Chhattisgarh	1.43	1.18	0.49
8.	Dadra and Nagar Haveli	0.02	0.05	0.03
9.	Daman and Diu	0.02	0.05	0.28
10.	Delhi	1.52	2.46	1.50
11.	Goa	0.24	0.23	0.56
12.	Gujarat	6.00	5.93	24.56
13.	Haryana	2.39	2.34	3.83
14.	Himachal Pradesh	0.79	0.58	0.82
15.	Jammu and Kashmir	0.85	0.71	1.25
16.	Jharkhand	1.86	1.60	0.74
17.	Karnataka	5.56	5.80	4.00
18.	Kerala	6.10	6.16	6.53
19.	Lakshadweep	0.01	0.01	0.00
20.	Madhya Pradesh	5.33	4.18	1.55
21.	Maharashtra	8.44	8.70	10.01
22.	Manipur	0.25	0.29	0.10
23.	Meghalaya	0.24	0.24	0.07
24.	Mizoram	0.08	0.10	0.06
25.	Nagaland	0.11	0.21	0.19
26.	Odisha	4.34	4.13	0.19
27.	Puducherry	0.10	0.13	0.17
28.	Punjab	3.99	3.33	5.47
29.	Rajasthan	4.59	3.82	3.75
30.	Sikkim	0.05	0.10	0.01
31.	Tamil Nadu	9.13	10.06	11.46
32.	Tripura	0.27	0.22	0.10
33.	Uttar Pradesh	12.13	11.47	8.27
34.	Uttarakhand	1.03	0.86	0.89
35.	West Bengal	9.55	10.65	5.81

The location coefficient of employment of a state is the ratio of share of total employment in MSME sector in a state over the share of total MSME enterprises in the state.

Atypically, Industry Location Quotients are calculated by comparing the industry's share of regional employment with its share of national employment. Herein we computed States' labour and capital share vis-avis States' enterprise share to understand relative employment to units' ratio in a state versus other states, as also while carrying out the same exercise over censuses whether this ratio is going up or down. A similar exercise with respect to capital provides whether units in one state are more capital intensive than others and how the capital intensity in a state going up or down.

"Spatial distribution could indicate patterns of underlying process. Incidents exposed to the impact of similar process tend to follow similar locating pattern. Hence, study on spatial cluster could reveal information about the underlying geographical process that generates the spatial pattern, which can further aid the comprehension of underlying geographical process and its relationship with the phenomenon under investigation" (Lu 2016). As we do not have sufficient time series information for all the states, such cluster analysis is not possible. To study the concentration in the state hence, Hirchman Herfindahl Index has been constructed for the different censuses. The index is computed for the labour and capital per enterprise using equation

$$\mathrm{HHI} = \sum_{(i=0)}^{n} P_i^2/100 \tag{1}$$

where P_i = percentages are of the ith state to the total.

HHI constructed for an investment across states in different censuses present an upward trend ever since second census while labour HHI is experiencing a fall, and so also to certain extent, the number of enterprises (Fig. 1; Table 3). The trend clearly indicates capital stock compilation and concentration in some states while employment is much more diversified since second census. So far as number of enterprises is concerned, there are fluctuating trends with overall decline signifying overall diversification (non-concentration) of enterprises across states over the censuses.

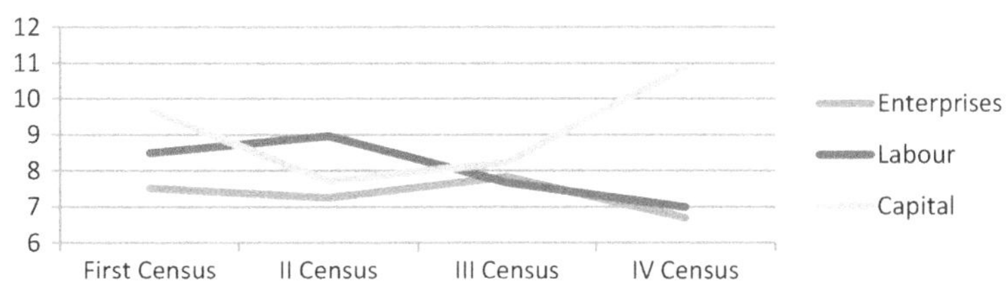

Fig. 1 Trend of HHI with respect of number of enterprises, labour and capital: first to fourth census

Table 3 HH index with respect to labour employed, investments, enterprises in different censuses

States	Enterprises	Labour	Capital
First census	7.52	8.49	9.68
II census	7.25	8.96	7.71
III census	7.83	7.67	8.23
IV census	6.69	6.99	10.89

Alternatively, the ***coefficient of specialization*** measures the degree to which a local or a regional economic system specializes in one or more economic sectors compared to the regional or the national economy (Rodrigue 2017). A value of zero denotes no *specialization* of the economy under study (compared to the reference economy).

$$\mathrm{SI} = \sum_i t_i^2 \Big/ \left(\sum_i t_i\right)^2 \tag{2}$$

where, t_i is share of employment per enterprise.

It is the total of squares of share of employment per enterprise in a state over the square of total employment per enterprise in the country as a whole. So, if the specialization index tends toward 1, such a result indicates that the terminal is highly diversified. If, inversely, the index tends toward 0, it means that the terminal's activity is specialized. Thus, the specialization index is called upon to appreciate the degree of specialization/diversification (Comtois 2017).

States/UTs	LSQ	CSQ
I census	0.04	0.06
II census	0.01	0.06
III census	0.14	0.08
IV census	0.07	0.14

LSQ (Specialisation coefficient of labour) has fallen from third census, but we found a gradual rise in CSQ (specialisation coefficient of capital), more rapid rise during third to fourth census.

Matching States quotient of Labour and Capital

So far as the relative coefficients of localisation of capital (CQ) and labour (LQ), the two major factors of production, namely, is concerned, the two coefficients have been juxtaposed in the following table to mark

1. Whether the two coefficients differed for different states, that is analysis pertaining to over different censuses, how were the values of LQ and CQ for different states varied; and
2. If there was a matching pattern of coefficients: that is, how across states LQ distribution is related with CQ distribution.

Table 4 K–S—Statistics for status of states* in terms of LQ and CQ in second, third and fourth census

States/UTs	Second census	Third census	Fourth census
	LQ versus CQ	LQ versus CQ	LQ versus CQ
D	0.17241	0.08600	0.31429
Critical Value	0.25255	0.22988	0.22988

*Status of states is 0: if value is less than Mean − 0.75 Std Dev
1: if value lies between Mean − 0.25 Std Dev to Mean − 0. 75 Std Dev
2: if value lies between Mean − 0.25 Std Dev to Mean + 0.25 Std Dev
3: if value lies between Mean + 0.25 Std Dev to Mean + 0.75 Std Dev
4: if value lies more than Mean + 0.75 Std Dev

We would be dealing the second question first that is to look into distribution pattern of CQ and LQ across states, and how the distribution pattern changed over time (over Censuses). For this, we used The Kolmogorov Smirnov D statistics. The Kolmogorov Smirnov D statistics defined as the maximum value of the absolute difference between two cumulative distribution functions measures the overall difference between two cumulative distribution functions (Table 4).

$$D = \max \; -\infty < x < \infty |\mathrm{SN1}(x) - \mathrm{SN2}(x)| \tag{3}$$

For comparing two different cumulative distribution functions SN1(x) and SN2(x), the K–S statistic indicates that there was not much of difference in the two coefficients during second and third census as the maximum difference value 'D' was below the critical value. But the fourth census atypically denotes a significant deviation from earlier two censuses as the 'D' has been found to be more than the critical value indicating localisation coefficients of labour distribution significantly differentiated from localisation coefficient of capital during the census.

Attempting analysis pertains to 'Whether the two coefficients differed for different states, that is analysis pertaining to over different censuses, how were the values of LQ and CQ for different states varied'.

(a) Spatial Cluster

"Spatial distributions with values at certain locations showing relationship with values at other locations are named spatial autocorrelation" (Lu 2016). Spatial cluster is positive spatial autocorrelation when similar values are spatially clustered together. On the opposite is the distribution with similar values separated/dispersed from each other, which is called negative spatial autocorrelation (Boots and Getis 1988; Lu 2016). For finding out spatial auto-correlation, co-variance is found out to LQ Values of different states as well as CQ Values of different states, in different censuses.

Changing Inter-state Differentials in LQ and CQ:

It is found that there is marked change in third and fourth census, particularly in fourth census with more states lying in categories of high labour-low capital or low capital-high labour. Thus in a way regional imbalances are on increase in the last census. A cross-check of states 'position on two factors of production' indicates the following:

States such as Maharashtra, T.N., Punjab, and Haryana had all high CQ and high LQ in the III Census; in the IV Census, all the four states had low LQ though high CQ. There was a major shift noted in case of Punjab and Haryana from II Census to III census, as these states shifted from low LQ and low CQ in II Census to high CQ and high LQ in the III Census. Another state which also was lying in low LQ and low CQ in II and III census but high CQ and high LQ in the last IV Census was J and K (refer Annexure).

A significant and notice worthy correlation trend between capital—labour ratio and labour productivity was found amongst three categories of states, viz. (1) High capital—low employment, states, (2) Low—capital and High labour states, and (3) other states. States with high capital and relatively low labour share, category 1 states, In this case the Pearson Correlation coefficient values between labour productivity and capital labour ratio '*r*' during fourth census was found to be 0.2313 (*T*-test value is 4.55076E−05). The value of '*r*' has declined from earlier period when it was 0.445522254 (*T*-test value being: 0.001180141). Correlation coefficient values between labour productivity and capital labour ratio are not only low but also have fallen from 0.44 in 2001–02 to 0.21 in last Census of MSME. These are the States of Maharashtra, Tamil Nadu, Punjab, Haryana, Jammu and Kashmir, and Pondicherry with high capital and relatively less labour share, which further could be significantly differentiated in terms of states having '*r*', value declining means as capital to labour ratio going up, labour productivity declining (This was indicative of capital—under use).

Second category of states, States with low capital but relatively high labour with the Pearson correlation '*r*', value 0.7764 (*T*-test value is 1.60626E−06) also experienced a decline from earlier period when it was 0.869747955 (*T* test value being: 0.002207113). Most of North East states and States of M.P, Chhattisgarh, Jharkhand are in this category. Herein, the correlation value between capital-labour ratio and labour productivity has been almost nearly 0.80 (declined marginally from 0.86 to 0.81).

For rest of the States: In this case the Pearson correlation '*r*' during fourth census was found to be 0.7989. *T*-test value is 0.00115622. The value of *r* has declined from earlier period when it was 0.835782715 (*T* Test value being: 2.53069E−06). Other states too have positive '*r*' and declining trend. Again '*r*' value is found to be nearly 0.80.

It is also noted that Pearson correlation '*r*' value between labour productivity and capital labour ratio differed significantly across states lying in three categories led us to make enquiry into the convergence and divergence trends in labour productivity among states (Fig. 2).

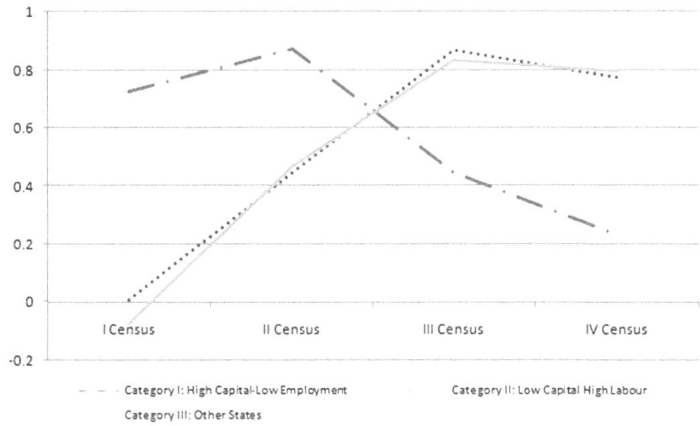

Fig. 2 Value of '*r*' capital-labour ratio as related to labour productivity trend for three types of states

3 Convergence and Divergence Trends: Changing Disparity Over Time and Its Correlates

The literature on disparities across Indian states is relatively scanty. Sarker (1994) studies the link between regional imbalances and plan outlays. He discovers a strong link between development (measured in terms of 14 variables including per capita consumption of electricity, percentage of villages electrified, per capita expenditure on health, effective literacy rates, etc.) and the plan outlays for the different states. He employs principal component analysis to construct a composite index of development according to which Punjab scores the highest and Bihar the lowest. The analysis is based on a study of 15 Indian states. Dholakia (1994) concludes in terms of a study of 20 Indian states over the period 1960–61 to 1989–90 that there are marked tendencies of convergence of long-term economic growth rates for the states. He identifies 1980–81 to the year of break in the trend of real incomes of India states. Several of the laggard states started growing after this date while the leaders began to stagnate (Dholakia 1994). Cashin and Sahay (1996) too claim absolute convergence on the basis of data relating to 20 Indian states over the period 1961–91, at the same time that the dispersion of real per capita income increased during the period. The present study seems to support the observations of Dholakia and Cashin and Sahay. In our analysis it is found that growth-differentials among regions prevail, as testing of tendencies of convergence/divergence according to Solow model gave us the following results.

Solow Model of Convergence and Factor Mobility:

$$\text{Standard Solow Model: } sf(k^*)/k^* = n \qquad (4)$$

where

s saving rate (herein, Capital Investment per enterprise)
k^* steady state capital stock (herein, Capital-Labour Ratio)
n rate of growth of population (herein, Enterprises).

Long run growth implication of (1) is the labour productivity is constant over the long run when technological growth is determined (or restricted to) endogenously. So far as growth rates are concerned, Solow model states the countries with differential capital-labour ratio will follow differential growth paths. Country having lower labour productivity will grow at a faster rate. Negative correlation between LP in 2001–02 and growth rate during 2001–02 to 2006–07 (third and fourth census) proves that. In fact it is found that the correlation coefficient is −0.071 between the two.

Thus the states with higher LP in Third Census had lower growth of labour productivity subsequently and vice versa. So far as LP is concerned it is found that LP growth rate (that LP growth during third to fourth census) is again negatively correlated with Initial labour per enterprise (labour intensity, henceforth LI) values, that is LP level in a state in the third census. Interestingly LQ growth rate too is negatively varying with initial level of LQs.

Thus, over time the regions would converge in terms of LP as well as LI and LQ: Negative '*r*' values for LQ depicted a mobility of labour from one state to another, from state with lower LQ in third to have more LQ growth, and those with higher values in third census to have lower growth during third to fourth census. Simultaneously, negative '*r*' values for labour intensity with respect to Labour intensity growth again reflect inter-firm mobility. *This is to equivalent to saying that from the states where per enterprise employment was more (alternatively, less), there is a mobility to the states with lower (alternatively, higher) average employment per enterprise indicating a convergence with respect to enterprise level employment. In the same way, the states having higher share of employment compared to enterprise share tend to move to lower share of employment compared to enterprise share, and* vice versa. *This again reflects state-level convergence.*

However, as regards per capita income across states conclusions opposed to ours are reached by Raman (1996), as well as Ghosh et al. (1998). They report significant divergence across Indian states. Marjit and Mitra (1996) raise an interesting question with regards to productivity, however, in the presence of perfect factor mobility (as should be the case between Indian states, reflected from our above analysis), they wonder how far the predictions of the convergence hypothesis are valid as then technologically similar regions must instantaneously achieve equality of labour productivity, thus removing any possibility of differential growth rates. Thus, the absence of imperfect factor mobility is a necessary condition for the convergence theory to hold. Alternatively, in the presence of factor mobility, differential growth rates across regions do not imply convergence (on account of diminishing returns). In other words, even if a negative relationship between initial per capita income and the overall growth rate is observed, it may not indicate convergence.

Our study does not seem to support the view of diminishing returns however. That is to say, study reflects a more or less static return to capital. This is attempted through comparing the growth of CQ as well capital per enterprise (capital intensity, (henceforth CI) values between the last two censuses (third and fourth census) against the growth of turnover per enterprise (production quotient, henceforth PQ) in the duration. Pearson coefficient value 0.96 in case of CQ and 0.68 in case of CI indicate almost unilateral growth though the relationship was insignificant as *P*-values was much more than required 0.15.

It is found that growth in production vary in tandem with growth in capital share to the units share, that is, higher is the production growth, capital share to the units share is higher, and vice versa. This is not only perceptible, over two periods, growth in fourth census over third census but also across states within a census. And thus, the observed convergence reported on basis of Tables 5 and 6 do not seem to support a perfect labour or capital mobility.

Table 5 Correlation between LP in 2001–02 and growth rate during 2001–02 to 2006–07

T-test: paired two sample for means	LP in 2001-02 and growth rate during 2001–02 to 2006–07
Pearson correlation	−0.071583374
t stat	6.242531132
$P(T <= t)$ one-tail	2.08916E−07
$P(T <= t)$ two-tail	4.17833E−07

Table 6 **a** Labour intensity in III census versus labour intensity growth third to IV census. **b** LQ in III census versus LQ growth during third to fourth census

(a)

	Labour intensity in III census
Pearson correlation	−0.6289
t stat	8.679036
$P(T <= t)$ one-tail	1.93E−10
$P(T <= t)$ two-tail	3.85E−10

(b)

T-test: paired two sample for means

	LQ in III Census
Pearson correlation	−0.62883
t stat	6.724959
$P(T <= t)$ one-tail	5.81E−08
$P(T <= t)$ two-tail	1.16E−07

Table 7 **a** CQ versus PQ. **b** CI versus PQ

(a)	
Correlation	CQ
Pearson correlation	0.957786031
t stat	0.267591207
$P(T <= t)$ one-tail	0.395315324
$P(T <= t)$ two-tail	0.790630648
(b)	
T-test: paired two sample for means	
	CI
Pearson correlation	0.678495
t stat	−1.82309
$P(T <= t)$ one-tail	0.03868
$P(T <= t)$ two-tail	0.07736

Another way to prove inter-unit returns was: To check production growth versus change in capital per enterprise, CI per se, across the states as well as change in two parameters between third and fourth census. A double differential equation is determined to understand β-convergence that is if there exist diminishing returns to capital per enterprise growth (Table 7).

Growth in production also varied positively with growth in capital share per unit, indicating higher production growth as the capital per unit was higher, and vice versa.

Convergence relative to states specific steady states

The total factor productivity growth (TFPG) in a large number of industries seems to have improved across most of the states. Technology acquisition, efficient utilisation of resources and infrastructure development are some of the factors which possibly contributed to the increase in TFPG (Mitra 1999). Nagaraj et al. (1997) considered the growth performance of Indian states on per capita SDP during the 1960–94 period and found evidence of conditional convergence, i.e., convergence relative to states specific steady states. They also assess the contribution of various indicators of physical, economic and social infrastructure to growth trends. Compared to this, our viewpoint is rather mundane. In fact the present study analyses the LP convergence across states with state specific initial levels of CLR (Table 8).

A negative '*r*' value between initial state CLR and LP growth between initial (third census) and final (fourth census) indicates some sort of non-convergence, that is, the states having high level of CLR does not have high productivity and those with low CLR low LP growth. There seems rather an inverse trend. Despite higher CLR, LP declines and vice versa. A similar trend was observed while comparing LP growth and steady state CI, that is, a negative relationship is found that between LP growth with initial CI values that is if initial level of CI is more, LP growth is less and vice versa.

Table 8 **a** '*r*' between CLR and LP growth. **b** '*r*' between CI and LP growth

(a)

'*r*'	Labour productivity changes III and IV census	CLR III census
LP changes between III and IV census	1	
CLR III census	−0.29584	1
Pearson correlation	−0.297566632	
t stat	−9.112016681	
P(*T* <= *t*) one-tail	7.8771E−11	
P(*T* <= *t*) two-tail	1.57542E−10	

(b)

	LP growth III to IV census	CI in third census
Mean	−0.657788757	2.360084192
Variance	0.048932488	11.49218739
Pearson correlation	−0.116374189	
df	33	
t stat	−5.141112355	
P(*T* <= *t*) one-tail	6.08424E−06	
P(*T* <= *t*) two-tail	1.21685E−05	

In particular, we have not been able to come to any definite way of establishing or rationalising the existence of the state specific steady states (see in this connection Quah 1993).

Rao et al. (1999) analyses the issue of inter-state variation in growth, from perspective of studying not only the convergence but also examining the reasons for the observed pattern. However, they found the states to follow divergent growth paths, which they try to explain in terms of other variables besides the initial level of capital per enterprise. As our analysis, indicates, a consensus is yet to emerge on the convergence issue relating to the Indian states. It is therefore worth our while to take a fresh look into the question.

Behaviour of Growth Rates

We begin our analytical description with growth rates enjoyed by the respective states overtime. Interestingly enough, even for a straightforward issue such as this, there seems to be no unique way of examining the matter.

While the growth rate of LP, on an average, appears to be around 0.065%, most of the North East states had lower growth of employment than the national overall growth excepting for States of Arunachal Pradesh and Nagaland. All the states in extreme North, Jammu and Kashmir, Punjab, Haryana and Himachal Pradesh had higher growth of employment than National overall. Other states having more than national employment growth were Goa, Dadra and Nagar Haveli, Kerala, Rajasthan and Pudduchery. Thus out of total 20 big states, other than the four on North, only three states Goa, Rajasthan and Kerala had more employment growth than all-India. As against the above growth, CLR growth was higher for some more states such as Chandigarh, Delhi, Maharashtra, Odisha, Tripura, Uttar Pradesh and West Bengal too. CQ growth also was negative in 17 out of 21 major states. A disturbing feature is that for almost all the states, LP growth was negative in the last census from previous one. There was a decreasing tendency throughout in 14 out of 22 major states with intermittent growth rates in rest.

So far as CAGR of LP, CQ and CLR are concerned, LP has had a negative growth rate in all major states excepting for Kerala. Gujarat had a much higher CAGR (0.42) compared to any other state followed by Kerala (0.20), Tamil Nadu (0.18), further by J and K (0.13), Himachal Pradesh (0.12). The only other states having positive CAGR of CQ are Jharkhand (0.06) and Karnataka (0.01).

Clearly so, the liberalisation of economy has had a special impact on the growth rates of all states. This observation leads one to expect that the capital investment should have played a significant role in the development of the states post-liberalisation. It is tempting to conjecture that the states which performed better in terms of the growth rates in LP, were perhaps better off in terms of their CQ and CLR levels. This conjecture though receives some support from the results reported but the analysis of the growth rates by computing the Census-to-Census growth rates for each state/union territory brought forth the facts: first, there are large fluctuations in these rates for each state (as reflected from Coefficient of Variation (henceforth CoV) of the CAGR of LP, CQ and CLR, (Refer Table 11), and secondly there is no state which did not experience a negative LP growth rates, during third to fourth census (Refer Table 9). To highlight these findings and to sharpen our understanding of the fluctuation in, the overall growth rates for each state (from first to fourth census: Refer Table 10) is brought out along with the standard deviation of growth rates between one census to next census across states, and so also the coefficient of variations of growth rates, and the maximum and the minimum CAGR (Table 11).

Correlation of LP CAGR with CAGR of CQ and CLR in nutshell proves that the states which performed better in terms of the growth rates in LP, were also better off in growth rates of CQ and CLR. But as the P-value for the CQ was more than 0.15, it was concluded that only CLR had a positive and significant correlation with LP growth rate. Hence, the developments post 2000s brings forth some positive

Table 9 CAGR of LP, CQ and CLR over censuses: states wise

States/UTs	Growth rate I and II census	Growth rate II and III census	Growth rate III and IV census	Growth rate I and II census	Growth rate II and III census	Growth rate III and IV census	Growth rate I and II census	Growth rate II and III census	Growth rate III and IV census
	LP			CQ			CLR		
Andhra Pradesh	0.182	0.088	−0.296	0.02	0.04	−0.17	0.09	0.21	−0.32
Assam	0.145	0.125	−0.288	0.03	−0.05	−0.04	0.11	0.14	−0.22
Bihar	0.099	0.122	−0.262	−0.02	−0.02	−0.08	0.09	0.19	−0.32
Chhattisgarh			−0.197			−0.08			−0.31
Gujarat	0.140	0.039	−0.128	0.02	−0.06	0.42	0.09	0.14	0.13
Haryana	0.148	0.113	−0.194	−0.01	0.05	−0.02	0.10	0.18	−0.16
HP	0.184	0.135	−0.105	0.07	−0.01	0.12	0.13	0.14	−0.09
J and K	0.133	0.137	−0.114	0.04	0.00	0.13	0.14	0.17	−0.10
Jharkhand			−0.154			0.06			−0.14
Karnataka	0.152	0.063	−0.141	0.00	−0.03	0.01	0.10	0.14	−0.20
Kerala	0.142	0.055	0.000	0.00	−0.06	0.20	0.13	0.13	−0.07
M P	0.170	0.079	−0.235	−0.06	0.02	−0.01	0.08	0.16	−0.26
Maharashtra	0.162	0.078	−0.225	0.02	0.01	−0.17	0.09	0.20	−0.26
Odisha	0.148	0.137	−0.331	0.04	0.01	−0.50	0.11	0.18	−0.56
Punjab	0.137	0.123	−0.170	0.00	0.05	−0.03	0.10	0.20	−0.17
Rajasthan	0.163	0.124	−0.250	0.03	0.04	−0.10	0.12	0.19	−0.24
Tamil Nadu	0.122	0.062	−0.089	0.02	−0.05	0.18	0.10	0.14	−0.05
Uttar Pradesh	−0.117		−0.239	0.01	−0.01	−0.06	−0.14		−0.27
Uttarakhand			−0.136			0.00			−0.25
West Bengal	0.117	0.154	−0.333	−0.03	0.05	−0.12	0.07	0.22	−0.27

results on account of labour productivity as capital vis-a-vis labour grows, though localisation of more capital does not indicate the same, significantly.[3,4]

Looking at the CoVs and the maximum and the minimum rates, we find large fluctuations among states in growth rates of LQ, CQ and LP. The fact that there could be alternative ways of calculating the growth rate of a variable over a given period of time and that one may arrive at divergent results depending on the formula used need emphasis. This preliminary investigation makes it evident that one should not hope to discover much homogeneity among the Indian states. Keeping this in mind, we proceed to investigate the convergence question a la Barro and Sala-i-Martin.

Another Analysis: α and β-Convergence

α-Convergence: As is well know, the concept of α-convergence does not relate directly to the growth rates of economies. Instead, it focuses attention on the

[3]In fact while correlating the LP with other variables like Location quotients of a Capital or Labour and lagged CLRs we found that P-value for the three censuses for all the relevant factors was observed to be much more than 0.15, we had to reconsider only the factors meeting criteria of *P*-value to be less than 0.15 and thus the above conclusion.

	Coefficients	Standard error	*t* stat	*P*-value
II census				
Intercept	4.57286104	0.67565688	6.76802258	5.3239E−07
CQ	0.84228019	0.70996803	1.18636355	0.24709074
CLR	−6.994E−05	5.0131E−05	−1.3951657	0.17574369
EQ	−0.3827057	0.77988853	−0.4907184	0.62808254
III census				
Intercept	5.42172098	0.40891236	13.2588827	2.4493E−13
CQ	−0.1102718	0.19778228	−0.5575414	0.58175107
CLR	3.2557E−05	2.0202E−05	1.61155858	0.11868795
EQ	0.01705631	0.01858035	0.91797585	0.3667595
IV census				
Intercept	3.818958	0.463308	8.242807	3.35E−09
CQ	−0.12369	0.147595	−0.83804	0.408637
CLR	1.9E−06	1.65E−06	1.147608	0.2602
EQ	0.58855	0.252571	2.330241	0.026709

[4]MitraArup and Prakash Singh, 'Trade liberalisation enhances productivity and wages at the aggregate level, and also in the case of basic goods and capital goods. However, in an attempt to raise productivity, firms may extract more work from those who are already engaged, and tend to pay them less than their due share in certain industry groups. Contractualisation and feminisation show similar effects for all the industry groups except the intermediate goods industries, and has a worsening effect on wages and also productivity'. Explanations Based on India's Industrial Sector: Why Wage Differences Exist across Sectors? Economic and Political Weekly, Vol. 51, Issue No. 38, 17 Sep, 2016).

Table 10 Overall growth rates between first and fourth census (1972–73 to 2006–07)

States/UTs	Overall growth rate			
	LP	EQ	CQ	CLR
Andhra Pradesh	0.061	0.01188	−0.00285	0.125
Arunachal Pradesh	0.087	−0.04021	0.03265	0.160
Assam	0.064	−0.00117	−0.01326	0.105
Bihar	0.049	−0.00383	−0.02764	0.113
Chandigarh	0.059	0.00802	−0.02447	0.116
Dadra and Nagar Haveli	0.119	0.01238	−0.00517	0.151
Delhi	0.059	0.01211	−0.00934	0.145
Goa	0.104	0.00053	0.01941	0.119
Gujarat	0.056	0.00034	0.03498	0.096
Haryana	0.079	0.00278	0.00971	0.114
Himachal Pradesh	0.121	0.02353	0.03974	0.111
Jammu and Kashmir	0.098	0.00203	0.03437	0.131
Karnataka	0.069	0.00219	−0.01029	0.101
Kerala	0.086	−0.01555	0.00412	0.112
Madhya Pradesh	0.066	0.00540	−0.01681	0.102
Maharashtra	0.064	−0.00722	−0.01431	0.120
Manipur	0.047	0.02021	−0.05319	0.059
Meghalya	0.054	0.01376	−0.02594	0.089
Mizoram	0.064	0.03315	−0.05168	0.019
Nagaland	0.080	0.02378	0.01755	0.137
Odisha	0.060	0.00256	−0.07596	0.122
Puducherry	0.120	0.01645	0.02019	0.109
Punjab	0.084	0.00267	0.01668	0.124
Rajasthan	0.079	0.01251	0.01609	0.127
Tamil Nadu	0.066	−0.00089	0.00949	0.098
Tripura	0.063	0.00950	−0.00453	0.127
Uttar Pradesh	0.065	−0.00312	−0.00915	0.123
West Bengal	0.054	0.00129	−0.01029	0.116

dispersion of per enterprise outputs over a cross-section of economies at each point of time. The economies are said to satisfy the condition of α-convergence if this dispersion decreases over time (EER 2017). A homogeneous group of sub-economies, such as regional subgroups within a national economy, are less likely to differ from each other on account of differences in parametric specifications or random causes. Consequently, they are expected to be α-convergence. This however, is not borne out by the Indian states.

Table 11 CoV, mean standard deviation, maximum and minimum of CAGR between censuses

CAGR	Particular	LP	CQ	CLR
Between I and II census	Mean	0.1411	*0.0189*	*0.0904*
	Standard deviation	0.0660	0.0538	0.0723
	Maximum	0.2550	0.1800	0.3000
	Minimum	−0.1170	−0.1000	−0.1400
	CoV	0.4676	2.8444	0.8006
Between II and III census	Mean	0.1158	0.0042	0.1703
	Standard deviation	0.0417	0.0523	0.0463
	Maximum	0.1880	0.0900	0.2600
	Minimum	0.0390	−0.1500	0.0400
	CoV	0.3598	12.4636	0.2721
Between III and IV census	Mean	−0.2168	−0.0682	−0.2326
	Standard deviation	0.0980	0.1862	0.1407
	Maximum	0	0.4200	0.1300
	Minimum	−0.3900	−0.5000	−0.5600
	CoV	−0.4521	−2.7292	−0.6049

We begin by calculating the CoV of LP across states for each census. Then, we fit a linear time trend over the series so generated. The striking result that emerges here is that the trend of the CoV is increasing. The adjusted R^2 values are found to be high and t-ratios for the intercept as well as the slope coefficient are highly significant. It is clear therefore that for the period under review, the Indian states do not exhibit convergence. In order to have deeper insight into the nature of convergence and divergence, the same CoV-trend analysis was carried out for other components of inter-state variations namely, CI, LI and LQ, where the last one was defined to include EQ to CQ on an average.

CoV was though fluctuated in case of CI but ultimately it too showed an increase from first to third and then to fourth census. Same holds truth for CQ. As against rise of CoV in case of CI, CQ and LP, there were marginal declines in case of LI, and LQ. As is anticipated with rise in CoV of CI and fall in CoV of LI, the CoV of CLR not only declined but also was negative in the fourth census. This conclusion is in concurrence with our earlier findings of simultaneous occurrence of convergence and divergence tendencies in factoral endowments through establishing negative and positive correlations between initial values of LP and LP growth rates, LQ and LQ growth rates, LI and LI growth rates, CI and CI growth rates, CQ and CQ growth rates. A CoV trend across census establishes strong evidence that the Indian states diverged in terms of labour productivity over the 35-years period under consideration. The details of the CoV are presented in Table 12 (Fig. 3).

Table 12 Coefficient of variation in different censuses

Parameters	CoV values			
	First census	Second census	Third census	Fourth census
CI	1.007	3.029	1.463	2.068
CQ	0.771	0.924	1.434	2.034
LP	0.329	0.658	1.048	1.613
CLR	1.359	0.776	3.352	−0.333
LI	3.041	3.895	3.029	3.018
LQ	3.014	3.226	2.980	2.963

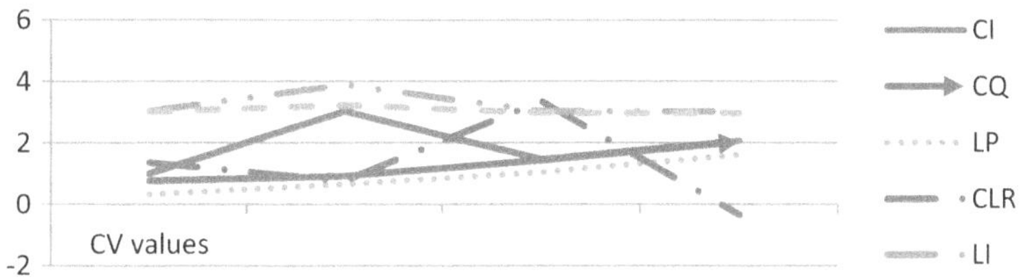

Fig. 3 Trend-lines of coefficient of variance over census

CoV in case of both LP and CQ is going up unabated from the first census to fourth. Labour Intensity variation across states however has mostly been at same level with intermittent rise during second census. Capital Intensity variation which exhibited a decline from second to third census again indicated a rise during third to fourth census. Thus the only CoV showing decline being the CLR, though during second to third census, there was a sharp rise, but a sharper decline was observed in the last census with overall CoV depicting a decline. It was found that the CoVs for CQ as well as LP have the positive trend, but for CLR shows a negative trend. Further, the values of R^2 were high in all cases.

β-Convergence

As already noted neo-classical theory suggests that at low levels of per capita output, an economy grows at a high rate and vice versa. If two economies, similar in terms of parametric specifications, differ only with respect to their per capita output levels at some initial point of time, then at any subsequent point of time, the economy that started off with a higher per capita output should grow at a slower rate. This leads to the hypothesis of absolute or β-convergence (Sharma 2013), which predicts a negative relationship between the rates of growth enjoyed by a cross-section of economies and the levels of their LP at a given initial point of time.

Our next step in this paper is to test for β-convergence amongst Indian states. Clearly, the results obtained so far lead us to believe that the hypothesis will be rejected. Nevertheless, academic rigour demands that this be actually verified. The problem was studied in two different ways. First, we looked at the secular behaviour of labour productivity by fitting a linear relationship of type $yt = \alpha + \beta yt - 1$. This was done through estimating LP in successive period LPs using equation LPs = $a + \beta$ LP$_i$ wherein initial LP, viz, LP in initial census (LP$_i$). However, LP$_i$ may be a weak indicator of initial conditions. Hence, an alternative indicator was tried, viz, measure of semi-log ($\ln yt = \alpha + \beta yt - 1$) trend to the data for each state for all the three series. For both forms, the estimated coefficients of LP during third census and LP during fourth census are positive and significant. This means that for all the states, LP had an increasing trend, though the R^2 values differ across them. The phenomenon of β-convergence occurs if the latter regression line yields a negative coefficient for LP$_i$.

It may well be seen that in all the cases, it is clear that there is no evidence of β-convergence. There is a positive and significant relationship between current censuses (IV Census) LP with last census (III Census) LP,[5] that is,

LP = 24.32858 + 0.290629 LP.

Even semi-log relationship in case of fourth census LP with third census LP also is found to be significant.[6]

5

Regression statistics	
Multiple R	0.588684
R^2	0.346549
Adjusted R^2	0.326128
Standard error	292.1858

	Coefficients	Standard error	t stat	P-value	Lower 95%	Upper 95%	Lower 95.0%	Upper 95.0%
Intercept	24.32858	70.03112	0.347397	0.730568	−118.32	166.9773	−118.32	166.9773
Labour productivity III	0.290629	0.070549	4.119556	0.00025	0.146926	0.434332	0.146926	0.434332

6And as a Semi log function:

Regression statistics	
Multiple R	0.662776
R^2	0.439272
Adjusted R^2	0.421749
Standard error	0.648952
Observations	34

	Coefficients	Standard error	t stat	P-value	Lower 95%	Upper 95%	Lower 95.0%	Upper 95.0%
Intercept	4.410074	0.155541	28.35317	3.03E−24	4.093248	4.7269	4.093248	4.7269
Labour productivity III	0.000785	0.000157	5.006864	1.95E−05	0.000465	0.001104	0.000465	0.001104

In LP = 4.410074 + 0.000785LP
Further for Third Census LP and while linear relationships stand as
LP = 24.01388 + 5.978579 LP
Second Census LP it is
LP = 44.29027 + 5.883493LP
Similarly, semi-log relationship for third census being
In LP = 5.548645 + 0.006274LP
And for Second Census
In LP = 3.700063 + 0.060392LP

The model of beta convergence can be used to analyze the development of economic levels only retrospectively (i.e. in the past). β values have all through been positive and this indicates the states labour productivity have divergence tendencies. The coefficients of the indices of initial LP are positive and significant at the 5% level in all the regressions. The relationship is significant in all cases excepting for the semi-log relationship in case of second census LP as correlated with LP of first Census. Further, the values of R^2 were high in all cases excepting again in cases of second census LP (both log linear, and semi-log relationships) correlated with first census. The relatively low values of R^2 in second census estimates suggest that there are other important factors that need to be taken into account in explaining the behaviour of LP growth rates.

Reasons for Differential Growth Rates: Correlates of Regional Imbalances: Factorial Analysis

As stated earlier, the literature on disparities across Indian states studies the link between regional imbalances and plan outlays Sarker (1994). Sarker discovers a strong link between development (measured in terms of 14 variables including per capita consumption of electricity, percentage of villages electrified, per capita expenditure on health, effective literacy rates, etc.) and the plan outlays for the different states. In our analysis, it is attempted to correlate the CQ growth first and then LQ growth with the different infrastructure and government initiatives, particularly road infrastructure, power supply, Unregistered enterprises growth (reflecting ancillarisation and non-formal sector growth in MSME sector) and investment per enterprise growth (last factor while comparing Labour Quotient growth).

However Principal Component Analysis carried out over the same factors, three most important factors contributing to the Labour Quotient being Per Capita Power, Change in Capital Intensity 2003–07 followed by Length of Roads CAGR 2003–08 (Table 13).

So far as CQ growth is concerned, the two most important factors that emerge are Per Capita Power and CAGR % unregistered enterprises 2002–2007 (Table 14).

Table 13 Percent of variance explained by different infrastructure and other factors in determining LQ

Component matrix		
	Component	
	1	2
Length of roads CAGR 2003–08	0.709	
Change in capital intensity 2003–07		0.788
Per capita power	0.843	
Extraction method: principal component analysis		
a. 3 components extracted		

Table 14 Degree of variance explained by different infrastructure and other factors in determining CQ

Component matrix		
	Component	
	1	2
Per capita power	0.812	
CAGR % un-registered enterprises 2002–2007		0.870
Extraction method: principal component analysis		
a. 2 components extracted		

4 Conclusions

The paper has the following findings in a nutshell:

- Capital Stock is found to be more concentrated in the States of Maharashtra, Tamil Nadu, Punjab, Haryana, Jammu and Kashmir, and Pondicherry while employment over years has diversified across almost all the states.
- In the latest Census of MSME, that is the fourth census, localization of labour has significantly deviated in the sense, it has not remained limited to the states, where capital has concentrated. This has resulted in increased number of States lying in categories of 'High Labour as against Low Capital levels' as well as 'low-labour high capital levels'.
- Pearson's 'r' coefficient between Capital Labour Ratio (CLR) and labour productivity was atypically low (0.21) in case of states with 'Low Capital - High Labour levels'. This was not so in cases of states with 'matching capital and labour levels', or States having 'High Capital but Low Labour levels' (in both cases, values being more than 0.84).
- As far as convergence and divergence trends are concerned, it is found that two types of convergence in employment seems to be occurring (a) enterprise level within a state, (b) state level. But the same does not seem to occur in case of

other factors of production, particularly, capital and this has also resulted in non-convergence in resultant productivity.

- Three most important determinants of MSME growth were found to be infrastructure development, in terms of power use per enterprise, road infrastructure levels in the states and capital intensity (capital per enterprise) growth rate. Yet it cannot be said for sure that which states are more benefited due to infrastructure spread among the three category states. Yet, on the whole this seems to lead to making certain policy prescriptions.

Annexure

Distribution of States According to LQ Versus CQ

	Census-II	Census-III	Census-IV	Remarks
Quadrant-1 (Low Labour and Low Capital)	M. P. (0.22,0.34) HP (0.58,0.72) Haryana (0.72,0.95) J and K (0.71,0.78) Mizoram (0.73,0.95) Punjab (0.72,0.78) Rajasthan (0.67,0.79) Bihar (0.83,0.60) Manipur (0.78,0.63) Meghalaya (1.03,0.95)	M.P. (0.55, 0.30) Bihar (0.58, 0.46) Chhattisgarh (0.60, 0.53) HP (0.77, 0.59) J and K (0.77, 0.78) Karnataka (0.96, 0.68) Uttarakhand (0.59, 0.85) Jharkhand (0.86, 0.29) Kerala (0.82, 0.43) Mizoram (0.75, 0.39) Assam (1.00, 0.67) Manipur (0.96, 0.70) Gujarat (0.93, 0.71) Arunachal (1.05, 1.08) UP (0.80, 0.94)	Arunanchal (0.38, 0.36) Assam (0.97, 0.56) HP (0.73, 1.04) Odisha (0.95, 0.04) Bihar (0.87, 0.31) Meghalaya (0.98, 0.28) Chhattisgarh (0.82, 0.34) M.P. (0.78, 0.29) Jharkhand (0.86, 0.40) Tripura (0.80, 0.36) UP (0.95,0.68) Karnataka (1.04,0.72) Rajasthan (0.82, 0.83) Uttarakhand (0.84, 0.8)	Five states, namely, Bihar, MP, Chhattisgarh, Jharkhand and HP in IV Census were still with low capital and low labour, and they were there in second and third census too While some of the states moved out from here: Andaman, J and K, Mizoram and Manipur appear only in census IV All the 5 States newly added to this category in Census III also figured in Census IV However 2 states newly figured in the category in Census III, Kerala and Gujarat moved out from the category in Census IV Rajasthan and Meghalaya figured in the category in Census II and re-appeared in Census IV Haryana moved out from this category Post-II census Odisha and Tripura were new additions in Census IV

(continued)

(continued)

	Census-II	Census-III	Census-IV	Remarks
Qudrant-2 (Low Labour and High Capital)	Karnataka (0.96, 1.02) Kerala (0.94, 1.05)	Rajasthan (1.03, 1.36)	Maharashtra (1.03, 1.19) T.N. (1.10, 1.26) Punjab (0.83, 1.37) Haryana (0.98, 1.60) J & K (0.84, 1.46) Goa (0.99, 2.37) Gujarat (0.99, 4.09)	There are different states figuring in the category in the three different censuses
Qudrant-3 (High Labour and High Capital)	Assam (1.24, 1.32) Odisha (1.33, 1.18) Goa (1.14, 1.68) Gujarat (1.28, 1.61) Delhi (1.93, 2.50) Maharashtra (1.89, 2.64) T.N. (1.49, 1.19) Tripura (1.98, 1.14) UP (1.66, 1.15) Nagaland (2.69, 2.5) Sikkim (2.41, 7.44)	WB (1.35, 1.18) Punjab (1.16, 1.62) Andhra (1.36, 1.75) Haryana (1.36, 1.80) T.N. (1.09, 1.54) Odisha (1.45, 1.38) Goa (1.73, 2.6) Maharashtra (1.69, 3.00) Nagaland (1.92, 4.20) Tripura (2.72, 2.97) Delhi (2.61, 8.4)	Nagaland (1.98, 1.75)	There seems a gradual reduction in this category of high capital intensity and high labour productivity Only Dadra Nagar Haveli, Damn and Diu, Nagaland and Pondicherry were consistently in this category for all the three Censuses; Chandigarh, Delhi, Goa, Maharashtra, Odisha, T.N., and Tripura were found to be in the category till III census
Qudrant-4 (High Labour and Low Capital)	Andhra (1.12, 1.00) WB	Meghalaya (1.21, 0.63) Sikkim (1.54, 0.79)	Manipur (1.17, 0.38) Andhra (1.23, 0.67) Mizoram (1.26, 0.74)	There is a general tendency of states to be appearing more and more in this category of high labour productivity and low capital intensity

(continued)

(continued)

	Census-II	Census-III	Census-IV	Remarks
			WB (1.12, 0.61) Kerala (1.01, 1.07) Sikkim (2.09, 0.23) Delhi (1.62, 0.98)	

Note Figures in parenthesis reflect: First Figure is: Capital LQs, Second Figure is: Employment LQ
Low Labour and Low Capital <=1.00, High Labour and High Capital >1.00
Red means present in II Census, Light brown means present in III census and IV census too, Purple means appeared in II and IV Census, Black means new inclusion

References

Barro, R., & Sala-i-Martin, X. (1995). *Economic growth*. New York: McGraw-Hill.

Boots, B. N., & Getis, A. (1988). *Point pattern analysis*. Newbury Park, CA: Sage Publications.

Cashin, P., & Sahay, R. (1996). Internal migration, centre-state grants, and economic growth in the states of India. *IMF Staff Papers, 43*(1), 123–171.

Comtois, C. (2017). *The specialization index and the location coefficient*. New York, USA: Department of Global Studies & Geography, Hofstra University.

Dasgupta, D. (2000, July 1). Inter-state disparities in India. *Economic and Political Weekly, 35*(7), 2413–2422.

Dholakia, R. (1994, August 21). Spatial dimension of acceleration of economic growth in India. *Economic and Political Weekly, 29*(35), 2303–2309.

Ghosh, B., Marjit, S., & Neogi, C. (1998, June 27). Economic growth and regional divergence in India, 1960 to 1995. *Economic and Political Weekly, 33*(26), 1623–1630.

https://msme.gov.in/about-us/about-us-ministry.

http://www.dcmsme.gov.in/ito_msme/censuses.htm.

Intellectual Capital Advisory Services Private Limited. (2012, November). *Micro, small and medium enterprise finance in India: A research study on needs, gaps and way forward* (pp. 23, 29). USA: International Finance Corporation.

Lu, Y. (2016). *Spatial cluster analysis for point data: Location quotients verses kernel density* (page 2 of 24). Buffalo: Department of Geography, State University of New York (http://dusk.geo.orst.edu/ucgis/web/oregon/papers/lu.htm).

Lessmann, C., & Seidel, A. (2017). Regional inequality, convergence, and its determinants—A view from outer space. *European Economic Review, 92*, 110–132.

Lucas, R. E. (1998). Ón the mechanics of economics development. *Journal of Monetary Economics, 22*(1), 3–42.

Marjit, S., & Mitra, S. (1996, August 17). Convergence in regional growth rates: Indian research agenda. *Economic and Political Weekly, 31*(33), 2239–2242.

Ministry of Micro, Small & Medium Enterprises. (2007). *Micro, small and medium enterprises in India: An overview*. Ministry of Micro Small and Medium Enterprise, Government of India.

Mitra, A. (1999, July 31). Total factor productivity growth and technical efficiency in Indian industries. *Economic and Political Weekly, 34*(31).

Nagaraj, R., Varoudakis, A., & Veganzones, M. A. (1997). *Long run growth trends and convergence across Indian states*. IGIDR, Mumbai (Mimeograph).

Quah, D. (1993). Empirical cross-section dynamics in economic growth. *European Economic Review, 37,* 426–434.
Raman, J. (1996). *Convergence or uneven development: A note on regional development in India.* USA: Valparaiso University (Mimeographed).
Rao, M. G., Shand, R. T., & Kalirajan, K. P. (1999, March 27–April 2). Indian states: A divergent view. *Economic and Political Weekly, 34*(13), 769–778.
Rodrigue, J.-P. (2017). The specialization index and the location coefficient in chapter 10 methods in transport geography. In *The geography of transport systems* (4th ed., 440 pages). New York: Routledge. ISBN 978-1138669574.
Sarker, P. C. (1994, March 12). Regional imbalances in Indian economy over plan periods. *Economic and Political Weekly, 29*(2), 621–633.
Sharma, N. (2013). *Growth and structural changes in Indian manufacturing since liberalization.* Discussion Paper No 6, in Development Economics and Innovation Studies, Centre for Development Economics and Innovation Studies, Punjabi University (https://www.scribd.com/document/311440162/6-Niharika-Sharma).
Solow, R. M. (1956). A contribution to the theory of economic growth. *Quarterly Journal of Economics, 70,* 65–94.
Subina, S. (2015). Role of MSMEs in the growth of Indian economy. *Global Journal of Commerce and Management Perspective, 4*(5), 40–43. ISSN: 2319-7285 (for 2, 3).

Growth and Structural Changes in Indian Economy—An Analysis

Anil K. Yadav and Jerry Joseph

1 Introduction

Economic development and structural changes are interrelated: if one changes the other also changes. On the other hand, growth is basically a part of the overall economic development. So all these attributes can be correlated on analytical grounds. This becomes very distinct from the work of Van Gamert (1986): 'Economic Development is strongly connected with the structural change and is the vehicle of economic growth and economic development induces structural changes'. Similarly, Clark (1940) tried to analyse the structural changes and attributed the pattern of structural transformation to the composition of demand as an outcome of increasing incomes and to the inter-sectoral variations in the rates of growth of labour productivity. The similar proposition has been shared by Urata (1987). Kuznets (1955–56 to 1966–67 in a series) based on the historical experience of the developed countries pointed out the changes in the structure of production and employment, shifting away from agriculture towards industry and later away from industry to services. Similarly, the trade structure also witnessed significant changes in export from primary goods to merchandised goods, etc. Kuznets (1966) had made the analysis of growth in different countries. He pointed out that the cycles common to countries experiencing modern economic growth could easily result in a decline of around 20% in real output in a short period of time. He further states that unless there is sustained growth, and the sharp cyclical decline would sweep away the past gains and revert the economy to the original economic status. Later, Chenery and Syrquin (1975) made the comparisons among countries and tried to

A. K. Yadav (✉) · J. Joseph
NILERD, A-7, Narela Institutional Area, Delhi 110040, India
e-mail: anil_doctor2005@yahoo.com

J. Joseph
e-mail: jerryjerry20042002@gmail.com

NILERD, *Reflecting on India's Development*,
https://doi.org/10.1007/978-981-13-1414-8_3

prove the set path in a quantitative manner. They further stated the stages of changes relating them to the income levels. Panchamukhi et al. (1986) had analysed the Indian and other developing countries data and found a completely different pattern from the one the developed countries had followed. They had established that in case of developing countries, the share of GDP is changing directly from agriculture to industry and as well as to services sector. They had also observed that in case of developing countries, the share is inclined more in favour of services sector as compared to industry. In a continued effort, Bhattacharya and Mitra (1990) had analysed the data on the services sector and viewed that there had been an excess growth as experienced by this sector. Further, Goldar and Mitra (2010) tried to study the sectoral shifts in relation to the increase in productivity and overall economic growth in India. They are of the view that there has been a major shift in favour of tertiary sector and this shift contributed immensely by economic growth. However, they further noted that between the secondary and trade-transport sectors, the former proved to be the lead sector for growth in medium and long run although the share of trade-transport in GDP has increased overtime. Therefore, they suggested that there is a need for a policy which could focus on the industrial sector. So far as the growth of the tertiary sector is concerned, they found that the productivity growth within the tertiary sector has possibly originated from the use of IT services. Papola (2012) has attempted to analyse the structural changes in Indian economy and has tried to capture the emerging patterns and its implications on the economy. He found that there has been an increasing trend in the import intensity of exports. He termed this a disturbing feature of the emerging trend in India's trade structure. Second, he also notes that there has been a faster growth of exports in services. The growth was much faster than merchandise exports and at the same time, it exhibited greater resilience and sustainability reflected in their robust growth even during the period of depression (2008) in the global economy. In an inter-state analysis of variations in the rates of GSDP growth, he found a strong association of rate of growth with the pace of industrial growth. He further noted that all states have undergone the structural changes, i.e. a decline in agriculture share in GSDP. More importantly, he noted that despite the fact that share of agriculture has fallen in all the states, the disparity among the states has not declined.

More recently, Bhalla et al. (2017) have analysed India's demographic dividend in a theoretical antecedent and with empirical evidence. Kuznets, Coale and Hoover recognised that it was quite possible for a country to experience a period of accelerating workforce growth and declining birth rates without being able to take advantage of this window of opportunity which will close, if and when birth rates become equal to death rates and population growth therefore ceases. This trio could foresee the metamorphosis of the Bretton Woods institutions into those of the Washington Consensus, not as their role as architects, arbiters and enforcers of neo-liberal macroeconomic policies in distant countries at diverse levels of economic and institutional development. However, in an exclusive effort, Joshi (2017) has tried to analyse the determinants of tertiary sector employment in India, she has used different variables in order to determine the employment in services sector. These determinants are size of population, urbanisation, female literacy rate, female education up to secondary level and over and above the sex ratio, etc. After regressing these variables, she could point out that the spread of literacy can prove to be instrumental for the employment generation. Apart from this, the urbanisation was also found supportive for the employment growth in the services sector. All the studies have shown a definite pattern of structural changes and growth in India and different other countries. All these above studies have certainly brought out greater clarity on the structural transformation. It needs further proving in the light of liberalisation and labour reforms.

In this paper, we seek to look into the growth and structural changes in Indian economy and further in 17 major states. Initially, we are taking year-to-year growth rates since 1950–51 till 2011–12. This is done in order to examine the year-to-year fluctuations in the growth rates and the probable reasons thereof. Secondly, plan-wise growth rates have also been considered. This has been taken in order to observe plan to plan performance. The paper considers the structures, i.e. the production structure mainly at the sectoral level and the employment structure among the three sectors. We have also calculated the productivity relatives. This has been done by dividing the production structure share of the sectors by employment shares of the sectors.

The paper has also looked into the state level structure of production and employment. An analysis has been made between the states with higher structural shifts and labour reforms. We would also be probing into the rural and urban composition of the population. We would be analysing the relationship between structural shifts in states and the nutrition level (calorie intake), the literacy level, monthly per capita consumption expenditure, per capita income in states (SGDP) and the inflation (consumer price index as proxy). Hence, we would try to test the following hypotheses:

1. Higher the structural shifts higher would be the consumption, nutrition and education development (literacy rate), urbanisation, per capita income and the inflation rate.

2 Database and Methodology

The data for the paper has been used from different sources such as censuses of India i.e. 1991, 2001 and 2011, National account statistics, various rounds of National Sample Survey Organisation (NSSO) on employment, and National Nutrition Monitoring Bureau, National Family Health Surveys and other related sources required for the analysis. The data has also been taken from Indiastats, a statistical database available with the institute. We have mostly used the percentage analysis. We have calculated the productivity relatives by dividing the share of

GDP/SGDP by the share of employment in that particular sector. Apart from this, we have used the correlation matrix to establish the relationship among the shifts in the shares of the sector and the monthly per capita consumption expenditure, nutritional level, literacy and the urbanisation level and inflation. Mostly the data on all these indicators has been taken from India stats database available in the institute (NILERD). The data on Consumer Price Index (Proxy for Inflation) has been taken from the Ministry of Statistics and Programme Implementation (MOSPI) database series.

3 Growth

The Indian economy has been growing with time. It has experienced the lows and highs as the time passed. Initially, it had been by around 3% or so and was termed as Hindu rate of growth (Raj Krishna). It may be observed that there are lots of fluctuations in the growth rates. The growth rates have been even negative for some years. These years are 1957–58 (−0.5), 1965–66 (−2.7), 1972–73 (−0.5) and 1979–80 (−5.1). These years had been the abnormal years as has been observed from the literature. There had been a war with Pakistan in 1965 and 1971 and the impact of that came on the next year's growth performance. The year 1979–80 was a draught year. Figure 1 shows the fluctuations. It is quite clear that there are lots of fluctuations in the growth scenario. The growth rates started improving in 1980s and kept on rising till the Eleventh Five-Year Plan. It may be observed that the growth rates changes as the base year changes. The growth rates were different with the base year 1980–81 (Yadav 1993, 1995a, b, 1999). The growth rates were on the higher side with base year 1980–81 as compared to 2004–05. The fluctuations are more as may be seen in Fig. 1 (Table 1).

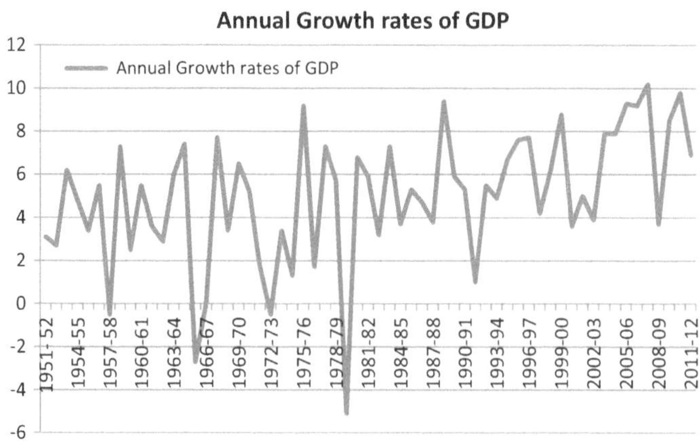

Fig. 1 The fluctuations in the growth rates

Table 1 Annual growth rates gross domestic product in India

Years	Growth	Year	Growth
1951–52	3.1	1982–83	3.2
1952–53	2.7	1983–84	7.3
1953–54	6.2	1984–85	3.7
1954–55	4.8	1985–86	5.3
1955–56	3.4	1986–87	4.7
1956–57	5.5	1987–88	3.8
1957–58	−0.5	1988–89	9.4
1958–59	7.3	1989–90	5.9
1959–60	2.5	1990–91	5.3
1960–61	5.5	1991–92	1.0
1961–62	3.6	1992–93	5.5
1962–63	2.9	1993–94	4.9
1963–64	6.0	1994–95	6.7
1964–65	7.4	1995–96	7.6
1965–66	−2.7	1996–97	7.7
1966–67	0.0	1997–98	4.2
1967–68	7.7	1998–99	6.2
1968–69	3.4	1999–00	8.8
1969–70	6.5	2000–01	3.6
1970–71	5.2	2001–02	5.0
1971–72	1.7	2002–03	3.9
1972–73	−0.5	2003–04	7.9
1973–74	3.4	2004–05	7.9
1974–75	1.3	2005–06	9.3
1975–76	9.2	2006–07	9.2
1976–77	1.7	2007–08	10.2
1977–78	7.3	2008–09	3.7
1978–79	5.7	2009–10	8.5
1979–80	−5.1	2010–11	9.8
1980–81	6.8	2011–12	6.9
1981–82	5.9		

Source Economic survey, 2015–16

Table 2 shows the planwise growth rates. It is understood that the growth rates had been on the lower side till the Sixth Five-Year Plan. It started rising from the Sixth Five-Year Plan onwards. It was 5.4% during the Sixth Five-Year Plan kept on rising and had been 7.8% during the Eleventh Five-Year Plan. One may note that growth rates are different since the base year is different. In the earlier base year, the First Five-Year Plan showed 5.1% rate of growth (Yadav 1993, 1995a, b, 1999), the Second Five-Year Plan showed 2.2% growth rate. The Third and Fourth Year Plan shows lower rate of growth as per the 2004–05 base. It means that as the base year changes the growth rates also changes.

Table 2 Planwise growth rates

Plan	Year	Annual average growth rates (in constant price)
First Plan	(1951–52 to 1955–56)	4.0
Second Plan	(1956–57 to 1960–61)	4.1
Third Plan	(1961–62 to 1965–66)	3.4
Three annual plan	(1966–67 to 1968–69)	3.7
Fourth Plan	(1969–70 to 1973–74)	3.2
Fifth Plan	(1974–75 to 1978–79)	5.1
Annual Plan	(1979–80)	−5.1
Sixth Plan	(1980–81 to 1984–85)	5.4
Seventh Plan	(1985–86 to 1989–90)	5.8
Two annual Plan	(1990–91 to 1991–92)	3.2
Eight Plan	(1992–93 to 1996–97)	6.5
Ninth Plan	(1997–98 to 2001–02)	5.6
Tenth Plan	(2002–03 to 2006–07)	7.6
Eleventh Plan	(2007–08 to 2011–12)	7.8

Source Economic survey, 2015–16

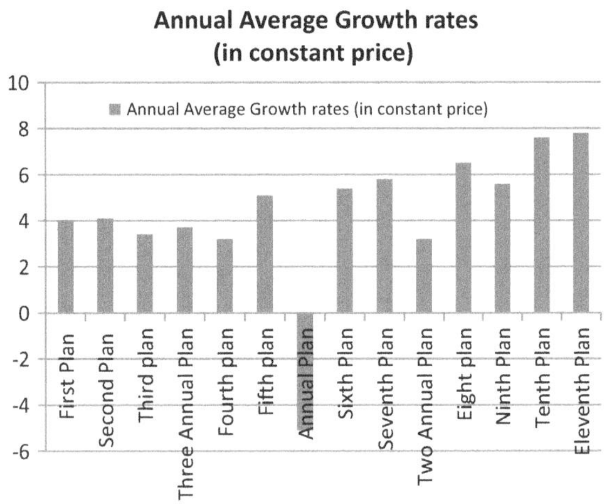

Fig. 2 The annual average growth rates. *Source* Drawn on the basis of Table 2

Figure 2 shows more clearly the performance of the economy during the plan periods, i.e. Five-Year Plans as well as the annual plans. This also clearly explains that the growth rates have increased from Fifth Five-Year Plan onwards.

4 Gross Domestic Product (GDP)

Table 3 shows the shares of gross domestic product over the 64 years starting from 1950–51 to 2013–14 among different sectors such as agriculture, industry and the services. It may be observed that the share of agriculture is falling in favour of

Table 3 Share of GDP in different sectors

	Years									
	1950–51	1960–61	1970–71	1980–81	1990–91	2000–01	2010–11	2011–12	2012–13	2013–14
Ag	53.71	49.79	43.86	38.031	33.00	25.22	16.84	16.48	20.87	20.43
Ind	14.35	17.92	21.42	23.04	24.15	24.30	25.67	26.10	28.89	28.61
Ser	31.94	32.29	34.72	43.96	42.85	50.48	57.49	57.42	50.24	50.96

Source Economic survey, 2015–16

industry and that more in favour of services sector. The share of agriculture had been 53.71% in 1950–51 and got reduced to 16.48% in 2011–12 and slightly moved up to 20.43% in 2013–14. It is a reduction in the share by around 31 percentage points from 1950–51 to 2013–14. This slight increase in the share of GDP in 2013–14 may have happened due to the change of base year. As against this, the share of industry as well as that of the services is increasing over time. The share of industry has increased from 14.35% in 1950–51 to 28.61% in 2013–14. This is an increase of around 14 percentage points. Similarly, the share of the services sector has increased from 31.94% in 1950–51 to 50.96% in 2013–14. The services sector has gained around 19 percentage points. This reflects that the Indian economy is fast moving towards a services economy.

5 Employment Structure

The employment structure has been shown in Table 4. It is evident from the data presented in the table that employment structure is changing over time period. It is changing although at a slow pace till 2004–05 and then changed at a relatively faster pace during 2004–05 and 2011–12. It may, however, be observed that the share of agriculture has shifted towards both the sectors, i.e. industry as well as services. The shift in industrial share is faster as compared to services sector during the same period as mentioned above, i.e. 2004–05 and 2011–12. The share of agriculture got reduced from 64.6% in 1993–94 to 49.4% in 2011–12. The share has changed by 15.2 percentages points. The share of industry got changed from

Table 4 Employment structure by sectors

	Years			
Sectors	1993–94	1999–00	2004–05	2011–12
Agriculture	64.6	62.3	59.1	49.4
Industry	14.2	15.2	17.6	23.7
Services	21.2	22.5	23.4	26.9

Source Different employment round, National Sample Survey Organisation (NSSO)

14.2 to 23.7% during the same period showing a gain of around 9.5 percentage points whereas the share of services sector has increased from 21.2 to 26.7%. It reflects a shift of 5.7 percentage points.

6 Productivity Relatives

Table 5 shows the productivity relatives in different sectors. As evident from the table, productivity relatives are lower in the agriculture sector and that too are falling subsequently. During 1990–91 it was 0.51 and fell to 0.33 in 2011–12. The productivity relatives do not come near to one (1) in agriculture sector. This is because it is employing comparatively more than it is producing. The agriculture sector is also having disguised employment. Second, it is also understood that the marginal physical productivity of an additional labour is zero and after some time, it becomes negative in the case of agriculture. As against this, the productivity relatives are on the higher side in the industry as well as in the services sector. The productivity relatives are highest in services sector. The productivity relatives lay between 1 and 2 in the case of industry whereas it lies between 2 and 2.5 as far as services sector is concerned. The productivity relatives are keeping on the lower side in agriculture sector as compared to industry and much lower to services sector. It is possible because of the fact that the share of services sector in GDP has been increasing significantly and the share of employment is not increasing to that extent.

7 State Gross Domestic Product (SGDP)

It may be seen from Table 6 that the shares are changing very fast after 1991. One may recall that it was a special year since the structural reforms and/or adjustments were introduced in this year. The share of agriculture is rapidly sliding down and that of services rising. The share of industry also increasing but at a very slow pace. The share of agriculture has gone down in the case of all the states except Bihar. In case of Bihar the share of agriculture has gone up in 2001. However, the situation improved and the share has declined in 2011–12. One may observe from the table that the share of services has increased sharply for all the states which is quite similar to the pattern of national level.

Table 5 Productivity relatives in different sectors

	Years		
Sectors	1990–91	2000–01	2011–12
Agriculture	0.51	0.41	0.33
Industry	1.70	1.60	1.10
Services	2.02	2.24	2.14

Source Derived from Tables 3 and 4

Table 6 Sectorwise share of SGDP in different states of India

		1990–91			2000–01			2011–2012		
Sr. No.	Name of the state	Ag	Ind	Ser	Ag	Ind	Ser	Ag	Ind	Ser
1	Andhra Pradesh	35.76	22.49	41.81	27.58	23.45	48.97	26.09	31.02	42.89
2	Assam	36.52	17.45	46.04	31.90	18.59	49.56	20.93	31.86	47.21
3	Bihar	36.28	32.28	31.44	36.93	11.02	52.05	24.67	18.10	57.23
4	Gujarat	23.61	38.34	38.05	13.69	40.99	45.47	18.56	41.95	39.49
5	Haryana	44.58	24.55	30.87	29.75	28.18	42.07	22.50	30.18	47.25
6	Himachal Pradesh	32.65	27.07	40.28	22.06	37.92	40.02	16.23	42.82	40.95
7	Jammu and Kashmir	–	–	–	27.90	24.03	48.07	16.99	27.26	55.75
8	Karnataka	31.76	26.53	41.72	26.68	24.69	48.63	12.87	27.74	59.39
9	Kerala	29.66	24.53	45.80	18.96	21.83	59.29	13.68	26.79	59.53
10	Madhya Pradesh	39.82	29.13	31.04	22.01	26.31	51.68	28.70	29.88	41.42
11	Maharashtra	19.75	37.06	43.19	14.41	27.86	57.73	12.26	34.37	53.37
12	Orissa	32.68	27.99	39.33	25.65	25.59	48.76	17.17	41.97	40.84
13	Punjab	46.73	24.33	28.75	36.25	23.27	40.48	29.69	24.49	45.82
14	Rajasthan	44.08	22.61	33.31	27.21	28.26	44.53	27.69	31.68	40.63
15	Tamil Nadu	20.77	35.51	43.72	15.20	31.01	53.79	12.24	32.78	54.98
16	Uttar Pradesh	40.75	22.17	37.08	45.41	18.74	35.85	26.28	26.91	46.81
17	West Bengal	26.18	30.60	43.20	25.75	18.99	55.26	–	–	–

Source Taken from Indiastats, a statistical database

8 Employment Structure

Table 7 shows the employment structure of different states. It may be noted from the table that the structure is changing over time. Although it is changing at a slower pace, the direction of change is from agriculture to industry and services. In some states, it has been observed that the change is taking place directly from agriculture to the services sector. One thing is clear from the data that the industry is absorbing less people as compared to agriculture and services sector. This has already been observed in an earlier study (Yadav 2005). This seems to be a universal truth barring few states.

9 Productivity Relatives

Table 8 shows the productivity relatives in three different sectors, i.e. agriculture, industry and the services. One may observe from the table that the productivity relative have lower values in agriculture and that of the industry and services is

Table 7 Sectorwise share of employment in different states of India

		1993–94			1999–00			2011–12		
Sr. No.	Name of the state	Ag	Ind	Ser	Ag	Ind	Ser	Ag	Ind	Ser
1	Andhra Pradesh	64.58	13.48	21.90	60.59	14.34	25.07	52.92	19.34	27.74
2	Assam	61.83	6.83	31.35	51.09	8.05	40.86	56.05	13.24	30.71
3	Bihar	67.43	10.03	23.10	63.04	12.70	24.26	62.37	16.01	21.62
4	Gujarat	61.53	18.40	20.03	60.04	16.18	22.88	48.78	26.37	24.87
5	Haryana	59.20	14.95	27.85	53.07	18.05	28.88	43.34	27.23	29.43
6	Himachal Pradesh	64.83	11.40	23.88	56.45	16.27	27.27	58.43	22.62	18.95
7	Jammu and Kashmir	60.50	12.28	27.18	59.04	14.24	26.72	42.48	29.91	27.61
8	Karnataka	66.20	14.05	19.68	63.37	14.38	22.25	49.94	19.11	30.95
9	Kerala	49.88	20.95	29.18	38.99	24.72	36.29	25.53	31.81	42.66
10	Madhya Pradesh	72.93	9.15	17.83	68.23	11.55	20.22	59.00	20.74	20.26
11	Maharashtra	64.70	13.55	21.90	61.68	14.14	24.18	49.10	19.05	31.85
12	Orissa	65.95	12.30	21.78	61.04	16.71	22.25	55.71	22.71	21.58
13	Punjab	58.35	14.90	26.83	55.09	16.96	27.95	36.45	31.52	32.03
14	Rajasthan	65.53	15.43	19.10	61.62	17.85	20.53	50.41	29.70	19.89
15	Tamil Nadu	56.30	21.08	22.10	52.21	23.06	19.08	35.16	33.87	30.97
16	Uttar Pradesh	63.90	13.55	22.53	57.86	16.93	25.21	52.41	26.34	21.25
17	West Bengal	49.43	23.08	27.40	47.43	22.82	29.75	39.23	31.33	29.44

Source Different employment rounds, NSSO

higher. As seen from the table that productivity relatives have been falling continuously for the agriculture and that of industry and service is rising. This is primarily happening due to the reason that the share of agriculture in SGDP is falling but of that employment is not falling at the same rate. Whereas the share of industry and also that of services in SGDP is rising at a faster rate than employment.

10 Sectoral Shifts in SGDP

In Table 9, sectoral shifts have been placed. It is observed that sectoral shifts are quite visible. The shifting is taking place from agriculture to industry and the services. As we had observed in national case so is happening for different states. It is evident from the table that the shifts are taking place more in favour of the services sector. One may understand that the services sector is expanding in terms of SGDP share and hence the growth is faster in it. Mostly, it has been observed that the agriculture sector shows the negative signs. It is in fact happening because of

Table 8 Statewise productivity relatives in India

Sr. No.	Name of the state	1990–91			2000–01			2011–2012		
		Ag	Ind	Ser	Ag	Ind	Ser	Ag	Ind	Ser
1.	Andhra Pradesh	0.55	1.66	1.90	0.45	1.63	1.95	0.49	1.60	1.54
2	Assam	0.59	2.55	1.46	0.62	2.30	1.21	0.37	2.40	1.53
3	Bihar	0.53	3.21	1.36	0.60	0.86	2.14	0.39	1.13	2.64
4	Gujarat	0.38	2.08	1.89	0.22	0.30	1.98	0.38	1.59	1.58
5	Haryana	0.75	1.64	1.10	0.56	1.56	1.45	0.51	1.59	1.58
6	Himachal Pradesh	0.50	2.37	1.68	0.39	2.33	1.46	0.27	1.89	2.16
7	Jammu and Kashmir	–	–	–	0.47	1.68	1.79	0.39	1.43	2.01
8	Karnataka	0.47	1.88	2.11	0.42	1.71	2.18	0.25	0.45	1.91
9	Kerala	0.59	1.17	1.56	0.48	0.88	1.63	0.53	0.84	1.39
10	Madhya Pradesh	0.54	3.18	1.74	0.32	2.27	2.55	0.48	1.44	2.04
11	Maharashtra	0.30	2.73	1.97	0.23	1.97	2.38	0.24	1.80	1.67
12	Orissa	0.49	2.27	1.71	0.42	1.53	2.19	0.30	1.84	1.89
13	Punjab	0.80	1.63	1.07	0.65	1.37	2.16	0.81	0.77	1.43
14	Rajasthan	0.67	1.46	1.74	0.44	2.70	2.16	0.54	1.06	2.04
15	Tamil Nadu	0.36	1.68	1.97	0.29	1.34	2.81	0.34	1.05	1.77
16	Uttar Pradesh	0.63	1.63	1.64	0.78	1.10	1.42	0.50	1.03	2.20
17	West Bengal	0.52	1.32	1.57	0.54	0.83	1.85	–	–	–

Source Derived from Tables 6 and 7

the fact that shifts are taking place from agriculture. It is interesting to note that it is positive in case of two states, viz. Bihar and Uttar Pradesh during 1991–2001. In Bihar, it is 0.65 percentages points while in Utter Pradesh it is 4.66 percentage points. It does means that these two states are not visualising the desired changes. Moreover, these two states are the part of the BIMARU states and also the most backward and highly populated.

11 Correlation Matrix

Table 10 shows the kind of relationship between shares of different sectors, i.e. agriculture, industry and services and various variables as described above in section I and II. It is observed that the share of agriculture is having a negative relationship with the share of industry, services, urban population and the literacy. It is having positive relationship with the calorie intake, monthly per capita expenditure and per capita SGDP. Similarly, industry is having a negative relationship with agriculture, services and calorie intake, monthly per capita consumption expenditure while it has positive relations with rest of the variables. This suggests that the industry and the literacy do go to gather. Similarly, the monthly per capita consumption expenditure has positive relationship with the share of agriculture,

Table 9 Percentage change in the share of GDP

Sr. No.	Name of the state	1991/2001			2001/2011		
		Ag	Ind	Ser	Ag	Ind	Ser
1	Andhra Pradesh	−8.18	0.96	7.16	−1.49	7.57	−6.08
2	Assam	−4.62	1.14	3.52	−10.97	2.34	−2.35
3	Bihar	0.65	−21.26	20.58	−12.26	7.08	5.18
4	Gujarat	−9.92	17.36	7.42	4.87	0.96	−5.98
5	Haryana	−14.83	3.63	11.20	−7.25	2.00	5.18
6	Himachal Pradesh	−10.59	10.85	−0.26	−5.83	4.90	0.93
7	Jammu and Kashmir	–	–	–	−10.91	3.23	7.68
8	Karnataka	−5.08	−1.84	6.91	−13.81	3.05	10.76
9	Kerala	−10.70	−2.70	13.49	−5.28	4.96	0.24
10	Madhya Pradesh	−17.81	−2.82	20.64	−6.69	3.57	−10.26
11	Maharashtra	−5.34	−9.20	14.54	−2.15	6.51	−4.36
12	Orissa	−7.03	−2.40	9.43	−8.48	16.38	−7.92
13	Punjab	−10.48	−1.06	11.73	−6.56	1.22	−5.34
14	Rajasthan	−3.91	5.65	11.22	0.48	3.42	−3.90
15	Tamil Nadu	−5.57	−4.50	10.07	−2.96	4.77	1.19
16	Uttar Pradesh	4.66	−3.43	−1.23	−19.13	8.17	10.96
17	West Bengal	−0.43	−11.61	12.06	–	–	–

Source Calculated on the basis of Table 6

calorie intake urban population and the literacy rate but has negative relationship with the other sectors. So far as the services sector is concerned it has negative relationship with rest of the variables except urbanisation and literacy rate. Whereas the calorie intake has negative relationship with the share of industry, services, urban population and literacy rate and per capita SGDP. It is interesting to note that literacy is having positive relationship with the share of industry, services, urban population and per capita monthly consumption expenditure and per capita SGDP.

The monthly per capita expenditure has positive relation with agriculture, calorie intake, share of urban population, literacy rate, and the per capita SGDP. The per capita SGDP has positive relation with most of the sectors and variables except services. This means that the per capita SGDP moves along with most of the sectors and the variable considered here for the analysis.

Table 11 shows the correlation among different variable for the year 2001. The data on calorie intake is not available and hence relationship with other variable cannot be ascertained. Nonetheless, it is interesting to observe that the share of agriculture is having negative relationship with all the variables. This clearly suggests that its share is falling. The industry is having positive relation with most of the variables and negative with agriculture and services sector. As against this, services sector is having positive relation only with urban population and the literacy and negative with rest of the variables and/or sectors.

Table 10 Correlation coefficient between different sectors and other variable, 1991

	Share of agriculture	Share of industry	Share of service	Calorie intake	Share of urban population	Literacy rate	Monthly per capita consumption expenditure	Per capita SNDP
Share of agriculture	1							
Share of industry	−0.708	1						
Share of service	−0.703	−0.0009	1					
Calorie intake	0.5551	−0.4039	−0.3921	1				
Share of urban population	−0.445	0.4714	0.1835	−0.3797	1			
Literacy rate	−0.4922	0.2204	0.4817	−0.3841	0.3183	1		
Monthly per capita consumption expenditure	0.3158	−0.3268	−0.1132	0.4819	0.0672	0.399	1	
Per capita SGDP	0.0292	0.1927	−0.213	−0.0809	0.5164	0.372	0.4864	1

Source Calculated on the bases of information taken from different source

Table 11 Correlation coefficient between different sectors and other variable, 2001

	Share of agriculture	Share of industry	Share of service	Calorie intake	Share of urban population	Literacy rate	Monthly per capita consumption expenditure	Per capita SNDP
Share of agriculture	1							
Share of industry	−0.5154	1						
Share of service	−0.5695	−0.2614	1					
Calorie intake								
Share of urban population	−0.5139	0.2484	0.2729		1			
Literacy rate	−0.6387	0.2664	0.3479		0.3996	1		
Monthly per capita consumption expenditure	−0.3179	0.3516	−0.0913		0.4625	0.6428	1	
Per capita SNDP	−0.3667	0.2994	−0.0705		0.5633	0.6929	0.8464	1

Source Calculated on the bases of information taken from different sources

Table 12 shows the correlation among the sectors and the variables. In this year's analysis yet another variable, i.e. consumer price index (CPI) (proxy for inflation) has been added for the analysis. It may be observed that the share of agriculture is having negative relation with most of the variable and sectors except calorie intake. The industry sector, on the other hand, is having positive relationship with all the variables and negative with the share of agriculture, services sector and inflation. As against this, the service sector is having a negative relationship with agriculture and industry sector and the calorie intake and positive with rest of the variables. However, the relationship of these variables with other variables is very different. For example, literacy has got a positive relationship with all the other variables except agriculture. Mitra (2017) also found the similar results whereby he says that the rural and urban growth also contribute to the urbanisation. Second, he also postulated that the work participation and the literacy among rural males also add to the urbanisation. This gets strengthen from the fact that the share of urban population is having a negative relationship with agriculture and the calorie intake, and it has a positive relationship with rest of the sectors and variables. It is very interesting to note that the Consumer price index is having a negative relationship with most of the variables and sectors except Share of service, urban population and literacy. It shows that whichever variable is increasing has a positive relationship with rest of the variables except agriculture.

11.1 Population Structure

Table 13 shows the rural–urban structure of population. One may observe that the rural–urban structure is changing over time. The population is getting migrated from rural to urban. The urban share of the population is rising and that of rural is declining. It may be noted that it is changing faster in some states and slower in the other. But the fact remains that it is changing. The states where it is changing faster are Tamil Nadu, Kerala, Maharashtra, Gujarat, Karnataka, Punjab, Haryana, Andhra Pradesh, West Bengal, etc. As against this, it is changing at relatively a slower pace in the state like Himachal Pradesh, Odisha, Bihar, Assam and Uttar Pradesh. It shows a very interesting result from the analysis that those states which are more industrialised and also where the literacy rate is higher the urbanisation is also higher. Whereas it is the other way round that those state where the literacy is lower and also the industrialisation is lower, it seems that the population has not moved from the rural areas to the urban areas much, i.e. not to the expectation level.

Figures 3, 4 and 5 clearly depict the changes in the rural–urban composition in different states. Figures below show the changes in the shares of rural and urban areas.

Table 12 Correlation coefficient between different sectors and other variable, 2011

	Share of agriculture	Share of industry	Share of service	Calorie intake	Share of urban population	Literacy rate	Monthly per capita consumption expenditure	Per capita SNDP	CPI
Share of agriculture	1								
Share of industry	−0.3971	1							
Share of service	−0.5524	−0.5407	1						
Calorie intake	0.2101	0.1395	−0.3416	1					
Share of urban population	−0.3366	0.0034	0.3298	−0.1879	1				
Literacy rate	−0.5918	0.3576	0.2137	0.0774	0.5565	1			
Monthly per capita consumption expenditure	−0.3427	0.0119	0.2985	0.255	0.6959	0.7048	1		
Per capita SNDP	−0.5461	0.328	0.2048	0.1522	0.7029	0.7414	0.8968	1	
CPI	−0.2705	−0.0353	0.2607	−0.63	0.2797	0.3159	−0.024	−0.034	1

Source Calculated on the bases of information taken from different sources

Table 13 Population structure in India (percent)

	1991		2001		2011	
States	Urban	Rural	Urban	Rural	Urban	Rural
Andhra Pradesh	26.89	73.11	27.30	72.70	33.36	66.64
Assam	11.10	88.90	12.90	87.10	14.10	85.90
Bihar	13.14	86.86	10.46	89.54	11.29	88.71
Gujarat	34.49	65.51	37.36	62.64	42.60	57.40
Haryana	24.63	75.37	28.92	71.08	34.88	65.12
Himachal Pradesh	8.69	91.31	9.80	90.20	10.03	89.97
Jammu and Kashmir			24.81	75.19	27.38	72.62
Karnataka	30.92	69.08	33.99	66.01	38.67	61.33
Kerala	26.39	73.61	25.96	74.04	47.70	52.30
Madhya Pradesh	23.18	76.82	26.46	73.54	27.63	72.37
Maharashtra	38.69	61.31	42.43	57.57	45.22	54.78
Odessa	13.38	86.62	14.99	85.01	16.69	83.31
Punjab	29.55	70.45	33.92	66.08	37.48	62.52
Rajasthan	22.88	77.12	23.39	76.61	24.87	75.13
Tamil Nadu	34.15	65.85	44.04	55.96	48.40	51.60
Uttar Pradesh	19.84	80.16	20.78	79.22	22.27	77.73
West Bengal	27.48	72.52	27.97	72.03	31.87	68.13

Source Various censuses Registrar General of India

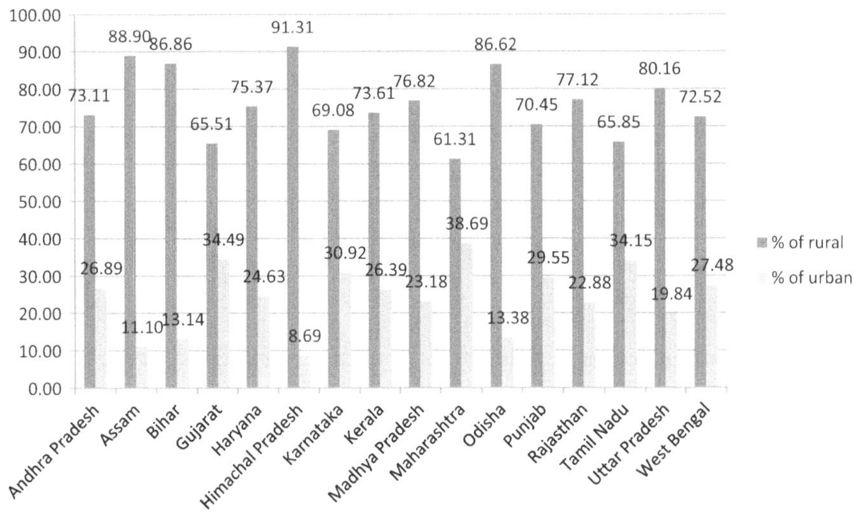

Fig. 3 Population structure of India, 1991

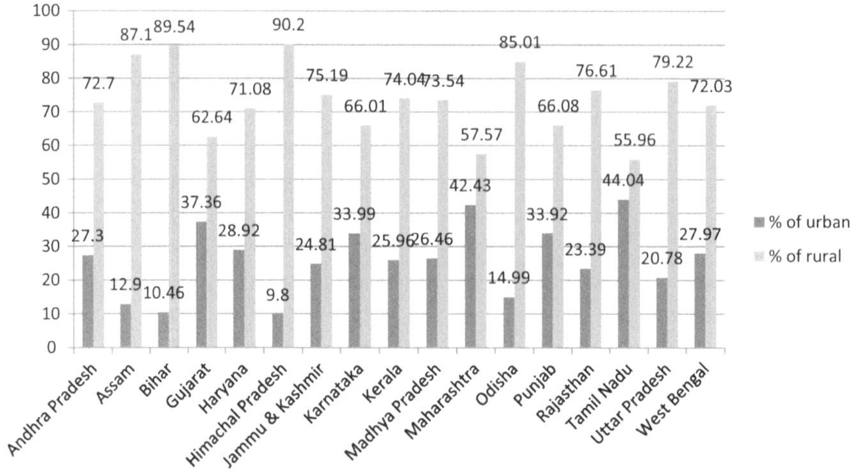

Fig. 4 The population structure of India, 2001

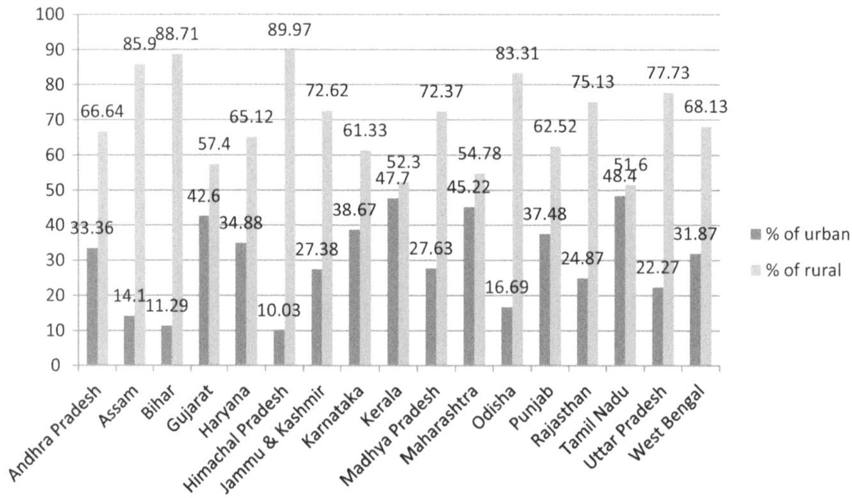

Fig. 5 The population structure of India, 2011

12 Sectoral Shifts and Labour Reforms

As we know that the labour reforms have taken place in Maharashtra, Gujarat, Madhya Pradesh, Rajasthan and Haryana. These changes are witnessed in the Industrial Disputed Act, 1947 which states that if an industry employs up to 300 employs, it may retrench and/or shut down the firm without government's approval. Second, about the Factory Act, the factories which employ 40 workers and the unit

Table 14 Sectoral changes in those states where labour reforms have taken place

Years	1991/2001			2001/2011		
Sectors/States	Ag	Ind	Ser	Ag	Ind	Ser
Gujarat	−9.98	17.36	7.42	4.87	0.96	−5.18
Haryana	−14.83	3.63	11.20	−7.25	2.00	5.18
Madhya Pradesh	−17.81	−2.82	20.64	−6.69	3.57	−10.26
Maharashtra	−5.34	−9.20	14.54	−2.15	6.51	−4.36
Rajasthan	−10.82	5.65	11.22	0.48	3.42	−3.90

Source Taken from Table 9

operating with electricity would be treated as a factory if employ 20 workers earlier. The overtime has been enhanced from 75 to 115 h. The contract Labour Act would apply on companies which engage 50 workers which on 20 workers earlier. Apart from this, there are state-specific amendments in the labour laws like Haryana has proposed incentives if the companies employ at least 70% of the semi-skilled workers from within the state. We have tried to understand the relationship between the sectoral shifts and labour reforms. We have chosen those states where labour reforms have taken place. Now the question arises as to whether the states where labour reforms have taken place are they the one where sectoral changes in SGDP are also higher. In a very cursory glance, one may observe from Table 14 that in three states, viz. Haryana and Madhya Pradesh and Table 14.

Rajasthan the one where sectoral changes is on the higher side during 1991–2001. Among all states, Madhya Pradesh had the highest changes during 1991–2001. It may, therefore, be stated safely that the states which had followed the labour reforms also have higher sectoral shifts. In addition to this, it may also be stated that Kerala and Tamil Nadu are the states which visualised higher sectoral shifts although they have not followed the labour reforms.

13 Conclusions

In this paper, we seek to analyse the growth pattern and the structural changes in the Indian economy and its major states. We have taken the GDP/SGDP and employment figures for the analysis. It is observed that the growth rates have been widely fluctuating on yearly basis and the growth rates have been negative for 4 years. It has happened mainly due to the three wars we fought with China and Pakistan and another being the draught year. As far as the shares of GDP are concerned, it is changing faster from agriculture to industry and also to the services sector at the national level. This is also quite similar in the case of the states. As against this, the share of employment is changing in a similar manner but relatively at a slower pace. Indeed, it is because of this reason that the productivity relatives have been keeping low in the agriculture and higher in the industry as well as the services sector. It is, in fact, the highest for the services sector.

The correlation matrix shows that the agriculture is having negative relations with most of the variables while the other two sectors, i.e. industry and the services, are having a positive relation. As far as the story of urbanisation is concerned, it seems to have been faster in those states where industrialisation and literacy rates are higher. We have also made an effort to relate the sectoral shift with that of Labour reforms. It has been found that where the labour reforms have been accepted, the sectoral shifts are also higher. If we go further, we may also say that in those states where urbanisation is higher the shifts in SGDP are also higher and they also followed the labour reforms. But the argument may be taken with some caution because there are some states where there are no labour reforms but the shift in SGDP as well as the shift in population structure is higher. These are Kerala and Tamil Nadu.

Looking at the results we may suggest that urbanisation may be encouraged so as to achieve higher literacy rates. Second, keeping in view that labour reforms have been beneficial in states where they were followed it may be safe to recommend for other states. This may result in faster sectoral shifts.

Acknowledgements We are thankful to Prof. Arup Mitra, DG, Dr. Kailash Pradhan, Joint Director Shri Marshall Birua, Shri Vijay Saxsena, both Assistant Directors and Shri Arun Kumar, Computer Assistant of NILERD, for their encouragement and help rendered at different stages.

Conflict of Interest

The authors are the Director and Assistant Directors in NILERD. The views expressed in this paper are of ours and not of the institute we are employed in.

References

Bhalla, S., Kumar, A., & Jatav, M. (2017). India's demography dividend: Theoretical antecedents and empirical evidence. In K. P. Kannan, R. P. Mamgain & P. Rustagi (Eds.), *Labour and development: Essays in honour of Prof. T.S. Papola*.

Bhattacharya, B. B., & Mitra, A. (1990). Excess growth in tertiary sector in Indian economy: Issues and implications. *Economic and Political Weekly, 25*(44), 2445–2450 November, 1990.

Chenery, H. B., & Syrquin, M. (1975). *Patterns of Development: 1950–70*. London: A World Bank Research Publication, Oxford University Press for World Bank.

Clark, C. (1940). *Conditions of economic progress*. London: Macmillan.

Goldar, B., & Mitra, A. (2010). Productivity increase and changing sectoral composition: Contribution to economic growth in India. In Government of India (2015–16), Economic Survey of India, Ministry of Finance (Ed.), *India's economy and growth: Essays in honour of VKRV Rao*. New Delhi: Sage publication India.

Joshi, S. (2017). Determinant of tertiary sector employment in India. In Dr. A. Mitra, (Ed.), *Economic growth in India and its many dimensions*. Delhi: Orient Blackswan.

Kuznets, S. (1955). Towards a theory of economic growth. In R. Lekachman (Ed.), *National policy for economic welfare at home and abroad*. Garden City, NY: Doubleday.

Kuznets, S. (1956). Quantitative aspects of economic growth of nations. In *Economic development and cultural change* (Vol. 1), October, 1956.

Kuznets, S. (1966). *Modern economic growth: Rate, structure and spread.* New Haven and London: Yale University Press.

Mitra, A. (2017). Growth, inequality, poverty and urbanisation, WPS 01/2017, Nilerd Working Paper Series.

Ministry of Statistics and Programme Implementation. (1993–94, 1999–00, 2004–05 2011–12). Various issues of the employment rounds, NewDelhi.

Panchamukhi, V. R., Nambiar, R. G. & Mehta, R. (1986). Structural change and economic growth in developing countries. In *The VIII World Economic Congress New Delhi.*

Papola, T. S. (2012). Economic growth and employment linkages: The Indian experience. *The Indian Economic Journal (Conference Volume)*, December, 2012.

Registrar General of India. (1991, 2001, 2011). *Census of India various tables on population, 1991, 2001 & 2011*, New Delhi.

Urata, S. (1987). Sources of economic growth and structural change in China 1956–1981. *The Journal of Comparative Economics.*

Van Gemert, H. G. (1986). *Structural change in OECD countries, some estimates of normal pattern.* Paper presented at VIII IEA World Congress, (Session 9, Theme 1), New Delhi.

Yadav, A. K. (1993). Structural changes in Indian economy: A comparative analysis among countries over time. A Ph.D. Thesis submitted to and Awarded by Gujarat University through Sardar Patel Institute of Economic and Social Research, Ahmadabad.

Yadav, A. K. (1995a). Growth and structural changes in the Indian economy. *Anvesak, 25*(1), January–June, 1995.

Yadav, A. K. (1995b). Agriculture and structural changes in Indian economy. January, 1995 for a project at Sardar Patel Institute of Eco. & Soc. Research, Ahmadabad, sponsored by Ford Foundation.

Yadav, A. K. (1999). *Structural changes in Indian economy.* Daryaganj, New Delhi: Northern Book Centre.

Yadav, A. K. (2005). Structural changes in the Indian workforce. In *Annual conference of the Indian Society of Labour Economics*, December 15–17, 2003 at Kolkata, and published in *Manpower Journal (XLII)*2, April–June, 2007.

Structural Transformation and Its Impact on Rural–Urban Households in India

P. C. Parida and K. C. Pradhan

1 Introduction

A topic that has been of long-running interest for researchers is to understand the implications of economic transformation of economies along the path of economic development. As documented in the literature, development process tends to create large-scale structural transformations in the form of transforming economies from agrarian to more industrial and service oriented. This relates to the famous Lewisian (1954) dual economy model which explains that a developing economy moves from a traditional agricultural base to a modern manufacturing led economy and in the process of such development surplus of unproductive labour in the agriculture sector would tend to move to productive manufacturing sector where wages are relatively high. In a similar line, the Harris and Todaro (1970) model discusses the structural transformation of the economy during a short period of time in the form of migration of labour force from rural to urban areas due to wage differential. The literature suggests that migration of labour force from rural to urban areas will have a positive impact on local development (Lucas and Stark 1985; Taylor 1992; Rozelle et al. 1999; Taylor and Martin 2001; De Brauw et al. 2001).

In the Indian context, the economy has witnessed a structural transformation over the past two decades particularly during the post-2000s period. Primary sector which played a dominant role in economic development of the country in terms of output and employment until the late 1970s has gradually decelerated over the period. On the other hand, the output and employment share of non-agriculture

P. C. Parida (✉) · K. C. Pradhan
National Institute of Labour Economics Research and Development (NILERD), Narela, Delhi, India
e-mail: paridapc@gmail.com

K. C. Pradhan
e-mail: kailasheco@gmail.com

NILERD, *Reflecting on India's Development*,
https://doi.org/10.1007/978-981-13-1414-8_4

sector has improved. It has been observed that the participation of rural households has declined in agriculture sector but expanded substantially in non-agriculture sector during the last two decades or so (Coppard 2001; Srivastav and Dubey 2002; Bhalla 2002; Bhaumik 2002; Chadha 2002; Sahu 2003). Given the half of the workforce in the country is still engaged in agriculture sector and more than 65% of population are living in rural areas, this structural transformation of the economy has potentially large implications on welfare of the people living in both rural and urban areas. Further, the country has experienced social transformation in terms of literacy, family planning, longevity and women's empowerment, etc., over the years which may have affected the well-being of the people. A more critical issue here is how the households in general and workforce in particular in the rural and urban areas adjust to such structural transformation in terms of their occupational choices, income, education and skill development, which in turn affect their livelihood. Whether such structural transformation has reduced or increased the welfare gap between the rural and urban households.

In this context, the present paper examines some of the key emerging issues such as (1) how has the sectoral transformation impacted the welfare of the people in rural and urban areas (2) how has the structural changes impacted wage rates and hence the welfare of the people (3) Does the changes of social transformation have any implications on welfare of households in rural and urban India? (4) Have these changes widened or squeezed the rural–urban welfare disparities?

The remaining structure of the paper is as follows. Section 2 presents a brief review of the literature. Methodology and data sources are analysed in Sect. 3. Section 4 covers descriptive analysis and empirical findings of the study. Section 5 concludes the paper.

2 Review of Literature

Some attempts have been made in the literature to examine factors that are responsible for rural–urban disparities. Nguyen et al. (2007) and Go et al. (2007) suggest that overall inequality in developing countries is driven primarily by welfare disparities between rural and urban areas. As such, understanding the sources of spatial welfare gaps is essential for policy purposes. Pervasive rural–urban welfare gaps have resulted due to a number of factors. One principal factor is the pursuit of urban biased industrialisation policies that resulted in stagnation of the rural agricultural sector and subsequently agricultural incomes (Chirwa and Matita 2009).

In a study for Veitnam, Nguyen et al. (2007) find that the sources of inequality between rural and urban households increased between 1993 and 1998, largely due to differences in returns to household endowments, particularly educational attainment of the household head. The effect of returns to characteristics was stronger at high quantiles. Conversely, they find that differences in household characteristics as a main source of inequality at lower quantiles. Thu Le and Booth

(2014) extend their analysis of Vietnam and study the period between 1993 and 2006, employing unconditional quantile regression decomposition based on re-centred influence functions. Thu Le and Booth (2014) conclude that rural–urban expenditure gaps result both from differences in observed characteristics of households and the returns to these characteristics. The key contributing factors to household inequality were found to be education, industrial structure and receipt of remittances (whilst remittances from domestic sources reduce inequalities, international remittances widen the gap). Chang (2012) finds that consumption inequality between non-farm and farm households in Taiwan is explained by differences in household endowments. The key determinants of the consumption gap include educational attainment, household income and the degree of urbanization. Fang and Sakellariou (2013) conclude that the narrowing of rural–urban inequalities (living standards) in Thailand, between 1990 and 2006, is explained by both changes in household characteristics and the returns to these characteristics. Improvement in educational attainment in rural areas was important to the reduction of inequality in Thailand (Fang and Sakellariou 2013). Frank et al. (2017) examined the determinants of household consumption expenditure and factors that explain rural–urban welfare gaps between 1998 and 2013 in Ghana using the unconditional quantile regression. They find the significant spatial differences in consumption expenditure across selected quantiles, with rural–urban inequalities driven largely by differences in returns to households' endowments.

In case of India, Azam (2012) examines differences in welfare between social groups. The study concludes that inequality in rural India is larger at higher quantiles. Inequality across distributions is significantly explained by differences in the returns to endowments. Cain et al. (2010) confirm the importance of returns to household characteristics to welfare gaps between households in India. The returns to education, which increased due to economic liberalization, tend to increase disparities in household expenditures, especially in urban areas. Hnatkovska and Lahiri (2012) examined the gaps between rural and urban. They have used household survey data from successive rounds of the NSSO for the period 1983–2005 and find that a significant narrowing of the differences in education, occupation distribution, and wages between individuals in rural India and their urban counterparts during this period.

Although the present study does not wholly differ from the above studies particularly from Hnatkovska and Lahiri (2012) in terms of issues, it examines the impact of structural transformation on welfare of the households in rural and urban areas slightly in a different context. First, the study uses the updated information to capture the impact of structural transformation on welfare of households in rural and urban India. Second, methodologically, the paper examines the issues using both cross section and pooled data in order to authenticate the findings. Third, definition wise, the study differs from earlier studies in terms of selecting the decision maker of the household. The present study uses the principal earner of the household as the decision maker instead of previous studies who have invariably taken head of the household as the decision maker.

3 Data Source and Methodology

The determinants of welfare of rural and urban households were identified by using cross section and pooled data obtained from two quinquennial rounds of National Sample Survey (NSS) namely 61st (2004–05) and 68th (2011–12). The study uses per capita household consumption expenditure to measure the welfare of the households and identified some of the key demographic and economic parameters to explain it. The variables considered in the model were:

- Dependent variable—Per capita household consumption expenditure
- Explanatory variables—the numbers of persons living in the household (household size), the age of the principal earner of the household, the education level of the principal earner (illiterate = 1, literate & up to primary = 2, secondary = 3, under graduation = 4, graduation & above = 5), the gender of the principal earner (female = 1), occupations (agriculture = 1, industry = 2, service = 3) of the principal earner and per capita wage of the household, and a dummy variable (urban = 1) was introduced in the model to estimate the rural/urban consumption gap in case of cross section data and a dummy variable for time period (2011–12 = 1) was introduced in the model to estimate the time impact on consumption expenditure in case of pooled data.

The paper uses demographic and economic characteristic of the principal earner of the household because we believe that the principal earner of the household may have more influence in family decision-making, even if that person is not designated as household head. In addition, NSSO data shows out of total sample size, about 68% principal earners were household head in 2004–05 and about 70% principal earners were household head in 2011–12. Further, the estimation excludes the sample size of households in which the principal earner is engaged in household enterprises (self-employed) as NSSO data shows wage rates are not available in this case.

The estimation of consumption function for rural, urban and aggregate level has been carried out in two steps. In the first step, we estimate the following consumption models:

(1) Using the cross section data for two time periods, i.e. 2004–05 and 2011–12

$$\begin{aligned}\mathrm{PCE\_}r_i = {} & \alpha_0 + \beta_1\mathrm{PE}_i + \beta_2\mathrm{SE}_i + \beta_3\mathrm{UG}_i + \beta_4\mathrm{GT}_i + \beta_5\mathrm{HS}_i \\ & + \beta_6\mathrm{AGE}_i + \beta_7\mathrm{GEND}_i + \beta_8\mathrm{IND}_i + \beta_9\mathrm{SER}_i + \beta_{10}\mathrm{PCW}_i + \varepsilon_{1i}\end{aligned} \tag{1}$$

$$\begin{aligned}\mathrm{PCE\_}u_i = {} & \alpha_1 + \gamma_1\mathrm{PE}_i + \gamma_2\mathrm{SE}_i + \gamma_3\mathrm{UG}_i + \gamma_4\mathrm{GT}_i + \gamma_5\mathrm{HS}_i \\ & + \gamma_6\mathrm{AGE}_i + \gamma_7\mathrm{GEND}_i + \gamma_8\mathrm{IND}_i + \gamma_9\mathrm{SER}_i + \gamma_{10}\mathrm{PCW}_i + \varepsilon_{2i}\end{aligned} \tag{2}$$

$$\begin{aligned}\mathrm{PCE}_i = {} & \alpha_2 + \eta_1\mathrm{PE}_i + \eta_2\mathrm{SE}_i + \eta_3\mathrm{UG}_i + \eta_4\mathrm{GT}_i + \eta_5\mathrm{HS}_i + \eta_6\mathrm{AGE}_i \\ & + \eta_7\mathrm{GEND}_i + \eta_8\mathrm{IND}_i + \eta_9\mathrm{SER}_i + \eta_{10}\mathrm{PCW}_i + \eta_{11}\mathrm{D}_u + \varepsilon_{3i}\end{aligned} \tag{3}$$

where i = 1, 2, 3, …, n number of households. PCE_r, PCE_u and PCE are real per capita household consumption expenditure in rural, urban and aggregate level, respectively. PE is literate up to primary level, SE is literate at secondary level, UG is literate at under graduate level, GT is graduation and above, HS is household size, AGE is age, GEND is gender, IND is industry occupation, SER is service occupation, PCW is real per capita wage earnings and D_u stands for dummy for the urban households. As per the theory, the signs of β_1, β_2, β_3, β_4, β_6, β_7, β_8, β_9 and β_{10} are expected to be positive and the sign of β_5 is expected to be negative. Similarly, in Eqs. (2 and 3), except γ_5 and η_5 the sign of coefficients of all other variables are expected to be positive.

(2) Using the pooled data (combining both 2004–05 and 2011–12)

$$\begin{aligned}\text{PCE\_}r_{it} &= \alpha_0 + \delta_1\text{PE}_{it} + \delta_2\text{SE}_{it} + \delta_3\text{UG}_{it} + \delta_4\text{GT}_{it} + \delta_5\text{HS}_{it} + \delta_6\text{AGE}_{it} \\ &\quad + \delta_7\text{GEND}_{it} + \delta_8\text{IND}_{it} + \delta_9\text{SER}_{it} + \delta_{10}\text{PCW}_{it} + \delta_{11}\text{DT}_{it} + u_{1it}\end{aligned} \tag{4}$$

$$\begin{aligned}\text{PCE\_}u_{it} &= \alpha_1 + \phi_1\text{PE}_{it} + \phi_2\text{SE}_{it} + \phi_3\text{UG}_{it} + \phi_4\text{GT}_{it} + \phi_5\text{HS}_{it} + \phi_6\text{AGE}_{it} \\ &\quad + \phi_7\text{GEND}_{it} + \phi_8\text{IND}_{it} + \phi_9\text{SER}_{it} + \phi_{10}\text{PCW}_{it} + \phi_{11}\text{DT}_{it} + u_{2it}\end{aligned} \tag{5}$$

where i = 1, 2, 3,…, n number of households and t = 2004–05 and 2011–12. The sign of δ_1, δ_2, δ_3, δ_4, δ_6, δ_7, δ_8, δ_9, δ_{10} and δ_{11} are expected to be positive and the sign of δ_5 is expected to be negative. Similarly, in Eq. (2), except ϕ_5, the signs of coefficients of all other variables are expected to be positive.

We have converted the nominal consumption expenditure and wage earnings of households into real term deflating by consumer price index (CPI, base year 1986–87). Further, CPI agricultural labourer and CPI industrial workers are used for rural and urban areas respectively to convert nominal consumption expenditure and wages into real term.

In the second step of estimation, we make an attempt to find out how the relationship between log (PCE) and household characteristics (determinants) defers between rural and urban areas. Therefore, we used B-O decomposition to decompose changes in the mean of log RPCE due to household characteristics between rural and urban areas. The B-O decomposition is done by using the following linear regression model:

$$Y_j = X_j'\beta_j + \varepsilon_j,\ E(\varepsilon_j) = 0 \quad j \in (R, U) \tag{6}$$

where Y is the log of RPCE, X is vector of household characteristics and a constant, β contains the slope parameters and the intercept, and ε is the error. R and U explain the rural and urban households, respectively. The mean difference of log of RPCE of urban and rural household's can be expressed as:

$$R = E(Y_U) - E(Y_R) = E(X_U)'\beta_U - E(X_R)'\beta_R \tag{7}$$

because

$$E(Y_j) = E\left(X_j'\beta_j + \varepsilon_j\right)) = E\left(X_j'\beta_j\right) + E(\varepsilon_j) = E(X_j)'\beta_j \tag{8}$$

where $E(\beta_j) = \beta_j$ and $E(\varepsilon_j) = 0$ by assumption.

To identify the contribution of urban and rural differences in predictors to the overall real per capita consumption difference, Eq. (7) can be rearranged as

$$R = \{E(X_U) - E(X_R)\}'\beta_R + E(X_R)'(\beta_U - \beta_R) + \{E(X_U) - E(X_R)\}'(\beta_U - \beta_R) \tag{9}$$

This is a 'threefold' decomposition, that is, the difference of the log of real per capita consumption of rural and urban households is divided into three components:

$$R = E + C + I \tag{10}$$

The first component, $\{E(X_U) - E(X_R)\}'\beta_R$, explains the endowment effects that is due to differences in the predictors. The second components $E(X_R)'(\beta_U - \beta_R)$ explain the differences in the coefficients (including differences in the intercept). The third component, $\{E(X_U) - E(X_R)\}'(\beta_U - \beta_R)$, explains interaction term accounting for the fact that differences in endowments and coefficients exist simultaneously between the urban and rural households.

The decomposition shown in Eq. (9) is formulated from the viewpoint of rural household. That is, the urban–rural differences in the predictors are weighted by the coefficients of rural household to determine the endowments effect (*E*). The *E* component measures the expected change of mean in per capita consumption of rural household if rural households had urban household's predictor levels. Similarly, for the *C* component (the 'coefficients effect'), the differences in coefficients are weighted by rural household's predictor levels. That is, the *C* component measures the expected change of mean in per capita consumption of rural household if the rural household had urban household's coefficients. Naturally, the differential can also be expressed from the viewpoint of urban households.

4 Results Analysis

The theoretical analysis suggests that economic welfare of households in terms of per capita household consumption expenditure is influenced by key economic, social and demographic factors namely education level, age, household size, gender, occupation and per capita wage earnings of households. But the degree of influence of these factors on per capita consumption expenditure of household is expected to vary from rural to urban areas due to variation in quality of education, female empowerment, types of occupation and level of wage rate and family planning. In this context, before examining the relationship between economic welfare and key economic, social and demographic factors, it is pertinent to understand the pattern of changes of these factors within and between rural and urban areas over the time.

4.1 Descriptive Statistics

Table 1 presents the summary statistics of some of these principal variables for rural and urban households in two different time points. Data shows that the level of per capita consumption expenditure (in nominal term) of urban household was 1.73 times more than rural household in 2004–05 which has slightly declined to 1.69 times in 2011–12. Over the period, the per capita consumption expenditure of rural household at all India level has increased by the extent of Rs. 815.95 from Rs. 657.70 in 2004–05 to Rs. 1473.65 in 2011–12 and it is statistically significant at 1% significance level. Similarly, the per capita consumption expenditure of urban household suggests that it has increased by Rs. 1350.32 between 2004–05 and 2011–12 and it is statistically significant. This suggests that although the level of per capita consumption expenditure of rural household is lower than urban household it has grown at a higher pace than the latter, suggesting a positive sign of gradual convergence of rural consumption towards the urban consumption level. Higher increase of rural household consumption expenditure in the recent time could be due to multiple factors such as increase of minimum support prices of agricultural produce, migration to urban areas for jobs, penetration of services activities, increase of agricultural wage income, etc. Data shows that the average per capita wage income of rural household has increased at compound annual growth rate of 14.4% between 2011–12 and 2004–05 as compared to 14% in case of urban household during the same period. We also find that more and more principal earners of the households in the rural areas are willing to work in non-agriculture sector than the agriculture sector. For example, the occupation data reveals that the urban to rural ratio in agriculture sector has increased from 0.11 in 2004–05 to 0.15 in 2011–12. On the other hand, the ratio shows opposite trends in case of industry and services sector during the same period, indicating the urban–rural gap is gradually squeezing with respect to wage rates and occupation choices.

As compared to urban, rural areas also witness improved trends in human capital in the form of expansion of education. The percentage of illiterate has declined at compound annual growth rate (CAGR) of 4.5% between 2004–05 and 2011–12 in rural areas as compared to 3.8% in urban areas. More importantly, as we move on from lower to higher education, except graduate and above, in all other cases, i.e. secondary, higher secondary and undergraduate, the percentage of literate people in the rural areas has increased at a higher pace than urban. As educated youth in rural areas are unwilling to work in agriculture sector, instead of preferring employment opportunities in non-agriculture sector, the percentage of principal earners employed in agriculture sector has declined at CAGR of 7.1% in rural areas during

Table 1 Descriptive statistics (2004–05 and 2011–12)

Variables	2004–05				2011–12				Rural	Urban
	Rural	Urban	Total	Diff. (U-R)	Rural	Urban	Total	Diff. (U-R)	Diff. (two rounds)	Diff. (two rounds)
Per capita consumption (Rs.)	657.70	1136.98	862.64	479.28***	1473.65	2487.30	1928.04	1013.65***	815.95***	1350.32***
	(2.67)	(15.39)	(6.82)	(13.65)	(7.40)	(14.88)	(8.13)	(15.72)	(7.41)	(21.46)
Illiterate (%)	31.39	15.27	24.50	−16.12***	22.75	11.63	17.77	−11.12***	−8.64***	−3.64***
	(0.25)	(0.23)	(0.18)	(0.35)	(0.25)	(0.21)	(0.17)	(0.34)	(0.36)	(0.31)
Literate and up to primary (%)	25.09	21.17	23.42	−3.92***	23.38	16.15	20.14	−7.23***	−1.71***	−5.02***
	(0.24)	(0.26)	(0.18)	(0.35)	(0.25)	(0.24)	(0.18)	(0.35)	(0.35)	(0.36)
Secondary (%)	24.95	29.62	26.95	4.67***	29.34	29.42	29.38	0.08	4.39***	−0.20
	(0.24)	(0.29)	(0.18)	(0.37)	(0.27)	(0.30)	(0.20)	(0.40)	(0.36)	(0.42)
Under graduation (%)	9.23	13.47	11.04	4.24***	11.09	14.46	12.60	3.37***	1.86***	0.99***
	(0.16)	(0.22)	(0.13)	(0.26)	(0.19)	(0.23)	(0.15)	(0.29)	(0.24)	(0.32)
Graduate and above (%)	9.34	20.46	14.10	11.12***	13.44	28.34	20.12	14.90***	4.09***	7.87***
	(0.16)	(0.26)	(0.14)	(0.29)	(0.20)	(0.30)	(0.18)	(0.35)	(0.25)	(0.39)
Age	36.68	37.38	36.98	0.70***	38.22	38.33	38.27	0.11	1.54***	0.95***
	(0.06)	(0.07)	(0.05)	(0.10)	(0.07)	(0.07)	(0.05)	(0.10)	(0.09)	(0.10)
Household size	5.04	4.57	4.84	−0.47***	4.72	4.30	4.53	−0.42***	−0.32***	−0.26***
	(0.01)	(0.01)	(0.01)	(0.02)	(0.01)	(0.01)	(0.01)	(0.02)	(0.02)	(0.02)
Female (%)	14.77	13.73	14.33	−1.04***	14.48	13.10	13.86	−1.39***	−0.29***	−0.63**
	(0.19)	(0.22)	(0.14)	(0.29)	(0.21)	(0.22)	(0.15)	(0.31)	(0.29)	(0.31)
Agriculture (%)	38.59	4.41	23.97	−34.18***	23.10	3.41	14.27	−19.69***	−15.49***	−1.00***
	(0.27)	(0.13)	(0.18)	(0.33)	(0.25)	(0.12)	(0.15)	(0.30)	(0.37)	(0.18)

(continued)

Table 1 (continued)

Variables	2004–05				2011–12				Rural	Urban
	Rural	Urban	Total	Diff. (U-R)	Rural	Urban	Total	Diff. (U-R)	Diff. (two rounds)	Diff. (two rounds)
Industry (%)	24.23	33.75	28.30	9.52***	38.42	34.58	36.70	−3.85***	14.19***	0.83***
	(0.23)	(0.30)	(0.19)	(0.37)	(0.29)	(0.31)	(0.21)	(0.43)	(0.37)	(0.43)
Service (%)	37.18	61.84	47.73	24.66***	38.48	62.01	49.03)	23.54***	1.30***	0.17
	(0.26)	(0.31)	(0.21)	(0.40)	(0.29)	(0.32)	(0.22)	(0.43)	(0.39)	(0.44)
Per capita wage (Rs.)	33.65	62.77	46.10	29.12***	86.52	156.99	118.11	70.47***	52.87***	94.22***
	(0.25)	(0.53)	(0.27)	(0.54)	(0.67)	(1.60)	(0.82)	(1.62)	(0.67)	(1.63)
No. of observation	33,485	25,015	58,500		28,423	23,093	51,516			

Standard errors in parentheses
***$p < 0.01$, **$p < 0.05$, *$p < 0.1$

2004–12. On the other hand, the percentage of principal earners in rural areas employed in industry and services has witnessed an increase at compound growth rate of 6.8 and 0.5%, respectively, during 2004–12 as compared to 0.3 and 0.04% in urban areas during the same period.

In addition to the above analysis of changes in trends of key variables, the paper also tries to find out how the distribution of household consumption expenditure has changed with respect to key explanatory variables. Table 2 reports the per capita household consumption expenditure (in nominal term) across key socio-economic and demographic parameters. In case of education, the data for 2004–05 shows the per capita consumption expenditure was more than one time higher in case of rural households whose principal earner was literate up to primary level as compared to rural households whose principal earner was illiterate. This ratio of per capita consumption expenditure of households whose principal earner is illiterate to the principal earner is having higher level of education tends to increases as the level of education of the principal earner increases. The similar trends are also found in the case of urban households for the same period. Interestingly, like the case of 2004–05 periods, data for 2011–12 also shows similar trends of consumption expenditure with respect to education but the ratio has declined in the latter period. Further, between rural and urban areas, it is found that the ratio of urban to rural household consumption expenditure has declined from 2004–05 to 2011–12 as far as the education of the principal earner is concerned. It suggests that consumption expenditure of rural households has increased at a higher rate than their urban counterparts.

Like the case of education, the data for occupation for 2004–05 suggests that households whose principal earner is working in industry spent money double than

Table 2 Per capita consumption by education, gender and industries[a]

Variables	2004–05			2011–12			U-R ratio	
	Rural	Urban	Total	Rural	Urban	Total	2004–05	2011–12
Illiterate	481.9	597.5	512.7	1097.0	1362.5	1174.9	1.2	1.2
Literate and up to primary	558.0	760.9	636.5	1203.2	1572.9	1336.1	1.4	1.3
Secondary	697.1	983.9	831.9	1455.9	2035.3	1716.0	1.4	1.4
Under graduation	939.0	1505.5	1234.5	1881.9	2754.9	2331.0	1.6	1.5
Graduate and above	1133.4	1907.7	1614.0	2284.1	3802.7	3243.1	1.7	1.7
Female	653.6	1188.2	872.7	1597.8	2711.9	2069.7	1.8	1.7
Male	658.4	1128.8	861.0	1452.6	2453.4	1905.2	1.7	1.7
Agriculture	494.9	599.3	503.1	1141.7	1540.0	1184.3	1.2	1.3
Industry	622.9	934.3	781.7	1285.4	2080.8	1621.3	1.5	1.6
Service	849.4	1285.9	1091.3	1860.9	2766.0	2374.1	1.5	1.5
Total	657.7	1137.0	862.6	1473.7	2487.3	1928.0	1.7	1.7

[a]Consumption expenditure is at current prices

the households whose principal earner is working in agriculture and allied sector. The ratio is found even higher in case of services sector. This is true for both rural and urban areas. Between urban and rural areas, the ratio of urban to rural consumption expenditure shows the principal earner's expenditure is 1.5 times higher in urban than rural areas. Consumption expenditure with respect to gender suggests that households whose principal earner is a male member consume equal level of consumption as compared households whose principal earner is a female member. Importantly, the latter groups of households have spent more in the recent time as compared to the former groups of households.

4.2 Estimated Results

The empirical findings of the paper are divided into two parts. In the first part, the paper presents results of rural and urban consumption functions using the cross section data for two data points, i.e. 2004–05 and 2011–12. In the second part, the study reports the results of consumption functions using the pool data of rural and urban areas.

Table 3 reports estimated results of consumption functions for rural, urban and aggregate at all India level using NSSO 61st round (2004–05) unit level data. In case of the rural areas, we found education at all levels namely literate and up to primary, secondary, under graduation and graduation and above in relative to illiteracy have a positive and significant impact on real per capita consumption expenditure of the household. More importantly, one could find that higher the level education of the principal earner of the household, higher is the per capita consumption of the household. The impact coefficients of literate and up to primary level, secondary, under graduation and graduation and above are found as 0.107, 0.232, 0.351, and 0.457, respectively. Similarly, another important factor that has positive and significant impact on per capita household consumption expenditure is the type of occupation pattern of household's principal earner. In the estimated model, out of three broad economic sectors, agricultural and allied sector is being taken as control variable. The results point to the fact that the principal earner's employment in industry sector has a positive impact of 0.095 on per capita household consumption expenditure. On the other hand, if the principal earner is working in the service sector, the impact is also found positive (0.161) and is relatively higher than industry. Since wage earning is higher in services sector followed by industry and agriculture sector in India, the impact of the former sector on consumption expenditure is expected to be higher than other two sectors. Unit NSSO level data suggests that wage rate of services sector was three times more than agriculture sector during 2004–05 but has declined marginally thereafter to below three times during 2011–12. Similarly, wage rate of industry was more than twice of agriculture sector during 2004–05, has slightly fallen thereafter during 2011–12. It suggests that although wage rate in agricultural sector has increased at a higher pace in the recent years, but still it remains much below of other two sectors'

Table 3 Consumption function of rural and urban households (2004–05)

Variables	Rural	Urban	Total
	Ln (Real per capita consumption)	*Ln* (Real per capita consumption)	*Ln* (Real per capita consumption)
Literate and up to primary	0.107***	0.125***	0.109***
	(0.00576)	(0.00935)	(0.00506)
Secondary	0.232***	0.273***	0.247***
	(0.00621)	(0.00910)	(0.00523)
Under graduation	0.351***	0.424***	0.390***
	(0.00890)	(0.0111)	(0.00693)
Graduate and above	0.457***	0.531***	0.518***
	(0.00933)	(0.0110)	(0.00699)
Ln (age)	0.0656***	0.0160*	0.0478***
	(0.00647)	(0.00922)	(0.00542)
Ln (household size)	−0.182***	−0.116***	−0.153***
	(0.00481)	(0.00580)	(0.00374)
Female	0.0732***	0.137***	0.105***
	(0.00617)	(0.00827)	(0.00506)
Industry	0.0948***	0.0897***	0.0625***
	(0.00553)	(0.0140)	(0.00512)
Service	0.161***	0.143***	0.111***
	(0.00583)	(0.0139)	(0.00515)
Ln (real per capita wage)	0.208***	0.364***	0.287***
	(0.00315)	(0.00382)	(0.00246)
Urban			0.0683***
			(0.00375)
Constant	4.511***	4.298***	4.460***
	(0.0246)	(0.0349)	(0.0202)
Observations	**33,485**	**25,015**	**58,500**
R-squared	**0.461**	**0.605**	**0.559**

Standard errors in parentheses
***$p < 0.01$, **$p < 0.05$, *$p < 0.1$

wage rates. Like occupation, the impact of wage earnings (in real term) of the household on real per capita consumption expenditure of the household is found positive and significant. The results show that 1% increase in real per capita wage rate leads to 0.21% increase in real per capita consumption expenditure. Besides the above variables, we also found other key variables such as age of the principal earner, female-headed household and household size influenced the per capita household consumption expenditure. As expected we found that while the sign of coefficients of age of the principal earner and female-headed households are positive, the sign of coefficient of household size is negative.

Like the case of rural areas, the estimated results of urban areas show different levels of education have a positive and statistically significant impact on per capita household consumption expenditure. But the impact of education on per capita household consumption expenditure is found relatively higher in the case of urban than rural areas, may be due to availability of better quality of education and job opportunities. The impact of principal earner's occupation either in industry or in services relative to agriculture sector on per capita household consumption expenditure shows positive sign and statistically significant. However, the impact of occupation of the principal earner of the household on household's consumption expenditure in urban shows is slightly lower than in rural areas. The reasons could be due to first, wage rates of industry and services sectors in rural areas have increased at a higher rate than their urban counterparts and second, households in urban areas usually spend less and save more than their rural counterparts. Although overall wage rate in urban areas has increased at a slower pace than rural areas, the impact of per capita real wage rate on per capita real consumption expenditure is however found relatively more in case of the former than the latter may be due to per capita wage rate of urban household is nearly two times higher than rural household.

At the aggregate level, the results show that factors such as education, occupation, age, gender, per capita wage and household size are important determinants of household consumption expenditure. The results also suggest that while factors such as education, occupation, age, gender and per capita wage rate are positively related with per capita household consumption, household size, on the other hand, is negatively related with per capita household consumption expenditure. A critical point needs to be drawn from the result is that as the level of education of the principal earner increases, its impact on per capita household consumption expenditure also increases. It points to the conclusion that higher is the level of education, better is the chances for getting a quality job and earning more income, which in turn positively affects the level of consumption. Our results support the findings of Robert Michael (1973), Sen (1999), Grossman (2005) and Hogan and Berning (2012) that education has positive impact on consumption. Another important finding of the paper is that urban dummy shows positive sign and statistically significant suggesting that per capita household consumption expenditure of urban households is significantly higher than the per capita consumption expenditure of rural households. The reasons could be due to that urban household's per capita wage earning in absolute value is relatively higher than its rural counterparts.

In nutshell, the above analysis points to the fact that rural and urban household consumption expenditure varies from each other. To understand it more precisely, the study conducts the B-O decomposition test on aggregate data for the period 2004–05.

Table 4 reports the results of B-O test. The lower part of the table explains mean predictions of consumption for two groups (rural and urban) and their difference. The results show the mean of per capita consumption is 5.426 for urban and 5.113 for rural, yielding a consumption gap of 0.313 which is statistically significant at 1% level. It means household consumption in urban was relatively more than rural

Table 4 Blinder–Oaxaca decomposition of consumption functions of rural and urban households (2004–05)

Variables	(1)	(2)	(3)	(4)
	Differential	Endowments	Coefficients	Interaction
Literate and up to primary		−0.00421***	0.00454*	−0.000710
		(0.000439)	(0.00276)	(0.000435)
Secondary		0.0108***	0.0102***	0.00191***
		(0.000914)	(0.00275)	(0.000536)
Under graduation		0.0149***	0.00670***	0.00308***
		(0.00101)	(0.00131)	(0.000633)
Graduate and above		0.0508***	0.00691***	0.00823***
		(0.00172)	(0.00135)	(0.00162)
Ln (age)		0.00162***	−0.176***	−0.00123***
		(0.000241)	(0.0400)	(0.000310)
Ln (household size)		0.0228***	0.0995***	−0.00832***
		(0.00103)	(0.0113)	(0.000993)
Female		−0.000763***	0.00945***	−0.000667***
		(0.000223)	(0.00153)	(0.000215)
Industry		0.00902***	−0.00124	−0.000487
		(0.000638)	(0.00365)	(0.00144)
Service		0.0397***	−0.00680	−0.00451
		(0.00158)	(0.00559)	(0.00371)
Ln (real per capita wage)		0.0803***	0.291***	0.0600***
		(0.00209)	(0.00928)	(0.00229)
Total		**0.225*** **	**0.0308*** **	**0.0573*** **
		(0.00352)	**(0.00577)**	**(0.00504)**
Prediction of urban	5.426***			
	(0.00433)			
Prediction of rural	5.113***			
	(0.00281)			
Difference	**0.313*** **			
	(0.00516)			
Constant			−0.213***	
			(0.0427)	
Observations	**58,500**	**58,500**	**58,500**	**58,500**

Standard errors in parentheses
***$p < 0.01$, **$p < 0.05$, *$p < 0.1$

areas during 2004–05 and it is statistically significant also. Now in the next step, the upper part of the table explains how much of this mean difference of predicted values of rural and urban consumption is attributed to variation of endowments (factors), coefficients and interactions of both. It is found that the predicted mean difference of rural and urban consumption 0.313 is largely (71.9%) attributed to endowment effect, followed by 18.3% by interaction effect coefficients and the remaining of 9.8% by coefficient effect. The mean difference of endowment effect between urban and rural would be minimised if both of them have the same characteristics. Within endowment effect, the results show differences exist between mean consumption of rural and urban and it is primarily due to variation in endowments such as wages followed by education and occupation.

Table 5 reports the estimated results of rural, urban and aggregate consumption functions at all India level for the period 2011–12. Results for rural indicate that education, occupation, wage rates, gender, household size and age are important determinants of rural household consumption. Similar to the findings for the period

Table 5 Consumption function of rural and urban households (2011–12)

Variables	Rural	Urban	Total
	Ln (Real per capita consumption)	*Ln* (Real per capita consumption)	*Ln* (Real per capita consumption)
Literate and up to primary	0.111***	0.114***	0.109***
	(0.00733)	(0.0117)	(0.00638)
Secondary	0.225***	0.261***	0.237***
	(0.00733)	(0.0108)	(0.00618)
Under graduation	0.333***	0.375***	0.355***
	(0.0100)	(0.0126)	(0.00783)
Graduate and above	0.407***	0.481***	0.465***
	(0.0103)	(0.0121)	(0.00772)
Ln (age)	0.115***	0.0423***	0.0863***
	(0.00816)	(0.0104)	(0.00651)
Ln (household size)	−0.246***	−0.181***	−0.217***
	(0.00596)	(0.00642)	(0.00440)
Female	0.104***	0.0801***	0.103***
	(0.00729)	(0.00919)	(0.00581)
Industry	0.0709***	0.0793***	0.0502***
	(0.00656)	(0.0171)	(0.00626)
Service	0.169***	0.140***	0.114***
	(0.00750)	(0.0171)	(0.00662)
Ln (real per capita wage)	0.196***	0.347***	0.275***
	(0.00364)	(0.00405)	(0.00273)
Urban			0.129***
			(0.00412)
Constant	4.549***	4.455***	4.575***
	(0.0321)	(0.0416)	(0.0252)
Observations	**28,423**	**23,093**	**51,516**
R-squared	**0.406**	**0.561**	**0.525**

Standard errors in parentheses
***$p < 0.01$, **$p < 0.05$, *$p < 0.1$

2004–05, the results for 2011–12 indicate higher is the level of education, better is the prospects of household consumption. In other words, the level of household consumption increases in synonymous with increase of education of the principal earner of the rural households. Within occupation, we found that employment in services in relative to agriculture sector tends to have more positive impact on household consumption than the industry sector. In case of urban, although we find a similar result like the case of rural in terms of relationship between consumption and explanatory variables, the impact of factors however varies from one to other. We found that the impact of wage rate of urban households on consumption is two times more than rural ones. Similarly, the impact of education on household consumption is slightly higher in case of urban than rural. At the aggregate level, which includes both rural and urban households suggest education, wage rate, occupation, gender, household size and age factors are important determinants of household consumption. Urban dummy, which is included in the aggregate consumption function to measure the differences between rural and urban household consumption, shows a positive sign and is statistically significant. It suggests that differences in household consumption between rural and urban households persist in India even if the consumption expenditure of rural households has increased at a faster rate in the recent years.

As there is evidence of differences exist between rural and urban household consumption during 2011–12, the B-O decomposition test shows the rural–urban consumption gap is 0.362 and it is statistically significant at 1% significance level (Table 6). Importantly, the result provides a vital point here is that the rural-urban consumption gap has slightly widened over the period from 0.313 during 2004–05 to 0.362 during 2011–12 and it is attributed largely to endowment effects (57.5%) followed by coefficients effects (26.7%) and interaction effect (15.8%).

As mentioned earlier, the second set of the result of the paper pertains to estimation of consumption functions based on pool data consisting of two data points (2004–05 and 2011–12) for both rural and urban household consumptions. The estimated results are presented in Table 7. In case of rural consumption, the signs of all determinants show same as the case of cross section data. The impact of education factor found positive and it increases as the level of education of the principal earner increases. Wages and occupations are also found statistically significant. In order to know the impact of time trends on consumption, a dummy variable for 2011–12 is included in the rural consumption function shows a positive sign and also statistically significant. It suggests that rural consumption has increased between 2004–05 and 2011–12 in India. The similar results are also found for urban consumption in which the time dummy variable for 2011–12 is found positive and statistically significant. But the coefficient of time dummy is lower in case of rural than urban indicating that the household consumption expenditure of the latter has increased faster than the former between 2004–05 and 2011–12. The signs of other determinants except household size are found positive and significant which is similar to the results obtained using the cross section for urban consumption.

The B-O decomposition results of rural consumption and its mean prediction values are reported in Table 8. The lower part of the table shows the difference of

Table 6 Blinder–Oaxaca decomposition of consumption functions of rural and urban households (2011–12)

Variables	(1) Differential	(2) Endowments	(3) Coefficients	(4) Interaction
Literate and up to primary		−0.00805***	0.000565	−0.000175
		(0.000657)	(0.00322)	(0.000996)
Secondary		0.000183	0.0105***	2.90e−05
		(0.000908)	(0.00383)	(0.000144)
Under graduation		0.0112***	0.00465***	0.00141**
		(0.00105)	(0.00179)	(0.000557)
Graduate and above		0.0606***	0.0100***	0.0111***
		(0.00212)	(0.00215)	(0.00239)
Ln (age)		0.000692**	−0.260***	−0.000437**
		(0.000317)	(0.0474)	(0.000213)
Ln (household size)		0.0302***	0.0942***	−0.00798***
		(0.00134)	(0.0127)	(0.00112)
Female		−0.00144***	−0.00350**	0.000334*
		(0.000333)	(0.00170)	(0.000178)
Industry		−0.00273***	0.00320	−0.000321
		(0.000394)	(0.00706)	(0.000707)
Service		0.0397***	−0.0112	−0.00682
		(0.00191)	(0.00717)	(0.00439)
Ln (real per capita wage)		0.0779***	0.342***	0.0600***
		(0.00220)	(0.0123)	(0.00251)
Total		**0.208*** **	**0.0967*** **	**0.0572*** **
		(0.00364)	**(0.00523)**	**(0.00406)**
Prediction of urban	5.700***			
	(0.00451)			
Prediction of rural	5.338***			
	(0.00315)			
Difference	**0.362*** **			
	(0.00550)			
Constant			−0.0939*	
			(0.0525)	
Observations	**51,516**	**51,516**	**51,516**	**51,516**

Standard errors in parentheses ***$p < 0.01$, **$p < 0.05$, *$p < 0.1$

mean prediction values of rural consumption is 0.226 for two data points, i.e. 2004–05 and 2011–12. This suggests that there is within the variation of consumption expenditure in rural areas which has increased by 0.226 between 2004–05 and 2011–12 and it is largely accounted to endowments effect (61%) followed by 36.5% by coefficients effect and the remaining by interaction effect.

Table 7 Consumption function of rural and urban households in case of pooled data

Variables	Rural	Urban
	Ln (Real per capita consumption)	*Ln* (Real per capita consumption)
Literate and up to primary	0.111***	0.120***
	(0.00455)	(0.00733)
Secondary	0.230***	0.269***
	(0.00474)	(0.00698)
Under graduation	0.342***	0.403***
	(0.00665)	(0.00831)
Graduate and above	0.431***	0.507***
	(0.00691)	(0.00811)
Ln (age)	0.0877***	0.0312***
	(0.00510)	(0.00690)
Ln (household size)	−0.209***	−0.146***
	(0.00376)	(0.00431)
Female	0.0885***	0.110***
	(0.00473)	(0.00616)
Industry	0.0842***	0.0871***
	(0.00420)	(0.0109)
Service	0.166***	0.142***
	(0.00462)	(0.0108)
Ln (real per capita wage)	0.203***	0.355***
	(0.00239)	(0.00278)
Year 2011–12	0.0849***	0.0855***
	(0.00331)	(0.00413)
Constant	4.483***	4.319***
	(0.0195)	(0.0268)
Observations	**61,908**	**48,108**
R-squared	**0.458**	**0.599**

Standard errors in parentheses
***$p < 0.01$, **$p < 0.05$, *$p < 0.1$

For urban consumption, the B-O decomposition results based on pooled data show that mean prediction value of urban consumption has increased from 2004–05 to 2011–12 as the difference between the two time points comes around 0.275 (Table 9). Further, it is found that the consumption expenditure gap for urban households is accounted more to endowments effect (67.6%) followed by 30% by coefficient effect and the remaining by interaction effect.

To sum up, the results of estimated consumption functions for rural and urban households using the cross section data for two data points 2004–05 and 2011–12 reveal three important points. First, factors such as education, occupation and wages

Table 8 Blinder–Oaxaca decomposition of consumption function of rural households (pooled data)

Variables	(1) Differential	(2) Endowments	(3) Coefficients	(4) Interaction
Literate and up to primary		−0.00184***	0.000989	−6.74e−05
		(0.000383)	(0.00234)	(0.000160)
Secondary		0.0102***	−0.00179	−0.000315
		(0.000877)	(0.00240)	(0.000423)
Under graduation		0.00654***	−0.00167	−0.000338
		(0.000874)	(0.00124)	(0.000253)
Graduate and above		0.0187***	−0.00470***	−0.00206***
		(0.00124)	(0.00130)	(0.000584)
Ln (age)		0.00314***	0.174***	0.00234***
		(0.000354)	(0.0369)	(0.000514)
Ln (household size)		0.00947***	−0.0961***	0.00333***
		(0.000760)	(0.0115)	(0.000472)
Female		−0.000212	0.00459***	−8.97e−05
		(0.000209)	(0.00141)	(9.26e−05)
Industry		0.0135***	−0.00579***	−0.00339***
		(0.000860)	(0.00208)	(0.00122)
Service		0.00209***	0.00277	9.66e−05
		(0.000635)	(0.00353)	(0.000127)
Ln (real per capita wage)		0.0817***	−0.0224**	−0.00471**
		(0.00191)	(0.00900)	(0.00189)
Total		**0.143*** **	**0.0877*** **	**−0.00521*** **
		(0.00302)	**(0.00354)**	**(0.00200)**
Prediction of rural in 2011–12	5.338***			
	(0.00315)			
Prediction of rural in 2004–05	5.113***			
	(0.00281)			
Difference	**0.226*** **			
	(0.00422)			
Constant			0.0382	
			(0.0404)	
Observations	**61,908**	**61,908**	**61,908**	**61,908**

Standard errors in parentheses
$^{***}p < 0.01$, $^{**}p < 0.05$, $^{*}p < 0.1$

have undergone sizable changes during the two data points and such changes have positively and significantly affected the consumption expenditure of households in both rural and urban areas. Second, the dummy variable for urban areas is found positive and significant indicating consumption expenditure at all India level is

Table 9 Blinder–Oaxaca decomposition of consumption function of urban households (pooled data)

Variables	(1) Differential	(2) Endowments	(3) Coefficients	(4) Interaction
Literate and up to primary		−0.00630***	−0.00249	0.000590
		(0.000647)	(0.00316)	(0.000752)
Secondary		−0.000541	−0.00364	2.43e−05
		(0.00114)	(0.00418)	(5.83e−05)
Under graduation		0.00420***	−0.00657***	−0.000484**
		(0.00135)	(0.00226)	(0.000227)
Graduate & above		0.0418***	−0.0102***	−0.00391***
		(0.00225)	(0.00335)	(0.00130)
Ln (age)		0.000466*	0.0938*	0.000764*
		(0.000272)	(0.0496)	(0.000410)
Ln (household size)		0.00570***	−0.0898***	0.00322***
		(0.000659)	(0.0119)	(0.000542)
Female		−0.000868**	−0.00784***	0.000361*
		(0.000430)	(0.00170)	(0.000194)
Industry		0.000745*	−0.00353	−8.68e−05
		(0.000405)	(0.00748)	(0.000189)
Service		0.000245	−0.00201	−5.58e−06
		(0.000633)	(0.0136)	(4.04e−05)
Ln (real per capita wage)		0.147***	−0.0368***	−0.00659***
		(0.00376)	(0.0125)	(0.00225)
Total		**0.192*****	**0.0885*****	**−0.00612*****
		(0.00495)	**(0.00424)**	**(0.00174)**
Prediction of urban in 2011–12	5.700***			
	(0.00451)			
Prediction of urban in 2004–05	5.426***			
	(0.00433)			
Difference	**0.275*****			
	(0.00625)			
Constant			0.158***	
			(0.0543)	
Observations	**48,108**	**48,108**	**48,108**	**48,108**

Standard errors in parentheses
***$p < 0.01$, **$p < 0.05$, *$p < 0.1$

positively linked to urban household consumption. And third, although the differences exist between urban and rural households consumption, the results show there is possibility convergence evidence between the two as the mean of endowment effect has declined over the period.

5 Conclusion

Indian economy has witnessed a structural change in various sectors during the post-economic reforms period. While the contribution of agriculture and allied sector to total GDP has declined considerably, its share in total employment has not. Since households in rural areas are invariably over dependent on agriculture and allied activities, the fall of income of this sector would adversely impact their consumption expenditure. However, the data shows that the occupation pattern of rural households is changing fast. Although agriculture remains the primary source of economic activities for rural households, people have chosen non-agriculture activities like construction and low skilled manufacturing jobs as secondary activities. Double earnings from both primary and secondary sources may have induced the consumption level of rural households. Further, wage rates in rural areas have also witnessed faster increase than urban areas. Given these underline changes of economic and demographic variables during the post-reform period, the present study makes an attempt to examine a pertinent issue of whether such changes have any bearing impact on level of consumption of households both in rural and urban areas. Second, whether these changes have led to possible convergence of rural consumption expenditure towards urban consumption expenditure.

The study finds that per capita consumption expenditure of households in urban areas was nearly double than rural areas both during 2004–05 and 2011–12. But the trend shows the ratio of urban to rural consumption expenditure has slightly declined during the latter period suggesting that rural consumption expenditure has increased at a faster rate in the recent years. The reason of high growth of consumption expenditure in rural areas could be due to multiple factors such as increase of education level of household members, changes in occupation pattern from agriculture to non-agriculture, increase of wage rates, decline of household size, etc. Although similar changes are evident in urban areas, the quantity of changes were rather low. The empirical findings of the study suggest that education level, occupation and gender of the principal earner of the household, average wage rate and size of the household are important determinants of per capita consumption expenditure of the households both in rural and urban areas. But the degree of impact of these variables on consumption expenditure varies from rural to urban. It is found from the cross section data that the impact of education, occupation and wages on per capita consumption expenditure is higher in case of urban than rural. Since there is evidence of differences exist between rural and urban areas, the issue has been examined in more details by applying the B-O decomposition technique.

The results of B-O decomposition test based on 2004–05 data indicate the mean differences of consumption expenditure of urban and rural households are 0.313 and it is largely explained by differences in endowment effect (71.9%). A similar test was also carried on 2011–12 data and found that the mean difference of consumption expenditure of urban and rural households is 0.362. In this case, also the urban–rural gap is explained largely by differences in endowment effects (57.5%). But the differences of endowment effect show that it has considerably declined between 2004–05 and 2011–12 suggesting that the sign of convergence of consumption expenditure between the rural and urban households has emerged in India.

We believe these results to be indicative of the fact that the massive structural changes that have been implemented in several sectors have different dimensional impacts on educational, occupation and earnings on workforce and hence on household consumption pattern in both rural and urban areas. Nevertheless, the results point to the fact that there is a possibility of convergence in consumption expenditure between rural and urban households in India which is similar to the fact presented by Hnatkovska and Lahiri (2012). The possible declining of welfare disparities between rural and urban areas has some important policy implications. First, with the rise of national income and growth, it may have positively impacted poverty reduction at a higher pace in rural than urban areas and hence contrasting the views of less inclusiveness of growth. Second, the rise of rural income and welfare would help the economy to generate more income and employment opportunities in the area, which in turn may discourse migration to urban areas. From the investment point of view, the rise of welfare in the rural areas provides a window of opportunities for corporate world to invest in the rural areas and maximise the returns.

References

Azam, M. (2012). A distributional analysis of social group inequality in rural India. *Journal of International Development, 24*(4), 415–432.

Bhalla, S. (2002). Rural non-farm employment and the unorganised sector in India. *The Indian Journal of Labour Economics, 45*(4), 695–717.

Bhaumik, S. K. (2002). Employment diversification in rural India: A state level analysis. *The Indian Journal of Labour Economics, 45*(4), 718–744.

Cain, J. S., Hasan, R., Magsombol, R., & Tandon, A. (2010). Accounting for inequality in India: Evidence from household expenditures. *World Development, 38*(3), 282–297.

Chadha, G. K. (2002). Rural non-farm employment in India: What does recent experience teach us? *The Indian Journal of Labour Economics, 45*(4), 663–694.

Chang, H. H. (2012). Consumption inequality between farm and nonfarm households in Taiwan: A decomposition analysis of differences in distribution. *Agricultural Economics, 43*(5), 487–498.

Chirwa, E. W., & Matita, M. M. (2009). *The rate of return on education in Malawi*. University of Malawi, Chancellor College, Department of Economics Working Paper, (2009/01).

Coppard, D. (2001). *The rural non-farm economy in India: A review of the literature*. Natural Resource Institute, Department for International Development (DFID), World Bank, NRI Report 2662 (2001).

De Brauw, A., Taylor, J. E., & Rozelle, S. (2001). *Migration and incomes in source communities: A new economics of migration perspective from China.*

Fang, Z., & Sakellariou, C. (2013). Evolution of urban–rural living standards inequality in Thailand: 1990–2006. *Asian Economic Journal, 27*(3), 285–306.

Frank, A.-T., Charles, G. A., & Derek, A. (2017). An unconditional quantile regression based decomposition of spatial welfare inequalities in Ghana. *The Journal of Development Studies*, 1–20.

Go, D., Nikitin, D., Wang, X., & Zou, H. F. (2007). Poverty and inequality in sub-saharan Africa: Literature survey and empirical assessment. *Annals of Economics and Finance, 8*(2), 251–304.
Grossman, M. (2005). Education and nonmarket outcomes. NBER Working Paper No. 11582.
Harris, J. R., & Todaro, M. P. (1970). Migration, unemployment and development: A two sector analysis. *The American Economic Review, American Economic Association, 60*(1), 126–142.
Hnatkovska, V., & Lahiri, A. (2012). *The rural-urban divide in India*. Working paper. International Growth Center.
Hogan, J. J., & Berning, J. P. (2012). Estimating the relationship between education and food purchases among food insecure households. In Selected paper prepared for presentation at the agricultural and applied economics association's 2012 AAEA Annual Meeting, Seattle, Washington, August 12–14, 2012.
Lewis, W. A. (1954). Economic development with unlimited supplies of labor. *The Manchester School, 22*(2), 139–191.
Lucas, R. E. B., & Stark, O. (1985). Motivations to remit: Evidence from Botswana. *Journal of Political Economy, 93*(5), 901–918. The University of Chicago Press.
Nguyen, B. T., Albrecht, J. W., Vroman, S. B., & Westbrook, M. D. (2007). A quantile regression decomposition of urban–rural inequality in Vietnam. *Journal of Development Economics, 83* (2), 466–490.
Michael, R. T. (1973). Education in nonmarket production. *Journal of Political Economy, 81*(2, Part 1):306–327.
Rozelle, S., Taylor, J. E, & de Brauw, A. (1999). Migration, remittances, and agricultural productivity in China. *The American Economic Review, 89* (2), 287–291. Papers and Proceedings of the One Hundred Eleventh Annual Meeting of the American Economic Association, American Economic Association.
Sahu, P. P. (2003). Casualisation of rural workforce in India: Analysis of recent trends. *The Indian Journal of Labour Economics, 46*(4), 927–939.
Taylor, J. E. (1992). Remittances and inequality reconsidered: Direct, indirect and intertemporal effects. *Journal of Policy Modeling, 14*(2), 187–208. Society for Policy Modeling.
Taylor, J. E., & Martin, P. (2001). Human capital: Migration and rural population change. In B. L. Gardner, & G. C. Rausser (Eds.), *Chapter in handbook for agricultural economics*. New York: Elsevier Science.
Thu Le, H., & Booth, A. L. (2014). Inequality in Vietnamese urban–rural living standards, 1993–2006. *Review of Income and Wealth, 60*(4), 862–886.
Sen, A. K. (1999). *Development as freedom*. Oxford University Press.
Srivastav, N., & Dubey, A. (2002). *Rural non-farm employment in India: Spatial variations and temporal change*. SSRN Scholarly Paper. Rochester, NY: Social Science Research Network, 1 Sept 2002. http://papers.ssrn.com/abstract=1825046.

Part 2

Skill Development Efforts in Higher Education to Fulfil the Objective of Make in India: Trends and Issues

G. P. Joshi and Sanchita Bhattacharya

1 Introduction

> Education, vocational training and lifelong learning are central pillars of employability, employment of workers and sustainable enterprise development
>
> —International Labour Organization.

The history of skill/technical education in India is very old. Various technical traits such as carpentry, black smithy, weaving, etc. were part of education. It has been witnessed from the archaeological remains of mediaeval India that during that period the vocational skill reached great heights. Indian archaeologists discovered two cities which were 4000 years old, which indicate an advanced civilization as compared to ancient Mesopotamia and Egypt. Mohenjo-Daro, the name was given by archaeologists of that time to the cities means 'hill of the dead,' and Harappa, after a nearby city.

The modern era of technical education in the country started with setting up of 'Survey School' at Madras by British traders. The Institution imparted training to Indians in land survey techniques. The effects of the Industrial Revolution had made a long-lasting impact on the socioeconomic and cultural conditions not only in the United Kingdom but spread to other countries of the globe.

It was a time when realized that the old system of training of artisans by only passing on knowledge and skills from generation to generation was not that useful. Because technological changes were having more influence, as a result, it was felt to develop a new learning system specially to have a technical system to meet the

G. P. Joshi (✉) · S. Bhattacharya
NILERD, Narela, India
e-mail: joshigp1960@gmail.com

S. Bhattacharya
e-mail: bsanchi@gmail.com

NILERD, *Reflecting on India's Development*,
https://doi.org/10.1007/978-981-13-1414-8_5

challenges of occupational needs in the industry and to maintain the innovative modern products. Thus, a new system of learning process was born while combining academic education with skill/technical training, especially tailor-made learning-training system designed for supply of technical trained (human resource) for the entire economy in multiple disciplines.

Soon after independence, the country has initiated a various number of projects to meet the needs of the people and to achieve self-sufficiency. The concept of technical education and skill education was related with acquisition of practical and basic scientific knowledge, which involves special manipulative skills, creative minds, and attitude relating to occupations in various sectors of economy and social life. At the same time the country had initiated an ambitious programme to expand the scope of technical education to meet the requirement as the country has the second- highest population of the working age (15–59) in the world but at the same time we have only about 10% of its total workforce with skill training. India being a growing economy needs for a large pool of skilled workers, to meet out the required demand by the various sectors of the economy.

To meet the requirements of technical/skilled human resource, the educational system expanded in the country at the following three levels during the past:

(1) To prepare skilled workers through Industrial Training Institutes(ITI),
(2) To prepare skilled manpower through advance level vocational courses (Diploma), and
(3) To prepare Professional for taking up planning, designing and production assignments (Degree Courses) through engineering colleges/technical department.

Keeping in view the global standard, skills/technical education has become a major driving force of economic development in the country. India is also destined to be a contributor to the global workforce pool on account of higher demographic dividend.

In today's age of globalization when each and every nation is moving very fast in technological development which is an important weapon to boost the efficiency and the quality of services for the competitive nature of productivity and economic growth as a whole. At present, India is one of the youngest nations in the world in terms of population dividend. It is an opportunity to reap the benefits of 'this dividend' while converting the young population into skilled/technical workforce. At the same time, apart from meeting its own demand, India has the potential to become the worldwide pool for outsourcing technical/skilled human resource. India is one of the few nations in the world where the working age population will be far in excess of those dependent on them (World Bank), this situation has to be continued for another three decades till 2040. This has been recognized as strength and a potential source of significant opportunity for the national economy, but this strength has to be converted into technically sound and continuously upgrade the skills of the available population in the working age group.

In recognition of these needs, the Government of India has adopted skill development as a national priority in coming years. To quote Hon'ble Prime

Minister of India, ***Shri Narendra Modi Independence Day 2014 Speech*** 'Today, the world and India need a skilled workforce. If we have to promote the development of our country then our mission has to be 'skill development' and 'Skilled India'. Millions and Millions of Indian youth should acquire the skills which could contribute towards making India a modern country. I also want to create a pool of young people who are able to create jobs and the ones who are not capable of creating jobs and do not have the opportunities, they must be in a position to face their counterparts in any corner of the world while keeping their heads high by virtue of their hard work and their dexterity of hands and win the hearts of people around the world through their skills'.

2 Review of Literature

An effort has been made to map the available literature to establish the available knowledge and ideas on technical and skill education in India. Okada (2012) reviews the current state of education, skills development, and employment for Indian youth, and considers the challenges facing India's skills development system. Sharing his experiences from the state of Karnataka, which has slightly better system of providing skill and vocational training as compared to other states, he commented that it has not sufficiently prepared its youth with the skills that the industries require. Pujani (2014) further investigated that whether the introduction of Make in India project and other initiatives taken by the central government is working as a key engine for India's economic growth or their contribution is not significant? At the same time, NITI Aayog report suggests that only 10% of the Indian workforce get formal training and against the actual industrial training requirement of 22 million workers, only 4.3 million workers are getting trained. An attempt has been made by Saini (2015) to examine the present skill capacity, issues of skill development initiative and their solutions. The skill capacity by Indian work force in the age group of 15–59 has been observed extremely low. Kapur (2016) investigated the different information about the concept of skill development in India as well as the programmes and policies that have been initiated. It was found in his study that skill development has been facilitated by the organization of their certain programmes, educational institutions and training centers. Rural masses in the country are still in a backward situation, steps therefore have been implemented to develop skills amongst them for the purpose of obtaining self-sufficiency in resource utilization, governance and leadership. Kanchan and Varshney (2015) in their study have analysed the present status of skill development and the challenges India has faced while implementation of different initiatives and strategies. They found during the course of study that about 80% of the workforce in the country (rural and urban together) does not possess any identifiable and marketable skills. Therefore, there is an urgent need to bridge this gap through various skill development initiatives to make India the global hub for skilled human resource, and also result in a surplus of skilled manpower of approximately 47 million by 2020. Deka and Batra (2016) have observed that there are ample employment opportunities in manufacturing establishment run by domestic and foreign entrepreneurs. Hence, labour force should acquire skill for making themselves employable. They also commented that skill developing initiatives needs to be implemented for lowing the skill gap between available and required skill. Kaur (2016) also tried to investigate the future demand of skilled labour in the manufacturing sector in the country and its corresponding supply. The author also investigated various obstacles in providing the requisite skills to the people of India and various initiatives taken by the government so far. With Make in India initiative, the job creation process is supposed to be going to accelerate. Skill India also needs to be on its mission to impart the skills to the Indian youth to reap the desired demographic dividend.

3 Status of Skill Development in India

The available statistical information indicate that the country is largely unskilled with little over 2.0% of its total workforce having gone through some kind of formal skill training, which is much lower compared to 68% in the UK and 52% in the US. Whatever may be the current availability of skilled workforce, the country has the enormous potential to become a skilled one. To leverage our demographic dividend more substantially, the government launched the Skill India campaign along with Make in India, a strategy that has its impact and connectivity towards various agendas. The government has introduced a couple of initiatives along with Make in India such as Digital India, Skill India etc. to strengthen Indian economy while making the technical people employable. One of the objectives of the initiative is to make the country a global manufacturing hub while attracting FDI (Foreign Direct Investment) and it has been assumed that there will be additional requirement of advanced technologies which will in a way boost up the requirement of highly qualified and technically sound talents.

In the past, the National Skill Development Policy (2009) had set a herculean target of skilling about 500 million people in the country by 2022. But more recently, study reports commissioned and released by Ministry of Skill Development, the Government of India has assessed an incremental human resource requirement across 24 sectors in the country was as 109.73 million by 2022 (Table 11).

It is scientifically true that the skill which required twenty years back might not be relevant to present scenario as a result nearly half of all the jobs are predicted to be at the risk of the automation. Keeping in view this fact into consideration and to bridge the gap, various measures have been initiated by the central government which includes National Skill Development Mission, National Policy for Skill Development and Entrepreneurship, 2015, Pradhan Mantri Kaushal Vikas Yojana (PMKVY), Skill Loan scheme, Rural India Skill etc. The objectives of all these initiatives are to enhance the skilling potential of the workforce so that the proportion of skilled working force could further increase and their contribution to the economy may also increase.

The National Skill Development Mission, a central government programme, was approved by the Union Cabinet on 01.07.2015, which was officially launched by the head of the government on 15.07.2015 on the occasion of World Youth Skills Day. The key objectives of the Mission were as follows:

(a) Institutional Training,
(b) Infrastructure,
(c) Convergence,
(d) Trainers,
(e) Overseas Employment,
(f) Sustainable Livelihoods, and
(g) Leveraging Public Infrastructure.

The scenario of technical/skill education in the country includes the first category of the technical education is the craftsmen training programme, which caters the needs of young people in the age group of 14–25 years. This training is organized through a network of Industrial Training Institutes (ITIs). The period of training and entry level qualifications for admission to various trades differ from course to course. Table 1 depicts the regionwise seating capacities with number of it is in India both at public as well as private sector.

Industrial Training Institutes of the country play a vital role in economy especially in terms of providing skilled human resource. It is seen from the above table that the northern region has the highest (34.8%) seating capacity followed by southern (26.5%) and western region (20.4%). The northern and western region has higher proportion of government ITIs, i.e. 35.6 and 36.1%, respectively, whereas, about 38.8 and 31.6% private ITIs were concentrated in both the region.

Technical Education & Vocational Training are often used synonymously. However, the term TE (technical education) indicates higher secondary courses of study along with practical training with an objective to make them employable as supervisors. Vocational Training refers to lower level education and training for skilled or semi-skilled workers in various trades/sectors.

Undergraduate technician, i.e. degree and diploma holders in engineering and technology covers various courses and programmes which includes various branches of engineering and technology, architecture, town planning, pharmacy and

Table 1 Distribution of ITIs by seating capacity (2014)

Name of the region	It is managed by govt. (no)	No of seats (govt.)	Private it is (no)	Seating capacity (private)	Total number of ITIs	Total number of seats
North	813	130,818	3757	458,837	4570	589,655
South	437	100,828	3056	347,926	3493	448,754
East	209	58,250	1569	250,301	1778	308,551
West	825	208,474	1298	137,402	2123	345,876
Total	2284	498,370	9680	1,194,466	11,964	1,692,836

Source Labour Bureau, the Ministry of Labour and Employment, GOI, 2015

applied arts and crafts, hotel management and catering technology as well as general management at undergraduate level. India is blessed with the population of about 70% below the age of 35 years which is strength for becoming a world power in the field of technical/skilled HR.

The technical education system in India can be broadly classified into three categories—Central Government funded institutions, State Government/State funded institutions and Self-financed institutions. The intake capacities of engineering colleges highlighted in Table 2 shows that in the year 2015–16, Tamil Nadu, Maharashtra and Uttar Pradesh have the highest share in total engineering colleges. The corresponding shares were 16, 12 and 9%, respectively. Tamil Nadu, Maharashtra and Andhra Pradesh have the highest share in total capacity among all engineering colleges in the same year.

Table 3 shows that the percentage share of number of engineering colleges to total was the highest in Andhra Pradesh followed by Tamil Nadu and Maharashtra during the year 2011–12. These three states are also having the highest share in total capacity also in the year 2011–12. So, during 2011–12 to 2015–16, the corresponding share of Andhra Pradesh has reduced from 21.05 to 7.75%.

In the year 2015, (Table 4) Karnataka's share has decreased from 15% in 2010 to 11% of total ITIs. The corresponding share for Uttar Pradesh has increased to 16% in the same year from 11% in 2010. Rajasthan's share in total ITIs has increased from 9% in 2010 to 13% in 2015. Uttar Pradesh, Rajasthan and Maharashtra bag the first, second and third position respectively in terms of seating capacity in 2015.

The share of Southern region was the highest in total (Table 5) ITIs followed by northern region in 2010 in India whereas the share of eastern region is the least in total number of ITIs in the same period. If we look at the respective share of states, we find that Uttar Pradesh tops the list followed by Karnataka. Around 32% of total seating capacity is bagged by southern region followed by northern region in 2010. Maharashtra, Andhra Pradesh and Karnataka occupy the first, second and third position among the states of India in terms of seating capacity in the same period.

Regionwise proportion of number of ITI Schools with seating capacities is presented in Fig. 1. North and southern region has shown higher proportion in terms of number of schools and seating capacity as compared to eastern and western region.

The percentage share of out-turn/pass-out students at undergraduate level in each stream of engineering disciplines to total engineering discipline is analysed to show the relative supply of engineering manpower from each stream of engineering. Table 6 depicts the Out-Turn/Pass-Out data for 2015–16. It has been found that in electronics engineering, the percentage of pass-out students is the highest, the corresponding share being 22%. The second major discipline showing a major share of out-turn is mechanical engineering. The percentage share of pass-out students in mechanical engineering is 20%. The third highest share of pass-out students is in computer engineering, the respective share being 19%.

If we compare the scenario of out-turn/pass-outs at undergraduate level in engineering discipline in 2015–16 with the scenario of out-turn/pass-outs in the

Table 2 Engineering colleges and their intake capacities in 2015–16

Sl. no.	State/UTs	No of colleges (govt. + pvt)	Intake capacity (no.)	States share in total colleges (%)	States share in total capacity (%)
1	Andaman and Nicobar Islands	1	360	0.02	0.01
2	Andhra Pradesh	500	298,982	7.75	9.50
3	Arunachal Pradesh	2	420	0.03	0.01
4	Assam	31	7967	0.48	0.25
5	Bihar	65	23,044	1.01	0.73
6	Chandigarh	10	3183	0.15	0.10
7	Chhattisgarh	91	35,004	1.41	1.11
8	Dadra and Nagar Haveli	1	330	0.02	0.01
9	Daman and Diu	2	540	0.03	0.02
10	Delhi	35	15,861	0.54	0.50
11	Goa	11	4211	0.17	0.13
12	Gujarat	234	148,594	3.63	4.72
13	Haryana	327	152,437	5.07	4.85
14	Himachal Pradesh	53	21,244	0.82	0.68
15	Jammu and Kashmir	41	9553	0.64	0.30
16	Jharkhand	45	16,834	0.70	0.54
17	Karnataka	506	214,341	7.84	6.81
18	Kerala	242	94,612	3.75	3.01
19	Madhya Pradesh	299	150,660	4.63	4.79
20	Maharashtra	801	365,295	12.41	11.61
21	Manipur	2	255	0.03	0.01
22	Meghalaya	4	800	0.06	0.03
23	Mizoram	2	140	0.03	0.00
24	Nagaland	3	360	0.05	0.01
25	Odisha	221	98,374	3.42	3.13
26	Puducherry	26	12,634	0.40	0.40
27	Punjab	242	115,715	3.75	3.68
28	Rajasthan	325	127,942	5.03	4.07
29	Sikkim	3	1299	0.05	0.04
30	Tamil Nadu	1030	537,474	15.96	17.09
31	Telangana	406	286,236	6.29	9.10
32	Tripura	8	1532	0.12	0.05
33	Uttar Pradesh	595	290,105	9.22	9.22

(continued)

Table 2 (continued)

Sl. no.	State/UTs	No of colleges (govt. + pvt)	Intake capacity (no.)	States share in total colleges (%)	States share in total capacity (%)
34	Uttarakhand	99	32,085	1.53	1.02
35	West Bengal	192	77,364	2.97	2.46
India		6455	3,145,787	100.00	100.00

Source Ministry of HRD, GOI, 2017

same discipline in 2011–12 (Table 7), we observe that the percentage share of pass-out students is the highest in electronics engineering followed by computer engineering and mechanical engineering. The respective shares are 27, 24 and 15%, respectively.

The available data on gender diversity in different streams in highlighted in Table 8.

Data depicted in Table 9 show that the percentage share of females to total ranges from 40 to 50% in computer engineering, architecture and IT computer in 2011–12. However, IT and computer was not included in the streams identified under engineering and technology in the same year. In 2015–16, the percentage share of females was the highest in architecture (54.99%) followed by information technology (51.65%) and computer engineering (49.36%).

Hence, it is found that women have the highest inclination for architecture, computer engineering and IT-related discipline and the trend remains unaltered over the years.

4 Diverse Realities, Common and Different Challenges

It is quite obvious that excellence in technical education only possible while initiating innovative teaching which includes theory and practical. This attempt would require changing the traditional way of imparting engineering education. A teacher's success depends on the ability of the students. However, there are teachers who have been successful to make the bad student a very good learner with the help of innovative teaching. It has been found in certain cases that teachers do not become successful to transfer knowledge even if they possess it personally. There are certain common challenges and realities are as follows:

- *Challenge of Proficiency in Language*: Some time students are from remote areas have done most of their studies in their local language and even the brightest of them find it difficult to understand modern language. Whereas the technical education is completely in English language,

Table 3 Engineering colleges and their intake capacities in 2011–12

Sl. no.	State/UTs	No. of colleges	Approved intake capacity (no.)	States share in total colleges (%)	States share in total capacity (%)
1	Andaman and Nicobar Islands	1	90	0.03	0.01
2	Andhra Pradesh	704	340,007	21.05	23.07
3	Arunachal Pradesh	1	216	0.03	0.01
4	Assam	11	3501	0.33	0.24
5	Bihar	19	5209	0.57	0.35
6	Chandigarh	5	1551	0.15	0.10
7	Chhattisgarh	53	24,479	1.58	1.66
8	Dadra and Nagar Haveli	–	–	–	–
9	Daman and Diu	–	–	–	–
10	Delhi	20	7981	0.60	0.54
11	Goa	4	1200	0.12	0.08
12	Gujarat	101	46,639	3.02	3.16
13	Haryana	166	64,280	4.96	4.36
14	Himachal Pradesh	21	7272	0.63	0.49
15	Jammu and Kashmir	9	2471	0.27	0.17
16	Jharkhand	14	6015	0.42	0.41
17	Karnataka	188	92,376	5.62	6.27
18	Kerala	148	52,211	4.42	3.54
19	Madhya Pradesh	227	96,536	6.79	6.55
20	Maharashtra	350	146,116	10.46	9.91
21	Manipur	2	155	0.06	0.01
22	Meghalaya	1	420	0.03	0.03
23	Mizoram	–	–	–	–
24	Nagaland	–	–	–	–
24	Odisha	101	45,434	3.02	3.08
25	Puducherry	13	6103	0.39	0.41
26	Punjab	105	43,408	3.14	2.94
27	Rajasthan	131	58,106	3.92	3.94
28	Sikkim	1	558	0.03	0.04
29	Tamil Nadu	498	236,417	14.89	16.04
30	Telangana	–	–	–	–

(continued)

Table 3 (continued)

Sl. no.	State/UTs	No. of colleges	Approved intake capacity (no.)	States share in total colleges (%)	States share in total capacity (%)
31	Tripura	1	300	0.03	0.02
32	Uttar Pradesh	329	136,417	9.83	9.25
33	Uttarakhand	33	13,430	0.99	0.91
34	West Bengal	88	34,973	2.63	2.37
Total		3345	1,473,871	100.00	100.00

Source Ministry of HRD, GOI, 2013

- *Challenge of Faculty Shortage*: There is an acute shortage of faculty as per Technical Education Quality Improvement Project (TEQIP) a study finding in 2009,
- *Challenge of Lack in Absorbing Capacity*: The classroom is a heterogeneous group of students whose marks range from as low as 40% to as high as 90%. Therefore, the absorbing capability of students is also varied,
- *Challenge of Lesser Exposure to Reality*: Technical subjects require that students be exposed to examples of the use of engineering principles as applicable in real life. This exposure is very limited at present.
- *Challenge of Lesser Industry Interaction*: Colleges try to organize Industrial visits for students to increase industry interactions, but it is rare and not as effective as it should be, especially in colleges in rural areas,
- *Challenge in Employability*: Only 10–25% of graduates are employable by the industry,
- *Challenge of Rapid Growth*: National Knowledge Commission (NKC) under Curriculum Reform in the Engineering Education recommends that industries participate in the education process. But the rapid growth of the number of Engineering Institutes in India makes this difficult,
- *Glaring Mismatch in Demand and Supply needs to be minimized*: A mismatch between education system and labour market needs is a serious threat to economic growth. The demand made by the industries and supply of labour-force mismatch leads to aggravate all types of skill development initiatives of the Government,
- *Skill development initiatives for women*: Women constitute about 48% of the total population of the country. According to India's constitution, women are legal citizens of the country and have equal rights with men. Because of lack of acceptance from the male dominant society, Indian women also require equally Empowerment through Skills Development & Vocational Education. The share of women workforce (between 25 and 54 years of age) is about 30% in 2010 as against 39% in 2000, which is quite below as compared to 82% in China and 72% in Brazil,

Table 4 Industrial training institutes and their seating capacities in 2015

Sl. no.	State/UTs	Total ITIs	% share of states to total ITIs	Total seating capacity	% share of states to total seating capacity
1	Andaman and Nicobar Islands	1	0.01	273	0.01
2	Andhra Pradesh	490	3.74	130,374	6.99
4	Arunachal Pradesh	6	0.05	608	0.03
5	Assam	36	0.27	6352	0.34
6	Bihar	873	6.66	129,870	6.96
7	Chandigarh	2	0.02	1192	0.06
8	Chhattisgarh	185	1.41	22,304	1.20
9	Dadra and Nagar Haveli	1	0.01	228	0.01
10	Daman and Diu	2	0.02	388	0.02
11	Delhi	82	0.63	17,272	0.93
12	Goa	15	0.11	3676	0.20
13	Gujarat	565	4.31	84,718	4.54
14	Haryana	308	2.35	51,946	2.78
15	Himachal Pradesh	228	1.74	30,480	1.63
16	Jammu and Kashmir	38	0.29	4197	0.22
17	Jharkhand	215	1.64	46,792	2.51
18	Karnataka	1481	11.30	134,944	7.23
19	Kerala	531	4.05	70,966	3.80
20	Lakshadweep	1	0.01	96	0.01
21	Madhya Pradesh	886	6.76	115,920	6.21
22	Maharashtra	863	6.59	166,252	8.91
23	Manipur	7	0.05	540	0.03
24	Meghalaya	7	0.05	942	0.05
25	Mizoram	1	0.01	294	0.02
26	Nagaland	8	0.06	944	0.05
27	Odisha	624	4.76	120,836	6.48
28	Puducherry	17	0.13	1940	0.10
29	Punjab	386	2.95	60,660	3.25
30	Rajasthan	1769	13.50	227,199	12.18
31	Sikkim	4	0.03	580	0.03
32	Tamil Nadu	722	5.51	92,390	4.95

(continued)

Table 4 (continued)

Sl. no.	State/UTs	Total ITIs	% share of states to total ITIs	Total seating capacity	% share of states to total seating capacity
33	Telangana	280	2.14	24,876	1.33
34	Tripura	13	0.10	1888	0.10
35	Uttar Pradesh	2185	16.67	270,654	14.51
36	Uttarakhand	131	1.00	16,625	0.89
37	West Bengal	142	1.08	26,404	1.42
India		13,105	100.00	1,865,620	1,865,620

Source Ministry of HRD, GOI, 2017

- *Private sector participation*: The present situation with respect to the participation of the private sector in curriculum development and policy formulation is negligible. The concentration of private sector institutions in urban locations as a result, rural population remains out of their purview. Second, due to the high cost of these institutes, the weaker or disadvantaged section also unable to get proper skill training,
- *Placement-linked Challenge*: In our country, the linkage between training, education and placement of the trained workforce is not adequate. This insufficient linkage is apparent from the examples of India and China. In India, there are about 120 vocational training courses which are mostly of long duration. In contrast to this, in China, there are almost 4000 modular courses which are of short duration and impart skill related to specific requirements of the job.
- *Informal and Formal Sector Skill Gap*: As the Government of India has set up a target to provide skill training to 500 million people by 2022, whereas in reality, the country is facing a significant skilled HR challenge. Around 93% of the Indian workforce is employed in the unorganized or informal sector, which lacks any kind of formal skill development training. This indicates that a lot of efforts are needed to make the youth skilled as per the data speak it does not imbibe any form of skill development—formal or informal.

5 Issues Remain Unaddressed

In a global scenario, India is today one of the leading economies in the world after China in terms of Human resource. But the other side of the coin is a substantial proportion of population are poor, deprived and suffering with malnutrition. The country still has one of the largest illiterate populations, both in terms of absolute size and in proportionate terms. Although, there has been a substantial increase in the number of institutions imparting technical education. But the real issues are still remaining unanswered. The issues which need to be resolved are as follows:

Table 5 Industrial training institutes and their seating capacities in 2010

Sl. no.	Region/states/ UTs	Total ITIs/ ITCs	Share of state in %	Total seating capacity	Seating capacity % share of states
Northern region					
1	Chandigarh	2	0.02	968	0.08
2	Delhi	73	0.84	15,336	1.26
3	Haryana	171	1.97	31,280	2.58
4	Himachal Pradesh	174	2.00	18,272	1.51
5	Jammu and Kashmir	38	0.44	4197	0.35
6	Punjab	277	3.19	39,444	3.25
7	Rajasthan	794	9.14	93,343	7.69
8	Uttar Pradesh	986	11.35	111,146	9.15
9	Uttarakhand	90	1.04	9361	0.77
Subtotal		2605	29.99	323,347	26.63
Southern region					
1	Andhra Pradesh	642	7.39	124,194	10.23
2	Karnataka	1318	15.17	115,040	9.48
3	Kerala	521	6.00	69,254	5.70
4	Lakshadweep	1	0.01	96	0.01
5	Puducherry	17	0.20	1924	0.16
6	Tamil Nadu	697	8.02	86,022	7.09
Subtotal		3196	36.79	396,530	32.66
Eastern region					
1	Arunachal Pradesh	5	0.06	512	0.04
2	Andaman and Nicobar Islands	1	0.01	273	0.02
3	Assam	34	0.39	5952	0.49
4	Bihar	376	4.33	60,210	4.96
5	Jharkhand	132	1.52	32,632	2.69
6	Manipur	7	0.08	540	0.04
7	Meghalaya	7	0.08	942	0.08
8	Mizoram	1	0.01	294	0.02
9	Nagaland	8	0.09	944	0.08
10	Orissa	588	6.77	104,452	8.60
11	Sikkim	4	0.05	580	0.05
12	Tripura	8	0.09	1040	0.09
13	West Bengal	75	0.86	14,516	1.20
Subtotal		1246	14.34	222,887	18.36

(continued)

Table 5 (continued)

Sl. no.	Region/states/ UTs	Total ITIs/ ITCs	Share of state in %	Total seating capacity	Seating capacity % share of states
Western region					
1	Chhattisgarh	136	1.57	16,112	1.33
2	Dadra and Nagar Haveli	1	0.01	228	0.02
3	Daman and Diu	2	0.02	388	0.03
4	Goa	14	0.16	3644	0.30
5	Gujarat	524	6.03	78,868	6.50
6	Madhya Pradesh	258	2.97	36,192	2.98
7	Maharashtra	705	8.12	135,852	11.19
Subtotal		1640	18.88	271,284	22.35
India		8687	100.00	1,214,048	100.00

Source Ministry of HRD, GOI, 2012

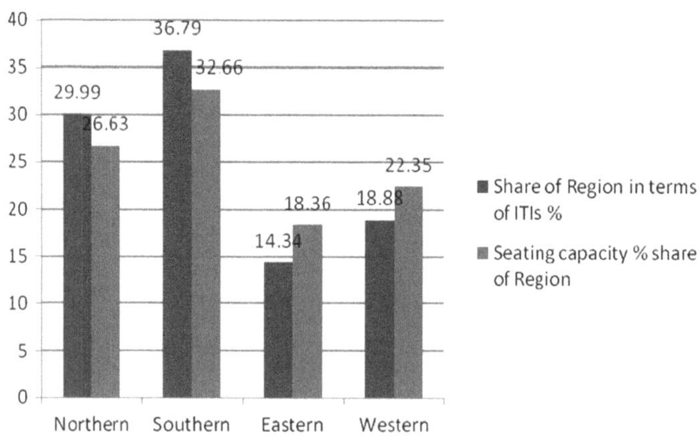

Fig. 1 Industrial training institutes and their seating capacities by region in 2010 *Source* Ministry of HRD, GOI

- How to integrate skill education with main stream general education to encourage students for skill education,
- What steps are needed to increase the intake proportion at senior secondary level in skill/vocational education,
- How to capture the changing labour market demand for skill and to introduce a mechanism for change in education system, and
- What can be an effective PPP model?

Table 6 Out-turn/pass-out students at undergraduate level in disciplines/subjects in higher education in India (2015–2016)

Sl. no.	Engineering and technology	Male pass-out	Female pass-out	Total pass-out	% respect of stream to total
1	Aeronautical engineering	2330	724	3054	0.36
2	Agriculture engineering	1772	975	2747	0.32
3	Architecture	3498	4274	7772	0.91
4	Chemical engineering	7333	2813	10,146	1.19
5	Civil engineering	74,709	19,452	94,161	11.08
6	Computer engineering	81,298	79,236	160,534	18.90
7	Dairy technology	307	114	421	0.05
8	Electrical engineering	70,911	26,001	96,912	11.41
9	Electronics engineering	106,125	80,883	187,008	22.01
10	Food technology	686	574	1260	0.15
11	Information technology	24,474	26,143	50,617	5.96
12	Marine engineering	1002	20	1022	0.12
13	Mechanical engineering	159,859	9823	169,682	19.97
14	Metallurgical engineering	2187	874	3061	0.36
15	Mining engineering	1122	58	1180	0.14
16	Other engineering and technology	40,499	19,246	59,745	7.03
17	Planning	97	72	169	0.02
All engineering and technology disciplines		578,209	271,282	849,491	100.00

Source Ministry of HRD, GOI, 2017

6 Overview of Skill Development Initiatives Taken by Other Countries

The efforts on making the skilled country successfully by some of the developed nations are depicted below:

Germany: In Germany, vocational education integrates work-based and school-based learning to prepare apprentices for a successful transition to full-time employment. Both the academic and practical training for a span of two to three and a half years for the admitted students has been fixed. On the basis of occupation decided by the student, every week, trainees spend 1 or 2 days in a vocational school and 3 or 4 days in the establishment they are attached with. Progress of the student is evaluated on the basis of his performance in theoretical as well as

Table 7 Out-turn/pass-out students at undergraduate level in disciplines/subjects in higher education in India (2011–12)

Sl. no.	Engineering and technology	Male pass-out	Female pass-out	Total pass-out	% respect of stream to total
1	Electronics engineering	92,516	54,644	147,160	26.81
2	Computer engineering	77,045	55,730	132,775	24.19
3	Mechanical engineering	78,737	5074	83,811	15.27
4	Electrical engineering	51,709	21,420	73,129	13.32
5	Other engineering and technology	36,547	19,161	55,708	10.15
6	Civil engineering	28,452	8402	36,854	6.71
7	Chemical engineering	4901	1711	6612	1.20
8	Architecture	2140	2067	4207	0.77
9	Agriculture engineering	1265	684	1949	0.36
10	Aeronautical engineering	1532	411	1943	0.35
11	Metallurgical engineering	1205	186	1391	0.25
12	Food technology	773	474	1247	0.23
13	Marine engineering	780	23	803	0.15
14	Mining engineering	690	26	716	0.13
15	Dairy technology	403	159	562	0.10
16	Planning	26	14	40	0.01
All engineering and technology disciplines		378,721	170,186	548,907	100.00

Source Ministry of HRD, GOI, 2013

practical knowledge gained during the academic session. The key objective of training in the dual system in the country is to achieve the skilled manpower as per the requirement.

South Korea: The technical education system in South Korea also highlights the example of developing economy while reaping the benefits through planned strategy. The country has a system of job oriented skill development programme, as a result, about 27% in training participation by employees and the number of employees trained by employers increased by almost 13 times is a unique example to learn from the country's technical education system.

China: China's Vocational Education & Training (VET) which includes pre-employment training/apprenticeship training/on-the-job training and retraining for the laid-off workers of the country. The entire process is managed by government employment training centers as well as non-governmental vocational training institutions. The country has made efforts even at the local government-level to

Table 8 Gender diversity in different streams in 2015–16

Sl. no.	Engineering and technology	Female as % to total
1	Aeronautical engineering	23.71
2	Agriculture engineering	35.49
3	Architecture	54.99
4	Chemical engineering	27.73
5	Civil engineering	20.66
6	Computer engineering	49.36
7	Dairy technology	27.08
8	Electrical engineering	26.83
9	Electronics engineering	43.25
10	Food technology	45.56
11	Information technology	51.65
12	Marine engineering	1.96
13	Mechanical engineering	5.79
14	Metallurgical engineering	28.55
15	Mining engineering	4.92
16	Other engineering and technology	32.21
17	Planning	42.60
Total in engineering and technology		31.93

Source Ministry of HRD, GOI, 2017

train unskilled and uneducated migrant labour for various sectors. This policy has also created a threat to India because there is a glut of Chinese products in the Indian market.

Singapore: In Singapore, the national framework for establishing standard in work performance is named as National skill Recognition System (NSRS). NSRS identifies skill job competencies and certifies skill acquisition. There is a collaboration of NSRS with employer group, industry associations, economic agencies and unions.

7 Interstate Disparities in Facilities for Technical/Skill Education in India

The enrolment data has revealed that only about 10.0% enrolment out of the total was in engineering and technology. But the situation varies from state to state, among the various states of the country, the major proportion of the technical educational institutions for vocational education are in (Northern region), i.e. Rajasthan state has the highest number followed by (Southern region) Karnataka. Four states namely Tamil Nadu, Karnataka, Maharashtra and Andhra Pradesh

Table 9 Gender diversity in different streams 2011–12

Sl. no.	Engineering and technology	Female as % to total
1	Electronics engineering	37.13
2	Computer engineering	41.97
3	Mechanical engineering	6.05
4	Electrical Engineering	29.29
5	Other engineering and technology	34.40
6	Civil engineering	22.80
7	Chemical engineering	25.88
8	Architecture	49.13
9	Agriculture engineering	35.09
10	Aeronautical engineering	21.15
11	Metallurgical engineering	13.37
12	Food technology	38.01
13	Marine engineering	2.86
14	Mining engineering	3.63
15	Dairy technology	28.29
16	Planning	35.00
17	Total	31.00
18	IT and Computer	46.22

Source Ministry of HRD, GOI, 2013

account for as much as 55.0% of engineering degree institutions. Besides, these states also account for about 50.0% intake of degree level in the country.

Whereas the out-turn is a concern, very few states contribute major share, i.e. about 17.0% which was highest proportion from the state of Tamil Nadu, in the year 2015–16, followed by 11.0% from Maharashtra, and 5.0% from Rajasthan.

Table 10 presents the top five states in India in gross enrolment ratios in different qualifications.

The above table depicts that the Gujarat state has shown all round progress in terms of GER as the state has represented almost in all level of qualification, on the other hand, one of the small state from north-eastern region, Arunachal Pradesh has also shown potential for the matter of comparison. It is seen from the above table that many major states are not seen in the above comparison.

8 Signals (Demand) from the Labour Market: Requirement of Skilled Manpower

It is well-known fact that the expansion in intake in technical education bears no relationship between labour market demands insofar as skilled manpower at different levels is concerned. A very small proportion of pass-outs are employable as a

Table 10 Top five states having highest gross enrolment ratios (GER) across educational qualification

Sl. no.	Academic qualifications							
	Ph.D.	M. Phil.	P.G.	U.G.	P.G. diploma	Diploma	Certificate	Integrated course
1	Arunachal Pradesh	Karnataka	Gujarat	Madhya Pradesh	Pondicherry	Karnataka	Mizoram	Uttar Pradesh
2	Gujarat	Uttar Pradesh	Karnataka	Jammu and Kashmir	Odisha	Gujarat	Tamil Nadu	Gujarat
3	Madhya Pradesh	Arunachal Pradesh	Uttar Pradesh	Arunachal Pradesh	Arunachal Pradesh	West Bengal	Karnataka	Rajasthan
4	Telangana	Telangana	Jammu and Kashmir	Karnataka	Chhattisgarh	Rajasthan	Telangana	Arunachal Pradesh
5	Karnataka	Gujarat	Arunachal Pradesh	Gujarat	Karnataka	Assam	Kerala	Chhattisgarh

Source All India senior secondary survey KMPG analysis, 2017

result, the number of unemployed technical people has been increasing over the years and at the same time intake capacities at all the levels have also increased. Why the technical people coming out from the institutions were not able to find the job? The probable answer could be the following:

(1) The intake capacities are higher than the market demands,
(2) Skill levels of the out-turn are different from the market needs, and
(3) The type of skill needed and the type of skill supplied are not matching.

The above-mentioned reasons could be responsible for the decreasing rates of absorption of technical people in the labour market. The Indian labour market has certain unique features such as the labour intensity in the agricultural sector in India is better, compared to other sub-sectors.

The country has visualized rapid growth in recent years, due to the growth in modern industries. The demand for a modern quality service has increased with the increase in purchasing power. But at the same time, the technical human resource available in the labour market was not found suitable as per the required skill. As a result, it is a wake-up alarm for introducing a required focus on the skill development for the young population of the country based on the market demand.

In order to utilize the available skill, Government of India has taken various measures to create adequate training for the youth to make them employable and develop required skills through various policy initiatives which are as follows:

- Prime Minister's National Council on Skill Development,
- National Skill Development Coordination Board,
- National Skill Development Corporation (NSDC),
- National Council for Vocational Training (NCVT).

However, there are many challenges that Skill India Mission faces, the most important being the insufficiency of funds to implement as ambitious and humungous a scheme such as this. A budget provision of Rs 17,273 Crore was made but the amount seems to be meagre one keeping in view the targeted beneficiaries in the country. Another area of concern is the existing wage structures. Several representatives of the workers' unions have pointed out that unless companies begin paying wages that commensurate with the skills of the workers, the Mission is not likely to leave any significant dent. Additionally, there is a need to ensure that labour laws are not violated as rampantly and with impunity as they are now. Thus, it is imperative that the workers' rights are protected, ample social security is provided and decent living standards are maintained.

India is a diverse country in terms of language, religion, income, caste, gender, geography, etc. This diversity also reflects disparity. To cater to all sections for skill development is a challenge that needs to be addressed in an inclusive manner so that there is equitable access for all.

It has been observed that the fresh technical graduates are also lacking the understanding of basic concepts such as, lack of client-handling skills and insufficient knowledge across domains, etc. are some of the skill gaps areas which need to be addressed before coming out in the labour market. In view of these constraints, there would be additional requirements of skilled workforce in various sub-sectors of the economy as depicted in Table 11. Further, the value-added industries are also being given a policy push under the 'Make in India' initiative, as a result, highly skilled workforce would be required in high-end industries of the country, and the technical institutions have to consider this fact while covering the curriculum in various stream.

The above-mentioned requirement of skilled manpower was projected by the newly created central ministry if Skill Development. The requirement of skilled manpower by 2022 was projected about 560.5 million in the country that is about 110 million incremental requirement in total as a whole. The ministry has also projected the incremental manpower requirement for various other sectors of the economy which is presented in Table 12.

About 110 million incremental requirement of skilled manpower from the year 2013 to 2022 indicates that substantially a higher proportion was projected for the sectors like Building, construction and real estate, retail sector, textile and clothing, transportation and logistics, beauty and wellness, and electronics—IT hardware.

It is crucial to capture the demand side signalled from job market along with supply side to throw light on the skill scenario of the country. It is difficult to get data to capture demand, however, some surveys are being undertaken to understand the market trend. One of such surveys is a joint study by CII, PeopleStrong, Wheebox and Linked in and their findings are published in their report titled India Skill Report 2016. It has been mentioned in the report that sectors like retail, e-commerce, BFSI, pharma, telecom and other manufacturing lead the way with an increase of over 20% in hiring persons in 2016 compared to that in 2015. It is closely followed by the sectors—BPO/KPO/ITES Core sector, where hiring numbers have increased by more than 10% in 2015–16 period. In sectors like FMCG, hospitality and software and IT where the percent share of hiring has remained the same in 2015–16. It has been expected in the study that the percent increase in industrial sectors is expected to reflect upon positively on the hiring trend. The data for percent increase in industrial sectors have been used from Department of Industrial Policy and Promotion (DIPP) for estimating the hiring trend. Hence, it can be said that software and IT sector having the potentiality to absorb engineers and technicians show an increase in hiring numbers of 0–5% during 2015–16. The engineering and automotive sector which also have requirement for engineering and technical manpower exhibit a growth rate in hiring number of 5–15% (Table 13).

Some basic and general requirements need to be fulfilled for meeting the hunt of skill in the job market. Some of these factors can be enumerated as:

(a) **Standardization in certification and assessment at entry and exit point**: There is no effective entry gate and exit gate assessment of students entering higher education beyond the top schools. Institutions like IITs/IIMs choose between tight entry gates and wide open exit gates or chartered accountancy institutions choose open entry gates and tight exit gates. However, lack of competition has led to the system of wide open entry gates and wide open exit

Table 11 Incremental human resource requirement across sectors by 2022

Sl. no.	Sector	Employment in 2013 (million)	Projected employment by 2022 (million)	Incremental requirement from 2013 to 2022 (million)
1	Auto and auto components	10.98	14.88	3.9
2	Beauty and wellness	4.21	14.27	10.06
3	Food processing	6.98	11.38	4.4
4	Media and entertainment	0.4	1.3	0.9
5	Handlooms and handicrafts	11.65	17.79	6.14
6	Leather and leather goods	3.09	6.81	3.72
7	Domestic help	6.0	10.88	4.88
8	Gems and jewellery	4.64	8.23	3.59
9	Telecommunication	2.08	4.16	2.08
10	Tourism, hospitality and travel	6.96	13.44	6.48
11	Furniture and furnishing	4.11	11.29	7.18
12	Building, construction and real estate	45.42	76.55	31.13
13	IT and ITES	2.96	5.12	2.16
14	Construction material and building hardware	8.3	11.0	2.7
15	Textile and clothing	15.23	21.54	6.31
16	Healthcare	3.59	7.39	3.8
17	Security	7.0	11.83	4.83
18	Agriculture	240.4	215.6	24.8
19	Education/skill development	13.02	17.31	4.2
20	Transportation and logistics	16.74	28.4	11.66
21	Electronic and IT hardware	4.33	8.94	4.61
22	Pharma and life sciences	1.86	3.58	1.72
23	BFSI	2.55	4.25	1.7
24	Retail	38.6	55.95	17.35
Total		461.1	581.89	120.79

(continued)

Table 11 (continued)

Sl. no.	Sector	Employment in 2013 (million)	Projected employment by 2022 (million)	Incremental requirement from 2013 to 2022 (million)
Removal of duplication in retail sector		(10.37)	(21.43)	(11.06)
Total requirement		450.73	560.46	109.73

Source Ministry of skill development and entrepreneurship, 2015

Table 12 Incremental human resource requirements across sectors by 2022

Sl. no.	Segment	Employment base in million		
		2013	2017	2022
1	Building, construction and real estate	45.42	59.40	76.55
2	Automobile and auto component	10.98	12.18	14.88
3	Banking, financial services insurance	2.55	3.20	4.21
4	Textile and clothing	15.23	18.06	21.54
5	Pharmaceuticals	1.86	2.60	3.58
6	Electronics—IT hardware	4.33	6.24	8.94
7	Retail Sector	38.6	45.11	55.95
8	IT and ITES	2.96	3.86	5.24
9	Food processing	1.75	2.65	4.40
10	Beauty and wellness	4.21	14.27	10.06
11	Electronic and IT hardware	4.33	8.94	4.61
12	Transportation and logistics	16.74	28.4	11.66
13	Healthcare	3.59	7.39	3.8
14	Handlooms and handicrafts	11.65	17.79	6.14
15	Telecommunication	2.08	4.16	2.08
16	Pharma and lifesciences	1.86	3.58	1.72
17	Education/skill development	13.02	17.31	4.29
18	Leather and leather goods	3.09	6.81	3.72
19	Security	7.0	11.83	4.83
20	Furniture and furnishing	4.11	11,29	7.18
21	Tourism, hospitality and travel	6.96	13.44	6.48
22	Gems and jewellery	4.64	8.23	3.59
23	Domestic help	6.0	10.88	4.88

Source Ministry of skill development and entrepreneurship

gates resulting in poor signalling. Higher signalling value of degrees or standard exit assessments with would reduce the costs and increase efficiencies in recruitment.

(b) **Language proficiency and Digital Literacy**: Language diversity in India requires a common medium of conveying thoughts and interaction among

Table 13 Distribution of per cent increase in deployment professionals in various sectors

SL No	Sectors	Hiring numbers per cent increase (in %)
1	Consumer goods and durables	0–5
2	Hospitality (including aviation, tours and travels, hotels)	0–5
3	Software and IT	0–5
4	Others and diversified	0–5
5	BPO, KPO and ITES	5–15
6	Core sector (oil and gas, power, steel, minerals, etc)	5–15
7	Engineering and automotive (auto and auto components)	5–15
8	Banking, financial services and insurance	15–25
9	Other manufacturing (not including FMCG)	25% and above
10	CD, automotive and engineering, pharma and healthcare	25% and above
11	Retail, e-commerce, transport and logistics	25% and above
12	Telecom and allied activities	25% and above

Source CII, people strong, Wheebox and Linkedin and published in their report titled India skill report 2016

several institutions, students and teachers. Proficiency in English/Hindi may be considered an essential yardstick for being selected in the job market. Proficiency in English is still considered having an edge in high-end services whereas knowledge of Hindi is required for unorganized services like security, door to door sales, electricians, etc. and other informal services.

The telecom and IT revolution are driving a massive recognition for digital literacy. The requirement for digital literacy and skills in digital marketing have given rise to lots of entrepreneurs in addition to wage employment.

(c) **Soft Skills**: **Soft** skills like skills in communication, teamwork, problem-solving, leadership, etc. are also intensely required in the job market. Employers in the modern-day job market look for the ability in, willingness to learn and inculcate a positive attitude to these soft skills from the jobseekers. So, these skills need to be incorporated in the training/education module and need to be integrated with other parts of the curriculum and embedded rather than delivered separately.

(d) **Relevant Industry Skills**: a relevant skill for a particular field is the most important prerequisite for matching the demand-side requirement. The world of work changes at a much more rapid pace than the static academic and learning structure. So, there is a constant need for training and retraining to suit the skill requirement. The changing global scenario through globalization, deregulation and competition changes expectations from employers faster than teaching modules of educational institutions. A close linkage with employers and educational institutions is the need of the day for driving curriculum reviews and upgrading staff training.

(e) **Social perception**: Perception about vocational training in India needs to be changed keeping in mind the emerging trends. Vocational training should not be looked down upon by institutions and society. Vocational stream should be brought in the main stream of educational structure and should have a channel to acquire higher degree or better placement in the job market.

(f) **Financing Options**: We need to provide financial facilities or training of existing employees, students and self-employed people. Scholarships and collateral free loans should be made available in a larger scale to enhance the skill of jobseekers and for meeting the skill requirements at different levels.

9 Weak Spots and Future Initiatives Needed to Meet Today's and Tomorrow's Skills Needs

Employment composition in India is dominated by unorganized sector work force (93.0%). If the decade of 1990s was one of the jobless growth and the growing the actualization, the first decade of the current century is set to witness a gradual further reduction of organized sector employment. The supply of technical/skill is not as per the labour market demand.

The Indian labour market will need a really high number of well trained as per the demand and qualified engineering graduates. Is India ready for it? Unfortunately, the facts look a bit dismal. Of the existing seating capacity of ITI (1,865,620) in 2015 Table 4, about 3,145,787 intake capacity in engineering graduates in 2015–15 (Table 2), about 849,491 engineering graduate were passed out in the year 2016 (Table 6), comparatively a lower number is categorized a kind of high quality graduates in the labour market. The required supply as per the demand is meagre.

Majority of the technical institutions (public and private) need to improve the quality as per the demand of the labour market. A majority of these institutions are affiliated to universities and teach the curriculum developed by the affiliating university. As a result, they lack the incentive to continuously improve the quality not geared to adapt to the changing needs of the job market.

The formal technical education system is producing enough engineers, diploma holders and certificate holders to cater for the growing needs of the 1.3 plus billion population of the country. But, many of these trained people do not find practicing what they were taught, because of the lack of industry–institution networking. Hundreds of thousands of technically qualified join the job market, with skills many employers do not want them because they are lacking the applied kind of skill. There is an urgent need for these young people to upskill themselves to stay relevant in today's fast-changing workplace.

Certain weightage is also to be given to the fast-growing digital Indian economy and increasing demand for highly skilled technical workers. This is amply evidenced by the fact that the gap between the technical training provided by the existing infrastructure and skill requirement of the labour market is still wide and needs to be addressed by the policy planner in technical education in the country.

10 Summary and Conclusions

The existing skill development policy in India needs an urgent relook as the government has initiated various skill development programmes. The existing institutional structure needs to be converted on the demand basis to cater to the requirement of the labour market. For the success of 'Make in India' project, it is important to equip India's youthful millions with the right skills to compete in a global job market. The current infrastructure facility available in the technical educational institutions is inadequate considering the requirement of the job market. Another crucial aspect in skill development is the 'Train the Trainers'. The trainer should be able to assess the needs of the students keeping in view the labour market situation.

The demand made by the labour market and supply of labour-force mismatch lead to defeat all types of skill development initiatives of the Government. This is an indication that there is a lot of scope to initiate requirement based approach for skill development keeping in view the demand and supply. Majority of formal institutions either in public or private sector is located around urban areas. It is necessary that the Government along with its partner agencies should set up more standardized skill-based institutions or skill development centers across the country.

The private it is in the country are more in number as compared to government-owned ones, on the other hand, the student intake capacities are higher in state-owned ITIs than their private counterparts. The ITI infrastructure in the country has been seriously affected by an acute shortage of qualified teachers, infrastructure for hands-on facility leading to the poor employability of passed out. As per the available infrastructure, the country has the capacity to train up to 3.1 million people per annum, which is about 24.2% of the 12.8 million new entrants to the workforce every year in the country. It is another other issue that the existing limited capacity may also remain underutilized in several segments.

One of the biggest challenges in skills development in the country is to impart requisite skills to this unorganized non-factory sector which deploy a sizeable workforce. The training needs of the unorganized sector are expected to be addressed by all formal training agencies including government institutes, private agencies and civil society organizations.

Annexure-1

Industrial Training Institutes and their Seating Capacities by Region in 2010

Sl. no.	Region	Total ITIs/ ITCs	Share of state in %	Total seating capacity	Seating capacity % share of states
1	Northern	2605	29.99	323,347	26.63
2	Southern	3196	36.79	396,530	32.66
3	Eastern	1246	14.34	222,887	18.36
4	Western	1640	18.88	271,284	22.35
All India		8687	100.00	12,14,048	100.00

Source Ministry of HRD, GOI, 2012

References

Deka, R. J., & Batra, B. (2016). The scope of skill development, employability of Indian workforce in context of make in India: A study. *International Journal of Engineering Technology, Management and Applied Sciences, 4*(4), 275–282. Retrieved from: http://www.ijetmas.com/admin/resources/project/paper/f201605021462179221.pdf.

Kanchan, S., & Varshney, S. (2015). Skill development initiatives and strategies. *Asian Journal of Management Research, 5*(4), 666–672. Retrieved from: http://www.ipublishing.co.in/ajmrvol1no1/volfive/EIJMRS5242.pdf.

Kapur, H. (2016). "Skill India" programme: A compliment to "Make in India" campaign. *Global Journal for Research Analysis, 5*(1), 84–86. Retrieved from: http://worldwidejournals.in/ojs/index.php/gjra/article/view/1989/2001. *International Journal of Enhanced Research in Management & Computer Applications, 6*(10), 113. ISSN: 2319-7471, October 2017, Impact Factor: 3.578.

Kaur, R. (2016). Skills development in India. *International Journal of Transformations in Business Management, 4*(2), 25–33. Retrieved from: http://www.ijtbm.com/images/short_pdf/1426172413__Kaur_8.pdf.

Okada, A. (2012). Skills development for youth in India: Challenges and opportunities. *Journal of International Cooperation in Education, 15*(2), 169–193. Retrieved from: http://home.hiroshimau.ac.jp/cice/wp-content/uploads/publications/15-2/15-2-10.pdf.

Pujani, K. K. (2014). A study on the requirement of skills development for the success of "Make in India" project. *Tactful Management Research Journal*. Retrieved from: http://tmgt.lsrj.in/SeminarPdf/299.pdf.

Saini, V. (2015). Skill development in India: Need, challenges and ways forward. *Abhinav National Monthly Refereed Journal of Research in Arts & Education, 4*(4), 1–9. Retrieved from: http://home.hiroshimau.ac.jp/cice/wp-content/uploads/publications/15-2/15-2-10.pdf.

Nurturing Skill Development in Organized Sector—Chaos in Institutional Set-up: Experiences from an Industrial Region in India

M. R. Prasad, Shachi Joshi, D. Indrakumar, V. K. Saxena and Tapas Kumar Sarangi

1 Introduction

Apprenticeship is envisaged to provide competency based set of skills through formal skill training in a large pool of establishments. To meet the growing need for skilled personnel in modern processes and technology-intensive industries, there is a need for young technical professionals to achieve last mile skilling. This is facilitated through a policy push by amending the Apprentices Act, 1961 in 1973, and creating autonomous structures called Board of Apprentice Training (BOAT) separately in three regions of India, i.e. Mumbai, Chennai and Kanpur, and another body called Board of Practical Training (BoPT) at Kolkatta. This facility of skill development is aimed at outgoing graduates of all Engineering Colleges, and Polytechnics in India. Later on, the purview of this facility is extended to 10 + 2 Vocational School streams by another amendment to Apprentices Act during 1983. Thus, the scheme is popularly known as National Apprentice Training Scheme (NATS).

Though, apparently, the NATS is facilitating last mile skill development to the youth entering into labour market, the scheme is plagued by many drawbacks.

M. R. Prasad (✉) · S. Joshi · D. Indrakumar · V. K. Saxena · T. K. Sarangi
NILERD, Narela Institutional Area, Delhi, India
e-mail: mrp489@gmail.com

S. Joshi
e-mail: shachi.joshi7@gmail.com

D. Indrakumar
e-mail: dindrakumar@gmail.com

V. K. Saxena
e-mail: vijaysaxena.iamr@gmail.com

T. K. Sarangi
e-mail: sarangi.tapas@gmail.com

NILERD, *Reflecting on India's Development*,
https://doi.org/10.1007/978-981-13-1414-8_6

Some of them are (i) lack of coordination and absence of linkage between establishments and institutional set-up, (ii) wastage of skilling infrastructure at establishments due to non-response from graduates, (iii) preference of fresh graduates for white-collared jobs among other issues. Thus, the actual scenario is captured in this paper by tapping all the stakeholders of NATS.

2 Salient Features of NATS

Main objectives of NATS are (i) to abridge the gap in skills, in so far as the practical/hands-on experience of fresh graduate engineers, diploma holders in engineering are concerned, which they do not acquire during their regular studies under normal practice, (ii) to secure facilities for training in different establishments, both in government and private domain.

All the pass-outs from engineering colleges, polytechnics, and vocational schools are eligible to enrol in NATS up to three years from the year of graduation. Tenure of the apprentice training is one year. Monthly rate of stipend is Rs. 4984/-, 3542/- and Rs. 2758/- for degree, diploma and school leavers, respectively. The enrolled candidates in the establishments are called Graduate Trainees, Technician Trainee and Technician (Vocational) Trainee during the tenure of the training.

At the end of one-year training, trainees are awarded proficiency certificate on the recommendations of the establishment where the training took place, by the respective BOAT/BOPT depending on to which Board, the trainees are enrolled. This one-year training certificate is treated at par with the full-fledged industrial experience certificate. This is a major turn-around for the young engineers who have acquired one-year experience in the latest technologies, and processes, acquired latest skills, and skill enhancement in order to obtain gainful employment as skilled professionals in the industries.

The employment avenues of such candidates improve enormously such as (i) they shall be absorbed in the same establishments where they obtained training depending on their performance, demand of skilled manpower in the same firm, (ii) retention of these trained personnel on further probation and further in-house training of the firm to mould the skilled personnel to the needs of the firm, (iii) enhanced chances of ex-trainees in the labour market in similar kind of establishments, for a gainful and suitable job.

2.1 Coverage and Outreach of NATS

At the national level, the total pool of 12,000 establishments running with modern technology spreading in a wide spectrum of activities under primary, secondary and tertiary sector are registered as eligible and fully equipped for the training of apprentices of NATS. These establishments have the cumulative training capacity

Table 1 Comparative Figures of All India and Western Region

Comparison	Number of establishments	Training seats capacity	Number of institutions
All India availability	12,000	250,000	2900
BOAT (WR)	4180	66,209	600

Source Annual Report of BOAT (WR), 2017 and website of All India Council for Technical Education (AICTE). MHRD, Govt. of India

of more than 250,000 seats. This is augmented by a total number of 2900 Institutes/ Colleges preparing technical graduates eligible to enrol as Apprentices, out of which, 600 are located in the Western Region. At the BOAT (WR) purview, there are 66,209 seats, majority of them in Maharashtra state, and 4180 establishments majority of them are in the private sector. Majority of the establishments are in the private domain (Table 1).

3 Evaluation of NATS of BOAT (Western Region)

As stated earlier, the NATS has evolved with a purpose of preparing high-end skilled personnel by facilitating last mile skilling of fresh graduates of technical institutions. Through one-year industrial training of NATS, the technical graduates are entering into labour market with skill enhancement satisfying 'industry-ready/work-ready/ job-ready' attributes. The NATS scheme is a potential vehicle of skill enhancement among the youth having sufficient technical educational background. However, there are varied signals coming out from the labour market about the employment prospects of such NATS-trained graduates. There is a need to look at the ground realities based on the empirical evidences. Hence, this study is being undertaken.

Statistics of NATS reveals that there is underutilization of capacity of training slots in establishments which can be seen as wastage of capacity and resources of skilling. On the other hand, graduates from institutions are remained unemployed and not enrolling with NATS. Therefore, the scheme has the scope and potential to bring out more effectiveness. For example, the capacity utilization of the scheme is around 57%, though the eligible youth joining labour force every year is more than 10 times the intake capacity of NATS. There are apparent signals that vocational school system is dysfunctional in every state. There were also signals of poor absorption rate of successful trainees in the same establishment though there is demand for skilled human resources. All these issues are cropping up in a highly industrialized region, i.e. Western Region, that has the concentration of heavy and technology-intensive industries. This region is supposed to provide very good opportunities for skill development, and job opportunities in organized sector for high-end skilled personnel.

Against this background, it is intended to go into the issues and problems hampering the implementation of NATS in the Western Region. This region covers industrially active states like Maharashtra, Gujarat, and states like Chattisgarh and Madhya Pradesh which are rich in mining and subsidiary units, Goa and Dadra Nagar Haveli which attracts industries due to local incentives. NATS is executed in this region by BOAT (WR), having its headquarters at Mumbai.

4 Objectives and Study Design

4.1 Objectives of the Study

a. To assess the impact of NATS training on employment, skills of targeted beneficiaries
b. To identify the bottlenecks in implementation of the NATS
c. To recommend remedial steps to improve the effectiveness of NATS

Inter-alia, the following issues centred around the study were covered in detail through the above objectives.

1. To gauge the impact of skill development/skill enhancement by tracking the employment opportunities of beneficiaries
2. To examine the absorption rate of the ex-trainees in comparison with the non-beneficiaries
3. To examine the implementation process of the scheme at BOAT (WR) level, i.e. administrative issues of implementation
4. To identify regulatory hurdles hampering training and functional efficiency of employers
5. To identify measures to enhance the popularity of the scheme
6. To assess the training infrastructure at workplace, and the tangible gains in new skills and skill enhancement by trainees
7. Outreach efforts by the implementing agency, i.e. BOAT (WR).

4.2 Methodology

The study covered all the states falling under the jurisdiction of BOAT (WR). The study extensively covered the key stakeholders of NATS, i.e. (i) Industrial Establishments, (ii) Direct Beneficiaries, i.e. Trainees, current and former, (iii) Institutes, (iv) faculty. In addition, few control group elements from each of the above are also taken.

Structured and comprehensive questionnaire to each of the above-stated stakeholders concerned with the study was canvassed and their views, and opinions were recorded about the in-depth functioning of BOAT (NR) vis-à-vis effectiveness of

NATS. In addition, Focused Group Discussions (FGD) were conducted separately with each of the stakeholders, i.e. Training Managers of Establishments, Placement-incharges of Institutes, Faculty, Outgoing students, Trainees of NATS.

4.3 Coverage and Sampling Frame

In each state, two places of industrially active zones were identified for the field survey. These establishments were a blend of (a) type of management, i.e. Central Public Sector Undertakings (CPSU), State Public Sector Undertakings (SPSU), Private Establishments, Government Organizations, (b)type of activity, i.e. manufacturing/processing/automobiles, IT/IT-enabled services, Power Generation/ Distribution Companies, Mining/Mineral industries, (c) size of establishment, i.e. medium, heavy industries, etc. Among the beneficiaries, both current (on-roll) trainees, and ex-trainees with due weightage to each type of trainee (graduate, diploma and vocational school pass-outs), gender were given. In case of Institutes, all kinds of Institutes, i.e. Degree and Diploma Institutes located in both rural and urban areas were covered. Details of the sampling frame are given in Tables 2, 3, 4 and 5.

Table 2 State/UT-wise distribution responded establishment by sector

State/UT	CPSU	SPSU/State Govt.	Private Estt	Total
1. Chhattisgarh	3	1	6	10
2. Dadra Nagar Haveli	–	–	3	3
3. Daman & Diu	–	–	3	3
4. Goa	2	–	7	9
5. Gujarat	–	1	8[a]	9
6. Madhya Pradesh	1	–	14	15
7. Maharashtra	4	2	3	9
Total	10	4	44	58

Note [a]Out of 8, one establishment is Cooperative Society.
Source NILERD Survey, 2017

Table 3 State- and gender-wise distribution of on-roll trainees (within brackets indicate %age)

Sl. No.	States	No. of on-roll trainees		
		Male	Female	Total
1.	Chhattisgarh	12 (75.0)	4 (25.0)	16 (100.0)
2.	Dadra & Nagar Haveli	14 (82.3)	3 (17.7)	17 (100.0)
3.	Daman & Diu	3 (30.0)	7 (70.0)	10 (100.0)
4.	Goa	13 (65.0)	7 (35.0)	20 (100.0)
5.	Gujarat	21 (70.0)	9 (30.0)	30 (100.0)
6.	Madhya Pradesh	30 (100.0)	0 (0.0)	30 (100.0)
7.	Maharashtra	21 (70.0)	9 (30.0)	30 (100.0)
Total		114 (74.5)	39 (25.5)	153 (100.0)

Source NILERD Survey, 2017

Table 4 Distribution of NATS completed trainees (tracer study)—absorbed by States/UTs, social category and gender

States/UTs	No. of NATS completed trainees—absorbed by social category and gender									
	General		Schedule Castes		Scheduled Tribes		Other Backward Classes		Total	
	Male	Female	Male	Female	Male	Female	Male	Female	Male	Female
Chhattisgarh	6	–	–	–	–	–	6	–	12	–
Dadra & Nagar Haveli	6	–	–	–	1	1	4	–	11	1
Daman & Diu	–	–	–	–	–	–	–	–	–	–
Goa	3	–	1	–	1	–	1	–	6	–
Gujarat	4	2	–	–	–	–	3	–	7	2
Madhya Pradesh	5	–	3	–	–	–	–	1	8	1
Maharashtra	3	2	1	1	–	–	1	4	5	7
Total	27	4	5	1	2	1	15	5	49	11

Source NILERD 2017

Table 5 Distribution of responded institutions in Western Region

States	Responded			
	Engg. Colleges	Polytechnics	Voc. Schools	Total
Chhattisgarh	2	5	–	7
Dadra & N Haveli	–	1	–	1
Daman & Diu	–	–	–	–
Goa	3	4	1	8
Gujarat	8	6	–	14
Madhya Pradesh	5	3	3	11
Maharashtra	6	2	3	11
Total	24	21	7	52

Source NILERD, Survey, 2017

5 Results and Discussion

5.1 Survey of Establishments—Nurturing Skill Development

5.1.1 Profile of Sampled Units

Out of the 58 sampled respondents, 44 are in the private sector, followed by 10 in CPSUs. In case of activity status of establishments, 37 out of 58 are falling in the manufacturing sector, followed by Services. In services, majority of them are in IT/ Software Development companies. 33 establishments are employing more than 500 skilled & highly skilled professionals. Among them, the share of private establishments is more than 60%. There is a lack of diversity in enrollment among the trainees with the skewed ratio of gender by merely 15% enrollment of females.

5.1.2 Overachievement by Private Units

The cumulative enrollment figures in these 58 surveyed establishments for the base year of 2014–15 were commendable with graduates enrollment exceeding the capacity of utilization by 40%. This overachievement is in private sector and that too in the manufacturing and IT sector which are playing commendable role in skill facilitation to the young graduates. In case of diploma and vocational school seats, there is underutilization.

5.1.3 Shortage of Skilled Personnel in the Units

There is acute shortage of skilled personnel in the establishments. There is also dearth of apprentices in many establishments, due to preferences by apprentices to enrol only in selected units such as CPSUs, reputed IT companies.

5.1.4 Reasons for Seats Remaining Vacant

Low stipend, no job guarantee/no guarantee of absorption after training, skills mismatch with the academic degree/specialization, lack of awareness about the benefits of NATS. It is pertinent to mention here that, after brainstorming with the stakeholders, it was found that, the perception of fresh graduates about the NATS is driving them to shy away from it, as it is viewed as a last mile option of career rather than last mile skill enhancement. The young graduates are driven by cushy jobs in corporate sector, high salaries/package at the beginning itself, high expectations of career from the beginning itself, attraction towards management education after graduation, etc.

In case of diploma holders, due to increased seats under lateral entry into degree course, and increased campus interviews from infrastructure companies, the diploma slots are lying vacant. In case of school vocational slots, it is a dying system and nowhere it is working up to the mark.

5.1.5 Stipend Issues

It is a meagre amount from the point of view of trainees. Many large companies are paying at par with minimum wages for skilled workers. The policy makers are of the view that stipend is only a subsistence allowance or pocket money to attract fresh graduates for last mile skilling and to gain industrial experience, so as to increase the scope and opportunities for jobs.

5.1.6 Status of Core and Complimentary Facilities at Worksite

Among the surveyed units, the core skilling facilities in large firms, and CPSUs are in place as per the standards and norms. Apprentices are enjoying the complimentary benefits such as free hostel, subsidized canteen and transport facilities.

5.1.7 Fitness for Absorption After Training in the Same Establishment

This is a vital parameter of measuring the effectiveness of NATS. Therefore, a detailed analysis was done after taking the feedback from the establishments. The views are classified into three types (with %age of units in the brackets), i.e. (a) fully fit for absorption (78%), (b) partially fit for absorption (20%), and the trainees need further exposure to skilling, and (c) not fit for absorption (2%). In case of responses of units on partial fitness of trainees, they were of the opinion that the trainees need some more exposure, ranging from another one year to two years for complete fitness. Only negligible section of industries opined that the trainees are not fit in their own firms. This is due to their own personal, technical reasons, as the companies are running with stiff competition, and they need a new set of skill attributes in their companies.

It is another fact that though, majority of the firms are satisfied with the trainees performance, and skill base, they are unable to absorb them into their companies due to various reasons, such as (a) stringent cost-cutting measures, and internal readjustment of skilled human resources, (b) looking for cutting-edge skilled personnel from job market to counter stiff competition from their peer-companies.

5.1.8 Skills Acquired by Trainees in Colleges—Views of Establishments

Establishments for one-year were observing the trainees in their problem solving, analytical capability, application of competencies and skills at the worksite. Therefore, their views are used to assess the competencies grasped at institutional level in order to link the demand–supply gaps and deficiencies between industry expectation, and institutional preparation of graduates. The issue is segregated into three major problems as illustrated below:

a. matching reforms—connecting supply to demand, i.e. employment reform. This needs minor reforms with minor reforms in syllabi at institutional level in association with industry,
b. mismatch reform—repairing supply to demand, i.e. employability reform. This needs Industry–Institute collaboration to mould the graduates during the last one or two semesters,
c. pipeline problem—preparing supply for reform, i.e. education reform. This needs a thorough overhaul of technical education to keep pace with the modern technologies and processes.

Above problems were universally acknowledged as perennial problems in technical and vocational education by other empirical research studies.[1] On the above issues, three-fourths of the establishments opined that mismatch problem is dominant at Institutional level, and wants industry's active involvement in the last semester to decide the syllabi, course content, skills to be imparted to outgoing graduates.

---

[1]India Labour Report-2008. Team Lease Report.

5.2 Feedback of On-Roll Trainees—Last Mile Skill Enhancement by Trainees

5.2.1 Profile of On-Roll Trainees

Opinion of 153 on-roll trainees, and 60 ex-trainees were gathered in the study. 65% of them are hailing from manufacturing sector, followed by services (mainly IT/ software services). By type of management, they are all working in private sector. An enquiry was made on the aspects such as socio-economic background of these trainees, perception of trainees regarding the core skill facilities, tenure of training, skill ecosystem prevailing at the workplace that promotes them towards skill development etc.

One-third of the respondents are from rural background. One-fifth of their parents' occupation is agriculture, and half of respondents' parents are managing petty businesses and petty services (broadly classified as service sector). More than 50% of their family income is around Rs. 10,000/- per month.

5.2.2 Views on Skill Upgradation

Two-thirds of the currently enrolled trainees have expressed their full satisfaction about the skill upgradation at workplace, and they are confident to gain a decent job after the training. Remaining one-third of the trainees desired the tenure to be extended by another year for better skilling. All of the trainees expressed that stipend is too low. They were not properly sensitized that the stipend is merely an encouraging incentive for skill enhancement after graduation to enable them to compete in the job market.

5.3 Feedback of Ex-Beneficiaries (Ex-Trainees) on Skill Enhancement Through NATS

This is done by trailing them to their place of job after training in the surrounding industrial hubs, and few ex-trainees who have been absorbed and enrolled as full-time employees of the host-establishment. Achievement in last mile skill development is up to 75% as per the ex-trainees. They gained confidence to face the interviews, and compete with other jobseekers having couple of years of experience. Significant development is the reduction in waiting period of ex-trainees in getting a suitable job compared to non-NATS graduates. Ex-beneficiaries of NATS got employment within 6 months, whereas, the non-beneficiaries are waiting for more than 2 years for gainful employment.

5.4 *Present Scenario at Institutional Set-up—Skill Crisis at Supply Side*

All India figures of total enrollment in technical education, and campus placement data show that 80% of the graduates are going out of Institutes without any job, and that too without complete skill sets to meet the expectations of industries. Current scenario of technical education, as per the official website of AICTE[2], is illustrated in Table 6.

There are few disturbing signals captured during the visits to sampled Institutes and from the above table, such as:

(a) Majority of the Institutes are located in rural areas and under private domain established during the past one and half decades. They have no proper infrastructure and latest equipment, and managing with half-qualified faculty.
(b) Campus placement in Western Region is merely 23% leaving the remaining 77% of the graduates going out without any job, and without proper skill acquisition.
(c) Looking at the intake capacity and enrollment figures, nearly half of the seat capacity is being wasted in the Institutes. This is not only wastage of resources at Institutes, but affecting the revenue inflow by way of fees, which further deteriorating the quality of technical education, as there are no funds for upgradation of infrastructure.

Thus, the competencies expected by the industries, and the fast-changing technologies at the industries are throwing major challenge to Institutions to reform the syllabus at supply side. There is a turmoil in technical education due to large number of Institutes started in rural areas under private domain. There are no sufficient facilities for the nourishment of skills. The vocational schools under government management are suffering with policy paralysis due to their stagnation in skills, and due to demand of modern skill set in the labour market. The current findings are in synchrony with the latest empirical studies,[3,4,5,6] There is urgent need to reform the technical education system to improve employability and skills by several reputed agencies such as

---

[2]Latest figures available at official website of AICTE. https://www.aicte-india.org/.

[3]Aspiring Minds (2016)—National Employability Report-Engineers 2016-Annual Report.

[4]See Aspiring Minds (2016).

[5]See Bijeesh (2016).

[6]See Aiyar and Ashoka (2011).

Table 6 Technical education in Western Region

Type of parameter	Western Region	All India	Share of Western Region in %age
Total Institutes[a]	2069	7956	26
Intake capacity	858,384	2,951,604	29
Enrollment	372,488	1,585,250	24
Campus placements	86,514	511,108	17

[a]Engineering Colleges offering Under Graduate Programs + Polytechnics offering Diploma Programs in Engineering and Technology Courses, AICTE Website

5.4.1 Stigma Associated with NATS

In spite of insufficient and incomplete skills associated with the outgoing graduates, as stated in the previous section, the graduates are reluctant to enrol for NATS training due to the following reasons, (i) too low stipend, and comparing the stipend with lucrative job offers in the campus interviews, (ii) preference for management education after graduation, (iii) absence of guarantee of absorption in the company after training, (iv) Institutions deliberate discouragement of NATS among their students, as it is viewed as the last mile option of career to students when all options are closed.

5.5 *Vocational School System—Suffering with Policy Paralysis*

Syllabus of vocational school system is overlapping with Craftsmen Training System (CTS) of Industrial Training Institutes/Industrial Training Centres (ITI/ITC) which is administered by Ministry of Skill Development and Employment. There is no coordination and mutual cooperation at the apex level to strengthen the vocational courses at the school level. Many courses in the field of Hospitality and Tourism, Health care, Textiles and Tailoring, Costume Design, IT, Retail, Banking and Accounting, Insurance, etc. are also nurtured in urban centres under the new-age private and MNC managements with their own branding and certification. This is the result of liberalization of technical and vocational education and training to private players. There is no rigid regulatory mechanism for the vocational courses at school level manned by MHRD. As a result, these private agencies have adopted newer methods of pedagogy, learning methods and industry collaboration to attract youth towards them. In other words, the private players have responded to the skill ecosystem revolving at the school level.

As a result, the vocational streams at 10 + 2 level under government control have badly suffered. They did not change the syllabi for the past two decades. During this period, there were generic changes in skills and technology associated with the school vocational streams which were not attended to. Therefore, the 10 + 2 vocational system is crippling and crumbling down.

5.6 *Efforts of BOAT (WR) to Revive the NATS*

Board, in short, is under the administrative control of MHRD which is struggling hard to revive the NATS with all the teething problems at its end. The hierarchy and strength of the Board were decided four decades back at the time of its inception, keeping in view the prevailing conditions at that point of time. Now, the scope, gamut of the Board has increased manifold in terms of coverage of Institutes, Graduates, and Establishments. In spite of these inherent problems, the Board is struggling hard to reach the entire region to all the stakeholders and to enhance the effectiveness of NATS. Board is adopting the innovative methods to improve the brand image of NATS, and to increase the enrollment under NATS. Following are the some of the steps taken by Board.

a. Career Guidance Program for outgoing graduates
b. Supervisory Development Program for Establishments
c. Entrepreneurship Development Program for Institutions and students
d. Awareness Camps about NATS for Institutions
e. Industry–Institute Interaction Meetings/Workshops on core skills and NATS
f. Bharti Melas—Enrollment Melas by bringing Establishments, Institutes, and Graduates under one platform.

6 Policy Recommendations

a. MHRD, the anchoring and administrative authority shall intervene and increase the stipend at least at par with minimum wages to attract fresh graduates from Institutions to enrol for NATS.
b. NATS is a potential vehicle towards last mile skilling of high-end professional graduates. The tenure may also be increased to 2 years, to adjust the competency deficit prevailing at Institutional level. This will attract the serious aspirants who want to start their career by skill enhancement and full-fledged training exposure at establishments.
c. BOAT (WR) may be strengthened by increasing the strength of officers, by at least one enforcement officer to one big state, in order to devote and cover all the major establishments in industrially active zones in all the states.
d. There should be regular tracer studies to review the status, and monitoring and evaluation studies to give regular feedback on implementation framework, and bottlenecks associated with NATS.

References

Aiyar, S., & Ashoka, M. (2011). *The demographic dividend: Evidence from Indian States*. Working Paper No. WP/11/38. Washington D.C.: International Monetary Fund.

Aspiring Minds. (2016). *National Employability Report—Engineers 2016—Annual Report*. New Delhi: Aspiring Minds.

Bijeesh, N. A. (2016). *How can Indian graduates improve their employability*. The paper was accessed from the http://www.indiaeducation.net/interviews/himanshu-aggarwal-ceo-aspiring-minds.html on 2nd May, 2017.

Technology Transfer to the Farmers and Role of KVKs

Shachi Joshi, D. Indrakumar and Neha Kumra

1 Introduction

Agriculture sector contributes only 17% to Gross Domestic Product (GDP) in the country. Boosting agricultural growth is essential for inclusive growth as it provides livelihood to about 50% of the population. Agriculture growth is also critical to meet the food and nutritional requirements of the growing population. This necessitates increased agriculture productivity using new technologies.

The Indian economy is moving towards modern and mechanized farming but the change is very slow and happening only in some regions of the country. Various types of technologies are available for pre and post harvest operations such as plough, harrow, seed driller, threshing machines, tractor, power tiller, implements (for clearing, depositing seeds, seeds sowing etc.), cane crusher, combined harvest, post harvest processing machineries, dairy equipments, irrigation technology etc. There are a lot of innovations that have the potential to make a huge impact on farming, e.g. mobile/IT and energy spaces, smart power systems, precision agriculture tools, farm management software, and affordable sensors are all within reach of even the smallest farmers today. Soil testing, drip irrigation, rainwater harvesting, etc. contribute to the farming sector in a big way.

S. Joshi (✉) · D. Indrakumar · N. Kumra
NILERD, Sector A-7, Institutional Area, Narela, Delhi 110040, India
e-mail: shachi.joshi7@gmail.com

D. Indrakumar
e-mail: dindrakumar@gmail.com

N. Kumra
e-mail: neha.kumra@gmail.com

NILERD, *Reflecting on India's Development*,
https://doi.org/10.1007/978-981-13-1414-8_7

Numerous research papers measuring returns to investment on agricultural research and technology transfer for a wide range of commodities and countries have shown high social payoffs, suggesting the beneficial impact of increasing investment on agricultural research and technology transfer (Akino and Hayami 1975; Arndt 1997; Evenson and Jha 1973; Lindner and Jarrett 1978; Ruttan 1982).

Adoption of new technology has been the major driving force for increasing agricultural productivity and promoting agriculture development. In the past, the choice of technologies and their adoption was to increase production, productivity and farm incomes but now agriculture has to fulfil diverse objectives, it has to be competitive globally, produce high-quality agricultural products and also meet sustainability goals. In order to remain competitive, agricultural producers need rapid access to emerging technologies. The new knowledge-intensive technology requires both strong laboratory research and a well-developed extension system to disseminate the knowledge with proven results.

Agriculture extension plays a critical role in dissemination of inventions and innovations to the farmers by demonstrating and refining it to suit the local needs. Agricultural extension, or agricultural advisory services, comprise the entire set of organizations that support people engaged in agricultural production and facilitate their efforts to solve problems, link to markets and other players in the agricultural value chain and obtain information, skills, and technologies to improve their livelihoods (Glendenning, Babu, Asenso-Okyere, 2010).

ICAR is the apex body at the centre to promote, undertake and coordinate research in all fields of agriculture in the country and renders vital support in agricultural development through its outreach services which are of 'front-line' nature, that is, developing, testing and mainstreaming innovative approaches for extension and rural advisory services. Several innovative extension approaches piloted by ICAR include Farmers FIRST (2016) which focuses on farmer's farm, innovations, resources, science and technology; Mera Gaon Mera Gaurav (2015) which seeks to promote the direct interface of scientists with farmers to provide information, knowledge and advise to farmers; and ARYA (2015) to attract and empower the youth in rural areas to take up agriculture (Singh et al. 2016).

Besides several institutions involved in Agriculture extension, in order to assess, refine and demonstrate the agricultural technologies in micro-farming situations of the farmers under various production systems operated under different agro-ecologies in the country, the ICAR has created a network of 681 Krishi Vigyan Kendras (KVKs) in all the rural districts of the country. KVKs, an integral part of the National Agricultural Research System (NARS), aim at the assessment of location-specific technology in agriculture and allied enterprises, through technology assessment, refinement and demonstration. KVKs have been functioning as Knowledge and Resource Centres of agricultural technology supporting initiatives of public, private and voluntary sector for improving the agricultural economy of the district and linking NARS with extension system and farmers. These institutes also produce quality technological products (seed, planting material, bio-agents, livestock) and make it available to farmers, organize front-line extension activities, identify and document selected farm innovations and converge of ongoing schemes and programmes within their mandate. They also build capacity of farmers and extension personnel to update their knowledge and skills on modern agricultural technologies.[1]

As new research/innovation on agriculture and allied sectors is a continuous process in the country, the paper attempts to analyse whether and how these changes are known to farmers, and whether these changes are accessible to farmers and help them. Role of KVKs is important here.

In this paper, data from a study conducted by NILERD on KVKs Impact on Dissemination of Improved Practices and Technologies has been utilized. The information on various indicators such as infrastructure, activities performed by KVKs, coverage and impact if any of these activities was collected from KVKs as well as beneficiaries (farmers). To know the impact, control group of farmers who were not receiving any benefit from KVKs were also interviewed. Stratified random sampling has been used to collect primary data. For a nationally representative sample, the whole country was divided into five regions: North, South, Central, West and East/North East. One state from each region was selected on the basis of random sampling. A sample of 48 KVKs consisting of various types of management such as Government, State Agriculture Universities, and NGOs were selected. To assess the impact of technology transferred by these institutes, farmers from each selected district were interviewed. To serve as counterfactual farmers who were not availing services of KVKs were also interviewed (control group of farmers to see the change brought about by KVKs). In all, 1870 farmers were covered. The combination of quantitative and qualitative methods was adopted to observe the results of interventions of KVKs.

In view of the crucial role played by KVKs in technology dissemination, this paper assesses the impact of the technology and knowledge transferred. The next section provides a brief review of literature on agricultural technology, and is followed by several sections providing an analysis of various aspects of data collected in the field survey (information need of farmers, availability of resources, coverage, service delivery and farmers' feedback). The penultimate section provides an analysis of the impact of KVK activities on farm practices and farmers. The last section concludes with an analysis of the key findings.

2 Literature Review

The process of innovation involves constant experimentation, improvisation, adaptation and simultaneous rejection of certain results either partly or completely depending upon individual or collective feedback. Many times, while searching for innovations, people have drawn negative inferences about the innovative potential

[1]https://kvk.icar.gov.in/aboutkvk.aspx.

of peasants. They were either looking for the wrong things, or looking through inappropriate prisms, or asking the wrong questions in the wrong places (Gupta, A.K.[2]).

A review of available literature on innovations and technology sharing in Agriculture brings to the fore related themes such as the need for a more nuanced understanding of the underlying institutional environment and constraints in adoption of agricultural technology (Gesellschaft 2016), innovations in agricultural research (Yadav and Sharma 2017), adequate and sustained investment in agricultural R&D (Shetty et al. 2014) and a policy framework for the agricultural Information Technology sector (Patil 2008). These themes cut across the three pillars of a developed agricultural system: knowledge, infrastructure and a robust delivery mechanism (Seth and Ganguly 2017).

The growth in agricultural production in India, in the two decades following independence, came from increase in cultivable area which was thereafter replaced by increased focus on agricultural productivity. A series of steps were taken by the Government in this regard including land reforms, the inauguration of Agricultural Price Commission with the objective to ensure remunerative prices to producers, new agricultural strategy, investment in research and extension services, provision of credit facilities, and improving rural infrastructure (Nerker et al. 2013). The experience from Green Revolution showed that besides technological advancements, supporting institutions like credit, land reforms etc., as well as incentives like prices, are of great importance for technology-led growth in agriculture. Sustainable security in food production, it is argued, will require emphasis on two cereals (which are rice and wheat) as well as utilization of frontier technologies, viz. biotechnology, nanotechnology, remote sensing, GIS, genome sequencing, market assisted technology, weather modelling, etc. In essence, a significant growth in agriculture requires the united efforts of all the stakeholders with innovations in research, policy and institutional dynamics (Yadav and Sharma 2017). Additionally, in the context of increasingly knowledge-intensive and high-tech agriculture, Gesellschaft (2016) argues that rather than assuming that an information and communication technology (ICT) approach will always be cost-effective and yield a better outcome, a more nuanced understanding of the underlying institutional environment and constraints is warranted.

Seth and Ganguly (2017) argue that to strengthen the supporting framework for growth, it will be important to focus on creating new physical markets, improving storage and transport facilities, making better roads and ensuring a continued electricity and water supply. In this regard, they mention that the public policy regime in India has been supporting technology-led agricultural growth and has been increasingly developing new institutions to ease access and affordability of technology adoption among farmers.

E-Agriculture, which involves the conceptualization, design, development, evaluation and application of innovative ways to use Information and

[2]Farmers' Innovations and Agricultural Technologies (A.K. Gupta).

Communication Technologies (ICT) in the rural domain with a focus on agriculture, is an emerging field focusing on the enhancement of agricultural and rural development through improved information and communication processes. It is argued that ICTs are highly relevant for Agricultural Extension scientists, researchers, functionaries and organizations. Nevertheless, 60% of farmers in India remain unserved by any extension agency or functionary and 40% have some access to Agricultural Information, the major sources of this information are radio and television (Singh et al. 2015).

With regards to agricultural innovations, Kumar and Sinha (2014) find that while the number of same has increased, i.e. seeds, pesticides, mechanization, demonstrating positive growth in agriculture; constraints with regards to measuring innovation, for example in the seed industry, remain. Innovations extending to agricultural credit markets are mentioned by Thejeswini et al. (2014), including the inventory/warehouse receipt financing, supply/value chain financing, leasing, contract farming and producer companies.

In light of the potential role of innovations in driving growth in agricultural production, Shetty et al. (2014) argue for adequate and sustained investment in R&D in agriculture, increasing from the present 0.6% of agricultural GDP to 2–3 times more. Data is presented showing that whereas India invested $0.40 for every $100 of agricultural GDP in 2008, this was lower compared to China ($0.50), Brazil ($1.8) and Japan ($4.25) in 2008, and the average of $0.56 for developing countries in 2000 (Beintema and Stads 2010).

Last but not the least, Patil (2008) suggests a policy framework for the agricultural Information Technology sector. It is suggested that human capital enhancement is the main remedial factor for the low rate of ICT adoption and its effectiveness at present. It is found that while market information and weather updates are of prime interest with regard to ICT; illiteracy, cost and lack of awareness are the major adoption constraints.

The literature indicates that availability and transfer of technology to the farmers is critical for boosting farm income. It is with the use of technology that we can achieve the target of doubling farmers' income by 2022. The next section deals with understanding the information requirements of farmers and various types of information requests received by KVKs.

3 Information Need for Farmers

Farmers require a diverse range of information to support their farm enterprises. Information is needed not only on best practices and technologies for crop production, which the traditional public-sector extension system provided during the Green Revolution, but information about post-harvest aspects including processing, marketing, storage, and handling is also needed. Farmers require information related to the following (Van den Ban 1998)

Table 1 Category of requests from farmers

Nature of request	Number of requests received from farmers
1. Information on crops	1632
2. Seeds/planting material	1711
3. Quality of animals	0068
4. Demonstration of new technology	0217
5. Assistance in implementing/adopting the new technology disseminated by KVKs	0345

- Most appropriate technological options
- Management of technologies, including optimal use of inputs
- Changing farm system options (mixed farming and diversification, animal husbandry, fisheries)
- Sourcing reputable input suppliers
- Collective action with other farmers
- Consumer and market demands for products
- Quality specifications for produce
- Time to buy inputs and sell produce
- Off-farm income-generation options
- Implications of changing policies (input subsidies, trade liberalization)
- Access to credit and loans
- Sustainable natural resource management and coping with climate change.

The information requirement the farmers about new technology differs between categories of farmers such as their location, holding size etc. Factors such as literacy or access to resources will have a large impact on information needs, searching behaviour, access, and use.

Table 1 details the various types of information requests received from surveyed KVKs. These requests comprised of information on crops, seeds/planting material, quality of animals, demonstration of new technology, assistance in implementing/ adopting the new technology disseminated by KVKs, etc. Highest number of requests was received in the category—seeds and planting material—which is integral for cropping.

To examine the role of KVKs in farm technology transfer such as availability of resources, activities performed by these institutes and also the outcome of these activities was investigated. Next sections throw light on these indicators.

4 Availability of Resources

KVKs require a host of resources for performing their activities. An assessment of the human, physical as well as financial resource available with surveyed KVKs is discussed below:

Availability of Human Resource

The number of extension personnel in India is only one-sixth of that in China. With this meagre number of extension personnel, serving widely dispersed farmers with diversified information needs is a really hard task. Most of the extension personnel are involved in multiple roles and hence overburdened. In addition, the public extension system largely concentrates on on-farm activities though farmers also need information on the food and agriculture value chain, starting from forecasts of weather conditions to market prices of the produce (Glendenning et al. 2010).

Each KVK has sanctioned 16 staff members comprising scientists, technical support staff and other staff including a Programme Coordinator (PC) and 6 Subject Matter Specialists (SMS) and other technical and non-technical staff. In the selected KVKs, it was observed that in general the KVKs are short of staff at all levels—to the tune of 23% among Scientists and 22% in Technical Support staff (Fig. 1). Shortage of staff affects the performance as it hampers the delivery of services.

Availability of Financial Resources and Utilization

Keeping in view the role of KVKs in farming sector, budget allocations are increasing. During the 12th Five-Year Plan period, first three years (2012–13 to 2014–15) witnessed an increasing allocation of Rs. 435.96 Crores, Rs. 496.88 Crores and Rs. 586.50 Crores respectively.

During 2013–14, the surveyed KVKs had an average annual budget of Rs. 83.4 lakhs and spent 90.0 lakhs achieving utilization of 108% during 2013–14 (Table 2). The higher utilization of resources is from the financial resources generated by these institutions through various activities undertaken by them such as production and sale of seeds, samplings, etc.

Availability of Infrastructure

Infrastructure such as Office building, Demonstration Units, laboratory and farmers' hostel are important components for efficient delivery of services by KVK. Hence, the opinion of 48 surveyed KVKs was sought regarding the availability of

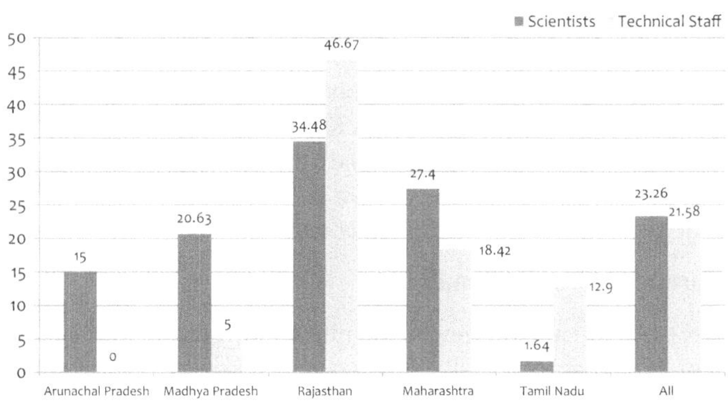

Fig. 1 Vacant positions (%) in KVKs

Table 2 Average budget and expenditure per KVK (2011–12 to 2013–14)

Year	Budget per KVKs (average, Rs. lakhs)	Expenditure per KVK (average, Rs. lakhs)
2011–12	71.5	71.5
2012–13	70.1	71.4
2013–14	83.4	90.0

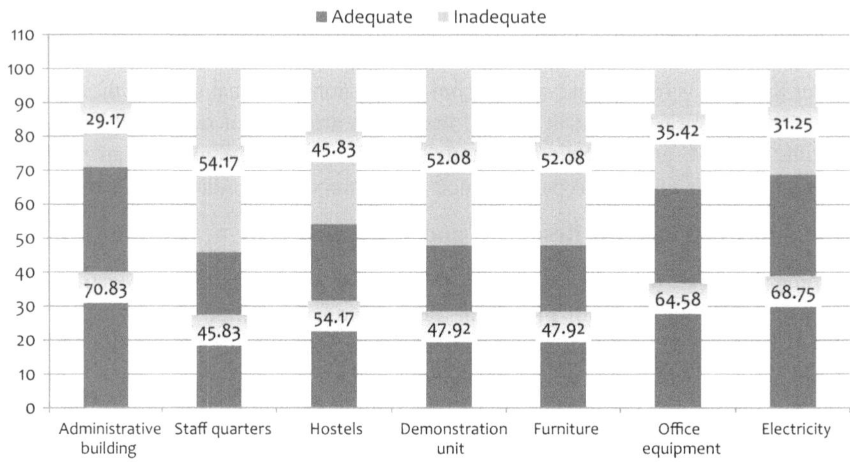

Fig. 2 Adequacy of infrastructure at the KVKs (%)

infrastructure facility with them. The details are given in Fig. 2. Generally, the KVKs are fully or partly satisfied regarding the various infrastructure facilities available with these institutes.

5 Coverage by Surveyed KVKs

During the 5 years preceding this survey, both the number of villages covered and the number of farmers covered by the KVKs increased steadily over the 5 years 2009–10 to 2013–14, at a CAGR of 16.2 and 10.3%, respectively (Table 3). As the number of KVKs selected remained constant at 48 through this 5-year period, these trends are true of the per KVK performance also.

Age Structure of Surveyed farmers

An effort was made to capture agewise distribution of surveyed farmers in farming. Age profile of farmers reveals that younger people do not find agriculture attractive as a profession. It was observed that only 5% of the farmers were youth in the age group of 15–24 years, which is also evident from our discussions with stakeholders

Table 3 Growth rate of coverage by KVK during (2009–10 to 2013–14)

Heads	5 year average annual growth rate (%)
Total villages visited	16.2
Total farmers covered	10.3
Villages covered by each KVK	16.2
Farmers covered by each KVK	10.3

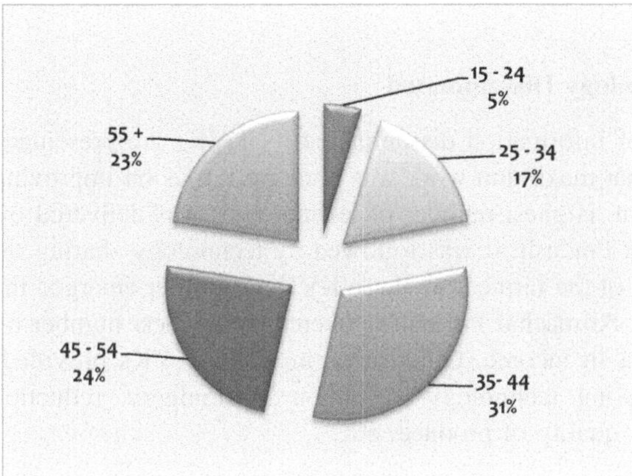

Fig. 3 Age wise distribution of farmers

indicating low motivation among youth to take up farming as an occupation (Fig. 3). There is a need to make farming profitable to attract more and more youth adopting farming.

6 Delivery of Services by KVKs

Various mandated and non-mandated activities are undertaken by KVKs to facilitate farmers. Mandated activities are crucial. On-farm testing which aims to assess the location-specific technologies under various farming systems is a mandated activity of KVKs. The Table 4 reveals that on an average 6 OFTs were carried out by KVKs in each district. Front-line demonstrations (FLDs) are conducted by KVKs to establish the production potential of the technologies on the farmers' fields. It has been observed that 116 FLDs were conducted by KVKs. Farmers training and awareness generation helps in adoption of new and refined technology and also makes them aware of the do's and don'ts. Table 4 details the number of various activities delivered by KVKs in their coverage areas.

Table 4 Activities carried out by KVKs

Core activities carried	No. of programmes carried during five years	Average per KVK
1. On-farm trial	0297	006
2. Front-line demonstration	5328	116
3. Farmers training	8049	175
4. Awareness programmes	1630	035

Type of Technology Disseminated

Various types of information disseminated by KVKs are presented in Table 5. It was observed that maximum work was done by KVKs on improving productivity/yield of the farm. Highest number of technologies was delivered by KVKs in the state of Madhya Pradesh. It was followed by technology sharing on the improvement of income of the farmers by these KVKs, it further emerged that amongst the surveyed states, Arunachal Pradesh delivered the highest number of technologies, for enhancement in income. Other areas in which KVKs provided their services include time-saving technology, reduction in drudgery, reduction in wastage, improvement in quality of produce, etc.

Table 5 Statewise number of technology disseminated by KVK by type during the last five years (2010–11 to 2014–15)

Type of technology disseminated for making impact on farming community	No. of technologies reported by KVKs					Total
	Arunachal Pradesh	Madhya Pradesh	Maharashtra	Rajasthan	Tamil Nadu	
1. Reduction in cost	66	44	7	12	7	136
2. Improved productivity/yield	70	86	21	21	17	215
3. Time saving	48	17	6	8	7	86
4. Multiple cropping	67	8	4	6	3	88
5. Less labour intensive operations	48	16	7	8	4	83
6. Confidence of farmers developed	70	8	6	10	7	101
7. Quality of product improved	66	52	11	10	10	149
8. Enhanced income	70	31	8	17	11	137
9. Less drudgery	47	7	4	5	3	66
10. Reduction in wastage	46	7	4	6	9	72
11. Enhanced marketability	66	8	6	7	9	96
Number of KVKs covered	06	10	10	10	40	46

Table 6 No. of entrepreneurial programmes organized and its outcome (2010–11 to 2014–15)

State	No. of programmes organized	No. of women participants[a]
Arunachal Pradesh	11	600 (1024)
Madhya Pradesh	73	1574 (5586)
Rajasthan	39	2058 (4390)
Maharashtra	98	1568 (6832)
Tamil Nadu	38	2233 (8096)
Total	259	8033 (19,318)

[a]Total participants, men and women, in brackets

Entrepreneurial Development Programmes organized:

One of the given mandates of KVKs is to organize capacity building programmes for the farmers, youth and women. The entrepreneurial training is provided to the farmers to facilitate their pursuit of the chosen lines of self-employment.

Average Number of Persons Covered by EDP Programmes of KVKs Annually is 19,318. During the period out of this, the highest number of programmes was organized in Tamil Nadu followed by Maharashtra. KVKs organize training programmes for women in several areas such as value addition, tailoring, food and nutrition, etc. It was observed that highest number of women capacity building courses was conducted in Tamil Nadu followed by Madhya Pradesh. Some of the technologies related to value addition and post-harvest management like fruit and vegetable preservation, rural crafts, tie and dye, tailoring and stitching, etc. Other technologies related to making of handicrafts from jute, bamboo, cotton, foam and rubber, nutritional management, kitchen gardening, Azolla cultivation, value addition in potato, soybean, wheat, gram rice, red gram, spices and other had helped women (Table 6).

It was observed that KVKs also provide various support service to the farmers in the field of assistance in getting loans, guidance regarding marketing of produce, post-harvest crop management, procurement of raw material, etc. which help farmers in starting their self-employment ventures. This leads to an enhancement in the income of farmers and improving their quality of living.

7 Farmers Feedback

An attempt has been made to identify a group of farmers who were relatively unexposed to KVKs and compare their experiences with those farmers who had interactions with KVKs, the former serving as a counterfactual in impact assessment.

The results show that 21% of the farmers (Table 7) were not aware of the existence and the activities of the KVKs. Training and demonstration by the KVKs was the main source of this knowledge. However, it is interesting to note the

Table 7 Percentage distribution of farmers about knowledge of activities of KVKs

State	% of those with no knowledge
Arunachal Pradesh	16.00
Madhya Pradesh	28.00
Maharashtra	15.00
Rajasthan	19.00
Tamil Nadu	22.00
Total	21.00

knowledge spin-off, i.e. about 18% of the farmers had acquired this knowledge from fellow farmers.

Variety of agencies are involved in dissemination of agricultural technologies. Apart from KVKs, the district agricultural office, NGOs and some industries engage in transferring new technologies to farmers in furtherance of their own organizational objectives. Table 8 provides source of knowledge to surveyed farmers. More than 50% of the farmers obtained knowledge training and demonstration from KVKs while District Agriculture offices accounted for 11.6%. It is seen that KVKs are the front-runners in knowledge transfer to the farmers.

Time Taken in Adoption of New Technology by Farmers:

The survey revealed that about 40% of the farmers adopted new technology immediately, 23% adopted during next season, 13% waited for the impact to be visible then they adopted while only 5% adopted after a long time (Table 9). A study conducted by Kumbhare and Khonde showed that 59% of farmers adopted the recommendation of KVK at medium level, while the others were in low and high level (Kumbhare and Khonde 2009).

Table 8 Distribution of farmers who acquired knowledge about technologies by source

Source of knowledge	% of farmers acquiring knowledge about technology from the source
Training at KVK	28.2
KVK demonstration	22.9
District agricultural office	11.6
Kishan call centres	6.4
NGO	3.2
Industry sources	1.0
Fellow farmers of KVK trained	12.9
Other fellow farmers	7.2
Own decision to change	5.0
Others	1.6

Table 9 Statewise distribution of farmers in adoption of new technologies and time gap

States	Status of adopted by time gap					
	Immediately	Next season	After seeing impact	After one year	After long time	Total
Arunachal Pradesh	015	004	004	01	001	025
Madhya Pradesh	262	095	032	26	123	538
Maharashtra	129	145	069	21	039	403
Rajasthan	138	107	032	26	109	412
Tamil Nadu	203	081	109	16	083	492
Total	747	432	246	090	355	1870
% Distribution	39.95	23.10	13.16	04.81	01.82	100

Table 10 Statewise distribution of farmers who made changes in farming practices during the last 5 years (%)

State	Farmers who made changes
Arunachal Pradesh	84.00
Madhya Pradesh	88.29
Maharashtra	95.53
Rajasthan	82.52
Tamil Nadu	83.54
Total	87.27

Total farmers surveyed were 1870, from 5 states

There were many farmers falling under the category of control group were of the view that they can increase their yield, income if they get training from KVKs in latest farming methods, latest seeds, etc. Some of them informed that while there are many farmers with land holdings in the range of 5–10 ha and willing to invest in agriculture, there is no expertise available to them. The KVKs may identify and reach out to such farmers.

About 87% of farmers made changes in farming practices during the 5 years period under consideration which is given in the Table 10:

In the earlier section of this paper, an effort has been made to highlight the services/activities performed by these institutions to improve the agriculture sector such as technology dissemination and capacity building. The following section will throw a light on the impact of these activities on farmers and farming.

8 Impact Assessment

Impact of technology sharing and dissemination depends not only on the availability of suitable technology but also on the willingness of farmers to adopt the technology accompanied by availability of low-cost inputs. This leads to an uncertainty of outcome which may vary differently for farmers depending upon previous experience, immediate past experience; future expectations of returns, etc.

To assess the role of KVKs, an enquiry on how the implementation of the new technologies transferred benefited the farmers who implemented these was sought. The parameters covered were—how the new technologies impacted farmers' productivity, incomes, reduced drudgery, etc. The information indicated a number of positive impacts. About 42% farmers responded that after the intervention of KVK, productivity increased and cost of production as well as wastage were reduced. 31% of the farmers highlighted that with the guidance of KVKs they were able to improve quality of products leading to enhanced income. About 19% expressed that interventions of KVKs have lead to time-saving and drudgery reduction of farmers (Fig. 4).

Most of the KVKs mentioned that the technologies had helped in reduction of drudgery, income enhancement and developed self-confidence among women. A number of technologies, such as energy saving charcoal sarai cooker, environment-friendly stove, and integrated nutrient management had helped women in carrying out their household activities. Lightweight tools like serrated sickles, wheel hoe, foot sprayer, maize sheller, groundnut pod stripper and coconut tree climber could be easily operated or handled by the farm women. Similarly, change of water and pheromone lures was also very easy for women. Vermicompost production technology was very easy and low cost, and raw material required for the production of vermicompost was available in the villages (Table 11; Fig. 4).

A range of impacts post KVK intervention were analysed in terms of the frequency with which they were cited by the farmers. Only in Arunachal Pradesh, reduction in cost ranked lower than increase in production/yield which elsewhere in the other four states ranked as the second most important impact cited by farmers (Table 8). This may potentially be attributed to the unique topography of the state and the attendant high costs of agriculture.

However, when level of satisfaction was analysed in terms of services provided by KVKs, it was observed that the maximum (84%) proportion of farmers in Arunachal Pradesh were satisfied while this figure was only about 66% in the state of Madhya Pradesh (Table 9).

Table 11 Statewise type of impact after the intervention of KVK

Type of impacts	States				
	Arunachal Pradesh	Madhya Pradesh	Maharashtra	Rajasthan	Tamil Nadu
1. Increase in production/yield	37.74	28.93	31.46	28.87	27.56
2. Improvement in quality of produce	28.30	17.36	13.04	14.40	16.62
3. Reduction in cost	15.09	37.13	39.73	40.86	38.31
4. Increase in income	7.55	11.51	11.16	13.07	13.42
5. Started self-employment	7.55	4.20	3.98	1.40	2.31

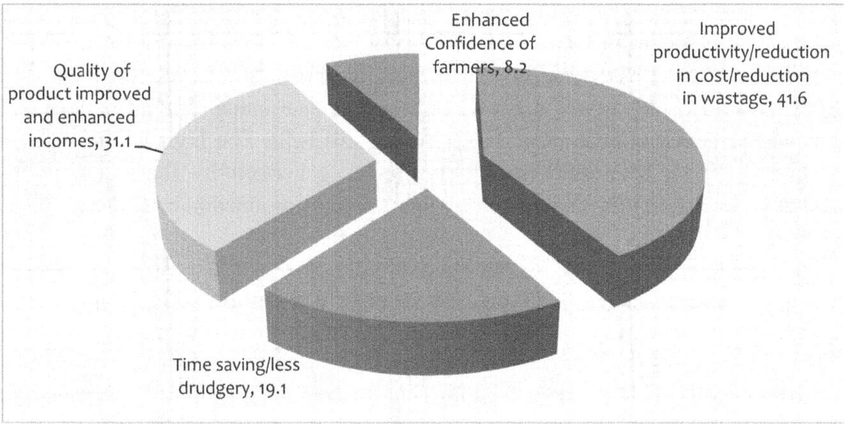

Fig. 4 Impact of KVKs (%)

Table 12 Genderwise outcome of training programmes organized by KVKs

Gender	Average number of persons trained by each KVK in a year	Percentage of those who started the business
Male	75	25.3
Female	33	22.6
Persons	108	24.5

Nevertheless, close to three-quarters of the farmers reported satisfaction with the services of KVKs, such as trainings, demonstration and staff visits to the fields and seed availability (Tables 9 and 10). 87% of farmers had made changes in farm practices during the last 5 years with 40% of the farmers adopting technology immediately.

Table 12 gives a summary of training programmes organized by KVKs and the outcome of these programmes.

9 Conclusions

KVKs have an edge in technology transfer over other service providers by virtue of their having better technical expertise and demonstration units. In the selected KVKs, it was observed that in general, the KVKs are short of staff at all levels—to the extent of 23% among scientists, 22% in technical support staff (22%) and about 86% among other staff.

Infrastructure is essential components for delivery of services by the KVKs. KVKs can give their best if they have timely availability of financial resources, human resources and physical resources. It was found that generally the KVKs are fully or partly satisfied regarding the various infrastructure facilities. Some of them lack building, labs, hostel, etc.

12th Plan period has witnessed an increasing allocation of financial resources. During 2013–14, the surveyed KVKs had an average annual budget of Rs. 83.4 lakhs and achieved utilization of 108% during 2013–14. The higher utilization of resources may be from the financial resources generated by these institutions through various activities undertaken by them such as production and sale of seeds, samplings etc.

During the 5 years, both the number of villages covered and the number of farmers covered by the KVKs increased steadily at a CAGR of 16.2 and 10.3%, respectively.

The information requirements of farmers differ between categories of farmers such as location, holding size, education, etc. Factors such as literacy or access to resources will have a large impact on information needs, searching behaviour, access and use. The survey results revealed that the requests received from farmers comprised of information on crops, seeds/planting material, quality of animals, demonstration of new technology, assistance in implementing/adopting the new technology disseminated, etc. Among all the requests received, highest number of requests received were in the category—seeds and planting material—which is integral for cropping.

On an average, 6 OFTs and 116 FLDs were conducted in each district. On an average, about 117 training programmes for farmers and 35 awareness generation programmes were carried out during the period under consideration.

It was observed that maximum work was done by KVKs on improving productivity/yield of the farm. The highest number of technologies was transferred in the state of Madhya Pradesh. This was followed by technology sharing on the improvement of income of the farmers. Furthermore, amongst the surveyed states Arunachal Pradesh delivered the highest number of technologies for enhancement of income. Other areas in which KVKs provided their services include time-saving technology, reduction in drudgery, reduction in wastage, improvement in quality of produce, etc.

19,318 capacity development programmes were organized during the period under consideration. Out of these, the highest number of programmes was conducted in Tamil Nadu followed by Maharashtra. KVKs organize training programmes for women in several areas such as value addition, tailoring, food and nutrition, etc. It was observed that highest number of capacity building courses for women was conducted in Tamil Nadu followed by Madhya Pradesh.

Some of the technologies related to value addition and post-harvest management like fruit and vegetable preservation, rural crafts, tie and dye, tailoring and stitching, etc. Other technologies related to making of handicrafts from jute, bamboo, cotton, foam and rubber, nutritional management, kitchen gardening, Azolla cultivation, value addition in potato, soybean, wheat, gram rice, red gram and spices have helped women.

Besides availability and dissemination of technology, the adoption depends on active participation of target groups in various activities and their willingness to use new knowledge and skills, available resources with farmers to use new technology is also an important ingredient for the impact of the activities undertaken by these institutes.

A range of impacts post KVK intervention were analysed in terms of the frequency with which they were cited by the farmers. Only in Arunachal Pradesh, reduction in cost ranked lower than the increase in production/yield which elsewhere in the other four states ranked as the second most important impact cited by farmers. This may potentially be attributed to the unique topography of the state and the attendant high costs of agriculture. It is also notable that 84% of the farmers in the state do not have machinery.

About three-quarters of the farmers reported satisfaction with the services of KVKs, such as trainings, demonstration, staff visits to the fields and seed availability. 87% of farmers had made changes in farm practices during the last 5 years with 40% of the farmers adopting technology immediately.

There were many farmers falling under the category of control group were of the view that they can increase their yield, income if they get training from KVKs in latest farming methods, latest seeds etc. Some of them informed that while there are many farmers with land holdings in the range of 5–10 ha and willing to invest in agriculture, there is no expertise available to them.

National, regional and international organizations have been emphasizing the importance of innovation and technology adoption for growth and employment in less developed countries (LDCs). The consensus is that promoting innovation and technology adoption is essential for growth and jobs in developing countries (Commission for Africa 2015).

There are several empirical evidences that KVKs have played a significant role in the overall development of agricultural sector. Recent innovative initiatives taken by the KVKs include upgrading the Lead and Active Farmers to Integrated Farming System which enhances the flow of income of the farmers; farmers to farmers outreach; more affordable and sustainable techniques for economic use of available water and sustain with the climatic conditions—like mulching, trip irrigation, use of fertilizers and pesticides through the irrigation system; cost reduction techniques; encouraging farmers to use organic and bio-fertilizers/pesticides and minimum use of chemical fertilizers; boosting and supporting for value addition and processing of farm produce; timely advice about the market and price particulars to farmers for selling their produce; community based advice to conserve locally available water bodies, rainwater harvesting and building community wells; creation and development of farmers federations for better coordination among the farmers; convergence and linkages among similar organizations; better use of available information and communication sources etc.

There is a need to strengthen extension services in the country to enhance farm productivity and boost farm incomes. KVKs can play a vital role in this arena. With changing requirements of farming sector and changing role of KVKs, these institutes need to be strengthened to serve the farm community as these are the real carriers of technology and innovations to the last farmer.

References

Akino, M., & Hayami, Y. (1975). Social returns to agricultural research investment. *American Journal of Agricultural Economics, 57*(1), 1–10.

Arndt, T. M., Dalrymple, D. G., & Ruttan, V. W. (1997). *Research allocation and productivity in national and international agricultural research* (p. 617). Minneapolis, USA: University of Minnesota Press.

Beintema, N. & Stads. G. (2010). Public agriculture R&D investments and capabilities in developing countries: Recent evidence for 2000 and beyond, background note prepared for the Global Conference on Agricultural Research for Development. Montpellier, France, March, 28–31.

Commission for Africa. (2015). Report of the Commission for Africa.

Deutsche Gesellschaft. (2016). *Use of ICT for agriculture in GIZ projects—Status quo, opportunities and challenges. Sector Network Rural Development Africa (SNRD).* Bonn (Germany): Gesellschaft für Internationale Zusammenarbeit (GIZ).

Evenson, R. E., & Jha, D. (1973). The contribution of agricultural research system to agricultural production in India. *Indian Journal of Agricultural Economics, 38*(4), 212–230.

Glendenning, C. J., Babu, S., & Asenso-Okyere, K. (2010). *Review of agriculture extension on India: Are farmer's information needs being met*? IFPRI Discussion Paper No. 01048, International Food Policy Research Institute, Eastern and Southern Africa Regional Office.

Kumar, V., & Sinha, K. (2014). Status and prospect of research and development in agriculture in India. *Journal of Science Policy & Governance, 5*(1).

Kumbhare, N. V., & Khonde, S. R. (2009). Impact of KVK training on farmers adoption behaviour and knowledge gain. *Indian Journal of Extension Education, 45*(3&4).

Lindner, R. J., & Jarrett, F. G. (1978). Supply shifts and the size of research benefits. *American Journal of Agricultural Economics, 60*(1), 48–58.

Nerker, K. R., et al. (2013). The sustainable growth and development of Indian agriculture. *Asia Pacific Journal of Marketing & Management Review, 2*(6), 117–119.

Patil, V. C. (2008). *Adoption of Information and Communication Technology (ICT) for agriculture: An Indian case study*. Paper presented in World Conference on Agricultural Information and IT, August 24–27, 2008. Tokyo University of Agriculture, Tokyo.

Ruttan, V. W. (1982). *Agricultural research policy* (p. 370). Minneapolis, Minnesota, USA: University of Minnesota Press.

Seth, A., & Ganguly, K. (2017). Digital technologies transforming indian agriculture. In *The Global Innovation Index 2017: Innovation Feeding the World*, Ithaca, Cornell University, INSEAD, and WIPO Fontainebleau, and Geneva.

Shetty, P. K., et al. (2014). Innovations that shaped indian agriculture-then and now. *Indian Journal of Science and Technology, 7*(8), 1176–1182.

Singh, K. M., Kumar, A., & Singh, R. K. P. (2015). *Role of information and communication technologies in Indian agriculture: An overview*. Article published in researchgate.net assessed from website: https://www.researchgate.net/publication/273242368 on October 15, 2017.

Singh, R., Singh, A. K., & Sontakki, B. S. (2016). Innovations in knowledge sharing and technology application. In *4th International Agronomy Congress*, November 22–26, New Delhi, India (Lead Papers Vol. 4).

Thejeswini, R., et al. (2014). Agricultural credit in India—Innovations in design and delivery of products and services. *Agricultural Economics Research Review, 27* (Conference Number), 75–83.

Van den Ban, A. (1998). 'Supporting farmers' decision-making process by agricultural extension. *Journal of Extension Systems, 14*, 55–64.

Yadav, J. P., & Sharma, A. (2017). Transforming rural India through agricultural innovations: Some major startups. *International Journal of Advance Research and Innovative Ideas in Education, 3*(3), 3695–3702.

Impact of Education on Labour Market Outcomes in Rural and Urban India

K. C. Pradhan, P. C. Parida and Tapas Sarangi

1 Introduction

Education is the mirror which reflects the economic and social status of a country. It is one of the key factors of economic development and prosperity. A country with highly educated population and skilled labour force would be able to achieve higher productivity, efficiency and overall economic development. Sen (1999) points out that an educated individual is more likely to find a job and has an increased capacity to use acquired resources efficiently. Thus, education is critical to the ability of poor people to escape from poverty and hunger. Exiting literature suggests that education has substantial impacts on labour market outcomes such as earnings and employment as well as non-market outcomes such as health, longevity, civic participation and criminal activity (Card 2001; Grossman 2005; Oreopoulos and Salvanes 2009). Some studies found that education increases personal earnings, productivity and national economic growth (Schultz 1961, 1971; Becker 1994; Psacharopoulos and Patrinos 2004). Barro and Lee (2010) suggest that every additional year of schooling, the world economy grew by at least 2%. According to International Labour Organization (2015) the completion of secondary education alone was not enough to push young people in low-income countries towards obtaining a better labour market outcome and of course, quality higher education system could be of paramount importance in shaping labour market outcomes. Therefore, along with improving the quality of higher education, priority has also been given more on

K. C. Pradhan · P. C. Parida (✉) · T. Sarangi
National Institute of Labour Economics Research and Development (NILERD), Delhi, India
e-mail: paridapc@gmail.com

K. C. Pradhan
e-mail: kailasheco@gmail.com

T. Sarangi
e-mail: sarangi.tapas@gmail.com

NILERD, *Reflecting on India's Development*,
https://doi.org/10.1007/978-981-13-1414-8_8

strengthening the technical and vocational education system. Countries from Europe and Asia Pacific have achieved a great success in skill development and economic development as well (Maclean et al. 2013).

In the Indian context, the education system has seen remarkable changes since the inception of economic reforms in the early 1990s. Elementary level education was universalised in 2000–01 under the flagship programme of the Sarva Shiksha Abhiyan (SSA) with aim of making free and compulsory education for children between the ages of 6–14 to achieve higher enrolment, retention and quality education. Similarly, the secondary level education has got a big push through the Rashtriya Madhyamik Shiksha Abhiyan (RMSA) for enhancing the enrolment for classes IX–X and achieving universalisation of education at secondary level by 2017 and universal retention by 2020. At the higher education level, there is an increase in the number of degree, technical/professional colleges and overall enrolment also. Privatization of school and college education has attracted a large number of private players to enter into the education system. There are many private convent schools, colleges and universities have come up during the last two decades. Although the education system in the country has taken a new stride, the concerns still remain of getting appropriate skilled labour force to meet its demand in various sectors (Economic Survey, GoI, 2016–17). There seems an increasing sense of disconnect between higher education in terms of achieving the quantity and quality labour force.

It is found that a vast majority of workforce in India are unskilled and mainly engaged in agriculture and non-farm sectors, which are at a large extent informal in nature. As per the Twelfth Five Year Plan report, while 12.8 million people join the Indian workforce each year, the annual training capacity is less than half of that. Current studies indicate that net enrolment in vocational courses in India is about 5.5 million per year as compared to 90 million in China and 11.3 million in the United States.[1] A mere 2% of Indian workers are formally skilled (Chenoy 2012). Significantly, the bulk of the labour force in India—about 93%—who work in the unorganized sector are largely untouched by any kind of formal training. The Union and State Governments are making every effort to strengthen the skill development programmes through setting up of new ministries/department of skill development. Although it would take a long way for India to achieve what other East Asian countries have already been but surely the country has made a good progress in skill development so far.

With the changes of literacy and skill level of labour force, the choice of occupation has undergone a dramatic change during the post-reforms period. It has been observed that women are no more confined to household activities rather have been actively participating in both blue and white collar jobs. Youth from the rural areas are unwilling to work in agriculture sector instead have come forward to work in informal or formal manufacturing and services sector. In urban areas, youth are

[1]http://www.ey.com/Publication/vwLUAssets/EY-Government-and-Public-Sector-Reaping-Indias-demographic-dividend/$FILE/EY-Reaping-Indias-promised-demographic-dividend-industry-in-driving-seat.pd.

gradually moving towards self employment activities rather opting for regular wage activities in the organized sector. Such changes of occupational choices are having multiplier impact on employment structure of the economy.

It is evident that while employment has declined in agriculture and allied sector in absolute value from 241.5 million in 1993–94 to 231.9 in 2011–12, it has increased substantially in non-manufacturing sector during the same period with an annual compound growth rate of more than 7% during 2004–05 and 2011–12. Ironically, services and manufacturing sectors that contributes around 70% to the national GDP, contribute only 40% to total employment. The industry body argues that shifting agricultural labour directly to manufacturing or services sector (except manual work in manufacturing units, retail shops, small restaurants, domestic help activities etc.) is becoming a difficult as the latter sectors require semi-skilled or high-skilled workforce. This seems to be the reason why most of the agricultural labourers in the last decade or so, who have shifted to non-manufacturing sector particularly to construction industry which does not need skilled workforce for certain activities. As a result, the composition of informality within the formal sector workforce has increased during the last decade. Due to changes of occupational choices and employment structure, the impact of these changes is also visible on wage rates both in urban and rural areas. NSSO data points to the fact that wage rates in both rural and urban areas have continuously increased in absolute value but the growth rate of wage rate in rural areas has increased at a higher pace than its urban counterparts. It may be due to shortage of labour force in rural areas particularly in agriculture sector that has pushed the wage rates in the sector upward (FICCI 2015).

To sum up, the above discussion suggests that the changes that have been visible in occupation, wages and employment structure in the rural and urban economies in India are fully or partially inherited due to increase in the level of education of the labour force. But the impact of education on labour market outcomes may have varied from rural to urban areas due to disparity in availability and quality of education (Wu et al. 2006).

In this context, the present study makes an attempt to empirically examine the impact of various level of education on three labour market outcomes namely occupation, wages and employment in rural and urban India. The study also tries to find out whether the returns to education has increased or decreased with respect to various parameters of labour market outcomes using the latest available NSSO data. In order to get the robust result, the study incorporates other key demographic and social parameters along with education in the estimated models.

The rest of the paper is organized as follows. In section-II, the study presents a brief review of literature of existing studies followed by methodology and data source in section-III. The empirical findings of the study are discussed in section-IV and the final section concludes the study with some policy suggestions.

2 Review of Literature

There is rich literature available on returns to education or schooling for both developed and developing countries.[2] In the context of India and other developing countries, most studies of the returns to education consider only wage rates. In contrast the present study examines returns to education in case of three labour market parameters. A study by Duraisamy (2002) found that returns to education increases up to the secondary level and decline thereafter. It also reported that there is evidence of substantial gender and rural–urban differences in the returns to schooling. Investments in women's education, particularly at the middle, lower secondary and higher secondary levels are more profitable than that for men. There were huge gap exists in returns to education across gender, rural–urban markets, caste and skills. In fact, such disparities have widened considerably during the post-liberalisation period (Chamarbagwala 2006; Duraisamy 2002). Another study by Dutta (2006) found that the gap in returns to education between primary and graduate levels has increased at a large extent in the recent years. Regarding the issue of whether returns to education has increased or decreased in India, using various rounds of NSSO data Azam (2012) concluded that it has increased over the period.

In a similar line, Agrawal (2012) using the India Human Development Survey, 2005 data found that returns to education are positive and rising across the quantiles of the wage distribution although it varies widely between rural and urban India. Singhari and Madheswaran (2016) found that the rates of return to education for regular workers are the highest for diploma followed by graduation and above degree, and secondary education. The study concluded that (1) for regular workers, overall returns to secondary education is rising across the quantiles; while returns to higher secondary, diploma, graduation and above degree follow an inverted U-shape pattern and (2) for casual workers, overall returns to primary and middle education are rising across the quantiles. Vatta et al. (2016) found that the returns to education have improved for regular workers, indicating towards higher wages for higher education.

3 Variables and Methodology of Estimation

In this paper we make an attempt to quantify the effects of education on labour market outcomes namely employment, occupation and wages. For the analysis, we use the latest NSSO 68th round (2011–12) unit level information. To find out the returns of education with respect to labour market outcomes, we estimate wage, employment and occupation equations separately.

---

[2]For details see Sianesi and Van Reenen (2002), https://www.ifs.org.uk/wps/wp0205.pdf and Harmon et al. (2000) http://eprints.lse.ac.uk/19551/1/CEEDP05.pdf.

Employment numbers has been derived based on the principal and subsidiary status of the household members in age group 15 and above for three broad sectors such as agriculture, industry and services. In case of occupation, the paper uses 2-digit level of occupation categories. They are administrators, managers, professionals, associate professionals, clerks etc., sales & service worker, skilled agriculture & fishery workers, craftsmen, machine operators and labourers & unskilled workers. For wages, data on wage rate per day of workers is used for the analysis. Since data on wage earning is not available for household enterprises (self-employed), the same has been omitted from the analysis. Hence, the number of observations considered for wage equation estimation is expected to be less.

Explanatory variables used in the model are as follows: (1) education level of members of the households (illiterate = 1, literate & up to primary = 2, secondary = 3, under graduation = 4, graduation & above = 5), (2) average age of household members, household size, average land owned (in hectares) and female and male members in the households are some of the explanatory variables included to avoid the model specification bias. To differentiate the impact of education in rural and urban areas, a dummy variable for rural area is incorporated in the estimated model.

The proposed models to estimate the impact of education on wages, occupational patterns and employment are given below.

(1) ***Wage Equation***

The link between education and earnings could be dated back to Friedman and Kuznets (1954). However, the linear model developed by Jacob Mincer (1974) has been widely used in the literature. It states that (the log of) wages depending only on years of schooling and years of experience, with a linear relationship between schooling and wages. In equation form it can be written as:

$$\ln(w) = \alpha + \beta_1 S + \beta_2 E + \beta_3 E^2 + u \quad (1)$$

where, ln = national logarithm, w = wages, S = schooling (education), E = experience and u is error term. The detailed explanation of the theoretical foundations of the Mincer equation may be seen in Heckman et al. (2003). Since year of schooling data is not available in NSSO, deriving information on work experience hence would be a difficult proposition. The problem in Mincian type wage equation is that wage is only observed for those who worked for wages and the estimator would be biased. We do not know what the wage offer is for those who don't participate in the labour force. To take into account the sample selection bias, we use the Heckman two-step procedure. The procedure involves two stages: in the first stage, we estimated Labour force equation (selection), and second stage involves estimation of the wage equation.

$$\text{LF}_i = \alpha_0 + \alpha_1\text{ED}_i + \alpha_2\text{HS}_i + \alpha_3\text{Land}_i + \alpha_5\text{GEN}_i + \alpha_6 D + \alpha_7\text{ED}_i * D + e_i \quad (2)$$

$$\ln(w_i) = \beta_0 + \beta_1\text{ED}_i + \beta_2\text{HS}_i + \beta_3\text{Land}_i + \beta_5\text{GEN}_i + \beta_6 D + \beta_7\text{ED}_i * D + \varphi_i + u_i \quad (3)$$

where, ln w is the log of daily wage rate of member of the household, ED is education level of household members, HS is household size, Land is acres of land owned by households, GEN implies gender (Male and Female), D is dummy variable for rural areas, ED * D is interactive variable of education with rural dummy and Labour force (LF) is 1 if member of the household is in labour force, otherwise zero. The e and u are the error terms.

The solution here is therefore to predict the likelihood of participation in the labor force at first stage using a probit model, then we calculate the predicted inverse Mills ratio ($\hat{\lambda}$) for each observation. The inverse Mills ratio is defined as the ratio of the probability density function to the cumulative distribution function of a distribution. In second stage, we estimate the wage equation using the $\hat{\lambda}$ as a predictor in the model (Wooldridge 2009). If the coefficient on $\hat{\lambda}$ is statistically equal to zero, there is no evidence of sample selection (endogeneity), and OLS results are consistent and can be presented. If the coefficient on $\hat{\lambda}$ is statistically significantly different from zero, the coefficients from the corrected model need to be reported.

(2) ***Employment Equation***

As found by the existing studies that education has positive impact on labour market outcomes including employment, this study empirically examines the relationship between these two variables by estimating the following equation.

$$\Pr(\text{emp}_j = 1|Z_l) = \eta_0 + \delta_l Z_l + \psi \quad (4)$$

where emp_j is a vector of jth qualitative dependent variables defined in terms of dummies for employment of household members in agriculture, industry and services sectors. $\Pr(\text{emp}_j)$ is probability of getting employed in jth sector. Z_l is lth explanatory variables. In addition to different level of education and a dummy variable for rural and urban areas, the model also includes some of the variables such as age of the household member, household size, land owned in hectares, interactive variables of education with rural dummy to avoid model specification bias. Equation (4) is estimated using the multivariate logit regression technique.

(3) ***Occupation Equation***

The occupational choice model estimated in this paper is given below.

$$\Pr(\text{occ}_k = 1|Z_l) = \eta_0 + \delta_l Z_l + \upsilon \qquad (5)$$

where occ_k is a vector of kth qualitative dependent variable. It is defined in terms of dummies for the choices of occupations by household members. $\Pr(\text{occ}_k)$ is probability of choosing the appropriate occupation jth sector. Z_l is lth explanatory variables. Explanatory variables include the different level of education of household members, a dummy variable for rural and urban areas, some control variables such as age of the household member, household size, land owned in hectres, interactive variables of education with rural dummy to avoid model specification bias. Equation (5) is estimated using the multivariate logit regression technique. The coefficients of explanatory variables in a multinomial logit model are not interpreted like the linear regression model. A more prudent way to interpret coefficients of multinomial logit model is in terms of marginal effect that measures the *ceteris paribus effects* of changes in the regressors affecting the features of the outcome variable.

4 Results Analysis

In this section we discuss the results of estimated wage, occupation and employment equations. Prior to analyzing the results, it is important to discuss the descriptive statistics of all the variables that are included in the specified model. The descriptive statistics of all the key indicators are given in Tables 4, 5, 6, 7 and 8 in the Appendix. Table 4 provides information on wages, employment and occupation by different explanatory variables. In 2011, there were 55.24% wage earners in urban areas as compared to 44.76% in rural areas. Out of total wage earners (72,672), 19.82% were illiterate, 20.8% were literate up to primary level. Maximum of 29.1% were having secondary level education. Less percentage of wage earners were having education at higher secondary (11.93%) and graduation and above level (18.39%). Within gender, maximum wage earners were male members (78.3%) and the remaining were female members. In case of employment, out of total number of persons employed (1,71,391), maximum were engaged in services (38.54%) followed by agriculture and allied (35.95%) and industry (25.51%). Like the case of wage earners, employment data shows the share of male members is highest (73.15%) and maximum percentage of employment (64.57%) has been generated in urban areas. Occupation wise, out of total number of household members (1,70,824), highest percentage of members (28.28%) had chosen agriculture and fishery activities as the main profession in 2011. Other two important occupations in which more household members were engaged are craftsmen, machine operators and labourers and unskilled workers. It is found that least percentage of household members (2.62%) were engaged in clerical profession.

Distribution of information relate to wages, employment and occupation by gender points to the fact that the average wage of male members was Rs. 338.92 as compared to Rs. 229.28 of female in 2011–12 (Table 5). And it also found that the difference between the two is statistically significant. As far as employment is concerned, sector-wise data shows percentage of female members employed in agriculture sector is 23.88 percentage points higher than male members, which is found opposite in the case of services. In case of industry, the margin of difference between male and female members employed is 6.91 percentage points. Occupation-wise, while male members dominate the white collar job market, women members are engaged more in low skilled professions like agriculture and fishery and other low skilled activities.

As discussed earlier, wage earning varies within and between rural and urban India due to variation in quality and the level of education. Data shows while household members those are illiterate earned Rs. 145.05 as compared to Rs. 677.09 by highly educated members (graduate and above) during 2011–12 (Table 6). And moreover, as the level of education increases, wage earning is also increases. This is true at all India level and rural and urban areas also. Between rural and urban households, wage earning is found invariably higher at all levels of education for the latter group of households as compared to the former. It is also observed that higher level of education has enabled the people from urban areas engaged in more proportion in industry and services sectors than rural areas. Agriculture and allied sector continued to be one of the main sources of livelihood for the people in India in general and rural areas in particular. Data shows household members from rural areas those are illiterate or having education up to secondary level by and large are engaged in agriculture sector. In other words, least number of household members in higher education category are engaged in agriculture sector. In contrast, we find more number of household members in higher education category are engaged in industry and services sector (Table 7). This is true for urban areas also where more educated household members are employed in services and industry sectors.

Education of household members by occupations in rural and urban areas suggest that households members those are illiterate or having education up to secondary level are preferring agriculture and fishery and low skilled economic activities as the main profession both in rural and urban areas. High qualified persons (under graduate, graduate and above) are seen engaged mostly in professions like professionals, associate professionals and clerks (Table 8).

In the nutshell, the above discussion points to the fact that higher is the level of education, better is the earnings of the individual. This is found both in rural and urban areas. Further, the average wage earning of household members in urban areas is found comparatively higher than its rural counterparts. It is also evident that higher education offers an opportunity to the people to choose better quality jobs available in secondary and tertiary sectors instead of agriculture and allied sector. Data shows lower is the level of education, higher is the possibility of working in agriculture and low productive activities. Hence, these finding point to the fact that education plays a critical role in determining the quality of jobs, earnings and choice of occupation.

Econometric results

In this section, we have tried to explain the factors that explain the disparity in wages, employment and occupation between the rural and urban India. While we use Heckman two-step procedure to estimate the wage equation, a multinomial logistic technique is used to estimate the occupation and employment equation. In the present context, the multinomial logistic technique explains the probability of getting employed in industry and services or some other sectors or choosing a particular occupation in rural and urban areas resulted due to changes in education with assuming other factors remain constant.

As indicated in the methodology section, to avoid the selection bias in the estimation of wage equation, first we estimate a labour force equation to derive the value of inverse Mills ratio (lambda). The results of labour force equation are presented in Table 9 (see Appendix). In the second step, the wage equation has been estimated using the estimated lambda obtained from first step as an independent variable along with education and other variables. This stage estimation is carried out on household members only those who participate in wage work. Results of wage equation are reported in Table 1. In estimation, out of five categories of general education, illiterate is taken as control variable. Similarly, between urban and rural, the former is taken as control variable in order to avoid the dummy variable trap in estimation. Results show that all education variables i.e., literate up to primary, secondary, under graduation, graduate and above are positively associated with wage earning and statistically significant suggesting education of an individual plays a critical role in determining the wage earning. Importantly, coefficients of education variable point to fact that higher is the education, better is the wage earning. And the returns to education increases at an increasing rate as the level of education increases. We find a positive inverse Mills ratio which indicates that a shock to the selection equation that increases labour force participation also increases the conditional expectation of wages (Arrazola and de Hevia 2008).

Rural dummy is found negative and statistically significant indicating differences exist between rural and urban areas as far as wage earning is concerned. This supports our earlier findings that wage earning in urban area is higher than rural area (Kijima 2006). Whether the impact of education on wage earning in rural area is different to urban area has been captured through interactive variables. It is found that as compared to illiterate in rural areas, secondary, under graduate and graduate and above interactive variables in rural areas are negatively associated with wage earning. It means different levels of education in urban areas are positively associated with wage earning.

The estimated results of employment equation using the multinomial logistic regression are reported in Table 2. Employment equation is estimated for three sectors i.e., agriculture, industry and services separately. In case of agriculture sector, the results confirm that people those are literate or highly educated in relative to illiterate raises the probability of they may go out of the sector. This is also true for rural areas where the education interaction indicates that rural status increases the likelihood of higher educated people relative to illiterate to go out of agriculture sector. Other variables that are positively associated with employment in agriculture

Table 1 Wage equation

Variables	ln(wage)
Age	0.0208***
	(0.000789)
Household size	−0.0126***
	(0.00122)
Land owned (in hectares)	0.0270***
	(0.00255)
Male	0.592***
	(0.0310)
Literate & up to primary	0.178***
	(0.0132)
Secondary	0.518***
	(0.0158)
Under graduation	0.993***
	(0.0181)
Graduate & above	1.519***
	(0.0242)
Rural	−0.0374**
	(0.0153)
Literate & up to primary* rural	−0.00474
	(0.0162)
Secondary* rural	−0.0582***
	(0.0149)
Under graduation* rural	−0.0852***
	(0.0184)
Graduate & above* rural	−0.198***
	(0.0171)
lambda	0.253***
	(0.0463)
Constant	3.456***
	(0.0949)
Observations	72,672
R-squared	0.431
F-test	3931.68***

Standard errors in parentheses
***, ** and * indicates significant at 1%, 5% and 10%, respectively

sectors are age of the household member and household size but the impact of these two factors is marginal. With respect to gender, the study finds that male members are less likely to be employed in agriculture sector relative to female members. The opposite results are found in case of industry and services sector where the male dummy variable is positively associated with employment indicating that the probability of male members employed in industry and services sector is relatively

Table 2 Employment equation

Variables	Agriculture	Industry	Service
Age	0.00173***	−0.00409***	0.00236***
	(0.000107)	(9.36e−05)	(0.000112)
Household size	0.00922***	−0.00295***	−0.00627***
	(0.000550)	(0.000476)	(0.000567)
Land owned (in hectares)	0.142***	−0.106***	−0.0356***
	(0.00157)	(0.00188)	(0.00170)
Male	−0.212***	0.0862***	0.125***
	(0.00329)	(0.00244)	(0.00320)
Literate & up to primary	−0.0632***	−0.00768	0.0709***
	(0.00866)	(0.00595)	(0.00789)
Secondary	−0.133***	−0.0609***	0.194***
	(0.00772)	(0.00517)	(0.00708)
Under graduation	−0.232***	−0.105***	0.336***
	(0.00711)	(0.00512)	(0.00763)
Graduate & above	−0.320***	−0.161***	0.481***
	(0.00485)	(0.00390)	(0.00547)
Rural	0.371***	−0.000979	−0.370***
	(0.00514)	(0.00511)	(0.00644)
Literate & up to primary*rural	−0.0302***	−0.0319***	0.0621***
	(0.00987)	(0.00696)	(0.00998)
Secondary*rural	−0.0301***	−0.0547***	0.0848***
	(0.00921)	(0.00631)	(0.00912)
Under graduation*rural	−0.00479	−0.112***	0.116***
	(0.0141)	(0.00697)	(0.0128)
Graduate & above*rural	−0.00143	−0.143***	0.145***
	(0.0158)	(0.00689)	(0.0142)
Predicted probabilities	**0.326**	**0.264**	**0.409**
Observations	**61,616**	**43,722**	**66,053**

Standard errors in parentheses
***, ** and * indicates significant at 1%, 5% and 10%, respectively

higher than female members. Like the case of agriculture sector, the results of industry show that the probability of educated person relative to illiterate is less likely to be employed in the sector. Education interaction variables with rural dummy show higher is the education, lower is the probability of persons employed in industry sector. In contrast, it is found that education interactive variables with rural dummy are positively associated with employment in services sector implying higher is the education, the probability of getting employed in the sector is more.

The results of impact of education and households characteristics on choice of occupations are reported in Table 3. The results suggest that education (literate and up to primary, secondary, under graduation and graduate and above) is positively

Table 3 Occupation equation

Variables	Administrators, Managers	Professionals, Associate Professionals	Clerks etc.	Sales and service worker
Age	0.00196***	0.00153***	0.000276***	0.000429***
	(7.15e−05)	(5.47e−05)	(2.07e−05)	(8.02e−05)
Household size	0.00197***	−0.00370***	−0.000913***	−0.00155***
	(0.000348)	(0.000269)	(9.76e−05)	(0.000402)
Land owned (in hectares)	0.00604***	0.0152***	0.00184***	−0.0129***
	(0.00120)	(0.000682)	(0.000245)	(0.00150)
Male	0.0516***	−0.0402***	5.95e−05	0.0533***
	(0.00201)	(0.00190)	(0.000514)	(0.00219)
Literate & up to primary	0.0338***	0.0552***	0.0139***	0.0319***
	(0.00620)	(0.00941)	(0.00512)	(0.00629)
Secondary	0.0521***	0.148***	0.0574***	0.0540***
	(0.00557)	(0.0102)	(0.00901)	(0.00576)
Under graduation	0.0102	0.427***	0.152***	−0.0223***
	(0.00709)	(0.0240)	(0.0263)	(0.00659)
Graduate & above	0.0109*	0.605***	0.147***	−0.0721***
	(0.00662)	(0.0247)	(0.0251)	(0.00382)
Rural	−0.0857***	−0.0436***	−0.0213***	−0.117***
	(0.00633)	(0.00772)	(0.00616)	(0.00676)
Literate & up to primary* rural	0.000867	0.00630	0.00572	0.0150*
	(0.00701)	(0.00899)	(0.00599)	(0.00778)
Secondary* rural	−0.000494	0.00674	0.00545	0.0136**
	(0.00625)	(0.00777)	(0.00507)	(0.00689)
Under graduation* rural	−0.0259***	0.00618	0.00956	−0.000154
	(0.00622)	(0.00796)	(0.00662)	(0.00813)
Graduate & above* rural	−0.0559***	0.00553	0.00538	0.00164
	(0.00478)	(0.00791)	(0.00553)	(0.00936)
Predicted probabilities	**0.115**	**0.075**	**0.013**	**0.143**
Observations	**15,182**	**18,841**	**4474**	**18,764**

Variables	Skilled agriculture and fishery workers	Craftsmen, machine operators	Labourers, unskilled workers
Age	0.00296***	−0.00383***	−0.00332***
	(0.000109)	(8.94e−05)	(7.62e−05)
Household size	0.0131***	−0.00386***	−0.00504***
	(0.000546)	(0.000443)	(0.000389)
Land owned (in hectares)	0.182***	−0.0906***	−0.102***
	(0.00179)	(0.00188)	(0.00160)
Male	−0.185***	0.105***	0.0155***
	(0.00342)	(0.00221)	(0.00192)

(continued)

Table 3 (continued)

Variables	Skilled agriculture and fishery workers	Craftsmen, machine operators	Labourers, unskilled workers
Literate & up to primary	−0.0550***	−0.00480	−0.0750***
	(0.0103)	(0.00579)	(0.00366)
Secondary	−0.0976***	−0.0495***	−0.164***
	(0.00897)	(0.00493)	(0.00344)
Under graduation	−0.237***	−0.148***	−0.183***
	(0.00658)	(0.00377)	(0.00224)
Graduate & above	−0.280***	−0.200***	−0.210***
	(0.00400)	(0.00225)	(0.00213)
Rural	0.307***	−0.0744***	0.0348***
	(0.00642)	(0.00575)	(0.00346)
Literate & up to primary* rural	−0.0154	−0.00838	−0.00406
	(0.0115)	(0.00693)	(0.00534)
Secondary* rural	−0.0216**	−0.0110*	0.00725
	(0.0103)	(0.00632)	(0.00534)
Under graduation* rural	0.0195	−0.0271***	0.0179*
	(0.0157)	(0.00829)	(0.0104)
Graduate & above* rural	0.0153	−0.0186	0.0467***
	(0.0181)	(0.0119)	(0.0178)
Predicted probabilities	**0.298**	**0.199**	**0.158**
Observations	**48,316**	**32,002**	**33,245**

Standard errors in parentheses
***, ** and * indicates significant at 1%, 5% and 10%, respectively

associated with professions like managers, professional and associate professionals and clerks and sales services and negatively associated with agricultural and unskilled activities. Therefore, higher is the education, more is the probability that the household members may go for managerial and professional occupations. Interactions variables of education with rural dummy also point to the fact that education raises the probability of household members to choose managerial and professional occupations over the agricultural and low skilled activities.

To sum up the above discussion suggests that education, age, household size, gender are important determinants of wages, employment and occupations. The results show that education disparity exists between rural and urban India, wherein interaction variables of education with rural dummy are found negatively associated with wage rate. It is also found that as the level of education increases relative of illiteracy, the wage earning capacity of household members also increases. Higher education also raises the probability of getting employed in services sector relative to agriculture and industry. Interestingly, the similar type of outcome is also evident in the case of rural areas. Occupation wise, higher education enable the household members to go for managerial or professional occupations than agriculture or low skilled activities.

5 Conclusion

The existing studies opined that education plays a critical role in improving the empowerment, efficiency, productivity and overall economic development of the country. It also provides right bargaining power to labour force to demand for more wages, engage in quality jobs and choose a suitable occupation for their livelihood. To optimally utilize the manpower resources, the government of India has implemented various educational programmes at primary and secondary level. A question arises here that whether the impact of education on labour market outcomes has been uniform across sectors and regions or there are differences? In this context, this paper examines the impact of education and some of the household characteristics on three labour market outcomes namely wages, employment and occupation using the NSSO 68th round (2011–12) data. While wage equation is estimated using Heckman two-step procedure, employment and occupation equations are estimated using the multinomial logistic regression technique.

Findings of wage equation estimation tend to confirm that different levels of education, age, household size, acres of land owned, gender are important determinants of wages. Further, rural dummy which explains the hypothesis of wage income in rural areas is lower than urban area is found negatively associated with wages and statistically significant. As far as education variables are concerned, all of them (literate up to primary, secondary, under graduation and graduate and above) are positively associated with wages. Further the results show that returns to education increases at an increasing rate as the level of education increases suggesting that more attention needs be paid on improving the accessibility and quality of primary and secondary education that would help in containing the dropout level and improving the enrollment ratio of higher education. As far as the differential impact of education on wages is concerned, the study found that the impact of all education variables on wages is found relatively higher in the case of urban than rural areas. Results of employment model suggest that compared to illiterates, the chances of higher educated people going to agriculture sector is less. This is true even in the case of rural areas where the interactive variable (education with rural dummy) is found negatively associated with employment in agriculture sector. Instead, with the increase of education, the probability of getting employed in services sector is found high as the education interaction variables with rural dummy are found positively associated with employment. From the occupational choice model, it is again evident that an increase of education of rural people has a higher probability of joining the relatively better jobs such managerial, professional and associate professional, clerks or salesman services indicating that people having higher education relative to illiterate are better off in terms of choosing the occupation in the job market. Overall, the study finds that education plays a critical role in determining wages, employment and occupational choices both in rural and urban India. But its impact on the above three labour market outcomes varies from rural to urban and among different sectors and occupations. Its impact on wages is found higher in case of urban than rural areas. Higher educated people relative to illiterate both in rural and urban areas may have higher probability of getting employed in services sector and choose better occupations for their livelihood. From the policy prospective, the government need to make an effort to reduce the education disparity between rural and urban areas, create quality jobs in the rural areas and increase the agricultural wages at par with some of the industrial activities, which could prevent people of migrating to urban areas.

Appendix

See Tables 4, 5, 6, 7, 8 and 9.

Table 4 Descriptive statistics

Variables	Wage equation	Employment equation	Occupation equation
Average wage rate (Rs.)	315.11	–	–
Agriculture (%)	–	35.95	–
Industry (%)	–	25.51	–
Service (%)	–	38.54	–
Administrators, Managers (%)	–	–	8.89
Professionals, Associate Professionals (%)	–	–	11.03
Clerks etc. (%)	–	–	2.62
Sales and service worker (%)	–	–	10.98
Skilled agriculture and fishery workers (%)	–	–	28.28
Craftsmen, machine operators (%)	–	–	18.73
Labourers, unskilled workers (%)	–	–	19.46
Average age	37.05	38.56	38.56
Average household size	4.84	5.29	5.29
Average land owned (hectares)	0.30	0.77	0.77
Average number of months without work	0.56	–	–
Male (%)	78.28	73.16	73.15
Female (%)	21.72	26.84	26.85
Illiterate (%)	19.82	22.32	22.34
Literate & up to primary (%)	20.80	22.17	22.14
Secondary (%)	29.05	31.99	31.98
Under graduation (%)	11.93	10.91	10.91
Graduate & above (%)	18.39	12.62	12.63
Urban (%)	55.24	64.57	64.59
Rural (%)	44.76	35.43	35.41
Total observations	72,672	171,391	170,824

Table 5 Wage, employment and occupation distribution by gender

Variables	Male	Female	Total	Diff.
Average wage (Rs.)	338.92	229.28	315.11	109.64***
	(2.35)	(2.36)	(1.92)	(4.64)
Agriculture (%)	29.54	53.42	35.95	−23.88***
	(0.13)	(0.23)	(0.12)	(0.26)
Industry (%)	27.36	20.46	25.51	6.91***
	(0.13)	(0.19)	(0.11)	(0.24)
Service (%)	43.09	26.13	38.54	16.97***
	(0.14)	(0.20)	(0.12)	(0.26)
Administrators, Managers (%)	10.36	4.89	8.89	5.47***
	(0.09)	(0.10)	(0.07)	(0.15)
Professionals, Associate Professionals (%)	11.23	10.47	11.03	0.76***
	(0.09)	(0.14)	(0.08)	(0.17)
Clerks etc. (%)	2.96	1.69	2.62	1.27***
	(0.05)	(0.06)	(0.04)	(0.09)
Sales and service worker (%)	12.44	7.01	10.98	5.43***
	(0.09)	(0.12)	(0.08)	(0.17)
Skilled agriculture and fishery workers (%)	23.68	40.83	28.28	−17.15***
	(0.12)	(0.23)	(0.11)	(0.24)
Craftsmen, machine operators (%)	21.12	12.23	18.73	8.89***
	(0.12)	(0.15)	(0.09)	(0.21)
Labourers, unskilled workers (%)	18.21	22.88	19.46	−4.67***
	(0.11)	(0.20)	(0.10)	(0.22)

Standard errors in parentheses
***, ** and * indicates significant at 1%, 5% and 10%, respectively

Table 6 Average wage in rural and urban areas by general education

Variables	Average wage (Rs.)			
	Rural	Urban	Total	Diff.
Illiterate	138.29	161.07	145.05	−22.77***
	(0.82)	(1.94)	(0.82)	(1.78)
Literate & up to primary	167.67	192.40	176.73	−24.73***
	(1.29)	(2.05)	(1.12)	(2.31)
Secondary	230.08	288.84	256.63	−58.76***
	(1.96)	(10.83)	(5.01)	(10.07)
Under graduation	393.71	450.24	423.29	−56.53***
	(5.09)	(5.17)	(3.65)	(7.28)

(continued)

Table 6 (continued)

Variables	Average wage (Rs.)			
	Rural	Urban	Total	Diff.
Graduate & above	583.04	728.64	677.09	−145.60***
	(6.19)	(6.61)	(4.84)	(10.04)
Total	250.48	394.87	315.11	−144.39***
	(1.33)	(3.92)	(1.92)	(3.82)

Standard errors in parentheses
***, ** and * indicates significant at 1%, 5% and 10%, respectively

Table 7 Share of employment in the rural and urban areas by industrial classification

Variables	Agriculture (%)			
	Rural	Urban	Total	Diff.
Illiterate	34.25	27.85	33.67	6.41***
	(0.20)	(0.60)	(0.19)	(0.66)
Literate & up to primary	25.34	24.39	25.26	0.95
	(0.18)	(0.57)	(0.18)	(0.61)
Secondary	29.61	32.38	29.86	−2.77***
	(0.19)	(0.62)	(0.18)	(0.64)
Under graduation	7.16	8.43	7.28	−1.27***
	(0.11)	(0.37)	(0.10)	(0.36)
Graduate & above	3.63	6.95	3.93	−3.32***
	(0.08)	(0.34)	(0.08)	(0.27)
Total	50.61	9.24	35.95	41.37***
	(0.15)	(0.12)	(0.12)	(0.22)
	Industry (%)			
Illiterate	28.18	18.72	24.20	9.47***
	(0.28)	(0.29)	(0.20)	(0.41)
Literate & up to primary	30.08	24.45	27.71	5.63***
	(0.29)	(0.32)	(0.21)	(0.43)
Secondary	32.39	34.91	33.45	−2.52***
	(0.29)	(0.35)	(0.23)	(0.46)
Under graduation	6.44	11.25	8.47	−4.81***
	(0.15)	(0.23)	(0.13)	(0.27)
Graduate & above	2.90	10.68	6.17	−7.78***
	(0.11)	(0.23)	(0.12)	(0.23)
Total	22.88	30.30	25.51	−7.42***
	(0.13)	(0.19)	(0.11)	(0.22)

(continued)

Table 7 (continued)

Variables	Agriculture (%)			
	Rural	Urban	Total	Diff.
	Service (%)			
Illiterate	11.76	9.45	10.47	2.31***
	(0.19)	(0.15)	(0.12)	(0.24)
Literate & up to primary	17.97	13.72	15.61	4.25***
	(0.22)	(0.18)	(0.14)	(0.28)
Secondary	35.08	31.35	33.01	3.73***
	(0.28)	(0.24)	(0.18)	(0.37)
Under graduation	15.93	15.91	15.92	0.02
	(0.21)	(0.19)	(0.14)	(0.29)
Graduate & above	19.26	29.56	24.99	−10.30***
	(0.23)	(0.24)	(0.17)	(0.34)
Total	26.51	60.46	38.54	−33.94***
	(0.13)	(0.20)	(0.12)	(0.23)

Standard errors in parentheses
***, ** and * indicates significant at 1%, 5% and 10%, respectively

Table 8 Share of employment in the rural and Urban areas by occupational choices

Variables	Legislators, Managers (%)			
	Rural	Urban	Total	Diff.
Illiterate	14.69	7.74	10.73	6.95***
	(0.44)	(0.29)	(0.25)	(0.50)
Literate & up to primary	22.22	13.79	17.42	8.44***
	(0.51)	(0.37)	(0.31)	(0.62)
Secondary	39.73	32.98	35.88	6.75***
	(0.61)	(0.51)	(0.39)	(0.78)
Under graduation	12.90	16.28	14.83	−3.39***
	(0.41)	(0.40)	(0.29)	(0.58)
Graduate & above	10.46	29.20	21.14	−18.74***
	(0.38)	(0.49)	(0.33)	(0.65)
Total	5.92	14.31	8.89	−8.39***
	(0.07)	(0.14)	(0.07)	(0.14)
	Professionals, associate professionals (%)			
Illiterate	3.19	1.50	2.27	1.69***
	(0.19)	(0.12)	(0.11)	(0.22)
Literate & up to primary	6.02	3.14	4.44	2.88***
	(0.26)	(0.17)	(0.15)	(0.30)
Secondary	20.39	13.75	16.76	6.64***
	(0.44)	(0.34)	(0.27)	(0.54)

(continued)

Table 8 (continued)

Variables	Legislators, Managers (%)			
	Rural	Urban	Total	Diff.
Under graduation	23.91	19.79	21.65	4.12***
	(0.46)	(0.39)	(0.30)	(0.60)
Graduate & above	46.49	61.81	54.88	−15.33***
	(0.54)	(0.48)	(0.36)	(0.72)
Total	7.72	17.06	11.03	−9.33***
	(0.08)	(0.15)	(0.08)	(0.16)
	Clerks etc. (%)			
Illiterate	1.09	0.76	0.87	0.33
	(0.26)	(0.16)	(0.14)	(0.29)
Literate & up to primary	3.84	2.16	2.75	1.68***
	(0.49)	(0.27)	(0.24)	(0.51)
Secondary	27.29	20.67	22.98	6.62***
	(1.13)	(0.75)	(0.63)	(1.32)
Under graduation	32.09	24.37	27.07	7.72***
	(1.18)	(0.80)	(0.66)	(1.39)
Graduate & above	35.68	52.04	46.33	−16.36***
	(1.21)	(0.93)	(0.75)	(1.55)
Total	1.41	4.82	2.62	−3.40***
	(0.04)	(0.09)	(0.04)	(0.08)
Variables	Sales and service worker (%)			
	Rural	Urban	Total	Diff.
Illiterate	13.85	9.66	11.62	4.19***
	(0.37)	(0.30)	(0.23)	(0.47)
Literate & up to primary	22.89	17.00	19.76	5.89***
	(0.45)	(0.38)	(0.29)	(0.58)
Secondary	42.52	41.50	41.98	1.02
	(0.53)	(0.49)	(0.36)	(0.72)
Under graduation	13.12	16.87	15.11	−3.74***
	(0.36)	(0.38)	(0.26)	(0.52)
Graduate & above	7.61	14.97	11.52	−7.37***
	(0.28)	(0.36)	(0.23)	(0.46)
Total	7.97	16.48	10.98	−8.51***
	(0.08)	(0.15)	(0.08)	(0.16)
	Skilled agriculture and fishery workers (%)			
Illiterate	30.93	23.05	30.23	7.88***
	(0.22)	(0.64)	(0.21)	(0.73)
Literate & up to primary	24.44	22.61	24.27	1.83**
	(0.20)	(0.64)	(0.20)	(0.69)
Secondary	31.94	36.52	32.35	−4.58***
	(0.22)	(0.74)	(0.21)	(0.75)

(continued)

Table 8 (continued)

Variables	Sales and service worker (%)			
	Rural	Urban	Total	Diff.
Under graduation	8.32	9.82	8.45	−1.50***
	(0.13)	(0.46)	(0.13)	(0.45)
Graduate & above	4.37	8.00	4.69	−3.62***
	(0.10)	(0.41)	(0.10)	(0.34)
Total	39.91	7.07	28.28	32.84***
	(0.15)	(0.10)	(0.11)	(0.21)
	Craftsmen, machine operators (%)			
Illiterate	22.35	15.92	19.38	6.43***
	(0.32)	(0.30)	(0.22)	(0.44)
Literate & up to primary	29.38	25.23	27.46	4.15***
	(0.35)	(0.36)	(0.25)	(0.50)
Secondary	38.24	42.45	40.19	−4.21***
	(0.37)	(0.41)	(0.27)	(0.55)
Under graduation	7.74	11.31	9.40	−3.57***
	(0.20)	(0.26)	(0.16)	(0.33)
Graduate & above	2.28	5.08	3.57	−2.80***
	(0.11)	(0.18)	(0.10)	(0.21)
Total	15.58	24.49	18.73	−8.91***
	(0.11)	(0.17)	(0.09)	(0.20)
Variables	Labourers, unskilled workers (%)			
	Rural	Urban	Total	Diff.
Illiterate	41.30	34.45	39.33	6.85***
	(0.32)	(0.49)	(0.27)	(0.59)
Literate & up to primary	30.04	30.10	30.06	−0.06
	(0.30)	(0.47)	(0.25)	(0.56)
Secondary	24.57	29.33	25.94	−4.75***
	(0.28)	(0.47)	(0.24)	(0.53)
Under graduation	3.18	4.36	3.52	−1.18***
	(0.11)	(0.21)	(0.10)	(0.22)
Graduate & above	0.91	1.76	1.15	−0.85***
	(0.06)	(0.13	(0.06)	(0.13)
Total	21.48	15.78	19.46	5.70***
	(0.12)	(0.15)	(0.10)	(0.20)

Standard errors in parentheses
***, ** and * indicates significant at 1%, 5% and 10%, respectively

Table 9 Labour force participation

Variables	(1)
	Labor force participation
Age	0.0112***
	(4.33e−05)
Household size	−0.00837***
	(0.000311)
Land owned (in hectares)	−0.000101
	(0.000455)
Male	0.373***
	(0.00144)
Literate & up to primary	−6.97e−05
	(0.00406)
Secondary	0.133***
	(0.00399)
Under graduation	0.157***
	(0.00503)
Graduate & above	0.306***
	(0.00461)
Rural	0.120***
	(0.00342)
Literate & up to primary*rural	−0.0205***
	(0.00473)
Secondary*rural	0.00118
	(0.00467)
Under graduation*rural	−0.00547
	(0.00613)
Graduate & above*rural	0.00155
	(0.00691)
Observations	456,362

Standard errors in parentheses
***, ** and * indicates significant at 1%, 5% and 10%, respectively

References

Agrawal, T. (2012). Return to education in India: Some recent evidence. *Journal of Quantitative Economics, 10*(2), 131–151.

Arrazola, M., & de Hevia, J. (2008). Three measures of returns to education: An illustration for the case of Spain. *Economics of Education Review, 27*(3), 266–275.

Azam, M. (2012). Changes in wage structure in Urban India, 1983–2004: A quantile regression decomposition. *World Development, 40*(6), 1135–1150.

Barro, R., & Lee, J. (2010). A new data set of educational attainment in the world. NBER Working Paper Series 15902, National Bureau of Economic Research. Massachusetts Avenue Cambridge.

Becker, G. S. (1994). *Human capital: A theoretical and empirical analysis, with special reference to education*. Chicago: University of Chicago Press.
Card, D. (2001, September). Estimating the return to schooling: Progress on some persistent econometric problems. *Econometrica, 69*(5), 1127–1160.
Chamarbagwala, R. (2006). Economic liberalization and wage inequality in India. *World Development, 34*(12), 1997–2015.
Chenoy, D. (2012). *Skill development in India; A transformation in the making* (Chapter 18, IDFC). www.idfc.com/pdf/report/2012/chapter_18.pdf.
Duraisamy, P. (2002, December). Changes in returns to education in India, 1983–94: By gender, age-cohort and location. *Economics of Education Review, 21*(6), 609–622.
Dutta, P. V. (2006). Returns to education: New evidence for India, 1983–99. *Education Economics, 14*(4), 431–451.
Economic Survey. (2016–17). *Government of India*.
FICCI. (2015). *Labour in Indian agriculture: A growing challenge*. http://ficci.in/spdocument/20550/FICCI-agri-Report%2009-03-2015.pdf.
Friedman, M., & Kuznets, S. (1954). *Income from independent professional practice*. Cambridge: National Bureau of Economic Research (NBER).
Grossman, M. (2005). *Education and nonmarket outcomes*. NBER Working Paper 11582.
Harmon, C., Oosterbeek, H., & Walker, I. (2000). *The returns to education a review of evidence, issues and deficiencies in the literature*. Centre for the Economics of Education, London School of Economics and Political Science Houghton Street London WC2A 2AE.
Heckman, J. J., Lochner, L. J., & Todd, P. E. (2003). *Fifty years of mincer earnings regressions*. NBER Working Papers, no 9732, National Bureau of Economic Research, May.
ILO. (2015). *Global employment trend for youth 2015. Scaling up investments in decent jobs for youth*. Retrieved from http://www.il.org on April 18, 2016.
Kijima, Y. (2006). Why did wage inequality increase? Evidence from urban India 1983–99. *Journal of Development Economics, 81*(1), 97–117.
Maclean, R., Jagannathan S., & Sarvi, J. (2013). *Skills development for inclusive and sustainable growth in developing Asia-Pacific, technical and vocational education and training: Issues, concerns and prospects*. https://www.adb.org/sites/default/files/publication/30071/skills-development-inclusive-growth-asia-pacific.pdf.
Mincer, J. (1974). *Schooling, experience and earnings*. Cambridge: NBER.
Oreopoulos, P., & Salvanes, K. G. (2009). *How large are returns to schooling? Hint: Money isn't everything*. NBER Working Papers 15339.
Psacharopoulos, G., & Patrinos, H. A. (2004). Returns to investment in education: A further update. *Education Economics, 12*(2), 111–134.
Schultz, T. W. (1961). Investment in human capital. *The American Economic Review*, 1–17.
Schultz, T. W. (1971). *Investment in human capital: The role of education and of research*.
Sen, A. K. (1999). *Development as freedom*. Oxford: Oxford University Press.
Sianesi, B., & Van Reenen, J. (2002). *The returns to education: A review of the empirical macro-economic literature*. The Institute for Fiscal Studies, Working Paper 02/05.
Singhari, S., & Madheswaran, S. (2016). *The changing rates of return to education in India: Evidence from NSS Data*. The Institute for Social and Economic Change, Working paper 358.
Vatta, K., Sato, T., & Taneja, G. (2016). Indian labour markets and returns to education. *Millennial Asia, 7*(2), 107–130.
Wooldridge, J. M. (2009). *Introductory econometrics: A modern approach* (4th ed). Mason: South-Western, Cengage Learning.
Wu, K. B., Goldschmidt, P., Azam, M., & Boscardin, C. K. (2006). Girls in India: Poverty, location, and social disparities. In M. Lewis & M. Lockheed (Eds.), *Exclusion, gender and education: Case studies from the developing world*. Washington, DC: Center for Global Development.

Sarva Shiksha Abhiyan: Achievements, Problems and Future Prospects: A Comparative Analysis of Some Indian States

S. K. Yadav, Radhey Shyam Sharma and Marshal Birua

1 Background and Genesis

History of literacy rate in India has not been highly impressive because as per the 1951 population census, only 18.3% of the population was literate and thereafter, the rate increased over a period of time to 52.2% in 1991 and 74.0% in 2011 (Registrar General and Census Commissioner of India 2011). Although the country has made progress in improving the literacy rate, there is still a lot left to be done. 26.0% of the population not literate so far, amounts to 32.5 crores in absolute terms. The improvement in literacy rate has been achieved mainly due to the policy of Education for All (EFA)/Universal Elementary Education (UEE) and a great deal of interventions such as Sarva Shiksha Abhiyan (SSA) and District Primary Education Programme (DPEP) of the Government of India with the partnership of state governments. India's progress towards achieving the EFA goal has been remarkable. In spite of the progress made on several fronts, Universal Primary Education has not yet been achieved in India (UNESCO 2015).

SSA is a Government of India's flagship programme which has been operational since 2000–2001, and as an intervention programme since 2010 with the initial outlay of Rs. 7000 crores. SSA was launched for the achievement of universalisation of elementary education in a time-bound manner, as mandated by

S. K. Yadav (✉) · R. S. Sharma · M. Birua
National Institute of Labour Economics Research and Development
(NITI Aayog, Government of India), Delhi 110040, India
e-mail: sky_1960@yahoo.com

R. S. Sharma
e-mail: radheyshyam_1962@yahoo.com

M. Birua
e-mail: marshalbirua@yahoo.com

NILERD, *Reflecting on India's Development*,
https://doi.org/10.1007/978-981-13-1414-8_9

86th amendment of the Constitution of India making free and compulsory education for the children of 6–14 years age group, as a fundamental right (Issues of India 2014). The aims of SSA is to provide useful and elementary education for all children in the age group of 6–14 years by 2010 and to bridge social, regional and gender gaps, with the active participation of community in the management of schools. The programme covered the entire country with the partnership of state Governments (District Primary Education Department, Kaithal, Haryana 2017).

Overall goals of SSA[1] include universal access to and retention of education, bridging of gender and social category gaps in education and enhancement of learning levels among children. SSA provides for a variety of interventions, including inter alia, opening of new schools and alternate schooling facilities, construction of schools and additional classrooms, toilets and drinking water, provisioning for teachers, periodic teacher training and academic resource support, textbooks and support for learning achievement. These provisions need to be aligned with the legally mandated norms and standards and free entitlements mandated by the RTE Act, 2009 (Government of India, MHRD 2017a).

The law provides a legal framework that entitles all children between the age of 6–14 years free and compulsory admission, attendance and completion of elementary education. It provides for children's right to an education of equitable quality, based on principles of equity and non-discrimination. Most importantly, it provides for children's right to an education that is free from fear, stress and anxiety.

In 2010, the country achieved a historic milestone when Article 21-A and the Right of Children to Free and Compulsory Education (RTE) Act, 2009 became operative on 1 April 2010. The enforcement of the Article 21-A and the RTE Act represented a momentous step forward in our country's struggle for universalizing elementary education. The RTE Act is anchored in the belief that the values of equality, social justice and democracy and the creation of a just and humane society can be achieved only through provision of inclusive elementary education to all (Government of India, MHRD 2017b).

Specific objectives of SSA, laid down by the Government of India at the launch of SSA in 2001, were as follows:

- All children in school, Education Guarantee Centre, Alternate School, 'Back-to School' camps by 2003;
- All children complete 5 years of primary schooling by 2007;
- All children complete 8 years of elementary schooling by 2010;
- Focus on elementary education of satisfactory quality with emphasis on education for life;

[1]The information is from the Department of School Education—Punjab's 'Sarva Shiksha Abhiyan' homepage; http://ssapunjab.org/ssa/index.html.

- Bridge all gender and social category gaps at primary stage by 2007 and at elementary education level by 2010; and
- Universal retention by 2010 (Primary Education Department, RiBhoi District 2017).

With these objectives, the issues of quality education, equity and retention in schools are addressed squarely by transforming the SSA in a National Mission for Quality Elementary Education.

On the basis of past experience, from time to time, there have been modifications in the implementation of the programme. Still, a lot of work has to be done to improve the effectiveness of the programme. In view of the importance of the subject and involvement of huge funds, it is imperative to review and evaluate the programme from time to time. Due to the implementation of SSA, improvement has been seen in education indicators. Some of them are as follows:

Improvements in Education Indicators

According to Unified District Information System on Education (U-Dise) data 2015–16, out of 20.78 crore children in the age group of 6–13 years (census 2011), 19.67 crore children (94.65%) were enrolled in 14.49 lakh elementary schools on an average 136 children per school. This is in itself a significant achievement. Significant reduction in number of out of school children in the age group 6–14 years has been observed from 134.6 lakh in 2005 to 81 lakh in 2009 and further reduced to 61 lakh in 2014. Likewise, annual average dropout rate at primary level has also been reduced from 9.11% in 2009–10 to 4.13% in 2015–16. Another significant improvement recorded in respect of two education indicators such as transition rate from primary to upper primary has gone up from 83.53% in 2009–10 to 90.14% in 2015–16 and the Pupil–Teacher ratio (PTR) has improved from 32 in 2009–10 to 24 in 2015–16 (Government of India, MHRD 2017a).

SSA has achieved partially but considerable success in achieving the targets due to strict norms and monitoring process. However, it has not yet been succeeded in providing good quality education to a wide cross section of our children. The programme has not achieved successfully due to its own inherited and current problems in implementation. Many studies and reviews have been undertaken to monitor and assess the problems and shortcomings of the programme from time to time.

One such study was conducted by the Indian Institute of Management, Ahmadabad in 2006, which reported that SSA has met with considerable success quantitatively but not qualitatively.

The study documented that education was never so innovative: Schools in fishing boats, mobile schools in brick kilns; programmes like Meena campaign, Ujasbhani and Diwali camp for girl's education, special teachers for children with disabilities. These and many more innovations were made by the 4-year-old Sarva Shiksha Abhiyan to achieve universalisation of elementary education. The report highlighted best practices and innovations done by Andhra Pradesh, Delhi, Gujarat, Haryana, Karnataka, Kerala, Madhya Pradesh, Maharashtra, Odisha, Tamil Nadu, Uttar Pradesh, Uttarakhand and West Bengal.

While quality remains an area of concern, the SSA has been able to bridge the enrolment, retention and achievement gap between the sexes and among social groups. According to the study, out of school population had come down from 28.5% of the 6–14 years age group in 2001 to 6.94% by the end of 2005. Dropout rates at the primary level stand at about 12% and 190 out of the 400 districts were showing declining trends in 2005–2006. The SSA has been able to bring weak points pertaining to Scheduled Caste and Scheduled Tribes (SC/ST) in earlier efforts to universalize elementary education into the educational mainstream (Indian Institute of Management, Ahmedabad 2006). Many more studies were conducted to evaluate SSA Programme since monitoring and evaluation is a continuous process in the programme.

The paper tried to evaluate the SSA programme with specific objectives.

Objectives of the paper

The broad objectives of the paper are to:

Assess the targets and achievements of SSA;
Identify the Gap between targets and achievements;
Diagnose the reasons/problems for shortfall in achieving the targets, if any;
Suggest ways to overcome the problems; and
Assess the future prospects of SSA Programme.

Issues to be investigated:

i. **Quantitative Issues**
Whether the programme has achieved its goals quantitatively?
ii. **Qualitative Issues**
Whether the programme has achieved its goals qualitatively?

The quantitative issue investigated in the paper on the basis of empirical analysis while the quality issue investigated on the bases of literature/publications available on the subject matter.

The paper has drawn its conclusions on all India level and makes comparative analysis of some Indian states such as Gujarat, Haryana, Karnataka, Madhya Pradesh, Punjab and West Bengal. States were selected on the basis of their geographical location representing each zone of the country, viz. Northern, Western, Central, Eastern and Southern.

2 Targets and Achievements of SSA

Targets and achievements of SSA have been discussed under various components of SSA. These components are Budget and Expenditure, Opening of Schools, Construction of School building, Construction of Additional Classrooms, Training of Service Teachers, Distribution of Free Text Books, Establishment of Cluster and Block Resource Centres, Teachers' Appointments, etc. These are discussed as under:

Budget and Expenditure

In the beginning year of SSA (2001–2002), out of Rs. 49,837.06 lakhs of budget released, expenditure of only Rs. 17,204.06 (34.5%) was made at all India level. Among the states, the situation was also not so good. In states like Karnataka, Madhya Pradesh, Punjab and West Bengal, there was no expenditure made out of the released funds. Only in Gujarat and Haryana states, expenditure was made 59.7 and 5.8%, respectively. However, during 2003–2004, there was satisfactory progress in expenditure at the all India level. An expenditure of 61.7% was made which was higher than that of the previous years. Likewise, all states made good progress and tried for successful implementation of the SSA programme as shown in Table 1. Gujarat, Haryana and Karnataka made higher expenditures, i.e. 87.1, 88.2 and 89.3%, respectively, while the states like Punjab and West Bengal lagged behind in spending the amount, i.e. 35.7 and 14.5%, respectively. During the year 2004–2005, 85.3% of the available fund was spent at all India level. Among the states, the highest (87.1%) amount was spent by Karnataka followed by Madhya Pradesh (86.5%) and West Bengal (82.8%). The lowest fund was spent by Haryana (61.4%) followed by Gujarat (66.5%) and Punjab (76.3%) (Table 1).

During the year 2007–2008, good progress has been made and 72.9% of the approved outlay was spent at all India level. Among states, Karnataka was top in spending the amount (98.6%), which is higher than all India percentage followed by Gujarat (72.2%) and West Bengal (70.7%). Haryana state spent the lowest amount, i.e. 64.4% followed by Madhya Pradesh (67.4%), while Punjab (68.7%) spent below the all India percentage. During 2009–10, 77.1% budget was spent out of the total approved outlay at all India level. Punjab state spent the highest amount

Table 1 Funds released/available and expenditure under Sarva Shiksha Abhiyan (SSA) in selected states in India from 2001–02 to 2004–05 (Rs. in lakhs)

Sl. no.	State	2001–2002		2003–2004		2004–2005	
		Released	Expenditure	Available	Expenditure	Available	Expenditure
1.	Gujarat	2086.11	1246.16 (59.7)	16,906.21	14,717.12 (87.1)	28,029.32	18,632.5 (66.5)
2.	Haryana	365.02	21.20 (5.8)	10,341.71	9118.42 (88.2)	18,498.09	11,359.08 (61.4)
3.	Karnataka	2804.05	0	17,962	16,050.39 (89.3)	39,451.7	34,456.15 (87.1)
4.	Madhya Pradesh	2890.96	0	62,200.68	29,202.45 (46.9)	69,967.92	60,513.25 (86.5)
5.	Punjab	5709.33	0	12,439.85	4440.99 (35.7)	12,623.46	9636.55 (76.3)
6.	West Bengal	1618.70	0	45,321.62	6582.62 (14.5)	61,514.35	50,950.40 (82.8)
7.	All India	49,837.06	17,204.06 (34.5)	494,794.34	305,391.34 (61.7)	772,436.81	659,114.19 (85.3)

Note Figures within brackets indicate percentage of Targets achieved
Source Indiastat Website retrieved on 16th November, 2017

(99.6%) among the selected states followed by Madhya Pradesh (87.3%) and Karnataka (86.4%). Gujarat spent the lowest amount (72.2%) followed by West Bengal (74.9%) and Haryana (76.3%), which were below the all India percentage (Table 2).

During the year 2013–14, 83.7% of the allocated budget was spent at all India level. Among the states, Madhya Pradesh spent the highest amount (92.7%) followed by Punjab (86.9%) and Haryana (84.4%), which were above the all India percentage. Lowest spending was reported by Karnataka (77.5%) followed by West Bengal (78.4%) and Gujarat (80.7%), which were below the all India percentage. In the year 2014–15, 74.6% of the allocated fund was spent at all India level. Gujarat, Haryana, Karnataka and Punjab spent above the all India percentage. Gujarat spent the highest allocated amount (89.7%) and West Bengal the lowest (52.0%) (Table 3).

During the year 2015–16, 69.7% of the allocated amount was spent at all India level. Among the states, the highest amount (92.5%) was spent by Gujarat state which is much higher than other states and all India percentage followed by Karnataka (77.4%) and Punjab (66.6%). West Bengal spent the lowest amount (39.8%) followed by Madhya Pradesh (46.2%) and Haryana (47.2%). In the year 2016–17, 65.8% of the allocated amount under SSA was spent at all India level. Among the states, Karnataka spent the highest amount (68.5%) followed by Haryana (64.3%) and Punjab (56.6%), and lowest amount was spent by West Bengal (37.1%) followed by Gujarat (45.7%) and Madhya Pradesh (51.1%) (Table 4).

Outlay and Expenditure for Civil Works under SSA Programme

During the year 2007–08, 72.8% of targets were achieved at all India level in spending the approved outlay for civil works under SSA programme. Among the selected states, Karnataka achieved 100% target followed by Punjab (92.4%) and West Bengal (89.1%). Target achieved was lowest by Madhya Pradesh (37.9%) followed by Haryana (54.3%) and Gujarat (69.4%), which were below all India achievement. During the year 2008–09, almost same targets were achieved at all India level, i.e. 72.8% was spent of the approved outlay. Karnataka again spent 100% amount followed by Punjab (92.3%) and Gujarat (80.9%). Gujarat state improved its position. Lowest amount was spent by Haryana (52.0%) lower than the amount of the previous year followed by West Bengal (66.7%) and Madhya Pradesh (74.0%). During the year 2009–10, 66.9% targets were achieved in spending the approved outlay which is lower than the previous 2 years. Among the states, Punjab achieved 97.1% target followed by Karnataka (96.5%) and Gujarat (76.5%), which were above the all India percentage while the states such as Madhya Pradesh and West Bengal spent below the all India percentage.

It is observed from the analysis of the data that during each consecutive year the percentage of the amount spent on civil works has decreased from 72.8 to 66.9% at all India level. Four states improved their position in achieving their targets such as Madhya Pradesh, Punjab, Gujarat and Haryana, while Karnataka and West Bengal have gone down in achieving their targets (Table 5).

Table 2 Outlay approved and expenditure made under SSA in selected states in India from 2007–08 to 2009–10 (Rs. in lakhs)

Sl. no.	State	2007–2008		2008–2009		2009–2010	
		Approved outlay	Expenditure	Approved outlay	Expenditure	Approved outlay	Expenditure
1.	Gujarat	38,222.08	27,604.61 (72.2)	50,005.23	34,076.51 (68.1)	55,496	40,058.50 (72.2)
2.	Haryana	35,706.60	22,988.77 (64.4)	42,549.74	29,943.19 (70.4)	59,800.00	45,621.00 (76.3)
3.	Karnataka	69,746.00	68,739.93 (98.6)	96,014.08	89,806.77 (93.5)	96,104.08	83,028.29 (86.4)
4.	Madhya Pradesh	179,824.44	121,186.6 (67.4)	184,328.34	153,094.30 (83.1)	222,282	194,011.00 (87.3)
5.	Punjab	18,488.50	12,705.46 (68.7)	26,510.46	26,102.2 (98.5)	36,911.8	36,772.00 (99.6)
6.	West Bengal	143,876.18	101,725.2 (70.7)	173,779.34	124,384.2 (71.6)	216,762.6	162,540.00 (74.9)
7.	All India	2,135,955.99	1,556,557 (72.9)	2,410,946.99	1,905,652.00 (79.0)	2,727,210	2,103,527.00 (77.1)

Note Figures within brackets indicate percentage of Targets achieved
Source Indiastat Website retrieved on 16th November, 2017

Table 3 Fund allocation and expenditure made under SSA in selected states in India from 2013–14 to 2014–15 (Rs. in lakhs)

Sl. no.	State	2013–2014		2014–2015	
		Allocation	Expenditure	Allocation	Expenditure
1.	Gujarat	137,400.94	110,874.10 (80.7)	140,821.83	126,367.05 (89.7)
2.	Haryana	74,277.14	62,677.20 (84.4)	93,301.66	77,111.15 (82.6)
3.	Karnataka	118,216.08	91,639.10 (77.5)	133,978.35	103,546.41 (77.3)
4.	Madhya Pradesh	369,535.47	342,673.10 (92.7)	449,489.52	275,475.85 (61.3)
5.	Punjab	73,953.65	64,292.10 (86.9)	85,356.37	64,378.84 (75.4)
6.	West Bengal	362,860.28	284,664.50 (78.4)	476,627.83	250,940.93 (52.6)
7.	All India	4,771,745.1	3,994,752.30 (83.7)	5,613,726.43	4,190,986.17 (74.6)

Note Figures within brackets indicate percentage of Targets achieved
Source Indiastat Website retrieved on 16th November, 2017

Table 4 Fund allocation and expenditure made under SSA in selected states in India from 2015–16 to 2016–17 (Rs. in lakhs)

Sl. no.	State	2015–2016		2016–2017	
		Allocation	Expenditure	Allocation	Expenditure
1.	Gujarat	197,359.78	182,493.43 (92.5)	259,135.02	118,412.76 (45.7)
2.	Haryana	112,058.25	52,916.29 (47.2)	106,238.33	68,265.36 (64.3)
3.	Karnataka	154,580.82	119,636.52 (77.4)	187,896.99	128,686.02 (68.5)
4.	Madhya Pradesh	460,633.51	212,603.6 (46.2)	522,316.19	266,913.52 (51.1)
5.	Punjab	98,473.9	65,592.85 (66.6)	105,924.19	60,009.64 (56.6)
6.	West Bengal	429,479.85	170,734.26 (39.8)	468,849.08	173,945.6 (37.1)
7.	All India	6,341,298.94	4,422,718.23 (69.7)	7,424,868.77	4,885,824.93 (65.8)

Note Figures within brackets indicate percentage of Targets achieved
Source Indiastat Website retrieved on 16th November, 2017

Table 5 Outlay approved and expenditure made for civil works under SSA in selected states in India from 2007–08 to 2009–10 (Rs. in lakhs)

Sl. no.	States	2007–2008		2008–2009		2009–2010	
		Outlay approved	Expenditure	Outlay approved	Expenditure	Outlay approved	Expenditure
1.	Gujarat	17,274.02	11,986.94 (69.4)	17,304.83	14,003.44 (80.9)	17,634.44	13,489.89 (76.5)
2.	Haryana	9399.50	5101.26 (54.3)	14,357.66	7470.58 (52.0)	16,457.73	11,433.53 (69.5)
3.	Karnataka	23,681.81	23,681.82 (100.0)	30,239.44	30,247.64 (100.0)	19,877.15	19,186.75 (96.5)
4.	Madhya Pradesh	69,224.03	26,214.32 (37.9)	70,885.32	52,460.68 (74.0)	73,641.87	42,847.95 (58.2)
5.	Punjab	4189.80	3870.81 (92.4)	6404.87	5912.43 (92.3)	10,843.14	10,529.88 (97.1)
6.	West Bengal	69,006.16	61,484.52 (89.1)	44,568.95	29,725.40 (66.7)	63,030.75	37,924.74 (60.2)
7.	All India	766,638.56	558,453.58 (72.8)	807,492.58	599,469.99 (74.2)	773,583.77	517,531.41 (66.9)

Note Figures within brackets indicate percentage of Targets achieved
Source Indiastat Website retrieved on 16th November, 2017

Opening of Schools

During the year 2002–07, the target was set to open 240,072 schools in all states but only 186,985 (77.9%) schools were opened. No school was opened in West Bengal state. Punjab and Haryana state achieved 100% target in opening schools followed by Madhya Pradesh (76.8%) and Karnataka (67.3%). During 2002–07, Gujarat State achieved only 12.2% of target in opening schools. 77.9% of target was achieved at all India level during 2007–08, Haryana and Madhya Pradesh achieved 100% target followed by Punjab (50.0%) and West Bengal (24.9%). Data for Gujarat State was not available while Karnataka achieved nil. During 2010–11, there was a remarkable increase in achievement. 91.9% achievement was registered at all India level. 99.9% targets were achieved in Madhya Pradesh and West Bengal followed by Haryana (98.5%) and Karnataka (97.9%). Punjab achieved 92.6% of the target which was higher than its achievement during 2007–08 and lower than that during 2002–07.

It is observed from the analysis of the data that achievement of targets in opening schools at all India has shown an increasing trend from 77.9% in 2002–07 to 91.1% in 2010–11. States have also shown improvements in achieving targets. Data indicate quantitative success in achievement of targets (Table 6).

Teachers' Appointment

During the year 2002–07, 78.5% of target was achieved at all India level. Gujarat Haryana, Karnataka states achieved more than all India percentage of achievement,

Table 6 Targets and achievements in respect of opening of schools under SSA in selected states in India from 2002–07 to 2010–11

Sl. no.	States	2002–2007		2007–2008		2010–2011	
		T	A	T	A	T	A
1.	Gujarat	831	101 (12.2)	0	0 (0)	0	0 (0)
2.	Haryana	1993	1993 (100.0)	308	308 (100.0)	2598	2558 (98.5)
3.	Karnataka	8483	5708 (67.3)	1025	0 (0)	11,323	11,091 (97.9)
4.	Madhya Pradesh	49,990	38,385 (76.8)	1119	1119 (100.0)	54,321	54,289 (99.9)
5.	Punjab	1093	1093 (100.0)	10	5 (50.0)	2053	1901 (92.6)
6.	West Bengal	8122	0 (0)	1600	398 (24.9)	21,785	21,762 (99.9)
7.	All India	240,072	186,985 (77.9)	43,361	33,792 (77.9)	366,399	333,764 (91.1)

Note Figures within brackets indicate percentage of Targets achieved
T Target; *A* Achievement
Source Indiastat Website retrieved on 16th November, 2017

Table 7 Targets and achievement in respect of number of teachers appointments under SSA in selected states in India from 2002–07 to 2009–10

Sl. no.	States	2002–2007		2005–2006		2007–2008		2009–2010	
		T	A	T	A	T	A	T	A
1.	Gujarat	1848	1662 (89.9)	0	0	0	0	0	0
2.	Haryana	6104	6074 (99.5)	4629	2782 (60.8)	1980	0	0	0
3.	Karnataka	16,395	13,457 (82.1)	11,604	10,675 (92.0)	6009	6009 (100.0)	303	303 (100.0)
4.	Madhya Pradesh	90,477	80,316 (88.8)	89,072	86,874 (97.5)	2238	0	15	8 (53.3)
5.	Punjab	3070	1868 (60.8)	2660	1860 (69.9)	21	0	0	0
6.	West Bengal	87,881	30,333 (34.5)	73,536	17,018 (23.1)	4800	2314 (48.2)	2691	2282 (84.8)
7.	All India	1,012,103	794,535 (78.5)	770,316	354,859 (46.1)	122,840	69,905 (56.9)	8429	7765 (92.1)

Note Figures within brackets indicates percentage of Targets achieved
T Target; *A* Achievement
Source Indiastat Website retrieved on 16th November, 2017

while Punjab and West Bengal achieved less than the all India percentage. During 2005–06, targets achieved were very less, i.e. 46.1%. Haryana, Karnataka, Madhya Pradesh and Punjab achieved more and West Bengal achieved less than the all India percentage. During 2007–08, 56.9% of target was achieved at all India level, while Karnataka achieved more and West Bengal achieved less than the all India percentage. During 2009–10, 92.1% of target was achieved at all India level. West Bengal and Madhya Pradesh achieved less while Karnataka achieved higher than the all India percentage of target achieved (Table 7).

During the period 2009–10 to 2012–13, targets achieved in the appointment of teachers were very less, i.e. 33.0% in comparison of previous years at all India level. Among the states, Gujarat appointed the highest percentage of teachers, i.e. 75.1% followed by West Bengal (68.2%) and Punjab (45.7%). During the year 2010–11, 69.0% of target was achieved at all India level. Karnataka achieved the highest target, i.e. 89.3% followed by Haryana (80.1%) and Gujarat (75.1%). The lowest number of teachers were appointed in Madhya Pradesh (58.2%) followed by West Bengal (61.1%) and Punjab (68.1%). During 2013–14, 75.9% of target was achieved at all India level which is much higher than those of previous years. Among the states, highest target in appointing teachers was achieved by Punjab (100.0%) followed by Haryana (99.7%) and Madhya Pradesh (85.1%). During the year 2014–15, 79.9% of target was achieved at all India level. Among the states, Haryana achieved 86.4% of target followed by Karnataka (83.5%) and Gujarat (81.5%). The lowest target was achieved by West Bengal, i.e. 73.5% followed by Punjab (75.7%) and Madhya Pradesh (80.7%) (Table 8).

Table 8 Targets and achievement in respect of number of teachers appointments under SSA in selected states in India from 2009–10 to 2014–15

Sl. no.	States	2009–10 to 2012–13		2010–2011		2013–2014		2014–2015 (As on 30.8.15)	
		T	A	T	A	T	A	T	A
1.	Gujarat	20,052	15,052 (75.1)	20,052	15,052 (75.1)	58,688	48,751 (83.1)	53,688	43,751 (81.5)
2.	Haryana	4975	1062 (21.3)	11,157	8936 (80.1)	13,435	13,401 (99.7)	13,435	11,614 (86.4)
3.	Karnataka	11,299	2480 (21.9)	27,180	24,278 (89.3)	29,057	24,274 (83.5)	29,057	24,274 (83.5)
4.	Madhya Pradesh	85,948	19,615 (22.8)	168,888	98,287 (58.2)	173,855	147,972 (85.1)	178,928	144,372 (80.7)
5.	Punjab	14,839	6789 (45.7)	14,090	9594 (68.1)	14,090	14,090 (100.0)	14,090	10,661 (75.7)
6.	West Bengal	78,015	53,232 (68.2)	181,088	110,692 (61.1)	199,107	152,570 (76.6)	200,970	147,730 (73.5)
7.	All India	647,942	214,008 (33.0)	1,740,734	1,200,501 (69.0)	1,985,484	1,506,451 (75.9)	1,948,695	1,558,641 (79.9)

Note Figures within brackets indicate percentage of Targets achieved
T Target; *A* Achievement
Source Indiastat Website retrieved on 16th November, 2017

It is evident from the data that targets achieved in the appointment of teachers were minimum during the years 2009–10 to 2012–13 and it increased over a period of time, i.e. 79.9% during 2014–15 at all India level. More or less, the same situation was prevailing in states also. In some states, targets achieved were very high and on the other hand, in some states, the targets achievement was very low also.

Service Teachers' Training

Data in respect of Service Teachers' Training was available only for the year 2004–05. Analyses of data indicate that only 38.2% financial and 57.7% physical targets were achieved in respect of teachers' training at all India level. Among the states, highest financial targets were achieved by Haryana (68.5%) followed by Gujarat (48.1%) and Karnataka (42.9%). West Bengal achieved 26.9% while Punjab achieved very nominal financial target. Maximum Physical targets was achieved in Karnataka (100.0%) followed by Haryana (83.4%) and Madhya Pradesh (77.2%). Though Punjab achieved a very low financial target but achieved 62.5% physical target. West Bengal achieved 53.7% physical target which is lower than all India percentage. The lowest physical target was achieved by Gujarat state, i.e. 6.9% (Table 9).

Analyses of data on Service Teachers' Training indicate that there is no correlation between physical and financial target achievements. In states like Madhya Pradesh and Punjab, financial targets achieved were very low but physical targets achieved were much higher while it is reverse in the case of Gujarat.

Table 9 Targets and achievements in respect of physical and financial (Rs. in lakhs) progress of service teachers' training under SSA in selected states in India in 2004–05

Sl. no.	States	2004–2005			
		Targets		Achievements	
		Financial (Rs.)	Physical (No.)	Financial (Rs.)	Physical (No.)
1.	Gujarat	1828.97	130,642	880.08 (48.1)	9079 (6.9)
2.	Haryana	950.57	67,897	651.32 (68.5)	56,642 (83.4)
3.	Karnataka	2710.88	193,634	1162.19 (42.9)	193,634 (100.0)
4.	Madhya Pradesh	9295.28	97,480	605.06 (6.5)	75,295 (77.2)
5.	Punjab	1002.54	80,710	0.53 (0.1)	50,452 (62.5)
6.	West Bengal	1539.66	109,976	413.75 (26.9)	59,108 (53.7)
7.	All India	35,690.28	3,466,268	13,623.20 (38.2)	2,000,318 (57.7)

Note Figures within brackets indicate percentage of Targets achieved
Source Indiastat Website retrieved on 16th November, 2017

Setting up of Block Resource Centres

As per the available data of the years 2006 and 2010, more than 100%targets were achieved in setting up of Block Resource Centres (BRCs) at all India level and state level during the year 2006. Among selected states, all states except Madhya Pradesh (98.7%) achieved 100% targets. During the year 2010, a slight decrease in achievement has been observed from the year 2006. 95.5% target was achieved at all India level. Among the states, Haryana and West Bengal achieved more than 100% targets while Karnataka and Madhya Pradesh achieved hundred per cent targets. Gujarat and Punjab achieved slightly less than 100% target.

From the analyses of data, it can be concluded that BRCs were set up as per the targets. It shows good progress of work under SSA (Table 10).

Setting up of Cluster Resource Centres

Data on Establishment of Cluster Resource Centres (CRCs) indicate that 94.4% CRCs were established during the year 2006 which increased to 96.1% in 2010. State data indicates that 100% targets were achieved during the year 2006 in all the states except West Bengal in which only 33.8% target was achieved. During the year 2010, four states, viz. Haryana, Karnataka Madhya Pradesh and Punjab achieved 100% targets while Gujarat and West Bengal achieved 99.3 and 91.3% respectively.

Table 10 Targets and achievements in respect of block resource centres under SSA in selected states in India in 2006 and 2010

Sl. no.	States	As on 30 September 2006		As on 30 September 2010	
		T	A	T	A
1.	Gujarat	224	224 (100.0)	147	144 (97.9)
2.	Haryana	119	119 (100.0)	58	67 (115.5)
3.	Karnataka	176	176 (100.0)	90	90 (100.0)
4.	Madhya Pradesh	318	314 (98.7)	87	87 (100.0)
5.	Punjab	141	141 (100.0)	143	142 (99.3)
6.	West Bengal	707	707 (100.0)	250	269 (107.6)
7.	All India	6746	6771 (100.0)	3165	3024 (95.5)

Note Figures within brackets indicates percentage of Targets achieved
T Targets, *A* Achievements
Source Indiastat Website retrieved on 16th November, 2017

Table 11 Targets and achievements in respect of cluster resource centres under SSA in selected states in India in 2006 and 2010

Sl. no.	States	As on 30 September 2006		As on 30 September 2010	
		T	A	T	A
1.	Gujarat	3351	3351 (100.0)	1197	1189 (99.3)
2.	Haryana	1235	1235 (100.0)	565	565 (100.0)
3.	Karnataka	2269	2290 (100.0)	1411	1411 (100.0)
4.	Madhya Pradesh	6330	6330 (100.0)	613	613 (100.0)
5.	Punjab	1499	1499 (100.0)	1294	1300 (100.0)
6.	West Bengal	4212	1425 (33.8)	2734	2496 (91.3)
7.	All India	70,388	66,487 (94.4)	27,199	26,138 (96.1)

Note Figures within brackets indicates percentage of Targets achieved
T Targets, *A* Achievements
Source Indiastat Website retrieved on 16th November, 2017

Analytical review indicates that there was little shortfall in achieving the targets in both the years at all India level, while among the states, West Bengal was lagging behind (Table 11).

Free Text Books Distribution

According to the available data, during 2004–05, states like Haryana, Karnataka, Madhya Pradesh and Punjab achieved 100% targets while West Bengal achieved more than the set target. Data of Gujarat State of 2004–05 is not available. During the year 2006–07, Gujarat State achieved 86.0% target while all other states achieved 100% targets except Karnataka for which data are not available. Total target achieved during 2006–07 was 96.0% (Table 12).

Analyses of data indicate a little shortfall in target achievements which is only 4.0% at all India level in 2006–07. Quantitatively success rate is very high in this component.

Additional Classrooms

During the year 2002–07, Haryana State achieved more than the set target and Karnataka achieved 100% target. While Gujarat and Madhya Pradesh achieved 96.5 and 96.6% target, respectively. West Bengal achieved 93.8% in the construction of additional classrooms. 93.9% of target was achieved at all India level. During the year 2007–08 percentage of targets achieved has been decreased from 2002–07 periods in all the selected states as well as in India. Haryana and Punjab achieved 100% targets followed by Karnataka and Gujarat, i.e. 99.6 and 93.8%, respectively.

Table 12 Targets and achievements in respect of free text books to number of eligible children under SSA in selected states in India in 2004–05 and 2006–07

Sl. no.	States	2004–2005		2006–2007	
		Targets	Achievements	Targets	Achievements
1.	Gujarat	–	–	485,445	416,980 (86.0)
2.	Haryana	1,236,326	1,236,326 (100.0)	1,375,661	1,375,661 (100.0)
3.	Karnataka	304,671	304,671 (100.0)	0	0
4.	Madhya Pradesh	8,168,000	8,168,000 (100.0)	8,043,341	8,043,341 (100.0)
5.	Punjab	582,586	582,586 (100.0)	2,043,712	2,043,712 (100.0)
6.	West Bengal	621,350	4,379,887 (704.9)	3,120,658	3,120,658 (100.0)
7.	All India	71,182,407	70,491,639 (99.0)	66,870,135	63,991,054 (96.0)

Note Figures within brackets indicates percentage of Targets achieved
Source Indiastat Website retrieved on 16th November, 2017

West Bengal is lowest among the selected states. 87.9% of target was achieved in India during 2007–08. During 2010–11, West Bengal, Madhya Pradesh and Gujarat have shown an increase in achievements of targets as compared to that in 2007–08, while Haryana, Karnataka and Punjab have shown a decrease in their achievements. All India data has shown an increase in achievements as compared to 2007–08 periods (Table 13).

Analytical review of data indicates that some states achieved 100% targets while other states achieved little less. In India, a total of 93.8% target was achieved during 2010–11. The picture in this component in respect of target achievement is not so gloomy. But still, there is a need to fill the gap.

Drinking Water Facilities

According to the latest data available for the year 2009–10, targets achieved were very poor. 29.7% target was achieved at all India level. State-wise picture is also not so good. Gujarat State achieved highest 72.0% of target followed by Haryana (41.7%). West Bengal achieved only 3.0% of its stated target.

Analyses of data indicate that achievements of targets in drinking water facilities in schools were very poor (Table 14).

Toilet Facilities

As regards the construction of toilets, available data revealed that during the year 2006, 80.7% target was achieved at all India level. Among the states, highest target was achieved by Punjab (101.6%) followed by Gujarat (99.6%) and Madhya Pradesh (98.7%). The lowest target was achieved by West Bengal, i.e. 81.4%.

Table 13 Targets and achievements in respect of additional classrooms under SSA in selected states in India

Sl. no.	States	2002–2007		2007–2008		2010–2011	
		T	A	T	A	T	A
1.	Gujarat	14,270	13,775 (96.5)	7145	6705 (93.8)	30,157	29,973 (99.4)
2.	Haryana	10,126	11,158 (110.2)	4757	4757 (100.0)	24,162	23,342 (96.6)
3.	Karnataka	28,390	28,396 (100.0)	13,627	13,577 (99.6)	49,047	47,699 (97.3)
4.	Madhya Pradesh	37,052	35,792 (96.6)	15,559	13,986 (89.9)	113,993	109,530 (96.1)
5.	Punjab	13,702	13,394 (97.7)	4562	4561 (100.0)	22,122	19,952 (90.2)
6.	West Bengal	75,445	70,784 (93.8)	38,500	29,559 (86.8)	162,887	153,701 (94.4)
7.	All India	692,678	650,442 (93.9)	362,978	319,159 (87.9)	1,372,633	1,287,996 (93.8)

Note Figures within brackets indicates percentage of targets achieved
T Targets, *A* Achievements
Source Indiastat Website retrieved on 16th November, 2017

Table 14 Targets and achievements in respect of drinking water facilities under SSA in selected states in India

Sl. no.	States		2009–2010
		Targets	Achievements
1.	Gujarat	75	54 (72.0)
2.	Haryana	817	341 (41.7)
3.	Karnataka	0	0 (–)
4.	Madhya Pradesh	2024	0 (–)
5.	Punjab	0	0 (–)
6.	West Bengal	832	25 (3.0)
7.	All India	10,504	3119 (29.7)

Note Figures within brackets indicates percentage of targets achieved
Source Indiastat Website retrieved on 16th November, 2017

Table 15 Targets and achievements in respect of toilets under SSA in selected states in India

Sl. no.	States	As on 30-9-2006		2014–15	
		Targets	Achievements	Targets	Achievements
1.	Gujarat	8766	8727 (99.6)	773	103 (13.3)
2.	Haryana	15,518	13,693 (88.2)	0	0
3.	Karnataka	44,589	34,418 (77.2)	833	6 (0.7)
4.	Madhya Pradesh	41,171	40,652 (98.7)	15,529	6291 (40.5)
5.	Punjab	18,780	19,084 (101.6)	1463	469 (32.1)
6.	West Bengal	28,743	23,411 (81.4)	36,633	10,305 (28.1)
7.	All India	430,881	347,850 (80.7)	260,968	91,528 (35.1)

Note Figures within brackets indicates percentage of Targets
Source Indiastat Website retrieved on 16th November, 2017

Haryana and Karnataka achieved the targets of 88.2 and 77.2%, respectively. Targets achieved during the year 2014–15 show a very dismal picture in comparison to 2006. Only 35.1% target was achieved at all India level which is very less in comparison to the year 2006. Among the states, highest target was achieved by Madhya Pradesh (40.5%) followed by Punjab (32.1%) and West Bengal (28.1%). The lowest target was achieved by Karnataka, i.e. only 0.7%. Gujarat achieved only 13.3% target (Table 15).

Analyses of data conclude that targets achieved in respect of toilets are very poor in comparison to other components of SSA.

Construction of School Building

Data on the construction of school building were available for the year 2005–06, 2007–08 and 2010–11. During 2005–06, 94.5% of target was achieved at all India level. Among the states, Gujarat, Madhya Pradesh and Karnataka achieved higher targets than all India level, while Haryana and West Bengal achieved less than all India percentage. During 2007–08, 76.1% targets were achieved which is less than 2005–06. All states except West Bengal (42.0%) achieved more than all India percentage of achievement. States such as Haryana, Karnataka and Punjab achieved more than 100% target. During the year 2010–11, 93.3% target was achieved in the construction of school buildings. States such as Gujarat, Haryana, Karnataka and Punjab achieved more than all India achievement of targets, while Punjab and West Bengal achieved less than the all India achievement (Table 16).

Analyses of data indicate that among the 3 years, 2005–06 and 2010–11 targets were achieved more, while less target was achieved in 2007–08.

Table 16 Targets and achievements in respect of construction of school buildings under SSA in selected states in India

Sl. no.	States	2005–2006		2007–2008		2010–2011	
		T	A	T	A	T	A
1.	Gujarat	16	16 (100.0)	100	98 (98.0)	835	797 (95.4)
2.	Haryana	411	375 (91.2)	527	537 (101.9)	2284	2210 (96.8)
3.	Karnataka	616	614 (99.7)	743	763 (102.7)	3736	3733 (99.9)
4.	Madhya Pradesh	5524	5524 (100.0)	11,037	9695 (87.8)	43,703	43,703 (100.0)
5.	Punjab	NA	NA (–)	88	89 (101.1)	1486	1373 (92.4)
6.	West Bengal	215	180 (83.7)	288	121 (42.0)	14,362	7501 (52.2)
7.	All India	35,012	33,089 (94.5)	62,832	47,817 (76.1)	282,376	263,320 (93.3)

Note Figures within brackets indicates percentage of targets achieved
Source Indiastat Website retrieved on 16th November, 2017

3 Gaps in Targets and Achievements

It is evident from the available data that quantitatively there was a minimum gap in targets and achievements. In majority of the years since 2001, not much gap has been observed in targets and achievements. Most of the targets were achieved satisfactorily and success rate was very high in most of the targets in most of the years. It can be concluded that SSA programme has fulfilled its quantitative goals. In the beginning of the year, speed of achieving the targets was slow due to administrative reasons. During the years 2001–02, 2003–04 and 2004–05, lot of funds allocated was found unspent. After 2004–05, the speed of expenditure was increased. During 2006–07, 2007–08, 2008–09 and 2009–10, expenditure has reached up to 79.0% of the total funds allocated. The expenditure during 2013–14 and 2015–16 has been increased up to 83.7% at all India level as well as states also. In other components also, targets were achieved satisfactorily and gaps were minimum. Among the selected states in India, targets were achieved satisfactorily. In some years, in some states, 100% or more than 100% targets were achieved, which was a remarkable achievement.

In addition to budget and expenditure gaps, gaps in other components of SSA were also identified which are discussed as under:

- Very less target was achieved in respect of drinking water facilities, which is only 29.7%. Progress in the work of drinking water facility was very poor.

- Target achieved in the construction of additional classrooms was very much satisfactory. There was a very low gap between target and achievement, i.e. 6.2% only during 2010–11.
- Gap between target and achievement in opening of schools was also very low, i.e. only 8.9% during the year 2010–11.
- There is also a very small gap between target and achievement in the formation of Cluster Resources Centres. Only 3.9% of gap was identified during 2009–10. Likewise, in the formation of Blocks Resources Centres, only 4.5% of gap was identified at all India level during 2009–10.
- Huge gap was identified in achieving the targets in the construction of toilets, i.e. 64.9% targets during 2014–15 at all India level. But during 2005–06, the gap was not so high, i.e. only 19.3%.
- Only 4.0% gap was identified between target and achievement in respect of distribution of free textbooks during 2006–07. This gap was very narrow during 2004–05, i.e. only 0.8%.
- Gap between target and achievement was very high in 'training of teachers' component. During 2004–05, 42.3% of physical target and 61.8% of financial target were not achieved.
- Very narrow gap was identified in construction of school building. Only 6.7% of target was not achieved during 2010–11 at all India level.

4 Diagnostic Analyses of the Reasons/Problems in Shortfall in Achieving the Targets of SSA

The targets achieved in SSA were not so unsatisfactory. Gaps identified in various components were by and large narrow due to serious efforts made by government agencies to make the programme successful. But 100% targets were not achieved or in some of the components targets were not achieved fully. The paper tried to identify the reasons/problems for such an occurrence. Various studies have been undertaken in the past to evaluate the SSA programme. These studies highlighted various problems/constraints of SSA programme. Some of them have been discussed here.

Study conducted by Programme Evaluation Organisation (PEO) of erstwhile Planning Commission and presently NITI Aayog (2010) cited that regular teachers were not recruited for several years (due to court cases, weak state finances), there was lack of adequate number of teachers' training institutions in some areas, especially in the State of West Bengal, and teachers were unwilling to be posted in rural areas.

There is no separate permanent staff for SSA implementation at district level. District level staff, especially in Haryana, held additional charges. Inadequate manpower in Block Resource Centres and Cluster Resource Centres affects monitoring and capacity building.

Late disbursement and late receipt of funds lead to non-utilisation of funds at the end of the year. There are weak linkages in monitoring and supervising of SSA at district level. There is no clarity on roles, responsibilities of BRCs/CRCs (Programme Evaluation Organisation, Planning Commisssion 2010).

Comptroller and Auditor General (CAG) of India conducted an audit in Rajasthan State in 2007 which clearly indicates that delay in allotment of funds, shortfall in achieving targets, lack of basic facilities and unreliable child tracking system are some of the reasons of poor implementation of the programme. The report pointed out that thousands of schools in seven districts of Rajasthan in which the field study was conducted did not have basic facilities like building, drinking water, electricity, girl's toilets or playgrounds. The report also stated that financial management of the programme in the state was deficient as there were cases of excess charges of funds (Comptrollers and Auditor General of India 2007).

There is a lack of accountability under SSA which manifests itself in poor learning outcome and poor attendance rates of teachers (Abhimanuas.com/blogs/important-issues-detailed%20article/7310/sarva-shiksha-abhiyan–analyses).

Another problem lies in the provision of civil works which is not properly implemented by the concerned authorities as per the norms of SSA (Shodganga.inflibnet.ac.in/bitstream/1063/39731/9/09-chapter%201pdf).

Misuse of funds and lack of monitoring have resulted in making one of the government's most ambitious schemes of universal education a colossal failure, as reported in *India Today* (2006).

Diversion of funds in another scheme, underspending and non-release of funds in Madhya Pradesh in 2002–04 was reported in CAG Audit. States have routinely underfunded the SSA. Most of the states are adopting less qualified temporary shikshakarmi as teachers (www.thehidubussinesstimes.com/todays-paper/tp—,cag-terms—/article%201743449).

Lack of regular communication between central government, state governments and below is hampered by successful implementation of the programme (Singh and Gera 2015).

Lack of infrastructural facilities such as toilet, drinking water and classroom is the bottleneck in the implementation of the SSA programme.

Evaluation study conducted by the Department of Economic and Statistical Analysis of Haryana Government (2009) highlighted some of the shortcomings in the implementation of SSA in the state such as Non-utilisation of released funds; Violation of guidelines as well as norms fixed for implementation of the programme; lack of timely supply of free textbook to the targeted students; non-execution of Civil works as per the requirements; lack of maintaining of records relating to monitoring; lack of coordination between the members of Panchayati Raj Institutions and School teachers in execution of various activities of SSA; and lack of appropriate qualified and effective teachers' learning material and teachers' training (Government of Haryana, Department of Economic and Statistical Analysis 2009).

Study conducted by United Nations Educational, Scientific and Cultural Organisation (UNESCO) (2015) argued that states have not made optimum use of the technical expertise of local resources which have a wealth of experience (UNESCO 2015). A study conducted by Madhya Pradesh SSA (2017) observed that absenteeism is a more serious problem in rural areas in primary section (Sarva Shiksha Abhiyan Government of Madhya Pradesh 2017).

5 Strategies for Solution of Problems/Shortcomings and Way Forward

Many studies have been conducted in the past which suggested several strategies to remove the bottlenecks/problems of SSA in India. One such study was conducted by PEO of erstwhile Planning Commission and presently NITI Aayog (2010) which suggested that: recruitment of teachers to fill vacancies in minimum time; timely release of funds at all levels from central government to state governments and lowest level of governance; child-friendly curriculum and system of assessment to move from examination based to continuous appraisal; and also, there is a need to improve monitoring and supervision at all levels (Programme Evaluation Organisation, Planning Commission 2010). Regular monitoring at different levels by different agencies can energise the community to accept more responsibility towards schools.

Increasing the number of quality teachers, improving school and education system management, reaching disadvantaged and marginalised groups—all this will require more intensive and innovative ways to deliver learning opportunities. More funds should be invested in basic education to increase the quality of education such as the curriculum reform, the pedagogical supports and the pedagogical practices. Central government should have regular communication and interaction with states and UTs up to the lowest level of the unit, i.e. school (Singh and Gera 2015).

A study conducted by the Department of Economic and Statistical Analyses, Government of Haryana (2009) recommended that guidelines and norms laid down for implementation of the various activities under SSA should be strictly adhered to; the funds earmarked for the SSA should be 100% utilised to achieve the desired goal; any types of incentives in kind or cash should be provided with, at the beginning of the academic session; civil works like construction of school rooms. Urinals, toilets should be taken up as per requirement; coordination between members of Village Education Committee (VEC) and school teacher should be maintained so that the impediments coming in the execution of any activities can be avoided; teaching-learning material should be prepared keeping in view the prescribed syllabus of Class I–VIII and should be used while teaching the students and should not be stored in drawing rooms as well as halls; and the monitoring mechanism should be made effective as per provisions. Monitoring teams at state level, district level and block level should be constituted and records to this effect should be maintained for follow-up action (Government of Haryana, Department of Economic and Statistical Analyses 2009).

UNESCO case study of Madhya Pradesh and Rajasthan (2015) recommended that the EFA goals cannot be achieved through 'quick fix' strategies, but instead need long term, focused interventions (UNESCO 2015). To reduce absenteeism in rural area, the study conducted by Madhya Pradesh SSA (2017) suggested that school complex should be made more attractive; teachers should establish a good rapport with students and parents and bringing facilities in schools may be arranged (Sarva Shiksha Abhiyan, Government of Madhya Pradesh 2017).

While working on the suggestions and recommendations of various studies conducted in the past, Department of School Education and Literacy, Ministry of Human Resource Development, Government of India has taken some initiatives for Improvement of Quality of Elementary Education under SSA programme.

6 Recent Initiatives Taken by Government of India for Improvement of Quality of Elementary Education

Main objectives of these initiatives are to bring all students to one common platform; to share experience and learn from each other; to provide opportunities to the teaching fraternity to adopt better and more effective practices and to install a spirit of sharing, caring and togetherness. The following initiatives were taken by Government of India for improvement of quality of elementary education.

Grade-wise learning Goals and National Achievement Survey were two major steps taken by Government of India to improve the elementary education in India. Simultaneously, emphasis will be given on effective implementation of continuous and comprehensive evaluation of students in all schools and remedial classes for weak students. All school-going children has been linked up with Aadhar for effective monitoring of students in their academic progress and other benefits. Simultaneously all teachers were also linked up with Aadhar to prevent bogus teachers in the system. School location mapping website was also launched which shows the location of all schools on a map of India. Department of school education and literacy framed guidelines for partnership between schools and is preparing guidelines for rationalising and positive consolidation of small schools. Evaluation of teacher's performance in government-aided schools is being developed by National Council of Education and Training (NCERT) and training calendar for Head Master's training has been prepared by National University of Educational Planning and Administration (NUEPA). Use of E-governance was enhanced to facilitate faster and efficient decision-making. Guidelines are being framed for creation of separate cadre of school headmaster/principals in all states and UTs. Minimum tenure of teachers in one school has been advised in all States and UTs. Study on standardise all data definition, methodology of collecting all data and identifying critical data gap has been initiated. A plan is being finalised by NCERT, in consultation with Pandit Sundarlal Sharma Central Institute of Vocational Education (PSSCIVE), Bhopal for extension of scheme for vocationalisation at upper primary level. Stress was given on regular communication and interaction with States and UTs. In this regard, Secretary School Education and Literacy, Government of India communicated with Chief Secretaries of all States and UTs provided a letter dated 17 and 30 September 2016 on the national level reform agenda to improve the quality of schools education and performance of class 5 students in National Achievement Survey (Government of India, MHRD 2017a).

7 Subprogrammes Under SSA

The department of School Education and literacy also initiated subprogrammes under SSA to improve the quality of elementary education. The subprogrammes are as follows[2]:

The '**Padhe Bharat Badhe Bharat**' (PBBB) is a subprogramme of the SSA. In classes I and II, focusing on foundational learning in early grades with an emphasis on reading, writing and comprehension and Mathematics. States and UTs have been implementing specific interventions such as ABL in Tamil Nadu, Nalli Kali in Karnataka, Praya in Gujarat. Steps have been taken to develop specific teacher training modules for teachers teaching students in classes I and II. Punjab, Meghalaya and Delhi have introduced programmes for strengthening teaching of mathematics in classes I and II; in Sikkim, schools have set up reading corners for children in the foundational classes through support from community members.

The **Rashtriya Avishkar Abhiyan** (RAA) scheme was launched as a subprogramme under the SSA by Late Dr. A. P. J. Abdul Kalam, which aims to motivate and engage children in the age group of 6–18 years in Science, Mathematics and Technology by observation, experimentation, inference drawing and model building, through both inside and outside classroom activities. Schools have been adopted for mentoring by Institutions of Higher Education like IITs, IISERs and NITs. In some states, students have been taken for exposure visits to factories, research hub. Science and Mathematics clubs are being formed at the school level, and students are participating in competitions and exhibitions to showcase their innovations in Mathematics, Science and Technology.

Vidyanjali is a subprogramme under the SSA launched to enhance community and private sector involvement in Government-run elementary schools across the country under the overall aegis of the SSA. The aim of the programme is to strengthen implementation of co-scholastic activities in government schools through services of volunteers. So far, 3306 volunteers registered themselves for the

[2]As per the December 2016 press release by Ministry of Human Resource Development, Government of India (MHRD 2016).

programme creating 10,443 activities to be conducted in schools; 841 volunteers have gone to school and conducted activities (Government of India, MHRD 2017a).

8 Future Prospects

Despite the shortcomings of the programme, future prospects of SSA are bright in view of illiteracy rate of the young children as well as growing population in the age group 6 years and above. SSA programme is highly required in India with certain reforms. Shortcomings/bottlenecks of the programme should be removed with strong rides. Restrictions and regular monitoring are one ways to enhance the effectiveness of the programme. Transparent system must be the prime factor to improve the functioning of the programme. Regular strict auditing and follow-up action are also helpful in successful implementation of the programme. Efforts should be made for timely release of funds and funds must not be misutilised and diverted to other works. Civil works and infrastructure facilities make the programme successful in the future. Regular teachers should be appointed as per the norms and training should be imparted to them. Targets should be achieved maximum 100% in all components of SSA. Pupil–teacher ratio should be maintained. Teachers should make efforts to admit all eligible children to school and ensure that there is no subsequent dropout.

Quality is the biggest challenge for the SSA. Quality of teacher's training is an important issue. Quality of learning standard has to be improved so that children may not go to private tuitions; it clearly indicates that quality of education in school is not up to the mark (Sarva Shiksha Abhiyan (SSA) 2014).

UNESCO study (2015) in its midterm assessment of SSA revealed relatively poor progress in terms of quality improvement. The study recommended renewed focus on the quality of education in the second phase of SSA (UNESCO 2015). Quantitatively, targets have been achieved more or less satisfactorily but quality aspect lags behind. For the improvement of quality, several initiatives have been taken by the Government of India; these initiatives should be strictly adhered to.

Good results of initiatives taken on quality improvement have been noticed. The study conducted on SSA programme in Tripura State (2017) revealed that remarkable change has been found in the school infrastructure, dropout has been reduced remarkably, gender gap is almost declined, success rate is gradually improving, repetition rate is on the declining trend and there is a gradual increase in the transition rate. Another study conducted in Tripura state observed several causes of poor academic performance of students such as lack of quality and trained teacher, lack of motivation of teachers, lack of proper inspection and supervision of schools and no detention policy (Sarva Siksha Abhiyan, Governement of Tripura 2017).

9 Conclusions

On the basis of analysis of data and review of literature, the paper articulates the following major conclusions:

1. In view of 26% of illiterate population (32.3 crore) in India, there is still a need to continue the programme like Sarva Shiksha Abhiyan as a regular programme or till the alternate regular system be evolved to achieve the goal of universalisation of elementary education.
2. Quantatively, SSA programme has been quite successful and this fact has been supported by many research and evaluation studies conducted by reputed organisations like Indian Institute of Management (IIM), Ahmedabad.
3. Quality is a major concern in successful implementation of the SSA programme. Qualitatively, the programme has not been quite successful. Study conducted by IIM, Ahmedabad and other organisations made a serious observation on quality issues.
4. To improve the quality of the programme, the government has taken many initiatives due to which, improvement in quality of the programme is visible. More initiatives are needed to implement the programme successfully covering all the qualitative aspects.

In brief, the following conclusions have been emerged:

- Continuation of SSA programme is very much needed in view of the Indian education scenario and it should be continued as a regular programme to achieve UEE;
- Quantitatively, the programme achieved a higher success rate, but qualitatively, further improvement is needed;
- For improvement of the quality of the programme, various measures have already been taken by the Government of India from the year 2017 and the result of these initiatives is also visible.

References

Abhimanuas.com/blogs/important-issues-detailed%20article/7310/sarva-shiksha-abhiyan–analyses. Retrieved on dated 12.12.2017.

Comptrollers and Auditor General of India. (2007). *Rajasthan Sarva Shiksha Abhiyan—Shortage of targets*. Quoted from the website: archieve.indianexpress.com/…/rajasthan-sarva-shiksha-abhiyan-short%20of%20target-cag/276. Retrieved on 12.12.2017.

District Primary Education Department, Kaithal, Haryana. (2017). *Introduction to SSA*. Accessed from website: kaithal.gov.in/pdf/education/pdf/ssa/pdf. Dated 9.11.2017.

Government of Haryana, Department of Economic and Statistical Analysis. (2009). *Evaluation study of Sarva Shiksha Abhiyan, Chandigarh*.

Government of India, MHRD. (2017a). *Sarva Shiksha Abhiyan (SSA)*. Accessed from the website: pib.nic.in/newsite/print%20release/aspr. Retrieved on dated 25.9.2017.

Government of India, MHRD. (2017b). *Elementary education*. Accessed from the website: mhrd.gov.in/overview-se. Retrieved on dated 12.12.2017.

India Today. (2006). *Misuse of funds, lack of monitoring results one of the UPAs most ambitious scheme of universal education remaining a colossal failure*. Quoted from: indiatoday.intoday.in/story/misuse-of-funds-results-in-sarva-shiksha-abhiyan-failure///180453.html. Accessed on 12.12.2017.

Indian Institute of Management, Ahmedabad. (2006). *Shiksha Sangam—Innovation under the SSA*. Quoted from the website: digitallearning.eletsonline.com/2001/10/sarva-shiksha-abhiyan-brings%20innovation. Accessed on dated 26.9.2017.

Issues of India. (2014). *Sarva Shiksha Abhiyan: We should also see the positive side of SSA*. Accessed from website: https://www.socialissuesindia.worldpress.com/—/sarva-shiksha-abhiyan-ssa. Dated 9.11.2017.

MHRD. (2016). *Initiatives and achievements of Ministry of Human Resource Development, year end review 2016*. Ministry of Human Resource Development (MHRD), Government of India, 30 December; also accessible at http://pib.nic.in/newsite/PrintRelease.aspx?relid=155999.

Primary Education Department, RiBhoi District. (2017). *Sarva Shiksha Abhiyan—RiBhoi District*. Accessed from the website: http://ribhoi.gov.in/old/SSA/. Retrieved on dated 6.11.2017.

Programme Evaluation Organisation, Planning Commission. (2010). *Evaluation report on Sarva Shiksha Abhiyan*. PEO Report No.: 203, New Delhi. Quoted from the website: planning commission.nic.in/reposts/peoreport/peo-ssa2016pdf.

Registrar General and Census Commissioner of India. (2011). *Population census 2011*. New Delhi: Government of India. Extracted from the website: www.census2011.co.in. Accessed on dated 11.12.2017.

Sarva Shiksha Abhiyan (SSA). (2014). *A critical review of SSA*. SSA report. Quoted from website: socialissuesindia.files.wordpress.com/2014/03/ssa-report-2014 pdf.

Sarva Shiksha Abhiyan Government of Madhya Pradesh. (2017). *Research and evaluation, Bhopal*. Accessed from the web site: www.ssa.mp.gov.in. Dated 13.12.2017.

Sarva Siksha Abhiyan, Government of Tripura. (2017). *Research, Evaluation, Monitoring and Supervision (REMS), Agratala*. Accessed from the web site: www.ssatripura.com/mnuitems/13/researchwork.pdf. Dated 13.12.2017.

http://shodhganga.inflibnet.ac.in/bitstream/10603/115320/10/10_chapter%201.pdf. Retrieved on Dated 12.12.2017.

Singh, H., & Gera, M. (2015). Difficulties faced by teachers in successful implementation of Sarva-Shiksha-Abhiyan. *Indian Journal of Educational Studies, 1*, ISSN No. 2349-6908.

UNESCO. (2015). *Promising EFA practices in the Asia-Pacific Region, India. Sarva Shiksha Abhiyan, case study, Bangkok*. ISBN:978-92-223-514-7 (Print Version).

www.thehidubussinesstimes.com/todays-paper/tp—,cag-terms—/article%201743449. Retrieved on 12.12.2017.

Part 3

Tribal Research Institutes (TRIs) Revisited: An Outcome Perspective Analysis

A. P. William Wordsworth and Yogesh Kumar

1 Introduction

As the socio-political and economic environment is rapidly changing, countries are shifting towards regulatory mode of governance. However, just as the political affluence and patronage remain active in favour of people because of the existence of adult franchise, welfare domain remains an untouched area in democracies. In India, especially in the area of tribal welfare and development, all the while governments have adopted fair policies and practices, poverty level among tribal communities remains high as compared to other social groups[1] (Table 1). The demand for progressive changes in planning and much attention on implementation is widening. Tribal Research Institutes (TRIs) were instituted to diagnose the problems of tribal communities at grass-roots level.

The TRIs play multiple roles in bringing changes in the life of tribal communities through planning inputs at different levels. The first TRI came into being in the early 1950s to reflect the principle of Panchasheel by Jawaharlal Nehru, and eventually many more were established in different states, and the latest one started in 2018. At present, TRI scheme is considered one of the major activities of the Ministry of Tribal Affair.[2]

[1]The data reveals that the overall incidence of poverty has been reduced by more than half over the period from 1993–94 to 2011–12. There has been a more rapid decline in poverty since 2004–05. At the aggregate level, the decline in the poverty has been from 45.7% in 1993–94 to 37.7% in 2004–05 to 22% in 2011–12.

[2]Albeit MOTA supports to Anthropological Survey of India (ASI), Universities, research institutions and independent researches for pursuing on socio-cultural, anthropological, economic and related issues on tribal subjects besides TRIs.

A. P. William Wordsworth · Y. Kumar (✉)
National Institute of Labour Economics Research and Development, Delhi, India
e-mail: yogesh.vaish@gmail.com

A. P. William Wordsworth
e-mail: a.p.williamwordsworth@gmail.com

NILERD, *Reflecting on India's Development*,
https://doi.org/10.1007/978-981-13-1414-8_10

Table 1 Incidence of poverty between tribals and non-tribals

Year	1993–94			2004–05			2011–12		
Group	Rural	Urban	Total	Rural	Urban	Total	Rural	Urban	Total
Tribals	**65.9**	**41.1**	**63.7**	**62.3**	**35.5**	**60.0**	**45.3**	**24.1**	**43.0**
Non-tribals	48.4	31.6	43.9	39.4	25.4	35.6	22.9	13.3	20.0
Total	50.3	31.9	45.7	41.8	25.7	37.7	25.4	13.7	22.0

Source 50th, 61st and 68th Rounds, NSSO, Government of India

Government of India has recognized TRIs as knowledge and capacity building institutions for the tribal communities.[3] As of now there are 20 TRIs working in different states and UTs.[4] Despite these institutes came into existence at different periods, there are no temporal or spatial distinctions among the TRIs. Although the purpose of the TRIs is to ameliorate the overall living standard of tribal communities through better planning inputs from time to time, the absence of a unifying body, for research guidance and coordination, unduly delays and deviates from its main focus. Albeit the research works at TRIs encompasses variety of areas include socio-anthropological, cultural, behavioural, linguistic and ethnic aspects of tribal communities, besides administration as a major work, emphasis on livelihood aspects seems to be very little.

The efforts of TRIs are apparently a 'piecemeal', 'ad hoc' and random basis as there is no coordinated and standard research practices exist unlike the NSSO or CSO doing at national level. In a way he activities of TRIs are apparently far from correlating to or reflecting the reality of tribal life at grass-roots level. As the research confined to state or local area, there are no comparable standards at national level. A major problem faced by these TRIs is that integration of their activities from within and outside the state. As TRIs are engaged in standalone practices, not much attention is being made on standardization and integration at national level. Even if some common objectives are being fulfilled, they are yet to insinuate into a national platform particularly in research. In the absence of a dedicated '**Lead Research Centre**' for research guidance and directions (in addition to monitoring and supervision), the concomitant effort across TRIs seems to have been suffering.

This supposition emerges from the verification of qualitative data on TRIs vis-à-vis the level of tribal (human) resource development achieved or suffered across states. Somehow TRIs have overly focused on art, artefacts and cultural subjects, and a blurred focus on research. Understanding the nuances of economic disparities and poverty deprivation and appropriate intervention are the main thrust for

[3]Report of the High Level Committee on Socioeconomic, Health and Educational Status of Tribal Communities of India, Ministry of Tribal Affairs, Government of India, May, 2014.

[4]Twenty-one TRIs are, viz. Andhra Pradesh, Assam, Chhattisgarh, Jharkhand, Gujarat, Himachal Pradesh, Karnataka, Kerala, Madhya Pradesh, Maharashtra, Manipur, Orissa, Rajasthan, Tamil Nadu, Telangana, Tripura, West Bengal, Uttar Pradesh, Sikkim including the latest one in Jammu and Kashmir on 50:50 sharing basis between States and Centre. The TRI in the Union Territory Andaman and Nicobar Islands, in contrast, 100% grant is from Centre.

progress of tribal development. Even so, despite the serious claims and counter-claims, the relevance of TRIs cannot be obsolete.[5] Apart from some TRIs as an institute outlived much longer, with little or no accomplishment of goals, their deviations from its main focus require a complete revival. The need of this hour is to reshape its role and reinvigorate overall functioning of TRIs in order to cater to the complete well-being of the tribal societies.

TRIs as an institutions attempt to specialize and augment the tribal development process were established at different phases. Though the TRIs have same intent and objectives, TRIs at all the states were not created concurrently. Some of the States and UTs till date have not established their TRIs, which raises doubts about the over all tribal developments in the county.

In the initial years, soon after the establishment of TRIs the tribal communities were geographically scattered across unknown fields. The governance machinery itself was still-developing, complete enumeration of population and distinguishing the tribal communities from others were apparently a herculean exercise. Thus, the first-generation TRIs that were started in 50s had to deal with the difficult tasks of innumerable issues around tribal communities. However, *of late* as the intervention of Information and Communication Technology (ICT), the outlook now has changed the notion of time, distances and means of communication altogether. The twenty-first-century way of planning, evaluation and implementation of programmes and schemes have pruned away the age-old differences and practices, have brought in a system of functioning in a uniform and equal manner based on smart governance[6] principles. (Smart = Simple, Moral also Measurable, Accountable, Responsive and Transparent). Despite the working of some TRIs for a long time, there was no uniform pattern emerged or any progressive changes have taken place at the level of the 'administer' and the 'administered', i.e. MOTA and TRIs. Even if the developmental interventions for tribal development are taking place on multiple fronts, viz. central and states governments, NGOs, philanthropies, CSR activities, missionaries, including international aids etc., the socio-economic development of the tribes have not witnessed any measurable heights. These burning issues can never be out of focus for the TRIs rather than harbouring on anything else.

Similarly, there are no thematic differences between the TRIs established in the 1950s and now, as all the TRIs are experimenting with the same objectives and still have not located or rediscovered themselves to see substantial outcomes, apparently. Since all the TRIs follow objectives ditto, there seems no progressive milestones crossed. The 'ought to be' role played by TRIs, for the tribal community, is to (help in) eliminate the hindrances and make suggestions for

[5]TRI functions as prescribed by MOTA are (a) as body of knowledge and research (b) support evidence-based policy, planning and legislations (c) undertake capacity building of tribal people and personnel and institution associated with tribal affairs and (d) would be responsible for dissemination of information and creation of awareness.

[6]The convergence of good governance principles and processes, enabled by smart technologies, are the essential elements of Smart Governance required in a Smart Nation. Smart Governance in a Smart Nation A Singapore perspective.

socio-economic planning and development, but are now ostensibly being criticized for losing its focus.[7] Planning Commission (2013) observes that the potentialities of these institutions are not being harnessed fully.[8]

With this background, the current paper is organized into five sections with 'Introduction' as the first section. While the second section focuses upon the 'Generations of TRIs' delineate three categories of TRIs came into being in a different era, and the third section would discuss on the 'Locus and Focus of TRIs'. The fourth section is on the 'Analysis of TRIs' and the last and final section is on Summary and Recommendations.

2 Generations of TRIs

TRIs need to be classified into different cohorts for the purpose of understanding its impact during particular phase on the target group, and the manner of its own development from within. Despite the scope and coverage of problems of tribes varied from state to state and from time to time, invariably all the TRIs came into being in different generations, understanding the problems of the tribal communities remains at rudimentary stage as there are no significant milestones crossed.

The generations of TRIs thus can be classified into three distinct phases, viz. (i) Post-Independence era (1947), (ii) Post-States reorganization era (1965) and (iii) Post-Economic liberalization era (1991). These classifications enhance the understanding and gauge the levels of outreach of TRIs. These classifications also differentiate the progressive phases of development of TRIs from within and the objectives accomplished thereon. Though the generations and time dimension are changing constantly, the timeline for the TRIs remains static (Table 2).

The first-generation TRIs: In the Post-1947 Independence era, coincided with the first five-year plan (1951–1956), TRIs came into being in the four states like Odisha, Jharkhand (Bihar), Madhya Pradesh and West Bengal, respectively, in the year 1952, 1953, 1954 and 1955. While there seem to be no particular criteria adopted for selection of these states for setting up of TRIs, the benchmark for the selection of states undoubtedly should have been the highest concentration of tribal population in a state. For instance, West Bengal having 4.7% of tribal population surpassing all other states wherein the presence of tribal population is significantly high had managed to have a TRI. As per 1951 census (Table 3), baring the north-eastern states like Assam (with 19.19% tribal), Manipur (with 33.63% tribal) and Tripura (with 30.09 tribal) which were having highest concentration of tribal communities, the states of Odisha (with 11% tribal), Bihar (Jharkhand (with 10.07 tribal), Madhya Pradesh (with 11.66% tribal) and West Bengal (with 4.7% tribal)

[7]MOTA Minutes 9 July 2015, https://tribal.nic.in/DivisionsFiles/NCST-RM/6minutesofMeeting Research.pdf (accessed on 25 September 17).

[8]Twelfth Five-Year Plan (2012–2017), Social Sectors Volume-III, Planning Commission, Government of India.

Table 2 Generations/phase of TRIs

	Classification	Year
First-generation TRIs: Post-Independence Era, 1947		
1	Odisha	1952
2	Jharkhand (in united Bihar)	1953
3	Madhya Pradesh	1954
4	West Bengal	1955
Second-generation TRIs: Post-States Reorganisation Act, 1956		
5	Andhra Pradesh	1962
6	Gujarat	1962
7	Maharashtra	1962
8	Assam	1963
9	Rajasthan	1964
10	Kerala	1970
11	Tripura	1970
12	TN	1983
13	Uttar Pradesh	1987
14	Manipur	1987
Third-Generation TRIs: Post-Economic liberalization, 1991		
15	Himachal Pradesh	1994
16	Chhattisgarh	2004
17	Karnataka	2011
18	A&N Island	2014
19	Telangana	2014
20	Sikkim	2016
21	J & K	2018

Source Authors own compilation from TRI websites and input from officials in MOTA

were granted TRIs, although states like Maharashtra wherein (Coorg (with 9.19% tribal) and Bombay (with 9.43% tribal) equally had significant percentage of tribal communities did not get TRIs unlike West Bengal during the first phase.

Even, according to 2011 census, the ST population in West Bengal to the total states constitutes 5.80%. Albeit indiscriminate approach should have been followed in the selection of states—purely based on population parameter—creation of a TRI for West Bengal does not make much impact on the face of it. Sheerly for two reasons that (1) the relative deprivation of chances of a state with highest concentration of tribal population to have a TRI has suffered, and (2) while all the TRIs in other states invariably prefixed or suffixed TRIBAL in the title of Tribal Research Institute, the West Bengal TRI bears the title as, 'Cultural Research Institute'. As such in other cases there is dismal picture that emerges even while the TRIs overtly working for tribals, the name CRI which remotely reflects its works is being carried out for the tribal welfare, and hardly connects the activities around tribal

Table 3 State-wise schedule tribe population as per 1951 census

States/UTs	Scheduled tribes	% to total population
Uttar Pradesh	–	0
Bihar	4,049,183	10.07
Orissa	2,967,334	20.26
West Bengal	1,165,337	4.7
Chander Nagar	–	0
Assam	1,735,245	19.19
Manipur	194,239	33.63
Tripura	192,293	30.09
Sikkim	–	0
Madras	635,979	1.11
Mysore	15,310	0.17
Travancore Cochin	26,580	0.29
Coorg	21,084	9.19
Bombay	3,359,305	9.34
Saurashtra	38,849	0.94
Kutch	17,002	3
Madhya Pradesh	2,477,024	11.66
Madhya Bharat	1,060,812	13.34
Hyderabad	354,933	1.9
Bhopal	59,114	7.07
Vindhya Pradesh	418,282	11.7
Rajasthan	316,348	2.07
Punjab	2429	0.02
Patiala & East Punjab States Union	–	0
Ajmer	9816	1.41
Delhi	–	0
Himachal Pradesh & Bilaspur	–	0
Andaman & Nicobar Islands	–	0
India	19,116,498	5.36

Note These figures exclude the people living in Jammu and Kashmir state and part of part B tribal areas of Assam where the 1951 Census was not taken and they are exclusive also of 268,602 persons. Compiled from the statistics released by Census of India
Source https://www.indiastat.com/table/demographics/7/scheduledcastestribespopulation/249/21684/data.aspx

communities on the face of it. In reality, the actual functional aspects of CRI may need to be corroborated.

The second-generation TRIs came into being over a period of time (1962–1987) in 10 states such as Andhra Pradesh (with 7.00% STs), Gujarat (with 14.75% STs), Maharashtra (with 9.35% STs), Assam (with 12.45% STs), Rajasthan (with 13.48% STs), Kerala (with 1.45% STs), Tripura (with 31.76% STs), Tamil Nadu (with 1.10% STs), Uttar Pradesh (with 0.57% STs) and Manipur (with 35.12% STs) after the States Reorganisation Act, 1956. The significant development in this period is that between 1962 and 1987 there are more number of TRIs established. Out of these ten states, Uttar Pradesh had a negligible tribal population as 0.57% was the least percentage of tribal population in the state as well as in the country. Tamil Nadu (1.10%) and Kerala (1.45%) are the second and third lowest ranks in terms of tribal population in the state compared to the state population. Top three highest concentration of tribal population among these 10 states are being Manipur with 35.12%, Tripura with 31.76% and Gujarat with 14.75%, although, comparison of percentage of national-level tribal population with that of percentage with each north-eastern state, the percentage varies drastically, and in the mainstream states the variation is only minimum.

Whereas the states like Madhya Pradesh, Maharashtra, Orissa, Gujarat, Rajasthan, Jharkhand, Chhattisgarh, Andhra Pradesh, West Bengal and Karnataka are the states having larger number of scheduled tribes account for 83.2% of the total scheduled tribe population of the country,[9] of which the states like Orissa, Madhya Pradesh, Jharkhand and West Bengal have already established TRIs in the first phase. However, it seems that creation of TRIs after states reorganization Act, 1956 has no effect on all these tribal concentrated states forthwith. Karnataka was one such state had to wait in the third phase.

The third-generation TRIs came into being, after the 1991 economic liberalization, with the first one started in 1994 in Himachal Pradesh. Total of seven TRIs (Himachal Pradesh, Chhattisgarh, Karnataka, Andaman and Nicobar Island, Telangana, Sikkim and J & K) with a latest addition of one TRI in J&K in January 2018 are the third-generation TRIs. The TRI in Himachal Pradesh was established as ITSR (Institute of Tribal Studies and Research) as an autonomous institute under the administrative control of Himachal Pradesh University. Apparently, ITSR (TRI) is unique from others as it has been free from state control and offers academic programme such as postgraduate diploma in tribal studies and has its own functional autonomy.

In the third phase, a TRI for Chhattisgarh came into being in 2004, after 4 years of its formation as new state in the year 2000. The state of Telangana received its TRI in 2014 in the same year in which it was carved out as a new state from Andhra Pradesh. Whereas the TRI in Chhattisgarh was altogether a newly established institute, the TRI for Telangana was bifurcated from the existing TRI—Andhra Pradesh as corollary when the men and materials were bifurcated. Thus, the TRI, Telangana has also got its legal sanctity from the Ministry of Tribal Affairs in the same year.

Some imperative questions: Why there are no progressive advancements taking place in the functioning of the TRIs across India? Whether research is the core activity of TRIs as the title goes or it is secondary one. Why the sponsorships are

[9]http://censusindia.gov.in/Census_And_You/scheduled_castes_and_sceduled_tribes.aspx (accessed on 30 January 18).

going out from TRIs rather than organizing seminars/workshops on its own research findings? What are the impinging factors that retarding the research? When there are more than one activity is going on in the institute, why it should be called a research institute alone and why cannot the names be suitably modified to broaden its scope and be called as 'tribal cultural and research centres'? and, while, if the museum is an integral part of a research institute, then why the museums have not been highlighted in the title, can there be a uniform pattern of title of the institute across India?

Why there is a persistent delay in fulfilling the vacancies at TRIs? Why the ad hocism is allowed to continue on permanent basis? What are the skill enhancement trainings being given to the staff engaged in research, particularly in the area of research methodology? How far the idea of conferring the COE to few TRIs is appropriate?

Whether the backwardness and the poverty of the tribal are the matter of concern for TRIs? Whether TRIs dealt with or designed a plan for economic revitalization of tribal communities across states. Is there any skill gap analysis or demand for training programmes for the tribals is being contemplated at any of the TRIs that can be replicated by others?

Whether collaboration within the TRIs at zone/regional level is fulfilling the needs or has to look beyond? Why the state governments are not timely exploring and utilizing the potentials of TRIs? Why the MOTA make it compulsory to appoint the individuals from the academic background as directors of TRI instead of relying on bureaucrats? Whether the TRIs have adequate autonomy to deal with the subjects allocated, if no, what are the alternative means to empower and enhance the TRIs? In this section, there are several such questions being raised without clear answer, hope the paper further help the understanding of the reader.

Now the third section delves upon the geographical proximity as locational advantages for TRIs to work at comfortably on much concentrated tribal communities. The notional advantage of being nearer to the target population, disadvantage and actual focus of TRIs are being discussed.

3 Locus and Focus of TRIs

Locus of TRIs: Geographical proximity or strategic selection of location plays an important role in catering to smooth execution of tasks. The locational values determine the value of works accomplished in qualitative term.[10] With the limited resources and time when research is expected to accomplish, scientifically deduced

[10]Planning Commission observes that STs have traditionally been concentrated in about 15% of the country's geographical areas, mainly forests, hills, undulating inaccessible areas. The fact that most of them live in isolated groups in relatively remote areas has made it more difficult to deliver essential services to them and has also made it much more difficult for them to benefit from the acceleration of overall growth.

options such as 'being nearer' is the better choice to adopt. In the context of education of tribal children, Dr. B. R. Ambedkar in his words says, 'I would suggest that schools should be opened for them in their own locality or some central place....'[11] In the same parlance as the TRIs are recognized as knowledge and capacity building institutions, the location of TRIs in proximity to most populated tribal communities of that state/district would have been an ideal choice.

Locus of TRIs thrives upon some important exogenous considerations, viz. (i) while setting up the TRIs in each state whether due consideration was given about the existing tribal population at the time of creation of TRI in a state, (ii) even if a TRI was created, whether it was established in proximity to the district/city/ cluster where tribal population has highest concentration and (iii) whether in terms of accessibility and approachability the tribal community members are able to have smooth working relation with TRI and vice versa, and distances between the highest concentration of tribal belt and TRI, tribal population in a state and finally the threshold-gravitational analysis.

Though the percentage of tribal population in the cities, where the TRIs presently located, is not very high, the districts with highest percentage of tribal community are far away from the location of TRIs (Table 4). It appears that merely for administrative conveniences the TRIs were set up in the present location, which is either in state capitals or next biggest cities. The political precedence or haphazard decisions in selection of states have conveniently ignored the population parameters as basic criteria.

While the four north-eastern states like Arunachal Pradesh, Nagaland, Mizoram and Meghalaya, despite each one of them having more than fifty percentage of tribal population in seven or more districts, have not receive attention from the centre (Table 5),[12] Arunachal Pradesh in particular has fifteen tribal districts on its account, if put together the three more districts that falls under 25–50% category of ST population present in districts.

In contrast to this scenario, the states like Karnataka, Kerala, Tamil Nadu, Uttar Pradesh and West Bengal not a single one district falls under 50% and above category and not even 25% and above category. Except the state of Karnataka (with 6.95% of STs) and West Bengal (with 5.80% of STs) other three states, viz. Kerala, Tamil Nadu and Uttar Pradesh, each has less than two percent of the tribal population as a percentage to the total population (Table 6). Irrespective of the concentration of tribal population, these five states have got one TRI each in different years. While there is no denying the rights of all states to have one TRI, as it has been logically supported for TRIs to each one of the states, priority and due emphasis should have been based on population parameters. Elsewhere in this

[11]Essential Writings Of B. R. Ambedkar, Valerian Rodrigues,(Ed) Oxford University Press, Indian Paperback, 2005., And Action Points for Development of Schedule Castes and Schedule Tribes, written by Chandrapal, Adviser, Planning Commission, Government of India, 82 Action points.

[12]Census of India, 2011.

Table 4 Distance between TRIs and the district with highest percentage of STs in states

Districts	Total population	ST population	% of tribes in districts	Location of TRIs	Distance between TRI (KMs)
Churachandpur	274,143	254,787	92.9	Imphal, Manipur	65
The Dangs	228,291	216,073	94.6	Ahmadabad Gujarat	380
Jhabua	1,025,048	891,818	87.0	Bhopal, MP	330
Kargil	140,802	122,336	86.9	J&K (to be established)	475
Narmada	590,297	481,392	81.6	Ahmadabad Gujarat	200
Dohad	2,127,086	1,580,850	74.3	Ahmadabad Gujarat	200
Khunti	531,885	389,626	73.3	Ranch, JH	50
Simdega	599,578	424,407	70.8	Ranch, JH	120
Gumla	1,025,213	706,754	68.9	Ranch, JH	105
Dindori	704,524	455,789	64.7	Bhopal, MP	480
Dhar	2,185,793	1,222,814	55.9	Bhopal, MP	265
Nabarangapur	1,220,946	681,173	55.8	Bhubaneswar Odisha	570
Kandhamal	733,110	392,820	53.6	Bhubaneswar Odisha	280
Valsad	1,705,678	902,794	52.9	Ahmadabad Gujarat	335
Sundargarh	2,093,437	1,062,349	50.7	Bhubaneswar Odisha	360+
Koraput	137,9647	697,583	50.6	Bhubaneswar Odisha	500+
Anuppur MP	749,237	358,543	47.9	Bhopal, MP	550
Umaria MP	644,758	300,687	46.6	Bhopal, MP	585
Gadchiroli MH	1,072,942	415,306	38.7	Pune, MH	815
Chhindwara	209,0922	769,778	36.8	Bhopal, MP	290
Nashik MH	6,107,187	1,564,369	25.6	Pune, Maharashtra	215
Purulia	2,536,516	463,452	18.3	Kolkata, WB	300
Jalpaiguri	3,401,173	641,688	18.9	Kolkata, WB	590
Dakshin Dinajpur	1,503,178	242,317	16.0	Kolkata, WB	400
Paschim Medinipur	519,3411	772,177	14.9	Kolkata, WB	130
The Nilgiris	762,141	28,373	3.7	Nilgiris, TN	0

Source Compiled from various sources

Table 5 State-wise number of districts with ST population above 50% and between 25 and 50%

S. No.	State	No. of districts above 50%
1	**Arunachal Pradesh**	13
2	**Nagaland**	11
3	**Mizoram**	8
4	Odisha	8
5	Chhattisgarh	7
6	**Meghalaya**	7
7	Gujarat	6
8	Jharkhand	5
9	Manipur	5
10	Rajasthan	5
11	Assam	3
12	Himachal Pradesh	2
13	Jammu and Kashmir	2
14	Andaman & Nicobar Islands	2
15	Dadra & Nagar Haveli	1
16	Lakshadweep	1
17	Maharashtra	1
18	Sikkim	1
19	Tripura	1
	Total	90
S. No	State	No. of district 25–50%
1	Madhya Pradesh	13
2	Chhattisgarh	8
3	Jharkhand	6
4	Odisha	6
5	Assam	5
6	Gujarat	4
7	**Arunachal Pradesh**	3
8	Jammu and Kashmir	3
9	Maharashtra	3
10	Rajasthan	3
11	Sikkim	3
12	Tripura	3
13	Andhra Pradesh	1
14	Himachal Pradesh	1
	Total	62

Source census of India, 2011

Table 6 Highest and lowest proportion of STs in states/UTs

Top 5 states/union territories (%)		Bottom 5 states/union territories (%)	
Lakshadweep	94.8	Uttar Pradesh	0.56
Mizoram	94.4	Tamil Nadu	1.1
Nagaland	86.5	Bihar	1.28
Meghalaya	86.1	Kerala	1.45
Arunachal Pradesh	68.8	Uttarakhand	2.89

Source Census of India, 2011

paper, the emphasis has been on to the creation of one TRI for Bihar as tribal community in the state constitutes 1.28% of the total population.

Structure: Structurally, a tribal research institute supposedly consists of administrative wing, research and training wing, museum, library, conference hall and hostels, estate. Many of the campus indeed totally cut off from the main city. This has hampered the effective and efficient functioning of the institute.

TRIs entrusted with multiple tasks such as maintenance of museums, collection or live demonstration of artefacts, conducting training programmes, organizing melas (trade fair), capacity building for local functionaries and NGOs and so on so forth beside research. Though all these activities have been carried out under one roof, whether it is feasible to conduct research in a cordial manner, TRIs are just managing with the external support of manpower and resource persons on ad hoc basis. Thus, the need for rationally evaluating the TRIs emerges as the name, 'institutes of Tribal research', behold the crux of everything.

There is an urgent need to catch up with the trends in the centre level as the welfare schemes and approaches to human rights and development approaches are changing. In terms of functioning, there is not much difference between the TRIs of 1950s TRIs in 1991 and after. The functioning of the TRIs has not adequately yielded to the welfare need of the tribal communities per se, although in a piecemeal manner have advanced to house the tribal artefacts, the library and little of research advancement. Yet, the degree and the rate at which the TRIs ought to gauge their manner of functioning are unmeasured as the developmental activities from among the tribals are at slow phase.

Focus of TRIs: Whereas the social spending is the direct interventional measures intended to encounter and minimize the poverty and apathy of the targeted groups, the social planners design the means of development. In this regard, the institutions like TRIs play the role of facilitators in social planning with acumen. When such diagnostic process is skewed, the intervention and planning stages would be of ineffective.

The focus of TRIs is all about the progressive activities of the TRIs and its affect as commensurate impact or outcome. It is presupposed that TRIs setup in different phases/generations does not struck up with elementary levels of focus alone and with time reorient its interest to catch up with up-to-date development models for the benefits of target group. Whether any landmark developments down the line and different passing generations distinguish the TRIs from one another in the manner of working—is attempted based on certain parameters. There are three endogenous considerations, namely, capacity, ability and prevailing work environment within the TRIs would propel the studying of the TRIs and its impact. Additionally, the issues such as title of TRIs, title of Museum, existence and operation of website, contents in the website, downloadable contents aspect, optimality of resources and staff being used were considered.

Language–culture versus economic empowerment: Often the research studies to be conducted by TRIs, considering the poverty and backwardness of the tribes, need to give importance on livelihood and economic development of tribal community over language–cultural emphasis. Education and skill development, employment training and concerns on job opportunities would naturally encompass the development of language and culture.

Coverage of population: Population coverage of TRIs varies from maximum of 15,316,784 persons in Madhya Pradesh to a minimum of 28,530 in Andaman and Nicobar Islands (Table 7). The ratio of burden is 537:1 for Madhya Pradesh and Andaman, and Nicobar Islands is too wide when compared with the population in these two states. Such variation in numbers of population in different states apparently has different levels of burden on TRIs. It seems that there is no equal and level playing field exist for TRIs in states, and accordingly, the number of staff required in each TRI also varies from one another. The widespread tribal population and the quantum of workload on each TRI show prevalence of clear discrepancies within TRIs.

TRDI, Bhopal, a first-generation TRI in dealing with an amorphous tribal population spread across one of the biggest states, Madhya Pradesh for a quite long time despite its scarce manpower. As the TRDI has been grappling with huge tasks, it is surprising to note that it did not realize or react about its scanty manpower issues for such a long period. At least adequate research staff based on the size of the population of the state is must for a TRI. Whereas Andaman and Nicobar Islands having least population among the states/UTs has got its TRI in 2014, it is the biggest in terms of square kilometre spread among the UTs and is yet to begin its work.

Span of attention: The workload of the TRIs is determined by the local level machineries and functionaries that are either geographically or strategically located nearer to the much concentrated population yields to the effective span of attention. As the spread of tribal population across district or state varies from one TRI to another, the span of coverage is not equal across all states. Since the proportionate manpower determines the effectiveness, all the TRIs need to fulfil staff as per demand and need (Table 8).

Threshold point: As the geographical spread of tribal population varies from state to state, the population size also varies, not all TRIs by and large with adequate manpower, unable to cooperate with workload. The threshold levels of TRIs are apparently crossed in a few TRIs, which is also a major reason for not performing well (Table 9).

Table 7 Demographic status of total population & ST population (Census 1991, 2001 & 2011)

S. No.	India/State	ST Population		
		1991	2001	2011
	India	67758380	84326240	104281034
1	Andhra Pradesh	4199481	5024104	5918073
2	Arunachal Pradesh	550351	705158	951821
3	Assam	2874441	3308570	3884371
4	Bihar	6616914	758351	1336573
5	Chattisgarh	–	6616596	7822902
6	Goa	376	566	149275
7	Gujarat	6161775	7481160	8917174
8	Haryana	–	–	–
9	Himachal Pradesh	218.349	244587	382126
10	J & K	–	1105979	1493299
11	Jharkhand	–	7087068	8645042
12	Karnataka	1915691	3463986	4248987
13	Kerala	320967	364189	484839
14	Madhya Pradesh	15399034	12233474	15316784
15	Maharashtra	7318281	8577276	10510213
16	Manipur	632173	741141	902740
17	Meghalaya	1517927	1992862	2555861
18	Mizoram	653565	839310	1036115
19	Nagaland	1060822	1774026	170973
20	Orissa	7032214	8145081	9590756
21	Punjab	–	–	–
22	Rajasthan	5474881	7097706	9238534
23	Sikkim	90.901	111.405	206360
24	Tamil Nadu	574.194	651321	794697
25	Tripura	853345	993426	1166813
26	Uttarakhand	–	256129	291903
27	Uttar Pradesh	287901	107963	1134273
28	West Bengal	3808760	4406794	5296953
29	Andman & Nicobar Islands	26.77	29.469	28530
30	Chandigarh	–	–	–
31	Dadra & Nagar Haveli	109380	137225	178564
32	Daman & Diu	11724	13997	15363
33	Delhi	–	–	–
34	Lakshadweep	48163	57321	61120
35	Puducherry	–	–	–

States like Chhattisgarh, Jharkhand and Uttarakhand were created in the year 2000 after re-organization of the states of Madhya Pradesh, Bihar and Uttar Pradesh. Manipur (Excl.3 Sub-divisions of Senapati Distt)

Table 8 Size of the states and UTs

S. No.	Rank	State	Area (km^2)	% of national share
1	1	Rajasthan	342,239	10
2	2	Madhya Pradesh	308,252	9
3	3	Maharashtra	307,713	9
4	4	Andhra Pradesh	275,045	8
5	5	Uttar Pradesh	240,928	7
6	6	Jammu and Kashmir	222,236	7
7	7	Gujarat	196,244	6
8	8	Karnataka	191,791	6
9	9	Odisha	155,707	5
10	10	Chhattisgarh	135,192	4
11	11	Tamil Nadu	130,060	4
12	12	Bihar	94,163	3
13	13	West Bengal	88,752	3
14	15	Jharkhand	79,716	2
15	16	Assam	78,438	2
16	17	Himachal Pradesh	55,673	2
17	18	Uttarakhand	53,483	2
18	21	Kerala	38,852	1
19	23	Manipur	22,327	1
20	26	Tripura	10,486	0
21	27	Sikkim	7096	0
22	UT1	A & N Islands	8249	0

TRIs have been created to do a variety of works like providing planning inputs to the state governments by the way of conducting research and evaluation studies, collection of data, identify challenges in the field of socio-economic development of tribal community, preservation and promotion of the tribal culture, training and capacity building of stakeholders, and knowledge advocacy that would help to formulate evidence-based policy and planning, are the main activities. Apart from research, MOTA also supports the construction of tribal museums within the premises of the TRIs to preserve the tribal art, craft and culture.

With the limited research staff and lack of manpower in general, research works continue to suffer, which remain a challenge. This has caused a huge bearing on research output, which is evident in appraisal and evaluation research works passed on to the third party. On the face of it, it seems most of the TRIs are engaged in doing additional tasks from the state governments. For instance, verification of caste certificates, determination of ST status whether the claim and counterclaim of particular community under ST category is right and so on and so forth is the task accomplished through TRIs. There are several issues emerging from the functioning of TRIs both structurally and functionally. These are to be discussed in detail in the following.

Table 9 States with tribal population less than 10%

State	ST population			Decadal growth in % (from 2001)	% of STs in STATE to total state 2011	% of STs in state to total STs in India in 2011
	1991	2001	2011			
Karnataka	1,915,691	3,463,986	4,248,987	22.66	**6.95**	4.07
Kerala	320,967	364,189	484,839	33.13	**1.45**	0.46
Tamil Nadu	574,194	651,321	794,697	22.01	**1.10**	0.76
Uttar Pradesh	287,901	107,963	1,134,273	950.61	**0.57**	1.09
West Bengal	3,808,760	4,406,794	5,296,953	20.20	**5.80**	5.08

Source Census of India, 2011

Dynamics of TRIs: Ideally, there should have been phased manner progress in functioning of TRIs. However, it appears that there is no distinction between the TRIs of different generations. In other words, different generations of TRIs, as institutions working on a specific mandate, did not orient to specialize in understanding the gravity of the local issues of tribals.[13] Apparently, TRIs did not reinvent their own existence over a period of time by focussing on particular aspects of tribal issues, in order to reach up to the ebb of the issues such as poverty, illiteracy, poor health, skill gaps or augmenting to scholarly pursuit of tribal arts, etc. Approximately, the TRIs are acting as an extended arm of bureaucracy rather than an intellectual arm. The dynamism of TRIs ideally should reflect the corollary of improvement in the standard of living of tribal and vice versa. However, the majority of tribal population by and large remain at lower strata of economic hierarchy, and expecting them to contribute back to the welfare of TRIs is too much, although the nature of tribal society itself becomes the cause for the existence of TRIs.

Cultural empowerment versus entertainment: The tribal melas (trade fairs) and tribal cultural festivals are a kind of an entertainment, rather than empowerment of tribal communities organized across states, to popularize tribal culture mainly. However, the outreach of it cannot be compared with that of scholarly exponent of mainstream cultural heritage arts such as Hindustani or southern Carnatic classic music, dances, etc., in terms of volume of its recognition and promotional means and popularity it has.[14]

Although the tribal cultural festivals and programmes are aimed at promoting the indigenous tribal cultural talents, under the aegis of TRIs, there appears no recognition or award of scholarship for both (i) exhibiting artists talents and

[13]This is the outcome or impact of TRIs, which is understood from the perspective making vis-à-vis the progressive changes in the tribal life.

[14]Ministry of culture recognizes the scholarships mostly on classical and folk tradition but not of the tribal.

(ii) scholarly pursuit of tribal arts. There is a 'Best Janjatiya Achiever award' that is being instituted by MOTA, yet there is no regular scholarship scheme[15] available for tribal artists through TRIs at the centre level.[16] Similarly, no state governments have instituted regular scholarships at the state as well for the purpose of academic pursuit of tribal arts. Despite a thin layer of distinction between tribal arts (dances and music) and the folklore arts, seemingly there are 'NO' financial incentives available for pursuing the tribal arts.[17] While the existence of TRIs as an institutions bears appreciation for their contribution in promoting the cultural aspects of tribal communities, whether measures or research inputs by TRIs are made available to safeguard the tribals arts, literature and heritage by the way of recommending awards as regular institutional scholarships to the tribal artists is unclear.

Manpower shortage: The activities like libraries and museums, though to some extend few libraries and museums have outstandingly created the structures, outwardly not all the museums and libraries by TRIs are being utilized effectively, which are true from the available literature.[18] More often the answers for not being utilized fully unidirectionally leading to one answer, i.e. shortage of manpower. It is a common thing to observe that a persistent delay in filling the vacancies across TRIs is the main cause of the problem. According to a report by SCSTRTI, out of 109 sanctioned posts 59 posts are remaining vacant of which nearly about 30 posts are meant for research staff.[19] Minutes of action plans for TRIs by MOTA recorded the response by SCSTRTI, Odisha about meeting the issues of manpower shortage that 'it may not be solved immediately hence resourceful persons are hired from other institutions and engaged for activities'.[20] In a scenario like almost a major chunk of posts of research staff remain vacant, the outcome of the research managed with outsourcing and contracting may not yield fruitful result in the long run.

Veracity of research: A typical case of a first-generation TRI in Pune, Maharashtra named Tribal Research and Training Institute (TRTI) was on news for negative reasons. It was alleged that TRTI suffers lack of original research and training in the field.[21] Supposed reasons there on are that just 12 research studies

---

[15]Pre-metric, post-metric, overseas scholarships are not meant for culturally inclined tribal pursuing their artistic tradition as scholarship.

[16]https://tribal.nic.in/DivisionsFiles/NCST-RM/9NationalTrAwGuidlns.pdf (Accessed on 03 January 18).

[17]Central university of Jharkhand has started the course of 'Tribal-Folklore', gives opportunity to study tribal folklore. However, there is no special scholarship is available for tribal studies.

[18]Evaluation of Functioning of Tribal Research Institute (TRI) in Assam, November, 2011, National Council of Applied Economics Research (NCAER), 2011.

[19]A Journey Through Six Decades and Moving Ahead Schedule Castes and Schedule Tribes Research and Training Institute (SCSTRTI), 2017.

[20]MOTA Minutes 9 July 2015, https://tribal.nic.in/DivisionsFiles/NCST-RM/6minutesofMeetingResearch.pdf (accessed on 25 September 17).

[21]Partha Sarathi Biswas, State's apex tribal research institute under scanner for poor performance, The India Express, 31 May 2015 (Accessed on 05 August 2017) http://indianexpress.com/article/cities/mumbai/states-apex-tribal-research-institute-under-scanner-for-poor-performance/.

were conducted since its inception, only two research studies were conducted in the last 5 years, a study initiated in 2006 remained incomplete till 2014, the institute could evaluate only 11 out of the 171 schemes launched during the period from 2009 to 12 pertaining to social impact assessment of various welfare schemes of the state government.[22] However, it seems that the staff crunch and lack of skills were the cause of these problems as claimed by senior officials in TRTI, Pune. There is no such reports on other TRIs that are not available in the open domain.

Holistically, whether TRIs are enabling the tribal development or inhibits still requires a thorough probe as the MOTA observes that all the TRIs have lost their direction over a period of time.[23] Albeit, TRIs are not to be blamed for the present status of the tribal communities, as the activities of TRIs per se have direct consequences on ensuring the tribal welfare by keeping accounts of, and constant stock-taking of the field realities for planning inputs from various corners would have well augmented for a steady development and check if deviations any. In general, the onus remain with both the apex bodies, i.e. MOTA for lacking a solid monitoring and evaluation system and field office, i.e. TRIs as inadequate and incomplete data, piecemeal analysis, biased and selective approaches. Overall impression is that the frivolous and ad hoc approach in gathering field data on the issues of the tribal community seem to have diluted and undermined the real issues.

Locational advantages and disadvantages: It appears most of the TRIs are located ironically far away from tribal concentrated belts. While choosing the location for setting up the TRIs, population parameters were not taken into consideration. On an average, the areal distance between a TRI and the tribal concentrated belts varies from 200 to 500 KMs. However, the actual distance by road is much far away. Corroborated facts of location of some TRIs reveal that the actual distance varies from 50 to 850 KMs (refer Table 4), whereas Ranchi in Jharkhand and Imphal in Manipur were two exceptional TRIs whose distances are relatively less as 50 and 45 KMs. These two states are located very much in proximity to the district with highest percentage of tribal population.

In contrast states like Madhya Pradesh, Maharashtra and Odisha, they have remotely connected to tribal districts as the distance are too far. The distances between tribal concentrated districts and TRDI, Bhopal in Madhya Pradesh are viz. Jhabua (87.0%) 330 KMs, Dindori (64.7%) 480 KMs and Dhar with (55.9%) 265 KMs. The districts like Anuppur with 47.9% of tribal population measure the distance as 550 KMs and for Umaria with 46.6% of tibals distanced at 585 KMs. Although TRI in Madhya Pradesh was established at Chhindwara (36.8%) in 1954, later on it was shifted the TRI to Bhopal, and still the Chhindwara retains the TRI campus.

[22]Report of the Comptroller and Auditor General of India on General and Social Sector for the year ended March, 2014, Government of Maharashtra, Report No. 4 of the year 2015.

[23]MOTA Minutes 9 July 2015, https://tribal.nic.in/DivisionsFiles/NCST-RM/6minutesofMeeting Research.pdf (accessed on 25 September 17).

Whereas the location of TRI, Ranchi seems to be appropriate for it is accessible to highest concentration of tribal population in just 105 KMs away from Ranchi, i.e. Gumla with 710,000 population, the highest percentage of tribal population to the total population of the district also happened to in proximity to TRI, Ranchi, i.e. Khunti (73.3%) with 45 KMs.

In case of TRI, Jharkhand, the selection of the location was more appropriate and happened to find its location in the part of tribal concentrated Jharkhand side rather than elsewhere in undivided Bihar at the time of inception. States like Bihar though carved out from the Tribal state Jharkhand, the residual part of the leftover tribal population in Bihar state to total State constitutes 1.28% with a total of 1,336,573 population deserves to get a TRI in an appropriate district. Sooner or later, it is going to be a reality that setting up of a TRI, Bihar is also inevitable considering the tribal population in that states.

Of the total 9.35% of tribal population in Maharashtra, the highest concentration of tribal population falls in Gadchiroli district with 38.7% to the total population in the district. The distance from the present location of TRI in Pune to Gadchiroli is 815 KMs, which is a remotest area from the perspective of TRI, Pune for all practical purposes. The districts like Gadchiroli with the highest tribal population in the state of Maharashtra had been considered for setting up of TRI, sheerly for the high concentration of Tribal population as 38.7%; the developmental interventions would have minimized the overt activism of the tribal communities.

In case of Odisha, all the tribal concentrated districts are located in remote districts like Nabarangpur with (55.8%) located at 570 KMs away from TRI, Bhubaneswar, similarly Kandhamal (53.6%) at 280 KMs distance, Sundargarh (50.7%) at 360+ KMs distance and Koraput (50.6%) at 500 + KMs distances from Bhubaneswar. This is the case of persistent inaccessibility to both TRI and the tribal communities on the account of manoeuvrability.

4 Analysis of TRIs

Hitherto the discussions were about some exogenous factors such as notional features of the environment of TRIs and its outcome. Section four of this paper exclusively focuses upon the TRI specific issues across states. This section factually discusses the aptness and inappropriateness of structures and functions of TRIs on an outcome perspective, not only from the tribal prism but also in a general parlance.

'TRI' as the Title: The title of the tribal research institutes (TRIs) are not named uniformly. Few of the TRIs either prefixed the popular local leader in the state or included the Scheduled Castes (SCs) also in its title. A cursory look into the title appears that TRIs not only working on tribal subjects but on SCs as well. Let it be so, but whether or not TRI a typical professional research institute or it does something else also is not reflected in this present title. The case TRI, West Bengal though seems to be a research institution whether it is working on tribal culture is not clear as the title of the TRI, West Bengal is called 'Cultural Research Institute' rather than tribal research institute. This looks an inappropriate title and has the high scope of misleading. As such those organizations with overt name if the title of the institute does not adequately commit to the cause of tribal development, what else can be expected of from a cultural research institute? At least like the cases of TRI, Andhra Pradesh (The Tribal Cultural Research & Training Institute) and TRI, Tripura (Tribal Research and Cultural Institute), the key world 'tribal' should be imprinted on its forehead of the institute.

Notion of inclusion of SCs: With the inclusion of SCs in the title of tribal research institutes, the scope of TRIs appears to have been working on the subjects of SCs as well, but in reality it is not true. Even as the MOTA directions from time to time notify matters pertain only to STs but not on SCs. The issues emerged here are that the exclusive and focused attention on research and development on tribals welfare apparently has been reduced.

It could have been the reason that at the time of the creation of the TRIs under the aegis of the unified 'ministry of welfare' handled both the subjects—SCs and STs in an inclusive way. However, in the late 1990s the undivided ministry serving both SCs and STs wherein the Tribal Division was operating moved out and formed a separate ministry of Tribal affairs in October 1999.[24] Similarly, the national commission meant for SCs and STs was also bifurcated into two separate commissions in 2004.[25] The planners and think-tank paved the way to create a new body for a dedicated and committed apex organization for the cause of the tribal welfare. *Of late* the government posts meant for SCs and STs were also filled only with candidates from respective community and the practice of interchangeable and conversion of posts of SC into STs and vice versa are being abandoned. As such the increasing demand and volume of works on STs and SCs have increased; the need of a dedicated system in place is justified, wherein all the developmental apparatuses for both the communities are looked into separately.

Whereas MOTA in its official records the research institute is called TRIs, in few states the tile of the TRIs sounds different. Those states such as Assam (Assam Institute of Research for Tribals and Scheduled Castes), Kerala (Kerala Institute for Research, Training and Development Studies (KIRTADS[26]) of scheduled castes and tribes), Manipur (Directorate for Development of Tribals and Scheduled Castes), Orissa (Scheduled Caste and Scheduled Tribes Research and Training Institute) and Uttar Pradesh (SC/TC Research & Training Institute) carry the intertwined title of tribals and scheduled castes. It may be the reasons that the state governments do not different ministries for SCs and STs separately.

[24]http://socialjustice.nic.in/UserView/index?mid=1508, (accessed on 28 January 18).

[25]By the National Commission for Schedule Castes order dated 01 December 2004, created a new National Commission for Schedule Tribes, effectively came into being on 19 February 2004. http://ncsc.nic.in/files/ncsc/new3/150.pdf accessed on 28 January 18.

[26]KIRTADS is purely a governmental organization under the Scheduled Castes and Scheduled Tribes Development ministry and functions as a separate Directorate http://kirtads.kerala.gov.in/history/.

As such SCs do not fall under the purview of TRIs, inclusion of SCs in the title makes no meaning. But the case of TRI, Kerala is so sophisticated that the first part of the title is abbreviated as brand or trademark in a way that it does not capture the word tribal at the first instance. Subsequently, the acronym KIRTADS does not stand for TRI directly. KIRTADS has concealed and eclipsed the word ‘Tribe’ and thus the scope of TRI seems to have been distorted.

Whereas, with the progressing of time, the ministerial functions at the apex level, including the national commissions for SCs and STs, the development corporations for SCs and STs and other important functions have effectively been bifurcated, conveniently for the purpose of focused community planning and effective governance the TRIs still retaining the SCs in its title is an ambiguous pursuit. When all such divisions within the state machinery pointing towards particular pattern of functioning of the institutions pertain to tribal subjects, TRI still insists upon the scope of scheduled castes although there is no research works accomplished on the welfare of scheduled caste exclusively. This is because at state-level governments do not distinguish the tribes with that of castes. It seems that the state administration treat ‘tribes’ or ‘castes’ under ‘scheduled’ are alike, although approaches and treatments are independent from each other as they are not a homogeneous group.

Distinction of SCs and STs: Although the title of TRIs included SCs in its scope, the sole objectives reiterated its focus only on tribal subjects. MOTA administered a study through NCAER—a onetime evaluating of the functioning of the TRIs in Assam only to look into the tribal related affairs but not the SCs (NCAER, 2011). Even all the ministerial guidelines updated from time to time clearly streamlined its focuses around STs only.[27] Without any assumptions as to whether the TRIs mandates include the SCs in its scope, there is an urgent need to modify the title as to separate the scope of inclusion of SCs in its purview but also to delineate its scope to focus on the tribal subjects alone. This was essential to clearly reinvigorate the institute functions to achieve its given mandate in a quality manner. Second, the title across the states need to be standardized as merely prefixing or suffixing some prepositions or nouns does not differentiate its function from other TRIs. For instance, the TRDI, Bhopal (Tribal Research and Development Institute) does not have any development activities per se. Or if authorities consider if the term ‘development’ is a must term to be prefixed or suffixed in the title, it should be applicable to all the TRIs, unless there is a functional difference.

In case of TRI, Uttar Pradesh, the negligible amount of tribals’ population in this state though may not require a full-fledged TRI still there may be a separate provision for better management of tribal development affairs as in the case of Bihar as it deserves to have one. However, it is learnt through the telephonic interaction that the activities are held up for one or other reasons.

[27]Operational Guidelines for The scheme “Support to Tribal Research Institutes (TRI), 2017” Ministry of Tribal Affairs, Government of India, 14 December 2017.

Research: While the research on the vocabulary items, ethnographic details of the tribes including their present status, education, profession, food and culture, dress, festivals, custom, marriage and death ceremonies, nature of language maintenance and loss, etc. are seemingly the target of the TRIs, prospective plans are often a sort of a failure in the hands of the TRIs.

TRIs are not in a position to carry out full-fledged research activities on their own due to inadequate manpower capacity to undertake research studies. Even if few staff keen in conducting research, the academic freedom and their outreach is not as extensive as any academic institutions or universities. TRI, Assam study (NCAER, 2001) records that there was a general lack of motivation among all category staff, particularly acute among the research staff. Research staff expressed that the institute lacked an interactive environment (basically of the intellectual environment). Although research is a part of the institute, more often TRIs rather than conducting their own research works, resort to (a) outsources works to individuals in form of scholarships or one time package for engaging into doctoral, postdoctoral programmes, (b) engage independent researchers working on tribal related subjects, and (c) sanction funds to other institutions or universities by way of research projects on tribal matters. The qualifications of the researchers merely helps them at entry level but mostly engaged in administrative works. The study on TRI Assam (NCAER, 2001) affirms that the research staff in TRI, Assam although possess postgraduate qualification, do not have a research degree or formal research training.

FGD with officials in TRDI, Bhopal learnt that shortage of manpower and in the absence of an academic environment, institute is able to carry out only the limited administrative functions and not the full-fledged research as such. It was at the time of bifurcation of the state of Chhattisgarh from Madhya Pradesh, 23% of the staff strength and the resources were given to the new state. It was further stated that the security services and sweeping and cleaning works were assigned to private groups. It was in year 2000 the state of Chhattisgarh carved out, till date not filling the vacancies raises the eyebrow (IAMR field visit report, 2012). TRTI, Pune case also reveals that due to non-reconstitution of General Council, no subject(s) could be chosen by TRTI for research studies on its own during October 2004 to March 2014.

Publication: Since TRIs working under one roof, i.e. under government fold, receiving financial support from the central government for a specific purpose, there is a need for standardization of research publication, which comes from the standardization of the research process. As such there were no set guidelines and publication rules regarding publication of research outcomes. As of now, contents are being published arbitrarily. Though there are some publications like monographs, series, special publications, etc., placed on the respective websites of the TRIs, the copies are not readily available on net for access, except the scanned copies of cover pages. If not the complete text at least abridged version of content and accessibility details should be available to readers/stakeholders. For instance, a random look at the publications in the website of TRI Odisha shows that (SCSTRTI) (http://www.scstrti.in/publication.html), though the cover page preface and content in plain pages are uploaded, no content/text is available for access on net.

Similarly, TRI in the state of Gujarat has on its own displayed several publications[28] uniformly priced at Rs. 150 each publication, neither the cover pages nor any descriptive summary or reviews available for ready reference. Some of its research publications are although helpful in downloadable in MS Word format; the contents unpredictably give the title, year of publication authors, language of the text, etc. for innumerable variety of books. However, not a single text is readily available for consumption. While writing on TRI Manipur, about its publication of books in tribal languages, information/databank and documentation of tribal life, Zomminlun Gangte observes that although all these functions and aims look good on paper, ground reality is that little or nothing will be achieved until and unless the public take notice and give the institution the recognition that it deserves.[29]

While the above argument is true in case of states like Rajasthan and Kerala, websites of TRIs in these two states have become more complicated than websites of other states.[30] Although with difficulties for sometimes the websites were opened, the published materials uploaded are not available for access.

In case of Tripura TRI, a total of 144 publications (books reports monographs thesis, etc.) in the display under publication option in website of TRI, Tripura,[31] of which there are 31 documents show hyperlinked—downloadable option. Nevertheless, virtually not even a single downloadable option out of 31 successfully downloaded—The reasons being that the 404 server errors say, 'the resource you are looking for might have been removed, had its name changed, or is temporarily unavailable. However, whether all 144 publications displayed whether related to tribal community is uncertain. This fact may be corroborated from the domain server of the concerned website.

Field visit report to TRDI, Bhopal reveals that documentation works mostly published in Hindi language. Either a translator or an interpreter was not readily available for help. Amid other published documents, interestingly an important publication on tribal subject titled 'Basic statistics on STs of Madhya Pradesh', without the date of publication is readily available (Although, upon the query, authorities verified the date of publication as 2012) (IAMR field report, 2012), whereas the CAG about the TRTI, Pune observes that they have conducted only one benchmark survey in 1999–2000 which has also lost its relevance due to significant increase in tribal population since then.[32]

Museum: Museum accommodates innumerable items of tribal artefacts of which there are few articles which are of directly related to tribal communities and those

---

[28]https://trti.gujarat.gov.in/research.

[29]My encounter with the Tribal Research Institute (TRI), Manipur, http://e- pao.net/epPageExtractor.asp?src = education.Tribal_Research_Institute.html.(accessed on 22 January 18).

[30]Over a period of 4 months on regular basis, at least twice in a week, the author has attempted to open the websites.

[31]http://www.tritripura.in/new/publication.htm.

[32]Report of the Comptroller and Auditor General of India on General and Social Sector for the year ended March, 2014 Government of Maharashtra, Report No. 4 of the year 2015.

were not utilized by the tribals but by and large reflecting the tribal culture and models. While the nature of display explains the tribal hamlet, marriage, custom, festivals, different clans, etc., some of the displays project tribal community in a negative light. The way the tribal artefacts and replica are being projected shows that tribal costumes are extravagantly rich and the design qualities, etc. appear to be luxurious. It creates an impression that tribal culture very rich at least in the museums—which is an exaggerated hype. While invariably all the TRIs run museums alongside, museums do not appear to be part of the tribal research institutes. Even while the existence of a few museums as integral part of the institute has been reflected in the title, popularity of the museums is very limited.

An Indira Gandhi Rashtriya Manav Sangrahalaya (IGRMS), a museum by Ministry of Culture, is a sophisticated and rich museum housed innumerable artefacts pertain to different tribal cultures, represents a museum of man located in proximity TRDI (Tribal Research and Development) and looks like a model museum, whereas the museum managed by TRDI in Bhopal seem to be attracting very few visitors as compared to IGRMS. Although the TRDI deserves to house a museum, two museums running in proximity by and large on the same subjects are not justified. Merely for the sake of maintaining a museum need to be relooked or else it should be relocated to some other district. While some artisans are seen instantly involved in making the tribal artefacts of tribal culture in few TRIs, it should also be considered the scope of expanding the same as a skill development centres alongside.

Administration: TRIs receive 50% fund from the centre and are under the administrative control of state. The position of the Director by and large in all the TRIs is drawn from civil services, barring few exceptions. At times when a senior level civil servant becomes Director, visiting the TRI campus is seen to be difficult. More often long tenure of directors even beyond the superannuation or assuming the position of director after superannuation seems to be more officiating position of material convenience rather than serving for the real cause. Practically, Joint Director and Deputy Director who were drawn from the state civil services look into the day to day functions of TRI. Thus, functions of the TRI effectively being managed by a Joint Director.

Autonomy: TRIs are constantly under the influence of the state governments as the officials working in TRI drawn from state services. State government influences which means the TRIs are not free from the political influence. The political bind and the bureaucratic influence within the state restrain the officials and academics working in the TRIs to operate with complete academic freedom and autonomy. This is because of the officials drawn from the state services that appear to be having commitment and servitude towards reporting officials in the concerning ministry which more often serves vested interest. For instance, some of the states do not have independent website on its own and rather the activities of the TRIs are being coordinated with respective state departments only. Even some of the TRIs have independent website, the political influence is obvious in a manner that the ranks and file of all ministers and the chief minister imprinted in the web pages. TRIs as an academic research institute suffer as being influenced by the governments in the state. Even when a TRI looks into the affairs two or more states, the autonomy is often get diluted, as too many states influence TRIs. It is obvious that the TRIs suffer to establish its own identity in serving its interest, as they are not enjoying the functional autonomy. As far as financial autonomy is concern, getting funds from the state governments at times turn out to be a primary task of the TRIs as respective state governments do not release funds on time,[33] although there is no problem in getting the funds meant for salaries.

Whereas the Planning Commission high-level committee recommended to launch a Central Tribal Research Institute, as has been planned by the central government,[34] it is necessary to designate a TRI as a nodal agency representing the respective region—East, West, South, North-East and Central in order to ensure coordinated efforts of these TRIs.[35]

Training: Some TRIs in general give training to officials' engaged in tribal area. Very few TRIs organize training programmes to the students. For instance, TRI in Assam conducts regular training/coaching classes for competitive examinations to the unemployed ST students including the SCs. NCAER study report on TRI Assam observes that research staff do not have research degree or formal training. In such cases, either TRI staff would be facilitating the basic minimum training or engaging resource persons from outside on ad hoc basis.

Another aspect is that on whatever the subjects/area in which research and documentations are completed may be well appreciated as a part of the research activity but the relevance of the subjects considered is not chosen or approved by an academically empowered forum. Over a period of time, the reports and documents may have reinforced cultural aspects of the tribal life. But the need of the hour is to enable the tribal development through economic planning.

Utilization of Internet: It appears though some TRIs are in touch with tribal leaders, NGOs working on tribal welfare, tribal artists and others, communication means are very limited and not percolated to individual and family members of the tribes. Use of social media tools is not popularized to interact with TRIs. While maximum of the public utility services in the government are being computerized and the bank account, Aadhaar and PAN numbers have become compulsory to avail any benefits, including MGNAREGA and PDS subsidies, corollary that TRIs should also maintain such as online interactive facilities. Apart from maintaining individual records, an 'interactive web portal' wherein the beneficiaries, trainees, need to be captured on regular basis. Availing the benefit of e-governance to maintain the details of tribal clan, ethnic group and all other data could have readily be made accessible for reference purpose on various fronts. In case of any

[33]Almost all TRIs maintained that it take long time for them to get funds from the state government after Ministry sanctioned it to them.

[34]Report of the High Level Committee on Socioeconomic, Health and Educational Status of Tribal Communities of India, Ministry of Tribal Affairs, Government of India, May, 2014.

[35]Twelfth Five-Year Plan (2012–2017), Social Sectors Volume-III, Planning Commission, Government of India.

government welfare schemes and information maintained in other internet sources, such data should be linked to the TRI sites for ready reference.

Digitization: Almost all the libraries around the world have placed their documents on net for the wider use of the readers, while the old documents that were not produced after the intervention of information and communication network have been digitally converted and uploaded. Even if the contents are very old, they are being reproduced digitally. Invariably not a single content from any of the TRIs is readily available on net. It is a high time that the TRIs are required to digitize the data and place the contents on net, while introducing the interactive web portal for the beneficiaries and the subjects' studied.

Websites: World Wide Web is considered to be the window opening from where the communications with the stockholders are remotely accessible across. Much before the talk of digital India came into existence, the country has already placed all data and transactions through web such as MGNAREGA. Although some of the TRIs in few states have maintained official website on its own, not all the TRIs have websites. There could be different reasons for the delay in placing TRIs on web; however, the extended delay seems to be meaningless, as all the beneficiaries related to government welfare schemes are expected to transpire on net, and such research initiatives by TRIs go on web which is must advice (Table 10).

Notion of Centre of Excellence (COE): While the independent institutions like NGOs, universities/departments or institutes who are working voluntarily to study the conditions of tribals naturally qualified to get such excellence awards for their self-driven motivation, when too many stakeholders work in the same field, they as an entity with potential qualified to claim for the institution of excellences. Contrarily, the TRIs are specifically designed to undertake works exclusively on tribal matters, which is normally a regular and routine work. The TRIs are bound to work on continues basis irrespective of whether one gets COE status or not. Even, all the while, the secretary MOTA observes that TRIs as institutions have weakened and lost their direction that cannot contravene their inferences and confer the status of COE to some TRIs. Even if some so-called performing TRIs are awarded COE deliberately to boost up their morale, it would again remain a cause of demotivating other TRIs. More than awards the administrative missionary should see the results by setting new benchmarks.

5 Summary and Recommendations

It is obvious that the selection of states for setting up of TRIs was not sheerly based on the percentage of tribal community in a state. As a result, states have been choosen randomly rather than systematically. It also appears while considering a state for setting up of a TRI, and numerable other factors as well were taken into account. There were no fixed criteria in awarding number of TRIs in a year, thereby a prolonged delay in establishing TRIs in all the states. After the bifurcation of the state, Jharkhand from Bihar, the significant population of Bihar also deserves to

Table 10 State-wise TRI websites and their status

S. No.	State	TRIs in state	Availability of TRI website and link	Observations/remarks	Year of EST.
1	Andaman & Nicobar	Yes	Not Available	–	2014
2	Andhra Pradesh	Yes	http://www.aptribes.gov.in/tcrti/About.html	Since Telangana has initiated a new TRI in 2014, the old one is sided with Andhra Pradesh. There are no research contents seen in its website	1962
3	Assam	Yes	Not Available	–	1977
4	Bihar	No	Not Available	–	–
5	Chhattisgarh	Yes	http://cgtrti.gov.in/	All the contents are placed in Hindi and the title itself translates into 'schedule Tribe Research and Training Institute'. No publication is seen in the website and it seems mostly caste verification works are being assigned/undertaken toTRI	2004
6	Gujarat	Yes	https://trti.gujarat.gov.in/	Website shows some download hyperlink but the downloaded material has only reference about publication but no content	1962
7	Himachal Pradesh	Yes	Not available	–	–
8	Jammu and Kashmir	Yes	Not available	–	–
9	Jharkhand	Yes	http://www.trijharkhand.com/	'Sorry we are updating webpage we will come back soon'	1953
10	Karnataka	Yes	Not Available	–	2011
11	Kerala	Yes	http://www.kirtads.kerala.gov.in/	Though the page has pictures, not able to visit the publication page	1970
12	Madhya Pradesh	Yes	http://www.trdi.mp.gov.in/index.asp	Though separate publication division deals with different publication bulletins and compilation, none available on net	1954
13	Maharashtra	Yes	http://trti.maharashtra.gov.in/frm_HomePage.php	List of 229 published reports is placed in the website	1962
14	Manipur	Yes	http://www.trimanipur.com/	Website carry the details of publication but not the content	2007

(continued)

Table 10 (continued)

S. No.	State	TRIs in state	Availability of TRI website and link	Observations/remarks	Year of EST.
15	Odisha	Yes	http://www.scstrti.in/	Cover pages are uploaded but no review or abstract	1952
16	Rajasthan	Yes	http://tad.rajasthan.gov.in/tri/index.php/about-us/about-tri	Website has publication link but leads to nowhere	
17	Sikkim	Yes	Not Available	–	2016
18	Tamil Nadu	Yes	http://www.ooty.com/travel/tribalresearch.htm	Information is about tourism	1983
19	Telengana	Yes	http://twd.telangana.gov.in/tribal-cultural-research-and-training-institute-tcrti/	Telangana government site some introduction about TRI but not any published contents	2014
20	Tripura	Yes	http://www.tritripura.in/new/index.htm	144 publications available on the site of which 31 show downloadable hyperlink	1970
21	Uttar Pradesh	Yes	Not Available	–	1987
22	west Bengal	Yes	Not Available	–	1955

Source Compiled from individual websites and also corroborated from the data input from MOTA

have one TRI. There is no standard practice of effective monitoring and evaluation method followed for evaluating the performances of TRIs. In the absence of an autonomous body for coordinating the TRIs at the national level, all the TRIs have been practising ad hocsim and piecemeal performances. State governments seemingly do not provide full autonomy and functional freedom to TRIs and also there is no obligation on TRIs to carry out the regular and systematic research processes.

There is a need to revisit and reorient the functions and objectives of TRIs in the light of rapidly changing environment—*of late* with the advancement of information and communication technology—for the inclusive development of tribals from grass-roots level. The emphasis needed at focussing on skill and entrepreneurship development, economic, educational, health, nutritional and shelter need of tribal community. There is a need for coordinated efforts of dovetailing the welfare schemes and programmes with that of actual needs of the tribal communities, while TRIs need to delineate the data availability and shortages for better plan and development in a more inclusive way, keeping provisions for the monitoring and evaluation independently.

Suggestion for lead centre: In the absence of a permanent research coordination and data monitoring evaluation body at the centre level, the ad hoc manner of functioning of the TRIs did not find solutions to the issues of tribal backwardness for a quite some time.

The apex body MOTA need to set up a national-level autonomous lead centre or construe responsibility on pioneering research institutes like NILERD and convert all the TRIs as nodal centres for research and, M&E. This body would act as a coordinating agency and sanctions and approve all research-related matters in consultation with the guidance and of MOTA. The lead centre collects and compiles the real-time data through an interactive web portal directly feed by the beneficiaries/individual tribal community members. This would make obligation on the part of TRIs and nodal centres and corroborate the grass-roots developments and thereby better planning input can be ensured.

References

Minutes of the Meeting to Discuss the Action Plan of Tribal Research Institutes (TRIs), Centre of Excellences (COE) and Tribal Chairs, July 09, 2015.

Operational Guidelines for The scheme, Grant-in Aid to Tribal Research Institutes (TRIa), Research, Ministry of Tribal Affairs, Government of India. https://tribal.nic.in/writereaddata/Schemes/2-1RM-ResearchTraining.pdf. Accessed August 19, 2017.

Statistical profile of Scheduled tribes in India. (2013). *Ministry of Tribal Affairs, statistics division, Government of India, Designed and produced by DAVP, Ministry of Information and Broad casting*. Noida: Govt. of India and printed at Chaar Dishayen Printers.

TRI official Websites Consulted

TRI, Andhra Pradesh http://www.aptribes.gov.in/tcrti/About.html
TRI, Chhattisgarh http://cgtrti.gov.in/
TRI, Gujarat https://trti.gujarat.gov.in/
TRI, Jharkhand http://www.trijharkhand.com/
TRI, Kerala http://www.kirtads.kerala.gov.in/
TRI, Madhya Pradesh http://www.trdi.mp.gov.in/index.asp
TRI, Maharashtra http://trti.maharashtra.gov.in/frm_HomePage.php
TRI, Manipur http://www.trimanipur.com/
TRI, Odhisa http://www.scstrti.in/
TRI, Rajasthan http://tad.rajasthan.gov.in/tri/index.php/about-us/about-tri
TRI, Tamilnadu http://www.ooty.com/travel/tribalresearch.htm
TRI, Telangana http://twd.telangana.gov.in/tribal-cultural-research-and-training-institute-tcrti/
TRI, Tripura http://www.tritripura.in/new/index.htm

Gender Studies: A Theoretical Perspective

Indu Shekhar and Ruby Dhar

1 Introduction

Sociological theories through empirical evidence serve to explain social phenomena. The relationship between men and women through different periods has been explained by Engels in The Origin of the Family, Private Property and the State in 1884 through works of Morgan and the other nineteenth-century evolutionary anthropologists Agreeing with Morgan's classical outline of progress of human society through the stages of savagery, barbarism and civilization and the corresponding types of the governments, marriages and families largely dictated by the invention and discoveries, Engel systematically set out to provide a social explanation for the women's oppression by looking particularly at property as pivotal clue to the laws and principles of a gender theory. This was a shift from the religious ideology that women's inferiority was God-ordained or natural.

A look at evolution of Gender theories that explain the process of subjugation of women through social evolution is very important in today's times, where the blame for existing inequality is not seen in the social process but is put on the victims of this inequality.

In line with Marxists, the paper argues that while women are oppressed today and have been in the past, they have not always been so. This oppression arose at a particular stage of social development and was institutionalized through the particular form of the patriarchal family characteristic of that stage of social development. The objective of this paper is thus to trace the historical evidence of institutions that led to change from egalitarian relations to superior-subordinate

I. Shekhar (✉) · R. Dhar
NILERD, Sector A-7, Institutional Area, Narela, Delhi, India
e-mail: indusekhar.iamr@yahoo.co.in

R. Dhar
e-mail: ruby.dhar@nic.in

NILERD, *Reflecting on India's Development*,
https://doi.org/10.1007/978-981-13-1414-8_11

relations between men and women. For this purpose, the paper is divided into four sections. Section 2 traces the historical background of gender relations that resulted in subordination and subjugation of women drawing largely from works of Morgan and Engels. Section 3 challenges the conceptual and methodological framework used for gender studies. Section 4 looks at Anatomical, Hormonal and Cultural Hierarchy to understand the position of women and Sect. 5 presents the role of family, state and law in understanding gender studies.

2 Historical Background

The current discussions and debates about the study of gender anywhere make it necessary to include all kinds of knowledge for gender theorization. Gender theory cannot afford to be ahistorical, and gender historicity of practices has to be located in the development of institutions. The field of gender is too complex and contested, as everyday speech and grammer also show a sign of masculinization.

The gender relations during primitive society were egalitarian based on maternal clan as the basic unit of society. With the domestication of animals and accumulation of property, the ownership of the wealth began to shift from clan (gens) ownership into private ownership in the family. Women began to be exchanged as valued property and this changed the gender relations. This was accompanied by shifts in tracing the kinship line to emphasize the importance of paternity and the father, as well as a shift to monogamy in sexual relations.

Engels states "the overthrow of mother right was the world-historic defeat of the female sex" (Engels 1977). Men seized control over the households, women became degraded and slaves to men's lust and were the instruments for reproducing more children. In fact, the word family comes from the Latin term famulus which means household slave, and familia, the totality of slaves belonging to one man, the patriarch, who inherited all the wealth and wielded absolute power over all members of the household. This shift towards gender inequality was presented as a natural, not a social process.

The connectivity between early settlement and colonialism (as an antithesis) again as migration and its bearing upon the gender construction has not occupied the deserved spaces in the framework of the studies. Antithesis might have many layers and levels of responses to the existing one from very superfluous to deep structural one. Inventions may seem to be responsible for both settlement and (opposite of it) colonialism (as remigration) and should be seen in terms of the implications in the structure of kinship and property relationship between man and woman. The interaction of historical categories such as settlement, ancient societies, mercantilism, colonialism, decolonization, neocolonialism, modernization and globalization whether has influenced the social structure much or not should be the canvass and spectrum of gender both centrifugally and centripetally in order to understand how these have further marginalized women.

The years between World War I and World War II were marked by severe and prolonged unemployment in most of the advanced economies. "World War II marked the first time that nations with advanced economies had to mobilize all their resources. The United Kingdom and United States responded more effectively than Germany, whose Fuhrer did not encourage married women to leave their homes for paid employment" (Ginzberg 1975, p. 8). In the same way, with decolonization, a large number of countries with their independence in the late 1940s and 1950s set about to speed up their economic growth and modernize their societies, opened spaces for women participation in the formal sectors, an act that changed the route of humanity.

"In the United States, the dominant view was that the millions of married women who had responded to patriotic appeals by donning overalls and going to work would leave the labor force when hostilities came to an end. Of course, many did just that but war permanently altered the attitudes and behavior of married women toward work outside the home" (Ginzberg 1975, p. 8). After the overthrow of mother-right, the role of a woman labour has remained more or less the same, with unequal wages and spaces of sticky floors. Leaving the home and going for work outside, in modern times resembles, pre-settlement days when women were involved in gathering and hunting.

Now, we trace various theoretical perspectives that have led to change in relations and status of men and women.

2.1 Hetaerism

According to Bachofen, it is not the development of actual conditions under which men live, but the religious reflection of these conditions of life in the minds of men that brought about the historical changes in the mutual social position of man and woman (Engels, p. 10). In his view, the evolution from hetaerism to monogamy was a consequence of the evolution of religious ideas. Engels out rightly dismisses the argument because it is drawn from religious realm and further writes, "Clearly, such a conception-which regards religion as the decisive lever in world history-must finally end in sheer mysticism" (Engels, p. 11). Morgan, on the other hand, takes invention and discoveries and not materialism as a motor force of history. Determinations of what relations are biological, thus natural, and which are social, or cultural as a method of argumentations are required to avoid jumping from one to another. Methodology should be used to assume a more definitive importance in explaining what and how?

The journey from promiscuity to monogamy and theology to science and the rise of the middle classes have been dominated by institutional manipulations in an era of barter and digital in simultaneity. This can be the first thing in the prospectus of gender studies to see the ambit and gamut of the issues.

2.2 Matriarchate

It is argued that the first domestic institution in human history was not the family but the matrilineal—local clan, an argument augumented by continuous clannish-naming till date. However, this argument that early human kinship was matrilineal is nowadays widely discredited. Writing on Morgan, Engels opines, "He discovered that the gens, organized according to mother right, was the original form out of which developed the later gens, organized according to father right, the gens as we find it among the civilized peoples of antiquity" (Engels, p. 18). "The rediscovery of the original mother-right gens as the stage preliminary to the father-right gens of the civilized peoples has the same significance for the history of primitive society as Darwin's theory of evolution has for biology, and Marx's theory of surplus value for political economy" (Engels, p. 18).

2.3 Atonement

The publication of Bachofen's "*Mother Right*" can be said to be the beginning of the study of the history of the family. In the work, the author advances four propositions out of which; the first two are about "hetaerism" (promiscuity), third about gynecocracy and fourth about violation of a primeval religious injunction which is as such; "that the transition to monogamy, where the women belongs exclusively to one man, implied the violation of a primeval religious injunction (that is, in actual fact, the violation of the ancient traditional right of the other men to the same woman), a violation which had to be atoned for, or the toleration of which had to be purchased, by surrendering the woman for a limited period of time" (Engels, p. 10).

2.4 Child Bearing Altruism: Centrifugality of Love for Men

As stated earlier, for Engels, overthrow of mother-right was the cause of world historic defeat of the female sex and this was attributed to the onset of farming and pastoralism very rightly by Engels. However, the settlement might have been caused by childbearing consequence as well. "The mother-right gens has become the pivot around which this entire science turns; since its discovery we know in which direction to conduct our researches, what to investigate and how to classify the results of our investigation" (Engels, p. 18). "...gender relations are pivotal to the process of making "the world go round" (Beoku-Betts and Grant 2004, p. 409). He opines, "The social institutions under which men of a definite historical epoch and of a definite country live are conditioned by both kinds of production: by the stage of development of labour, on the one hand, and the family on the other" (Engels, p. 6).

The notion of conditioning can be developed by combining sensate and ideational together, for which both Bachofen and Briffault and Morgan and Engels need to be synthesized. For modern historical construction, rather doing with the opposition of sensate (material) and ideational (spiritual) in theories, to buy from Pitrim Sorokin has to be syenthesized.

For Levi Strauss, for the culture to emerge, groups of men must start to exchange women between themselves. This development was initiated by the establishment of the incest taboo. That implied to Lévi-Strauss that the men, instead of keeping all the women to themselves, gave them away to other men. The human society is always, according to Lévi-Strauss "*at first hand a masculine society*" (Lévi-Strauss quoted in Leacock 1981: 232). The concern of Levi-Strauss was with the basis of social organization in the exchange of women, arising out of the principle of exogamy giving rise to kinship system and structural patterns of larger structure which determines the permutations and combinations of every type of exchange. This is in tune with Morgan's understanding that society was based on sex (Levi-Strauss, 7. TESOK).

2.5 Can There Be an Antithesis of Exogamy-Endogamy?

Engels has raised a pertinent conceptual question of whether there can be an antithesis of exogamy and endogamy. One has to be very clear of the concepts of opposite, negation and binary set. Engels considers the antithesis between exogamy and endogamy as erroneous. "What Morgan only dimly surmised in 1871 is here developed with full comprehension. Endogamy and exogamy constitute no antithesis; up to the present no exogamous "tribes" have been brought to light anywhere" says Engels (Engels, p. 17). Levi-Strauss used the conceptual category of binary opposition instead of antithesis in his understanding of the elementary structure of kinship. It is his conceptual integrity that he places women in the category of nature and men in culture in binary construct.

3 Conceptual and Methodological Framework

In this section, we look at various conceptual and methodological frameworks adopted by thinkers for gender studies.

3.1 Individual Subjectivity to Plural Objectivity

Understanding the works of the giants of modern science and clear conceptualization remains at the core of every research, study and theorization. A blueprint of the framework and themes is more important than creating controversies surrounding the gender studies. The issue in the research on gender is not the schools, which come into existence, with scholars who foreground or mature any or gender studies and those who emphasize (plurality of variables) the intersection of caste, class, religion, age and language but in combining them altogether in a theoretical perspective historically. Gender might work in unison with caste in traditional society. Concepts have to be "causal" in nature so as to explore the consequences. The criticism against gender theorization is focused on descriptive and normative meanings. Comparative scholars tend to go one step beyond descriptive comparisons.

Attempt should be to explain the differences between cross-societal and national variation of the existing and normative levels of patterns and types of societies or governments, success and failure of a particular state policy, and the orchestration and occurrences of war and its impact on women. The job of the scholars should be to first singularize and then synthesize the demographic, technological and institutional assumptions in the direction of theory building beyond the caveats and specificity of societies and nation-states as done by Lewis Henry Morgan and Frederic Engels in their studies questioning the situation of women. Let us remember that the difference and classification are only initial building blocks of gender theorization to proceed to establish laws and principles. A semantic study of the nomenclature of the papers, modules and centres of gender study also can tell us about the state of affairs. Whether it is Gender Studies, or Women's Studies, or Women and Society, or Women's Question are different intonations. The work of an anthropologist could be to study the systems of kinship corresponding to the changing dimensions of the economic exchanges right from the inception. The studies of all the disciplines have to be reduced to the study of the mutuality of the relationship between man and woman to achieve theorization.

The social development in the process gave birth to two schools—Gynocentric emphasizing woman-centricism and Androcentric emphasizing man-centricism. The methodology of Durkheim, Marx, Weber and Freud has to be organized. Freud has become very significant to understand the exclusive right over each other in the journey from hetaerism to monogamy. Inescapability of Sigmund Freud to understand the mutuality between man and woman announced by Immanuel Wallerstein in the World Sociology Congress should become the scholarly duty. Gender has to be treated as a thing in Durkheimian conception of social fact having exteriority, constraint and generality. The Durkheimian relationship of Individual and collectivity should always be there while finding the locus of research. Beginning with the Weber' method of what it is not and his Theory of Action relating to all available phenomenological standpoints should be the backdrop of application. Phenomenology of Georg Wilhelm Friedrich Hegel, John Stuart Mill,

Adam Smith and symbolic interactionism of Irving Goffman should be theoretically synthesized. Once these pillars are founded, Subjective utility interpretation of Malinowski, External analogy of Evans-Pritchard and his concept of statelessness, Kinship and genetics of Robin Fox, rites de passage of Van Gannep and semantics of Noam Chomsky will work as frills and finials. A proper study of *Ancient Society* can give us the clue to the causal relationship between invention and discoveries on the one hand and the evolution of the subsequent institutions of family, property and the state on the other.

"For many of the scholars who reject a feminist epistemology, their unease arises from how the conceptualization of individuals is taken for granted in most of the feminist literature in countries such as the United States" (Purukayastha et al. 2003, p. 506). Either there has to be a study which emphasizes one unit and then synthesize with the whole or a variable which singularly remains and becomes encompassing. "A sharp distinction is assumed to separate the individual from any collectivity, between 'women' as an identifiable, embodied individual and women defined through multiple relationships" (Purukayastha et al. 2003, p. 506). Here, the difference of fundamental means of definition of two sexes should be borne in mind. "Such debates and disagreements on gender issues have to be understood with reference to the multilingual, multicultural nature of India, which has led to the development of different perspectives on gender, intersectionality, and power inequalities" (Purukayastha et al. 2003, p. 505). The different linguistic stock and types of speech never became a hurdle for Morgan to establish the stages. There may even be an analytical difference between intersectionality and interconnectivity.

Elson rightly finds a solution of dichotomies and nuances by combining the approach for theorization. "My research goal was to further elucidate the complicated interaction between the material body and the social body, and the findings lend support for a combined approach to theorizing gender identity" (Elson 2003, p. 766). The approach in my write up is to make it a plurality of approaches and not just combining the two. Along with woman as a body and woman as a society, the symbolic structures have to be read. Purukayastha et al. (2003) opine, "These authors, who described activism in post independence India, aimed at accessing social resources, collectively argued that women qua women make up an empty theoretical category and emphasized the interaction of class, gender, caste, religious, and regional specificities as key for understanding the conditions of women and men" (Purukayastha et al. 2003, p. 505). Do these intersections really count the mutuality of the relationship between man and woman?

3.2 Locus and Unit of Research

Locus of research is one of the central theoretical aspects for gender studies. Whether an individual or collectivity or an organization or institution should be the unit of study? As to the unit and locus of research, there cannot be any doubt that gender study has to consider individual, conjugal and communal (institution) to give meaning and interpretation to the existing and normative totality of the mutuality of relationship. In fact, there is no choice here but to consider all in a synthetic fashion to frame the understanding of the problem or solution. To do this, ambit and gamut of the categories with its connectivity to each other in terms of dependence and autonomy has to be set.

Yancey Martin in her work focusing on gender relations in organizations directs us to a level of reality that is, as she insightfully argues, hard to describe in text and hard to pin down in research. This practice of gender is local, subtle, often instantaneous, often barely noticed or made a theme in conversation. It is not what researchers can document in a questionnaire, not even (or not easily) in a retrospective interview" (Connell 2003, p. 370). These are must subjective orientations necessary to make the methods objective and develop further.

We have to include the practices as a variable in the study of gender. Yancey Martin is quite right when she says that gender practices "are guided only sometimes by intention relative to gender" (p. 355). That is to say, within a given practice, gender coexists with other determinants" (Connell 2003, p. 370). The other determinants could be what it is not. Let us see the dilemma of women in the professional career. This forces many women to forgo promotion and forces those women who do become managers to reconstruct their households so they can, "manage like a man" as Wajeman has suggested (Connell 2003, p. 371). Thus, "Patricia Yancey Martin gives us an exceptionally clear and useful review of the problems of theorizing gender in organizational contexts" (Connell 2003, p. 370). Such study on organization should be connected to the other levels and units of study. For example, let us not forget family.

Connell writes on Martin's Lecture, "She proposes the concept of a two-sided gender dynamic in organizational life: gendering practices, which embody institutionalized gender distinctions, and the process of 'practicing gender', in which particular people constitute gender relations in their continuing workplace activity" (Connell 2003, p. 370). This can be said to be a methodological venture in terms of classificatory attempts in the direction of theorization. "Most social—scientific accounts of 'practice' or 'action' are fundamentally individualistic, treating the person as the locus of subjectivity and agency. That goes for most theorizations of gender too, especially in the English-speaking world" (Connell 2003, p. 371). The study of individual should deal with the instinctual aspects while collective should deal with the adaptations of habituality leading to the formations of institutions. However, Connell possibly hints towards an overlapping in the method of defining the locus in the next sentence. "I think that Yancey Martin's theorization, despite her focus on organizational context, shares this individualized conception of what practice is" (Connell 2003, p. 371). Sartre made a distinction between levels of practice—individual practice the practico-inert, and developed the phenomena of groups. E. P. Thompson considers collectivities as the locus of subjectivity and agency.

3.3 *Glass Ceiling or Sticky Floor Hypothesis: Baxter and Wright*

"The "glass ceiling" is one of the most compelling metaphors for analysing inequalities between men and women in the workplace" (Baxter and Wright, p. 275). Baxter and Wright say that the metaphor of the glass ceiling seems to be confirmed by casual observation. Their claim, "It is a specific claim that the obstacles women face to promotion relative to men systematically increase as they move up the hierarchy" (p. 276). "In their recent article, Baxter and Wright (2000) argue that the metaphor of the glass ceiling does not accurately depict the barriers that women confront in the workforce" say Britton and William (Britton and Williams 2000, p. 804). They further write, "They suggest that barriers for women actually may be greater at the lower levels of job hierarchies than at the top" (Britton and Williams 2000, 804). "This is a controversial claim because it seems to suggest that attention to discrimination against women in upper management has been exaggerated and that there is no special problem requiring any special attention, as from the Federal Glass Ceiling Commission" (Ferree and Purukayastha 2000, p. 809). Critics do not agree with the notion of levels here. "We think that this misrepresents what is meant by a glass ceiling, because it assumes that each level is in some sense independent of each other level" (Ferree and Purukayastha 2000, p. 810). In reply to critics, Wright and Baxter continues, "We are interested in seeing whether the promotion obstacles across hierarchical levels faced by women relative to men are greater at the middle or top of organizations than at the bottom" (Wright and Baxter 2000, p. 818). Glass Ceiling Hypothesis is restricted to the corporate organization and does not help us in generalizing.

Drawing on a range of debates in an evolutionary frame from polygamy to monogamy and matriarchy to patriarchy, the attempt should be to sketch the existing theoretical issues of gender studies emanating may be first from the contradiction of biological or hormonal hierarchy and ritual or cultural hierarchy to deconstruct the jeopardy and situate the problem and offer solution.

4 Anatomical, Hormonal and Cultural Hierarchy

This section looks at some of the thinkers who placed anatomy, hormones and culture at the centre of women subjugation.

Hormonal consequence of childbearing added with the cultural hierarchy makes it a case of dilemma and jeopardy of double hierarchy. A myth of the sexual division of labour as the source of women' subjugation has to be demystified. Biologically, there is a psychic unity of mankind but there is a plethora of variations in cultural realm. It relates to the variations, specificity and generalizations in geographic region, caste, class, power, status, age, language, religion and race. It becomes a question of heterogeneity in terms of construction of rules, dominance, hegemony, patriarchy and the state. State's fellowship with men for war is being studied by many. "The demonization and regulation of women's bodies within religious patriarchies has been well documented in various religions" (Hartman and Marmon 2004, p. 389). The finding is a demand. "Feminist analysis has highlighted the extent of the oppression the various strictures surrounding the menstrual taboo effect-spoken and unspoken, encoded in texts, and transmitted orally" (Hartman and Marmon 2004, p. 389–390).

4.1 Social Fact

Gender is a social fact for being exterior, constraint and general. Gender as a social structure or gender function remains partial study. "Long historical precedent associates women's gender identities with their sexual/reproductive organs; uteruses and ovaries have even been employed as a synecdoche for women in their entirety" (Elson 2003, p. 753). The construction of gender identity based on reproductive organs is as old as human species. "Social theorists assert that gender identity is one of the most fundamental means by which individuals are recognized both by others and by themselves" (Elson 2003, p. 750).

Elson further writes, "What is the specific symbolic significance of ovaries to gender identity?" While the uterus, as the womb, may represent childbearing potential, the ovaries, generally perceived as sex hormone producers, may carry deeper gender significance" (Elson 2003, p. 751).

4.2 Sociology of Anatomy

Medical sociologists find biographical disruptions in the self. "As noted by several medical sociologists, medical events generate biographical disruptions or turning points; the individual's concept of who she or he is will never be the same as before" (Elson 2003, p. 753). Elson quoting Turner says, that a sociology of the body allows medical sociologists to appreciate "the intimate and necessary relationship between my sense of myself, my awareness of the integrity of my body and experience of illness as not simply an attack on my instrumental body (*Korper*) but as a radical intrusion into my embodied selfhood" (Elson 2003, p. 753). Embodiment and identity are related. Accordingly, "to change our embodiment is to change our identity" (p. 256). The moment we have culture, body is shaped. Foucault's work reinforces the extent to which "our bodies are trained, shaped, and impressed with the stamp of prevailing historical forms of selfhood, desire, masculinity, femininity" (Elson 2003, p. 753). Neither Sartre nor Foucault could give a theoretical breakthrough in understanding gender and it is better to hang around Morgan and Engels.

4.3 *Abomination of the Body*

To quote Elson again, "A female without a uterus or ovaries might carry a particular type of potential stigma-what Goffman referred to as an "abomination of the body" (p. 5) (Elson 2003, p. 753). A designation of hormonal hierarchy has been constructed. "These women constructed what I designate a *hormonal hierarchy*. This hierarchy constitutes what Bury might refer to as a necessary mobilization of resources to face the crisis in identity initiated by gynecological surgery" (Elson 2003, p. 754). Lived experiences of natural menopause have been studied. "Although feminist sociologists have undertaken extensive research on the lived experiences of "natural" menopause, they have not sufficiently explored the experiences of women who reach this stage through surgery" (Elson 2003, p. 754).

The interconnectivity of cultural backgrounds—the regional, the class and caste variations of patriarchal practices, communities, the state, and the status of women of different religious, ethnic and linguistic variations have been the concern of a significant group of writers on gender research. The origin, diffusion and impact of one domain over the next are deep structural one and very difficult to unravel in the course of development. It seems that straddling the opposition of sexes and matriarchy-patriarchy dichotomy to the level of symbols could be a theoretical possibility to work out. However, the facts should not be pressurized to fit the theory or forget those that do not fit in.

4.4 *Duality of Religious and Scientific Life*

The violation of a primeval religious injunction was used to establish male superiority. Scholars argue that religion is most rooted in South Asia which is irreducible. Let us remember that Morgan did not give importance to the regional religious specificity while Karl Marx coined an Asiatic mode of production what A. K. N. Karim calls a hydraulic society. Religious and scientific spheres are two distinct domains where the mutuality between man and woman is lurking the most. Sartre' notion of level is an existing and temporal fact. Homogeneity and heterogeneity of level across classes have to be bridged by a unified conceptualization which considers religion and science together and reduce to either law or principle. There may be the same principle working for the subjugation of women in the religious spheres to scientific domain.

Durkheimian definition of religion needs to be added with "a mechanism" (that controls) and not only as a system of belief. Science growing along with magic before established religion took over religion in most of the modernizing societies with the acceptance of science as a dominant principle in lives. "In early Eastern and Western cultures, rulers gained power and wealth from religion. Yet today, religion has waned, especially in highly developed nations. Now the favored method of control is through money" (Marrs 2013, p. 175). There has been a resurgence of both religiosity and women' participation in the last few centuries. "The religious resurgence, as we came to quickly understand, was not a consequence of Hindutva's poisonous political message alone" (Nair 2017, p. 36, EPW).

Religion was a form of governments in early civilizations. "These clerics got a taste of wealth and power, a taste they were loath to relinquish. Religion soon evolved into a rigid structure of dogmas, catechisms, tithing, and obedience" (Marrs 2013, p. 172). This created a respectful servitude among women. "Certain civilizations had firmly established the idea that the clergy could be the only religious authority and that kingship was a divine right" (Marrs 2013, p. 172). And the worst was the establishment of kingship which made women more miserable. The aura of Rites de Passage (birth, marriage and death) of Van Gannep revolves around religion. Once religion was well established, it started hobnobbing with the political systems.

4.5 Science as a New Magic

Arthur C. Clarke once stated that any sufficiently advanced technology is indistinguishable from magic. However, it should not be read as reversibility. A scientificity in religion (routinization) and religiousity in scientisim (ritualism of gadgets) can be observed from the modern habituality. Many ancient philosophers including Cicero also wrote that the occult mysteries had more to do with natural science than with religion. "Humanity appears to be in a footrace to see whether we will gain true freedom and liberty or submit to the technological and totalitarian world envisioned by Huxley and Orwell and promoted by Perkin's corporatocracy" (Marrs 2013, p. 338). Modern science is distinct in two ways—highest paid and heavily dominated by men. Modern nuclear science converges with the similar fear of state and religion of the past.

4.6 Embodiment to Entitlement: Plausible Possibility

Both the concepts of embodiment and entitlement evolved during the course of search signify the contextualization of the problem and solution to the gender issues. Elson suggests, "The only way to establish an embodied sociology, they claimed, is to shift from theorizing about bodies in a disembodied manner to perspectives of theorizing from lived bodies" (Elson 2003, p. 766). There is always a lust for hegemony. "Struggles for hegemony occur between groups of men who embody different masculinities and the bearers of different gender strategies" (p. 371). (Connell 2003, p. 370). Women are deprived of what becomes the reigning principle of organizing the collectivity individually or individual collectively. For example, the cases of magician, priestess and scientists? The actual and factual sense of ownership and possession of males of bows, soils, houses, cars, etc.

are infinite compared to women. A proper extension of Morganian techniques and skills of connecting the thread such as, inventions and discoveries as the elemental thing, irrespective of the types of governments, marriage and family across time and space should always be there in the back of the mind to find the causal concepts to situate the problem.

The levels of the countries may not be the same to the communities as it is difficult to summate the levels. Instead of that, it would be better to study three Is—Impulse, Instinct and institutions. A proper study of these three Is might give some light on the impermeable barrier for vertical mobility. Once the archaeology of a mind is set in the family, it will naturally extend to the institutional spaces. Family has to be particularly placed as one of the central variables in the schema of the construction of liberating framework.

5 The Family, State and Laws

Till now, we have looked at different ideologies to describe relations between men and women as well as the perspectives on subordination of women, but one needs to bear in mind that this dichotomous view of gender is not universal. In some cultures, gender is viewed as fluid. The practice of *berdache* (occasionally or permanently living and dressing as the opposite gender) has been noted among certain Aboriginal groups (Jacobs et al. 1997). Samoan culture accepts what they refer to as a "third gender." *Fa'afafine*, which translates as "the way of the woman," is a term used to describe individuals who are born biologically male but embody both masculine and feminine traits (Poasa 1992).

Assumptions about gender roles within marriage assume a prominent place in structural functionalism. Talcott argued that the contradiction between occupational roles and kinship roles of men and women in North America created tension or strain on individuals as they tried to adapt to the conflicting norms or requirements.

Critical sociologists, on the other hand, think that society is structured by relations of power and domination among social groups (e.g. women versus men) that determine access to scarce resources. Social problems and contradictions are created when dominant groups exploit or oppress subordinate groups.

Friedrich Engels who had studied the family structure and gender roles and suggested that the same owner–worker relationship seen in the labour force is also seen in the household, with women assuming the role of the proletariat. Women are therefore double exploited in capitalist society, both when they work outside the home and when they work within the home.

According to feminist theory, family plays an important role in perpetuating male dominance. In patriarchal societies, men's contributions are seen as more valuable than those of women. Additionally, women often perceive a disconnect between their personal experiences and the way the world is represented by society as a whole. Patriarchal perspectives and arrangements, widespread and taken for granted, are built into the relations of ruling. As a result, not only do women find it difficult to find their experiences acknowledged in the wider patriarchal culture, their viewpoints also tend to be silenced or marginalized to the point of being discredited or considered invalid.

Keeping in mind these broad perspectives, the paper argues how entitlements to women can be advanced by family, state and legal system.

5.1 Entitlement Begins in Family

Family is both an institution and association. It can well mediate between the two formal sides of school on the one hand, and state and work place on the other—the rationale for its centrality. Despite all the exclusiveness of an individual, family and society, one has to look for the laws on the structure and actions emanating from a gender perspective. And finally, the nature of the state matters a lot. The content analysis of the policies of the governments should be done. "Poverty and women are two closely connected themes in developing countries. Even in households with higher levels of living, intra-household inequality in terms of resources exists considerably, leaving women worse-off" (Mitra 2018, p. 1). He further says, "women in low-income households, particularly, undergo a great deal of struggle for survival in comparison to their male counterparts" (Mitra 2018, p. 1).

5.2 Entitlement Extended by State

To quote futuristic Morgan for the possibility, what Engels calls "verdict" on civilization, (Morgan 1877, p. 552) "The human mind stands bewildered in the presence of its own creation. The time will come, nevertheless, *when human intelligence will rise to the mastery over property*, (my italics) and define the relations of the state to the property it protects, as well as the obligations and the limits of the rights of its owners" (Engels, p. 175). The obligation of modern nation-states are constantly changing for welfare. "The interests of society are paramount to individual interests, and the two must be brought into just and harmonious relation. A mere property career is not the final destiny of mankind, if progress is to be the law of the future as it has been of the past" (Engels, p. 175). The destiny of mankind seems to be waiting for human intelligence. "It will be a revival, in a higher form, of the liberty, equality and fraternity of the ancient gentes" (Engels, p. 175).

5.3 Mediating Muddling Laws

In Haryana to protect the women from domestic violence has been studied by the scholars reflected an attrition rate of over 54%. "Most stakeholders interviewed stressed the need for shelter homes. The role of the police in the act's implementation also requires clarification" (Sakhrani 2017, p. 27). It also says, "There was low awareness amongst women about the right to free legal aid, despite established provisions for free legal aid". (Sakhrani 2017, p. 27) Not only has this, the inherent legal and policy biases been noticed by a study of the United Nations, the study quotes the Egyptian Penal Code No. 58 of 1937: "Article 237. Whoever surprises *his wife in the act of adultery* and *kills her* on the spot together with her adulterer-partner *shall be punished with detention instead of the penalties prescribed* in article 234 and 236". (Equality Now 2015, p. 39) And the interpretation is, "Article 237 of the Egyptian Penal Code *allows for a lesser punishment for men who kill their wives than for other forms of murder*" (Equality Now 2015, p. 39). Same is the case of its hoary counterpart. Indian Penal Code 1860, as amended by the Criminal Law (Amendment) Act No. 13 of 2013', "Exception 2. *Sexual intercourse or sexual acts by a man with his own wife, the wife not being under fifteen years of age, is not rape*" (Equality Now 2015, p. 34).

Various writers developed modified forms of evolutionism. Thus, there is the theory that social institutions do not develop in an upward straight line, but along a parabolic curve. Progression is neither unilinear nor reversal but a parabolic curve to D. N. Majumdar and T. N. Madan. An institution starts in a particular form, develops into its opposite and then further develops into its original form, but at a new, higher level. The earliest form of property ownership was undeliberate communal ownership. Later on, the institution of private ownership emerged, but the rational doctrines of property through the agency of the state again attempts deliberate communal ownership. The same way from promiscuity to monogamy to loosening of rigid sexual morality justified on various grounds can be seen. Lack of clothing to dressing of the whole body to nudism as a physical culture movement is obvious. Hypothesis is not of reversibility or degradation but parabolic curve in the progression of mutuality between man and woman. The nature of transitions in institutions strengthens the superiority of men over women by denying them the reigning principles—be it religious or scientific endeavors—two pillars of patriarchy pampered and perpetrated by the state. "The answer may be found by simply reviewing human history. We are taught that humans slowly evolved from hunter-gatherers to farmers who gathered in city-states, which became nations and empires" (Marrs 2013, p. 339). Historical tectonics is more important than the plate.

References

Baxter, J., & Wright, E. O. (2000). The glass ceiling hypothesis, a comparative study of the United States, Sweden, and Australia, *Gender and Society, 14*(2), 275–294.

Beoku-Betts, J. & Grant, L. (2004, December) Four years of books review in gender and society, similarities and differences in US focused and international works. *Gender and Society, 18*(3), 409–411.

Britton, D. M., & Williams, C. L. (2000, December). Response to baxter and wright, symposium. *Gender and Society, 14*(6), 804–808.

Connell, R. W. (2003, June). Developing a theory of gender as practice, notes on Yancey Martin's Feminist lecture. *Gender and Society, 17*(3), 370–372, 370.
Elson, J. (2003, October). Hormonal hierarchy, hysterectomy and stratified stigma. *Gender and Society, 17*(5) 750–770.
Engels, F. (1977). *The origin of the family*. Private Property and the State: Progress publishers, Moscow.
Equality Now, Words and Deeds. (2015, January). *Ending sex discrimination in the law*. www.equalitynow.org.
Ferree, M. M., & Purukayastha, B. (2000). Equality and cumulative disadvantage, response to Baxter and Wright. *Gender and Society, 14*(6), 809–813.
Ginzberg, E. (1975). *Human economy*. US: Mc-GrawHill inc.
Hartman, T., & Marmon, N. (2004, June). Lived regulations, systemic attributions, menstrual separation and ritual immersion in the experiences of orthodox Jewish women. *Gender and Society, 18*(3), 389–405.
Jacobs, S.-E., Thomas, W., & Lang, S. (1997). *Two spirit people: Native American gender identity, sexuality, and spirituality*. Champaign, IL: University of Illinois Press.
Leacock E. B. (1981). *Myths of male dominance*. U.S: Monthly Review Press.
Marrs, J. (2013). *Our occulted history*. New York: Harper Collins Publishers.
Mitra, A. (2018). Poverty, women, and dignity: Reflecting on the writings of Ashapurna Devi. In *Asia-Pacific Social Science Review 17*(3), pp. 1–14.
Morgan, L. H. (1877). *Ancient society, or researches in the lines of human progress from savagery through barbarism to civilization*. Macmillan & Co.
Nair, J. (2017). Faith, belief, piety and feminism, beyond an awkward relationship. *EPW, 52*(42–43).
Poasa, Kris. (1992). The samoan Fa'afafine: One case study and discussion of transsexualism. *Journal of Psychology and Human Sexuality, 5*(3), 39–51.
Purukayastha, B., et.al. (2003, August). The study of gender in India: A partial review. *Gender and Society, 17*(4), 503–524.
Sakhrani, M., et.al. (2017, November). Protection of women from domestic violence act (2006) in Haryana. *EPW, 3*(46).
Wright, E. O., Baxter, J. (2000, December). The glass ceiling hypothesis, a reply to critic. *Gender and Society, 14*(6), 814–821.

Websites

https://opentextbc.ca/introductiontosociology/chapter/chapter12-gender-sex-and-sexuality/. Accessed on April 24, 2018.
http://science.jrank.org/pages/9466/Gender-Studies-Anthropology-Feminist-Interventions-Legacy-Seventies.html. Accessed on April 24, 2018.

Gender Inequality: A Comparison of India and USA

Ruby Dhar, Ved Prakash and Bhoop Singh

1 Introduction

Social inequality is the existence of unequal opportunities and rewards for different social positions or statuses within a group or society, on the basis of this, gender inequality refers to the differential ability of men and women to access society's resources and to receive its privileges. Because historically men have garnered greater social power, gender inequality has systematically disadvantaged women. According to Collins, gender inequality is complicated, moreover, by the intersection of gender with race/ethnicity, social class, age and sexuality. That is, every individual, categorized as either male or female, also falls somewhere within a matrix of domination that includes these other dimensions.

Gender inequality is therefore a form of inequality which is distinct from other forms of economic and social inequalities. It dwells not only outside the household but also centrally within it. It stems not only from pre-existing differences in economic endowments between women and men but also from pre-existing gendered social norms and social perceptions. Gender inequality has adverse impact on development goals as it reduces economic growth. It hampers the overall well-being because blocking women from participation in social, political and economic activities can adversely affect the whole society.

Many developing countries including India have displayed gender inequality in education, employment and health. It is common to find girls and women suffering

R. Dhar (✉) · V. Prakash · B. Singh
NILERD, Sector A-7, Institutional Area, Narela, Delhi, India
e-mail: ruby.dhar@nic.in

V. Prakash
e-mail: ved_107@yahoo.co.in

B. Singh
e-mail: bhoopsingh.iamr@gmail.com

NILERD, *Reflecting on India's Development*,
https://doi.org/10.1007/978-981-13-1414-8_12

from high mortality rates. India's ranking on various gender indices present a very grim picture, India ranked 125 on Gender Development Index, out of 188 countries in 2015 (UNDP, HDR—2016). As per Global Gender Gap Report (2017) (WEF 2017), India stands at a rank of 108, out of 144 countries, showing that Indian women are at a disadvantage in several important ways. The index focuses not only on empowerment of women but on the relative gap between men and women in four fundamental categories—economic participation, educational attainment, health and survival, and political empowerment. India ranks 139 on economic participation, 112 on educational attainment, ranks world's fourth lowest at 141 on health and survival and 15 on political empowerment. India's ranking has improved from 113 (among 135 countries polled) to 108 (of 144 countries polled) largely due to its ranking in political empowerment.

The Organisation for Economic Co-operation and Development's Social Institutions Gender Index (SIGI) ranked India at 56 out of 86 countries in 2012, which was an improvement from its 2009 rank of 96 out of 102. The SIGI is a measure of discriminatory social institutions that are drivers of inequalities, rather than the unequal outcomes themselves, showing that social institutions can be a reason for gender inequalities in India.

According to a large number of studies, gender inequality impedes economic growth (Klasen 1999; Dollar and Gatti 1999; King and Mason 2001). Gender inequality in education lowers the average quality of human capital and thus negatively impacts economic growth. According to Mitra, labour market inequality spills over to inequality in education, health and political involvement (Mitra 2010). It is an accepted academic stand that sexism is systematic and structural, and that it involves the subordination of one group as a whole by another group which enjoys power and advantage in the system (Benatar 2012).

Despite numerous government and nongovernmental initiatives, laws that have being enacted for empowerment and protection of women from discrimination have not been able to make remarkable difference to position of women.

The present paper makes an attempt to compare gender inequality in India and United States of America (USA). USA was chosen for comparison with India first because both of them are largest democracies in the world and second because USA plays a dominant role in gender policymaking at international level and India on the other hand is a strong growing economy with a highly skewed sex ratio and having had women at both Prime minister and Presidential level in Government. For the purpose of comparison, data has been taken from Gender Data Portal of World Bank. Indicators related to Education, Health, Labour Force Participation and Political Involvement have been used. The focus is on data for the period 2007–2017.

There are many reasons to be concerned about existing gender inequalities in well-being-related dimensions such as education, health, employment, labour and politics. From a well-being and equity perspective, such gender inequalities are problematic as they lower well-being and are a form of injustice in most conceptions of equity or justice.

2 Education

Education is the basic requirement for human development, equally important to improve the women's status and autonomy. With education, employment opportunities are broadened and income levels are increased. The development of an individual and the progress of a nation depend on education.

The development of a society can be judged by measuring the issues related to educational inequality prevalent in the society. The prevalence of unequal distribution of education among male and female students hinders the development of a nation. In this section, we will look at few educational indicators to assess gender inequality in India and USA.

2.1 Government Expenditure on Education

Figure 1 shows government expenditure on education (as % of GDP) by India and USA for the year 2010–2014.

From the figure, one finds that USA spends much more than India on education; however, the expenditure on education shows a constant decline in USA while for India there has been increase in expenditure from 2011 to 2013, while the expenditure dropped by 0.03 points in 2014.

According to the United Nations Educational, Scientific and Cultural Organization (UNESCO), India has the lowest public expenditure on higher education per student in the world.

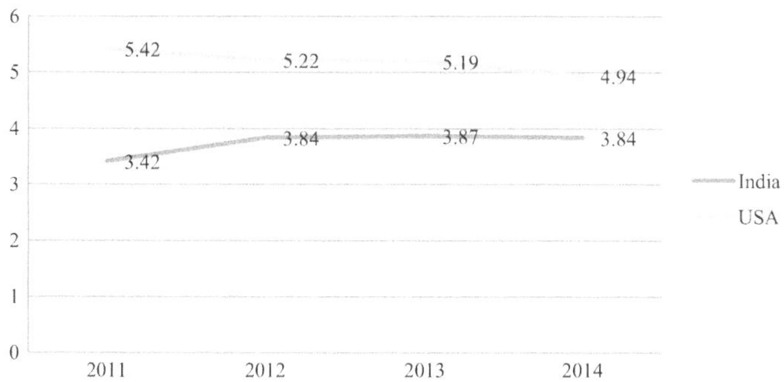

Fig. 1 Government expenditure on education (% of GDP)

2.2 *Out of Schoolchildren*

This is an important indicator to assess the situation of education in any country. A comparison of children out of school (primary) in both the countries is presented below in Table 1.

India has been able to reduce the number of female children out of school to 9.31 lakhs in 2013 from 22.48 lakhs in 2007, thus showing about 41% decrease in out of school female children, while the number of male children has increased from 15.43 lakhs to 19.55 lakhs during the same period.

In USA, one finds an increase in out of schoolchildren for both males and females. The number of out of school females was 2.49 lakhs in 2007 while it increased to 7.44 lakhs in 2013, an increase of about 33%. In the case of males, the total number was around 4.24 lakhs in 2007, while it was 7.73 lakhs in 2013, around 55% increase.

To have better understanding of situation of education, let us look at school enrolment in primary and secondary school.

2.3 *School Enrolment—Primary*

Enrolment of all eligible children of school-going age is an important step towards achieving 100% literacy.

A look at Table 2 also shows that female school enrolment at primary level has increased from 111.46% in 2008 to 114.95% in 2015 in India, while in USA the enrolment has decreased from 102.27% in 2008 to 99.4% in 2015. For male children, there is a decline in school enrolment for both India and USA; however, the decline is more sharp for India as compared to USA (Table 2).

Table 1 Out of school children (primary)

Year	India		USA	
	Male	Female	Male	Female
2007	15.43	22.48	4.24	2.49
2008	23.8	14.06	3.61	2.4
2009	36.36	18.65	6.13	3.41
2010	31.38	16.88	6.86	5.76
2011	36.9	16.95	8.44	6.37
2012	24.58	13.85	7.36	7.07
2013	19.55	9.31	7.73	7.44

Table 2 School enrolment—primary (Gross %)

	India		USA	
	Male	Female	Male	Female
2008	110.36	111.46	102.02	102.27
2009	108.39	110.93	101.01	101.56
2010	108.15	110.37	100.06	99.17
2011	106.9	110.04	98.53	99.12
2012	108.01	111.74	99.02	97.7
2013	104.85	116.98	98.62	97.99
2014	102.35	114.03	98.65	98.48
2015	102.71	114.95	99.16	99.4

Table 3 School enrolment—secondary (Gross %)

	India		USA	
	Male	Female	Male	Female
2008	64.01	56.76	94.52	94.22
2009	62.09	57.28	93.23	94.63
2010	65.5	60.87	92.51	93.58
2011	68.24	64.43	93.49	94.98
2012	70.79	67.39	93.92	94.35
2013	68.61	69.25	94.71	94.77
2014	73.82	74.8	95.41	96.38
2015	73.55	74.46	96.69	97.7

2.4 *School Enrolment—Secondary*

A look at secondary school enrolment figures (Table 3) shows nearly a 20% increase for Indian females from 2008 to 2015, while female enrolment in USA has increased only by about 2%. Male enrolment in secondary school has also shown an increase in both the countries. However, the increase is around 9% for India and only 2% for USA.

From the above figures, one can infer that initiatives of Indian government to increase enrolment of girl child in schools have shown positive results. Levy (1971) using data from 42 less developed countries tried to explore the relationship between social, political, economic and educational variables and the dropout rate from primary schools. It was found that school systems with high rates of repetition also have high dropout rates over the primary cycle. This suggests that automatic promotion may reduce educational wastage. Automatic promotion in form of non-repetition till class VIII was adopted by Government of India under The Right of Children to Free and Compulsory Education Act, which came into effect on 1 April 2010, this might be one of the reasons for drop in number of out of schoolchildren, mid-day meal scheme for children might be other reason. A UNESCO (2014) policy paper shows that increasing education expenditure and social cash transfers have led to increase in school enrolment. Increased enrolment of girls in India might be due to increased expenditure on education and government schemes like 'Ladli' which gives monetary benefits to parents of girl child.

In 2012, there were an estimated 1.8 million homeschooled students in the United States, which is an increase from 850,000 in 1999, when estimates were first reported. In addition, the estimated percentage of the school-age population that was homeschooled increased from 1.7% in 1999 to 3.4% in 2012 (US Dept. of Education). There was significant increases in homeschooling between 1999 and 2003 and between 2003 and 2007 (Redford et al. 2017).

2.5 *Female Teachers in Educational Institutions*

It is widely observed that dropout rates for girls are higher as compared to boys in most parts of the world. Chimombo (1999) observes that though the enrolment in school is almost same for girls and boys, boys have a higher likelihood of continuing school compared to girls. Holmes (2003) also found that girls overall attain less education and tend to drop out earlier as compared to boys. Secondary school enrolment is an indicator of this phenomenon.

From above tables on primary and secondary school enrolments, one finds that secondary school enrolment shows a decline when compared with primary school enrolment for both the countries. However, this decline is much more pronounced for India than USA.

Holcamp (2009) found that some socio-cultural factors highly impact girls dropout rate though those factors also contribute to boys dropout rate but to a lesser extent.

One of the factors that impact girls participation and enrolment at schools is availability of female teachers. Solotaroff et al. (2007) found that in Afghanistan, lack of female teachers is an obstacle to girls participation and enrolment in schools.

A look at availability of female teachers at Primary, Secondary and Tertiary education in India and USA (Table 4) shows that there is very wide disparity among both countries in percentage of female teachers at primary level, India has nearly 40% less teachers at primary level when compared with USA. At Secondary level, the gap has decreased to 17–19%, and around 9–11% at tertiary level.

Table 4 Availability of female teachers at primary, secondary and tertiary educational institutions (%)

	India			USA		
	2013	2014	2015	2013	2014	2015
Primary	48.184	49.488	49.49	87.156	87.159	87.147
Secondary	45.145	43.213	43.152	62.036	62.029	62.009
Tertiary	39.046	39.028	38.614	48.591	49.106	49.106

This is, however, in contrast to studies which state that one of the major factors that might affect enrolment of girls in primary schools is non-availability of female teachers, as the primary school enrolment in India has been increasing despite fewer number of female teachers.

From above, one can say that government expenditure on education is higher for USA. Primary school enrolment in USA is on the decline for both male and female, while India shows an increase in primary enrolment for girls and decrease for boys. Secondary school enrolment for girls and boys is on the increase; however, there is a gap of about 23% when compared with USA. The gap between female teachers in USA and India is maximum at primary level, which reduces at secondary and tertiary level.

3 Health

Economists and health experts have known for years that people who live in poorer societies live shorter lives. But research also points to an additional factor in explaining life expectancy: a society's level of inequality. People live longer in nations with lower levels of inequality.[1]

Thus, gender inequality continues to have a negative impact on many health outcomes. Gender-related power imbalances contribute to excess female mortality across the life cycle, and harmful gender norms affect men and boys by encouraging risk-taking and limiting health-seeking behaviours.

While gender equality has made the most progress in areas such as education and labour force participation, health inequality between men and women continues to plague many societies today. While both males and females face health disparities, girls and women experience a majority of health disparities. This comes from the fact that many cultural ideologies and practices have structured society in a way whereby women are more vulnerable to abuse and mistreatment, making them more prone to illnesses and early death. Kawachi et al. (1999) found that societies with high gender inequality are unhealthy for men and women.

Although women around the world share many similarities in terms of the health-impacting challenges, there are also many distinct differences that arise from their varying states of socio-economic conditions. The type of conditions in which women live is largely associated with not only their own socio-economic status but also that of their nation.

We use three measures of gender inequality in health outcomes, viz. the life expectancy advantage of women relative to men, infant and under-five mortality rate and the maternal mortality.

[1]For details refer https://inequality.org/facts/inequality-and-health/.

3.1 Life Expectancy at Birth

Research has shown that if men and women received similar nutrition, medical attention and general health care, women would live longer than men (Dennerstein et al. 1977). According to a WHO report (2009), females generally live longer than males—on average by 6 to 8 years. This difference is partly due to an inherent biological advantage for the female. But it also reflects behavioural differences between men and women. Newborn girls are more likely to survive to their first birthday than newborn boys are. This advantage continues throughout life: women tend to have lower rates of mortality at all ages, probably due to a combination of the genetic and behavioural factors.

Table 5 shows life expectancy at birth for males and females in India and USA. A look at life expectancy table shows it to be true for USA but for India this biological advantage of women is for about 2–3 years. According to Waldron (1983) when social discrimination decreases, women's life expectancy increases.

3.2 Infant and Under-Five Mortality Rate

However, Table 6 contradicts the above statement as one finds that female infant and under-five mortality rate in India is higher than male mortality rate under both categories, thus indicating that the natural biological advantage of girls is outset by social disadvantage accorded to them.

The statement, however, holds true for USA where the female mortality rate for infants and under five is lower than that of males, though the difference is not of 6–8 years as indicated by WHO. Thus, one can infer that apart from biological and behavioural factors there are socio-cultural factors that affect mortality rate.

Table 5 Life expectancy at birth

	India		USA	
	Male	Female	Male	Female
2008	64.84	66.83	75.6	80.6
2009	65.18	67.34	76	80.9
2010	65.49	67.84	76.2	81
2011	65.79	68.33	76.3	81.1
2012	66.08	68.78	76.4	81.2
2013	66.35	69.19	76.4	81.2
2014	66.61	69.56	76.5	81.3
2015	66.86	69.88	76.3	81.2
2016	67.09	70.17	76.3	81.2

Table 6 Mortality rate (per 1000 live births)

Mortality rate—infant					Mortality rate—under 5			
	India		USA		India		USA	
	Male	Female	Male	Female	Male	Female	Male	Female
2010	44.8	46.3	6.8	5.6	56	61.8	8	6.6
2015	36	36.3	6.2	5.1	43.9	46.7	7.2	6
2016	34.5	34.6	6.1	5.1	41.9	44.2	7.1	5.9

3.3 Maternal Deaths

It is often argued that number of maternal deaths [generally measured through Maternal Mortality Ratio (MMR)] is a reflection of gender inequality. Bhalotra and Gomes (2014) argue that as MMR is a woman-specific condition, public policy attention directed at MMR, and, accordingly, differences in life expectancy between women and men across countries are a reflection of differences in gender inequality across countries.

Maternal mortality reduction has been a priority under MDGs and now under SDGs. Sen, who in 1990, pointed out the phenomenon of 'missing women' further highlighted in 2001 that '[i]n some regions of the world inequality between women and men directly involves matters of life and death, and takes the brutal form of unusually high mortality rates for women …'. In fact, 'other than pre-birth and in early childhood, women are most likely to be missing relative to men in child-bearing years' (Duflo 2011).

A phenomenon clearly visible from data for India in Table 7 showing high incidence of maternal deaths. Although the number is continually declining over the years, it is alarmingly higher than USA, thus showing the gender disadvantage of women in India.

Bhalotra and Gomes (2014) in their study found that maternal mortality rates and female life expectancy advantage are significantly related to different measures—gender prejudice in society over and above income differences across societies, and shows that income by itself is insufficient in explaining cross-country differences in gender-unequal health outcomes. This has also been shown by Jayachandran (2014)

Table 7 Number of maternal deaths

	India	USA
2008	64,000	580
2009	60,000	600
2010	57,000	580
2011	54,000	580
2012	52,000	570
2013	49,000	570
2014	47,000	560
2015	45,000	550

who argue that poor countries have cultural features that exacerbate gender prejudice. 'Being poor is insufficient to explain parents' strong desire to have a son in China and India, for example'.

4 Labour Force Participation

As per ILO, last few decades have seen an increase in women's labour force participation across the globe. However, most of it is aimed at increasing women's employment but not necessarily improvement in quality of employment. The number of women in top positions is few and rare. Thus, gender equality at work is still a distant dream for many countries of the world.

For LFP, we compare India and USA on the following indicators: Labour force participation rate, wage and salaried workers, employment in agriculture, industry and services and self-employment.

4.1 Labour Force Participation Rate

Labour force participation rate (LFP) is the ratio of labour force (employed and unemployed but seeking work) to the population of respective age cohort. It is, therefore, a key determinant of the currently active population or an indicator of the magnitude of the supply of labour in the economy and a crucial component of long-term economic growth (Fig. 2).

Figure 2 shows that labour force participation rate has declined for all the four categories from 2008 to 2017. Labour force participation rate for Indian males is highest while for females is lowest. If economic growth was the only criterion for labour force participation, then there should not be disparity among LFPR of males and females in USA. However, one finds that LFPR for females is lower than that of males in USA reflecting disparity in LFP among males and females. In case of India, there is a wide disparity in LFPR of males and females reflecting that there are

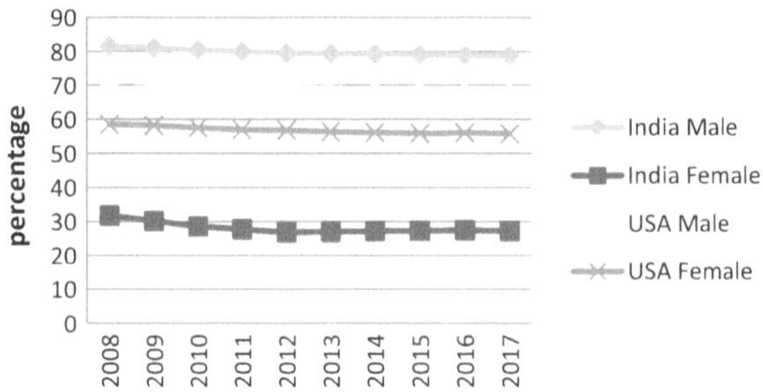

Fig. 2 Labour force participation rate

number of other factors than economic that may affect participation of women in labour force.

4.2 Sector-Wise Employment

Table 8 gives sector-wise employment for males and females in India and USA.

From the table, one finds that in India, highest percentage of women are employed in agriculture, although there is a decrease in their employment from 68.17% in 2008 to 56.36% in 2017. Their participation in services and industries shows an increase from 16.71% in 2008 to 25.94% in 2017 and 15.12% in 2008 to 17.69%, respectively. The same trend is seen for Indian males. A look at data for USA shows that service sector is dominated by females, as more than 90% are employed by services, followed by around 8% by industry and only 0.9% are employed by agriculture sector. This is understandable, USA being a developed country has moved from agriculture to service sector while India is still dependent on agriculture.

One interesting observation is that in USA the percentage of females in industries is much lower as compared to males, while percentage of females in services is much higher when compared with males, an examination of the same would make a good study.

4.3 Wage and Salaried Workers

A comparison between India and USA shows that more than 92% of females in USA are wage and salaried workers as compared to around 87% males (Table 9). India presents a very dismal picture as only around 21% of its males and 18.06% of females worked with wages and salaries in 2017. India has seen an increase in its wage and salaried workers since 2008 for both males (from 16.66% to 21.9%) and females (11.79%–18.06%); however, the increase is more in case of Indian females. No such phenomenon is observed in case of USA where the percentage of workers has remained more or less static during the studied period.

4.4 Self-employment

Table 10 presents interesting fact that about 81.94% of females in India were self-employed in 2017 as compared to only 7.34% in USA. The same is true for Indian males; this is an interesting finding as it explains the low percent of wage and salaried workers (both males and females) in India. However, a large number of these self-employed (more than 90%) run petty, unregistered enterprises/business

Table 8 Sector-wise employment (% of male/female employment)

Year	Agriculture				Industry				Services			
	India		USA		India		USA		India		USA	
	Male	Female	Male	Female	Male	Female	Male	Female	Male	Female	Male	Female
2008	47.7	68.17	2.17	0.77	22.75	15.12	29.95	9.06	29.55	16.71	67.88	90.17
2009	47.15	67.48	2.22	0.76	23.36	15.45	28.32	8.15	29.49	17.06	69.46	91.09
2010	46.49	66.75	2.31	0.84	23.83	15.68	27.72	7.92	29.68	17.57	69.97	91.25
2011	44.27	62.88	2.33	0.86	25.33	17.61	27.53	8.21	30.4	19.52	70.15	90.94
2012	43.01	59.7	2.19	0.84	26.05	18.96	27.26	8.24	30.94	21.34	70.55	90.92
2013	42.57	59.58	2.14	0.78	25.57	18.19	27.72	8.25	31.86	22.23	70.14	90.97
2014	41.31	58.73	2.2	0.81	25.79	18.14	28.02	8.41	32.91	23.14	69.78	90.78
2015	40.06	57.74	2.34	0.86	25.79	18.01	27.73	8.38	34.15	24.26	69.93	90.75
2016	39.07	56.92	2.32	0.88	25.68	17.7	27.73	8.25	35.26	25.38	69.95	90.87
2017	38.35	56.36	2.33	0.88	25.75	17.69	27.82	8.35	35.9	25.94	69.86	90.77

Table 9 Wage and salaried workers (%)

	India		USA	
	Male	Female	Male	Female
2008	16.66	11.79	87.09	92.51
2009	17.12	11.94	86.94	92.37
2010	17.97	12.53	86.84	92.28
2011	19.78	16.66	87.25	92.44
2012	20.03	16.83	87.47	92.33
2013	20.46	17.1	87.79	92.42
2014	20.86	17.29	87.92	92.61
2015	21.35	17.61	87.86	92.66
2016	21.86	18.03	87.94	92.76
2017	21.9	18.06	87.82	92.66

Table 10 Self-employment (%)

	India		USA	
	Male	Female	Male	Female
2008	83.35	88.21	12.91	7.49
2009	82.88	88.07	13.07	7.63
2010	82.03	87.47	13.16	7.71
2011	80.22	83.34	12.75	7.56
2012	79.98	83.17	12.53	7.67
2013	79.54	82.90	12.20	7.58
2014	79.15	82.71	12.08	7.39
2015	78.65	82.39	12.14	7.34
2016	78.14	81.97	12.06	7.24
2017	78.10	81.94	12.18	7.34

thus providing poor returns to the owners. On the other hand, the percentage of self-employed males and females is very low at 12.18 and 7.34%, respectively, in 2017 for USA.

In developing world, women continue to form a large majority of the world's working poor, earn less income and are more often engaged in the informal sector of the economy, thus affecting them by long-term unemployment when compared to men. Women often have less access to productive resources, education, and skills development and labour market opportunities than men in many societies. Furthermore, women continue to undertake most of the unpaid care work, which has become an increasing challenge in their efforts to engage in productive work, both in subsistence agriculture and market economy. This seems to hold true for India.

Duncombe and Marsden (1995) argue that women are subjected to 'triple shifts' this involves paid labour, domestic labour and emotional labour. The emotional labour refers to the care and attentiveness of the family unit, i.e. the social role of the woman being a wife and a mother towards the children and husband. According to Barren and Norris (1976), women are employed in unstable employment that is based on short-term contracts, lower pay and entail unskilled work with fewer prospects, they are therefore more likely to be made redundant and thus suffer from a decline in the labour market (cited in Sociology An Interactive Approach 1997).

Few theories emphasize that women's disadvantaged position in the labour market is caused by, and is a reflection of patriarchy as well as the subordinate position of women in society and in the family. In other words, the role of gender stereotypes held by employers and societies at large affect differential occupational attainment of men and women. These theories predict that women gravitate towards occupations that are most consistent with their 'female' characteristics, e.g. caring, nurture (Anker 1998).

Gender pay gaps persist around the world, including in the United States. In 2010, American women on average earned 81% of what their male counterparts earned (BLS 2010; DOL 2011). Women are 50% more likely to work in the public sector. Women surpass men on education attainment among those employed aged 25 and over: 37.1% of women hold at least a bachelor's degree compared to 34.9% for men (DOL 2011).

In 2010, there were approximately 65 million women in the labour force and 53% of these women were concentrated in three industries (a) education and health services, (b) trade, transportation and utilities and (c) local government (BLS 2011).

Women were overrepresented in several industries and underrepresented in others. For example, in 2010, women represented 79% of the health and social services workforce and 68.6% of the education services workforce. However, women represented only 43.2% of the professional, scientific and technical services sector and 8.9% of the construction sector (DOL 2011).

In terms of women in leadership positions, in 2009 only 24% of CEOs in the US were women and they earned 74.5% as much as male CEOs (BLS 2010, p. 9).

http://www.ilo.org/washington/areas/gender-equality-in-the-workplace/WCMS_159496/lang–en/index.htm accessed on 15 May 2018.

5 Political Participation

Countries with increased women's participation and leadership in civil society and political parties tend to be more inclusive, responsive, egalitarian and democratic.

Yet, women around the world are still largely absent from national and local decision-making bodies; struggle to have a voice in peace building transitions and

Table 11 Proportion of seats held by women in National Parliaments (%)

	India	USA
2008	9.1	17
2009	10.8	16.8
2010	10.8	16.8
2011	11	16.8
2012	11	18
2013	11	17.9
2014	11.4	19.3
2015	12	19.4
2016	12	19.4
2017	11.8	19.4

are excluded from political processes. Despite representing half the global population, women comprise less than 20% of the world's legislators. From discrimination and violence to a lack of support and resources, women face countless challenges to participation in the civic and political life of their countries (USAID).

Let us look at political participation of Women in India and USA (Table 11).

The table shows that India has less than 12% women representation in national parliament, while USA has around 19.5% representation of women in 2017.

Women's participation and access to formal political power structures vary across countries. Only three countries in the world have more than 50% representation of women in lower or single house, i.e. Rwanda (61.3%), Cuba (53.2%) and Bolivia (53.1%) (IPU 2018).

Many scholars have tried to explain the lack of women participation in politics. Rai maintains the conceptual basis of liberal theory that is inherently gendered in ways, which perpetuates patterns of patriarchy and ignores gender subordination in both polity and society (Rai 2000:2). Feminist theorists also challenged the notion of abstract individual in liberal theory and argued it is not a gender-neutral category. This is why despite women had the right to vote they were not able to impact public policy and could not bring private sphere in the preview of the public. Even western democracies left them dislocated on many fronts.

Bari (2005) argues that women's historic exclusion from political structures and processes is the result of multiple structural, functional and personal factors that vary in different social contexts across countries. However, beyond these specificities of national and local contexts, there is a generic issue in women's political participation that relates to the wider context of national and international politics, liberal democracy and development. The common pattern of women's political exclusion stems from (a) social and political discourses, (b) political structures and institutions, and (c) the socio-cultural and functional constraints that put limits on women's individual and collective agency.

Male domination of politics, political parties and culture of formal political structures is another factor that hinders women's political participation. Often male-dominated political parties have a male perspective on issues of national importance that disillusions women as their perspective is often ignored and not reflected in the politics of their parties. Also, women are usually not elected at the position of power within party structures because of gender biases of male leadership. Meetings of councils or parliamentary sessions are held in odd timings conflicting with women's domestic responsibilities (Bari 2005).

6 Conclusion

Gender equality (GE) is a critical component for societal and economic progress. Gender equality can promote economic performance through education, health and labour force participation. Gender equality in education increases human capital which in turn increases labour force participation of women.

As there is no country with perfect gender equality, all countries suffer some loss of human development due to gender inequality. India's goal of economic progress and development for all remains marred by a consistent rise in the level of gender inequality. This is evidenced by India's poor performance across various socio-economic indicators, reflecting a low female–male labour force participation rate, high maternal deaths, low educational achievements and a low representation of women in parliament as compared to USA. The government's low social and economic investment in promoting the freedom of women in both individual and social capacities, and ensuring equitable development, remain the key factors responsible for a rising gender imbalance (Deepanshu Mohan 2017).

India needs to pull up its efforts to bring about gender equality in education health and labour force participation because education inequality affects the average quality of human capital and reduces growth (Klasen 1999). Female education contributes to improvements in children's health, reductions in fertility rates and increases in labour force participation rates, and better quality of human capital of future generations (Mitra et al. 2015).

Annexure

Definitions of Indicators Used

1. Government expenditure on education: General government expenditure on education (current, capital and transfers) is expressed as a percentage of GDP. It includes expenditure funded by transfers from international sources to government. General government usually refers to local, regional and central governments.
2. Children out of school, primary (Number in Lakhs): Children out of school are the number of primary-school-age children not enrolled in primary or secondary school.

3. School enrolment in primary (%): Gross enrollment ratio is the ratio of total enrollment, regardless of age, to the population of the age group that officially corresponds to the level of education shown. Primary education provides children with basic reading, writing and mathematics skills along with an elementary understanding of such subjects as history, geography, natural science, social science, art and music.
4. School enrolment in secondary (%): Gross enrollment ratio is the ratio of total enrollment, regardless of age, to the population of the age group that officially corresponds to the level of education shown. Secondary education completes the provision of basic education that began at the primary level and aims at laying the foundations for lifelong learning and human development, by offering more subject- or skill-oriented instruction using more specialized teachers.
5. Female teachers in educational institutions: Share of female academic staff in education.
6. Maternal death refers to the death of a woman while pregnant or within 42 days of termination of pregnancy, irrespective of the duration and site of the pregnancy, from any cause related to or aggravated by the pregnancy or its management but not from accidental or incidental causes.
7. Employment is defined as persons of working age who were engaged in any activity to produce goods or provide services for pay or profit, whether at work during the reference period or not at work due to temporary absence from a job, or to working-time arrangement. The agriculture sector consists of activities in agriculture, hunting, forestry and fishing, in accordance with division 1 (ISIC 2) or categories A-B (ISIC 3) or category A (ISIC 4). The industry sector consists of mining and quarrying, manufacturing, construction and public utilities (electricity, gas and water), in accordance with divisions 2–5 (ISIC 2) or categories C-F (ISIC 3) or categories B-F (ISIC 4). The services sector consists of wholesale and retail trade and restaurants and hotels; transport, storage and communications; financing, insurance, real estate and business services; and community, social and personal services, in accordance with divisions 6–9 (ISIC 2) or categories G-Q (ISIC 3) or categories G-U (ISIC 4).
8. Labour force participation rate is the proportion of the population ages 15 and older that is economically active: all people who supply labour for the production of goods and services during a specified period.
9. Wage and salaried workers (employees) are those workers who hold the type of jobs defined as 'paid employment jobs', where the incumbents hold explicit (written or oral) or implicit employment contracts that give them a basic remuneration that is not directly dependent upon the revenue of the unit for which they work.
10. Self-employed workers are those workers who, working on their own account or with one or a few partners or in cooperative, hold the type of jobs defined as a 'self-employment jobs', i.e. jobs where the remuneration is directly dependent upon the profits derived from the goods and services produced. Self-employed

workers include four sub-categories of employers, own-account workers, members of producers' cooperatives and contributing family workers.
11. Women in parliaments are the percentage of parliamentary seats in a single or lower chamber held by women.

References

Anker, R. (1998). *Gender and jobs: Sex segregation of occupations in the world*. Geneva: ILO.

Bari, F. (2005). *Women's political participation: Issues and challenges*. United Nations, EGM/WPD-EE/2005/EP.12, 2005.

Barren, & Noris, cited in Jorgensen, N., Bird, J., Heyhoe, A., Russell, B., & Savvas, M. (1976, 1997). *Sociology: An interactive approach*. Collins Educational.

Benatar, D. (2012). *The second sexism: Discrimination against men and boys*. Wiley Blackwell.

Bhalotra, S., & Gomes, J. F. (2014). *Maternal mortality and female life expectancy: the importance of gender inequality*. Institute for Social and Economic Research, University of Essex, 20 Sept 2014.

BLS. (2010). *Highlights of Women's Earnings in 2009*. Washington, D.C.

BLS. (2011). *Women's Earnings and Employment by Industry, 2009*. Washington, D.C.

Chimombo, J. P. G. (1999). *Implementing educational innovations: A study of free primary schooling in Malawi*. Unpublished D. Phil. Thesis Submitted to the University of Sussex.

Dennerstein, L., Feldman, S., Murdaugh, C., Rossouw, J., & Tennstedt, S. (1977). *World congress of gerontology: Ageing beyond 2000: One world one future*. Adelaide: International Association of Gerontology.

Deepanshu, M. (2017). *Rising gender inequality leaves a dark mark on India's growth story*. https://thewire.in/economy/gender-inequality-labour-force.

DOL. (2011). *Women's Employment During the Recovery*. Washington, D.C.

Dollar, D., & Gatti, R. (1999). *Gender inequality, income, and growth: Are good times good for women?* Policy Research Report on Gender and Development Working Paper Series, No. 1. Development Research Group/PREMN, The World Bank.

Duflo, E. (2011). *Womens empowerment and economic development*. National Bureau of Economic Research: Technical Report.

Duncombe, J., & Marsden, D. (1995). 'Workaholics' and 'whingeing women": Theorising intimacy and emotion work: the last frontier of gender inequality. *Sociological Review, 43*(1), 150–169.

Global Gender Gap Report. (2017). *World Economic Forum*.

Holmes, J. (2003). Measuring the determinants of school completion in Pakistan: Analysis of censoring and selection bias. *Economics of Education Review 22*(3), 249–264.

Holcamp, G. (2009). *Researching the girls' dropout rate in Malawi. Why girls dropout of primary schools and in what way this rate can be reduced*. Master Thesis Special Education.

Inter-Parliamentary Union. (2018). *Women in national parliaments, as on 1st April 2018*. http://archive.ipu.org/wmn-e/classif.htm.

Jayachandran, S. (2014). *The roots of gender inequality in developing countries*. Technical report, National Bureau of Economic Research.

Kawachi, I., et al. (1999). Women's status and the health of women and men: A view from the states. *Social Science & Medicine, 48*(1), 21. As quoted in Van de Velde, S., et al. (2013). Macro-level gender equality and depression in men and women in Europe. *Sociology of health & illness, 35*(5), 682–698.

King, E. M., & Mason, A. D. (2001). Engendering development through gender equality in rights, resources and voices (summary). *A World Bank Policy Research Report*. Washington DC: The World Bank Group.

Klasen, S. (1999). *Does gender inequality reduce growth and development? Evidence from cross-country regressions*. Policy Research Report On Gender and Development Working Paper Series, No. 7. Development Research Group/PREMN, The World Bank.

Levy, M. B. (1971, Feb). Determinants of primary school dropouts in developing countries. *Comparative Education Review, 15*(1), 44–58.

Mitra, A. (2010). *Women's employment in Asia-Pacific, Asia-Pacific human development report background papers series*. Delhi: Institute of Economic Growth.

Mitra, A., Bang, J., & Biswas, A. (2015). Gender equality and economic growth: Is it equality of opportunity or equality of outcomes? *Feminist Economics, 21*(1), 110–135.

Rai, M. S. (2000). *International Perspective on Gender and Governance*. Great Britain: Macmillan Press.

Redford, J., Battle, D., & Bielick, S. (2017). *Homeschooling in the United States: 2012 (NCES 2016-096.REV)*. Washington, DC: National Center for Education Statistics, Institute of Education Sciences, U.S. Department of Education.

Sen, A. (1990). *More than 100 million women are missing*. The New York Review of Books.

Sen, A. (2001). *The many faces of gender inequality* (pp. 35–39). New republic.

Solotaroff, J. (2007). *Afghanistan gender mainstreaming implementation note series, no. 1: The world bank in South Asia*. https://siteresources.worldbank.org.

U.S. Department of Education Statistics About Non public Education in the United States. https://www2.ed.gov/about/offices/list/oii/nonpublic/statistics.html#homeschl.

UNDP, Human Development Report, 2016.

United Nations Educational, Scientific and Cultural Organization (UNESCO) 1989 and 2007. Statistical Yearbook Paris: UNESCO.

UNESCO. (2014). *Policy paper 14/fact sheet 28: June 2014 progress in getting all children to school stalls but some countries show the way forward*. http://unesdoc.unesco.org/images/0022/002281/228184E.pdf. Accessed on 5 May 2018.

Waldron, I. (1983). Sex difference in illness incidence, prognosis, and mortality: Issues and evidence. *Social Science and Medicine, 17*(16), 1107–1123.

World Health Organization. (2009). *Women & Health: Today's Evidence, Tomorrow's Agenda (PDF) (Report)*. WHO Press. Retrieved 5 May 2018.

World Health Statistics. (2009). Geneva: World Health Organization.

Websites

https://data.worldbank.org/topic/gender. Accessed on 26 May 2018.

https://www.usaid.gov/what-we-do/gender-equality-and-womens-empowerment/addressing-gender-programming/strengthening-womens. Accessed on 1 May 2018.

http://iosrjournals.org/iosr-jrme/papers/Vol-4%20Issue-6/Version-3/K04637583.pdf. Accessed on 1 May 2018.

http://www.ilo.org/employment/areas/gender-and-employment/lang–en/index.htm. Accessed on 5 May 2018.

Functioning of SHGs with a Special Focus on an Indian State

Ajjarapu Kamala Devi, Tapas Kumar Sarangi and Renu Lal

1 Introduction

Countries all over the world are developing by leaps and bounds in all spears, and globalization has helped economic development in this century in particular, but poverty still remains to be a major problem tagging at many countries in the world. So much so that in the year 2000 the united nations declared that by 2015 at least the people below the poverty line should be reduced to at least half the current level as part of the Millennium Development Goals (MDGs). In continuation to the MDGs, the UN declared Sustainable Development Goals (SDGs) where '*Ending poverty in all its forms*' is the first goal that every country including India has promised to be fulfilled by 2030.[1] Poverty is a human deprivation and restricts the access of the poor to mainstream institutions delivering services like education, health, nutrition, training, credit, market linkages and technology.

The poor and the underprivileged in the informal sector have to face a lot of difficulties to acquire finance from the formal lending channels. (1) SHG bank linkage programme (SHG-BLP) and Joint Liability Group Bank (JLG) lending programme where the banks lend through SHG; and (2) Lending through individual

[1]The target 1.4 of Goal-1 of SDGs emphasized, 'By 2030, ensure that all men and women, in particular the poor and the vulnerable, have equal rights to economic resources, as well as access to basic services, ownership and control over land and other forms of property, inheritance, natural resources, appropriate new technology and financial services, including microfinance'.

A. Kamala Devi (✉) · T. K. Sarangi · R. Lal
NILERD, A-7, Narela Institutional Area, 110040 Delhi, India
e-mail: kamalaupendranath@gmail.com

T. K. Sarangi
e-mail: sarangi.tapas@gmail.com

R. Lal
e-mail: renuj9@gmail.com

NILERD, *Reflecting on India's Development*,
https://doi.org/10.1007/978-981-13-1414-8_13

and group approach through Micro Finance Institutions (MFIs). SHG refers to Self-Help Groups (SHGs) formed by people in the unorganized sector to engage themselves in gainful employment to combat poverty and unemployment. SHGs become popular and gained momentum with more and more women joining the groups as a means to empowerment. It is therefore not strange if it is said that the SHG Bank linkage programme initiated by NABARD is the largest microfinance programme in the world. Not only are the bank's lending for viable economic activity but they are also lending monies to SHGs for meeting other responsibilities like buying cattle, procuring seeds and fertilizers and also performing marriages in the form of consumption loans. In addition to financial development, the members of SHGs are experiencing enhancement of organizational skills and management skills, group compatibility, etc.

The success of the SHGs as microfinance channels is evidenced by the fact that eight MFIs received permission by RBI to function as small finance banks and one MFI is already functioning as a Universal Bank. The SHG bank linkage programme has equally grown to touch the lives of individuals through SHGs with an outstanding loan portfolio of approximately 43,000 crores.[2] Microfinance has witnessed an explosion in popularity, with the total number of people served by MFIs or members of SHGs growing at more than 50% every year. The number of SHGs having savings linkage increased to 79.03 *lakh* as on 31 March 2016 from 76.97 *lakh* a year back. The fact that the domain of SHGs consists of 85.6% women groups brings home the point that empowerment of poor rural women has been achieved. NABARD and NRLM/SRLM working in coordination have ensured that SHGs got major chunk of Bank loans in the year 2015–16. It is also a matter worth mention that NRLM is working since April 2013 with an objective to cover 7 crore rural households through SHGs and federations with sustainable livelihoods.

DAY-NRLM is one of the flagship programmes of the Ministry Of Rural Development (MORD). This programme is aimed at poverty alleviation. Deendayal Antyodaya Yojana-National Rural livelihood mission is a restructured and reinvented programme of the erstwhile Swarnajayanti Gram Swarojgar Yojana which is implemented as a 'mission' with effect from June 2011 with specific time-bound targets. The DAY-NRLM aims at reducing rural poverty by enabling poor households to access gainful self-employment and skilled wage employment opportunities. The objective of the mission is to create efficient institutional platforms to enable the rural poor to increase their income and financial strengths by taking up sustainable livelihoods and also access financial services. To achieve this, objective rural poor are encouraged to form SHGs and they are trained to use the income generating asserts provided to them or buy such asserts by themselves by availing government subsidies and credit facilities provided to them. The programme envisages covering all poor households so as to ensure universalization with quality. Further, the poor would also have access to their rights and entitlement to public services. NRLM strives to bring out the inherent capabilities

[2]See The Bharat Microfinance Report 2015, Sa-Dhan and NABARD.

of the members and also complement them with capacities like information, knowledge, skills, tools, finance and collectivization. It is imperative to study the impact of the interventions taken up under NRLM on the coverage of the target households, revival of defunct SHGs, functioning of the SHGs and the socio-economic changes in the lives of the SHG members.

Objective:

The basic objective of the study is to critically evaluate the coverage of the target households and functional status of the SHGs.

The specific objectives of the study are

- To study the social mobilization and coverage of target households in the sample villages.
- To study the status and functioning of the SHGs in terms of opening bank accounts, receipt of revolving funds, rotation of funds, credit linkage, training, etc.
- To assess the ability of the SHG members in handling banking transactions and bookkeeping procedures.
- Check whether leaders alone or only a few members are taking key financial decisions. Check whether loans/bulk loans are sanctioned to only a few members and to assess the overall benefits received by the members after joining SHGs.

2 Study Area, Sources of Data and Methodology

Microcredit, routed through SHGs, has made considerable headway in Telangana. SHGs formed under Deendayal Antyodaya Yojana—National Rural Livelihoods Mission and are being in existence in the last 5 years and above have been chosen for the study. Three districts have been selected from 31 of the districts with socio-economic differentials in development. However, four SHGs which were formed recently were interested to participate. So they were also taken into consideration.

A purposive sampling procedure was adopted for the selection of the sample groups of SHGs. A total of 23 such groups covering three districts, i.e. Medchal, Ranga Reddy and Hyderabad districts, were selected for the purpose. While selecting the groups, it was ensured that all the groups have been functioning for at least the last 4/5 years. Out of the 25 SHGs, 4 groups exclusively belonged to the Below Poverty Line (BPL) category, while 12 groups were middle-income group and 9 groups are mixed in the sense that some members in the group belonged to the Above Poverty Line (APL) category while the remaining were from the BPL category. Of the total groups, only five (20%) have been working for less than 5 years; another 14 groups (56%) have been working for 15 years or more and 5 groups (20%) for more than 20 years. Only one group (4%) has been working for the last 5 years. These groups had a total of 272 members at the time of collection of information (see Table 1). It was observed that most of these SHGs are more or less homogeneous in terms of the socio-economic characteristics of their members.

Table 1 Salient features of sample SHGs in the study area

S. No	Name of the district	Name of the SHG	Mandal	Village	Year of starting	Number of members
1	Medchal	Vandana	Kapra	Vampuguda	2014	10
2	Medichel	Suryodaya	Kapra	Vampuguda	2016	11
3	Medichel	Annapurna	Kapra	Vampuguda	2013	10
4	Medichel	Pavani	Kapra	Vampuguda	2016	10
5	Ranga reddy	Padmavati	Ghatkesar	Venkatapuram	2003	10
6	Ranga reddy	Saraswati	Ghatkesar	Venkatapuram	1994	17
7	Ranga reddy	Prasanna	Ghatkesar	Venkatapuram	1994	14
8	Ranga reddy	Vanadurga	Ghatkesar	Venkatapuram	1996	14
9	Ranga reddy	Ambabhavani	Ghatkesar	Venkatapuram	2001	14
10	Ranga reddy	Pragati	Ghatkesar	Venkatapuram	2000	12
11	Ranga reddy	Omsai	Ghatkesar	Venkatapuram	2016	10
12	Ranga reddy	Swarnamaisamma	Ghatkesar	Swarnapuri	2017	10
13	Ranga reddy	Bhavani Priya	Ghatkesar	Swarnapuri	2009	10
14	Ranga reddy	Santoshlakshmi	Ghatkesar	Swarnapuri	2008	10
15	Ranga reddy	Vijetha	Ghatkesar	Swarnapuri	2003	10
16	Ranga reddy	Spurthi	Ghatkesar	Swarnapuri	2003	10
17	Hyderabad	Priyadarshini	Uppal	Habsiguda	2007	10
18	Hyderabad	IndiraPriya darshini	Uppal	Habsiguda	2007	10
19	Hyderabad	Nagini	Uppal	Habsiguda	2007	10
20	Hyderabad	Omsai	Uppal	Habsiguda	2007	10
21	Hyderabad	Mother Theresa	Uppal	Habsiguda	2007	10
22	Hyderabad	Tulasi-1	Uppal	Habsiguda	2007	10
23	Hyderabad	Tulasi-2	Uppal	Habsiguda	2007	10
24	Hyderabad	NTR	Uppal	Habsiguda	2007	10
25	Hyderabad	Ambedkar	Uppal	Habsiguda	2007	10

Source: Field Survey, 2018

Semi-structured interviews are conducted with 3–4 members in each sampled SHG in order to get insights regarding the changes in livelihoods and socio-economic lifestyles. Care has been taken to give due representation of different socio-economic categories. Focus group discussion was conducted in each selected SHG to elicit inputs regarding collective goals and objectives, achievements, empowerment, challenges, etc.

The study is limited to three districts, i.e. Medchal, Ranga Reddy and Hyderabad districts of Telangana state. Because of the time and financial constraint, the study is restricted to these three districts and purposive sample of the SHGs was taken. The study could not taken household information as the SHG members were busy with agriculture work and as an audit was going on discussion with district officials could not materialize.

3 Evolution of Self-Help Groups in India

SHGs movement has brought in remarkable changes in the socio-economic conditions of women especially in rural areas. A self-help group is a village-based financial intermediary committee usually of 10–20 local women or men. NABARD recognizes a self-help group as ‘a small economically homogenous and affinity group of rural poor voluntarily coming together to save small amounts regularly; to mutually agree to contribute to a common fund; to meet their emergency needs; to have a collective decision-making to solve conflicts through collective leadership and mutual discussion to provide collateral free loans with the term decided by the group at the market driven rates’.

The origin of SHG is from Gramin Bank of Bangladesh which was funded by the economist Prof. Mohammad Yunnes of Chittagong University in the year 1975. This was exclusively established for poor. The concept of SHGs was created with an assumption that through group effort problems related to poverty, illiteracy, health, lack of skills among rural families can be tackled. India’s self-help group movement is the largest and successful movement in the world. In India, Mysore Resettlement and Development Agency (MYRADA) an NGO located in South India was an early promoter of SHGs. By late 80s, MYRADA and the Bhagavatula Charitable Trust, of the Visakhapatnam district in Andhra Pradesh formed many SHGs known as the Credit management groups in rural areas, mostly among women. The outcome of this initiative was quite encouraging and attracted the attention of rural development departments of Government of India and saw an opening to bring the poor and the marginalized together and assist them to raise APL through the provision of microenterprise and invited NGOs, donors and bankers to explore the possibility of promoting savings and credit groups of women (Raja Reddy and Reddy 2012).

In early 90s, NABARD in consultation with RBI, Commercial Banks and NGOs launched the pilot project of linking the SHGs with commercial banks based on NABARD guidelines. By late 90s, the government had become a key promoter of

SHGs and they became visible across the country. By then, SHGs were not just savings and credit groups but were seen as common interest groups. SHGs began emerging up in many villages, with multiple SHGs being promoted in the same villages. SHG has become the largest microfinance initiative in the world with about 120 million poor people making up 1,618,456 SHGs by March 2005 (Ethiopian delegation 2014).

Restructuring from SJGSRY to DAY-NRLM:

Swarnajayanti Grameen Swarojgar Yojana (SGSY) was launched by MORD in 1999 at 75:25 costs sharing between Central and State Governments. After restructuring Integrated Rural Development Programme (IRDP) with an aim to promote self-employment among rural poor. In 2011, after addressing the shortcomings of SGSY programme based on the recommendations of Radha Krishna committee, the MORD introduced National Rural Livelihood Mission (NRLM) one of its flagship programmes with a budget of $5.1 billion. This is one of the world's largest initiatives to improve the livelihood of the poor. The guiding principles of NRLM are:

1. Poor have a strong desire to come out of poverty and they have innate capabilities
2. An external dedicated and sensitive support structure is required to induce the social mobilization, institution building and empowerment process
3. Facilitating knowledge dissemination, skill building, access to credit, access to marketing and access to other livelihoods services enables them to enjoy a portfolio of sustainable livelihoods
4. Social mobilization and building strong institutions of the poor is critical for unleashing the innate capabilities of the poor

Source: NRLM-MORD, Government of India

Later in 2015, the NRLM scheme became Deen Dayal Antyodaya Yojana (DAY). The aim of DAY is to uplift the urban poor folks by enhancing sustainable livelihood opportunities through skill development. The scheme is integration of the National Urban Livelihoods Mission (NULM) and National Rural Livelihoods Mission (NRLM). The unique features of DAY-NRLM are

- Based on saturation approach—seeks to cover all poor households in a phased manner, so as to ensure universalization with quality;
- Seeks to provide continuous handholding support to poor households for 6–8 years, till they come out of poverty;
- No one-time 'Capital subsidy'—continuous infusion of capital (own savings, inter-loaning, seed capital and bank credit);
- Promotes multiple livelihoods—farm and non-farm, skill based as well as self-employment;
- Building their own institutions/federations for long-term support.

Self-Help Groups (SHGs):

'SHG is a holistic programme of micro-enterprises covering all aspects of self-employment, organization of the rural poor into SHGs and their capacity building, planning of activity clusters, infrastructure build up, technology, credit and marketing' (Shodhganga.inflibnet).[3] A self-help group is a village-based committee usually composed of 10–20 local women or men. Most SHGs are located in India. It is not necessary that an SHG should be registered. SHGs are seen by government agencies as an instrument to empower women, developing leadership abilities among the poor and the needy people, increasing school enrolments and improving nutrition and the use of birth control.

The basic objectives of SHGs are:

- Inculcating in the members the habit of savings and banking;
- Helping the members secure financial, technical and moral strengths;
- Encourage the members to avail loans for productive purposes;
- Help them to increase their financial standing through loan/credit enabling the members to manage their own finance, use their collective wisdom in organizing and distributing the benefits among themselves;
- Create awareness among the women about the need and relevance of SHGs in gaining economic and social empowerment;
- Creating a feeling of 'one for all and all for one' among women;
- Helping the women enhance their capabilities, develop collective decision-making and thus gain confidence in themselves;
- Encourage women to accumulate their own capital resource base through their own savings;
- Motivating women to take up social responsibilities related to woman empowerment and development.

There are about 2.2 million (NABARD) SHGs in India. Many SHGs in India borrow from banks under SHG bank linkage programme, after building up their own capital through savings and repute for regular repayments. This programme has laid a secure path to deliver microfinance assistance to rural poor. Further, this system eliminates the need for collateral security for obtaining loan and reduces the transaction costs for both bank and the borrowers. The SHGs have helped in reducing the influence of informal lenders in rural areas.

The SHG bank linkage programme from its inception has been predominant in certain states like Andhra Pradesh, Tamil Nadu, Kerala and Karnataka. Around 57% of the SHGs credits linked are accounted by these southern states (Table 2).

As on March 2017, the number of SHGs in India maintaining savings bank accounts with the banking sector was about 19 crore. 'SHGs have been linked to banks over the years but a handful of states, mostly in South India over three fourths of this figure with Andhra Pradesh being an undisputed leader' (Anupam 2008). The region-wise growth of credit linked to SHGs can be observed that at all India level the growth between 2014–15 and 2015–16 is 12.67% while it has reduced to 3.59% by 16–17. Region-wise northeast recorded highest growth (38.56%) in 15–16 followed by eastern region (17.28%) and southern region (15.28%), whereas

[3]SGSY Programme and Self-Help Groups in Churachandpur District; Shodhganga.inflibnet.ac.in/bitstream/10603/169450/8/08_chapter 2.Pdf. Accessed on 28th March, 2018.

Table 2 Regional spread of credit linked SHGs in India

Regions	2014–15	2015–16	2016–17	Growth rate 2014–15 to 2015–16	Growth rate 2015–16 to 2016–17
North East	18,791	26,037	28,961	38.56	11.23
Northern	43,848	38,106	46,567	−13.10	22.20
Central	109,231	84,282	82,012	−22.84	−2.69
Western	97,341	112,525	106,825	−15.60	−5.07
Eastern	351,800	412,576	497,063	17.28	20.48
Southern	1,005,227	1,158,797	1,136,692	15.28	−1.91
All India	1,626,238	1,832,323	1,898,120	12.67	3.59

Source: NABARD

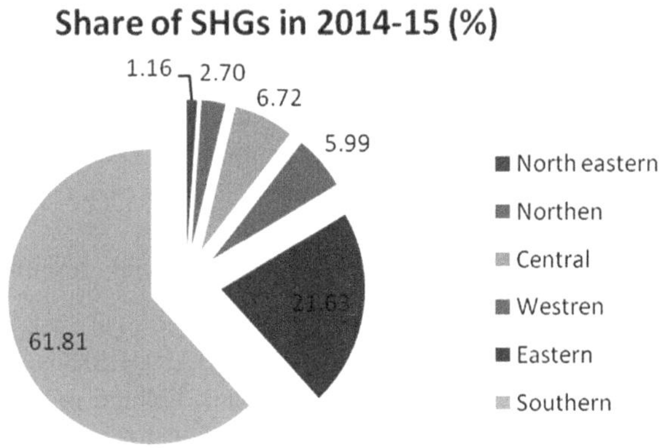

Fig. 1 Share of credit linked SHGs in the year 2014–15

northern, central and western region reported negative growth. During 2016–17, on the whole there is a decline in the credit link SHGs and western, central and southern regions indicated negative growth.

The region-wise share of credit linked SHG in all India during 2014–15 indicates that southern region contributes the highest share of SHGs with 61.81% followed by eastern region (21.63%) and central region (6.72%). The share of northern and northeastern is less than 3% (Figs. 1 and 2).

During 2015–16, it is observed that the share of southern region (63.24%), eastern region (22.52%) as well as western region (6.14%) has been increasing. However, the other three regions' share has reduced in comparison to 2014–15 (Fig. 3).

During 2016–17 although the share of southern region (59.89%), eastern region (26.19%) and western region (5.63%) as such was high, on the whole the share of credit linked SHGs has reduced. Microfinance alone cannot alleviate poverty. Microfiancé schemes need to be combined with complementary programmes addressing the social and cultural dimensions of want, privation, impoverishment and disposition (Khalil 2000).

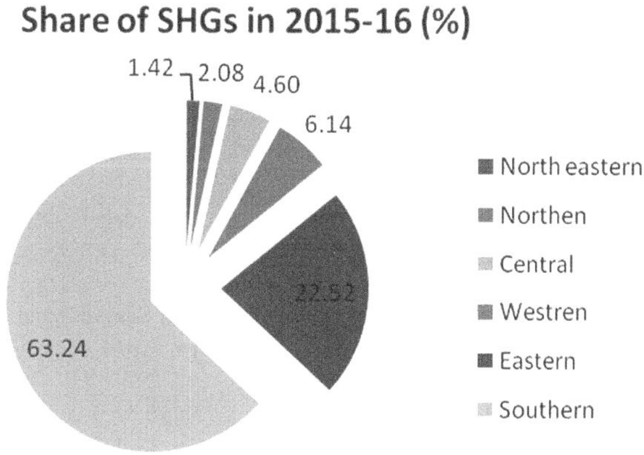

Fig. 2 Share of credit linked SHGs in the year 2015–16

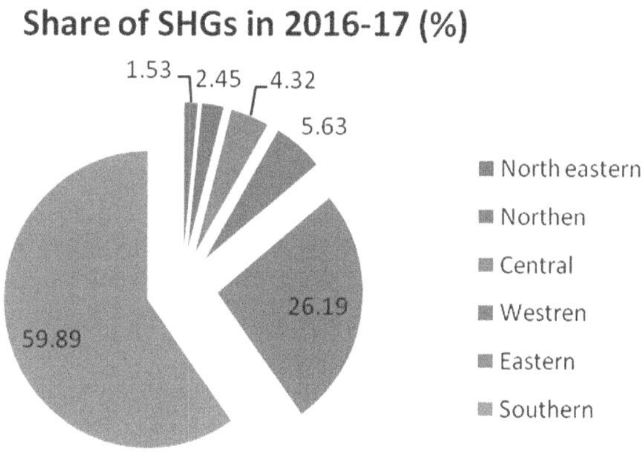

Fig. 3 Share of credit linked SHGs in the year 2016–17

In the newly formed state of Telangana also SHGs played a crucial role in social and economic upliftment of women. The state government feels that apart from thrift, empowerment of women and making them direct beneficiaries of material assets and financial allocation will lead to sustainable development. Prior to separation, the united Andhra Pradesh made efforts in encouraging rural women to farm SHGs and brought about 90% of the rural households into the fold of SHGs. To eradicate poverty through SHGs, Indira Kranti Patham (Srinidhi) has been launched with a special emphasis laid on the poorest and most vulnerable households. This programme is being implemented in all the villages in Telangana.

The aim of the DAY-NRLM Mission is to mobilize rural households into self-help groups in a time-bound manner. The objective is to encourage people to form SHGs and thus create livelihood opportunities. Universal mobilization of poor households into SHGs is the core objective of DAY-NRLM. In order to ensure that no poor family is left out, differential strategies are adopted for social mobilization of all poor families into functionally effective groups. However, it appears that social mobilization as envisaged is not happening (Table 3).

Table 3 Number of SHGs promoted under DAY-NRLM in Telangana (2013–14 to 2015–16)

	2013–14		2014–15		2015–16	
State	Target	Achievement	Target	Achievement	Target	Achievement
Telangana	NA	5600	2000	12,600	NA	6622
All India	313,427	181,931	279,707	187,076	303,086	344,412

Source: Lok Sabha unstarred question No. 1863, dated 5th May, 2016

Table 4 Number of SHGs promoted (New and Revived) and National Rural Livelihood Mission (NRLM) in Telangana (2014–2015 up to June 2016)

(In number)

State	Target			2016–17 April–June 2016
	2014–15	2015–16	2016–17[a]	
Telangana	12,600	6622	4000	1000

Source: Ministry of Statistics and Programme Implementation, Govt. of India
[a]Target
Lok Sabha unstarred question No. 3799 on 19th March, 2015
Lok Sabha unstarred question No. 573 on 23rd July, 2015

As can be observed in the year 2013–14, only 3.08% SHGs were promoted while in 2014–15 it raised to 6.73% and in 2015–16 the state experienced a drastic fall to 1.92%. Under NRLM, the social mobilization of SHGs in Telangana in the years 2014–15, 2015–16 and 2016–17 was 12,600, 6622 and 1000 (till April–June 2016), respectively (Table 4).

The decrees in the social mobilization of SHGs may be due to the state governments shift in the priority areas as the state was newly curved out from erstwhile Andhra Pradesh on 2nd June, 2014 (Table 5).

The exclusive women SHGs are predominant in Telangana as well as southern region, which indicates that SHGs are considered not as mechanism to eradicate

Table 5 Progress under microfinance savings of SHGs in Telangana and southern region as on March, 2017

Variables	Telangana	Southern Region	Share of Telangana
No. of SHGs	4839	377,152	1.28
No. of members	71,643	5,014,979	1.43
Savings amount	137.89	37330.2	0.37
Exclusive women's SHGs	4831	370,374	1.30
Women's Savings amount	127.2	36351.83	0.35
Share of women's SHGs (%)	99.83	98.20	–
Share of women's savings amount (%)	92.25	97.38	–

Source: NABARD

rural poverty but as a tool for empowering the women in rural areas. The women SHGs share in the total SHGs in southern region is 98% while in Telangana it is almost cent percent (99.83%). Similarly, the share of women savings in the savings amount in southern states put together is 97%, while in Telangana it is 92%, which is quite high. With regard to other variables like number of SHGs, members, saving amount, Exclusive women's SHGs and women's savings amount, the share of Telangana in southern region is not very encouraging. The state should soon (as stated by Telangana Minister for Panchayati Raj K.T. Rama Rao) 'become a role model for other states in motivating SHGs, initiatives aimed at women's empowerment…'. When the state of Telangana is part of Andhra Pradesh, the states' performance as far as SHGs are concerned the state is undisputed leader (Anupam 2008) in South India. Telangana state formed in 2014 and the formation of SHGs have come down from 12,600 in 2014–15 to 4000 in 2016–17 (refer Table 4). Looking at the decline, it is imperative to study the functioning of SHGs in Telangana.

4 Functioning of Self-Help Groups in Telangana

It is essential to assess the quality of the SHGs functioning in the villages and adherence of the functioning SHGs to democratic and microfinance practices. To understand the status of SHGs, a primary survey has been taken up and through focus group discussion with members of 25 SHGs opinion of the members was taken and elicited information relating to group homogeneity, functioning of groups, attitude of members, knowledge of various activities and educational level.

4.1 Formation of the Groups

Members of all the SHGs that were contacted in the three districts are mixed groups. Caste or economic conditions was not the criteria that were adopted to form the SHG group. It is the interest of the members, and proximity of residence to attend meetings was considered while forming the groups. Those who are living in the same lane or area were taken as members. They have refused to take some ladies as members as they are staying in some other colonies of the same village as these members felt that it is difficult organize meetings and ensure repayments if their members are staying in distance. Further, 75% of the groups' maintained only 10 members as they all felt it will be convenient to distribute the loan amount and manage the group. The age of the members in SHGs in Kapra and Malkajigiri Mandal was 20–55. But, in Ghatkesar Mandal the SHGs that were in existence for more than 20 years have one or two members who are 60 and above. They were not removed as they are very old members and they are given loans only from the group saving but they are not included in the bank loan. Most of the members in all the 25 SHGs are illiterate or literate up below primary level. All the members in the 25 SHGs were having BPL cards.

4.2 Continuity of the Members

It has been observed that most of the SHGs retained their original members. Only one member in one SHG in Vompuguda village reported to be left because of change of residence, two vacancies arised in one SHG in Venkatapuram village due to death of the members. However, the group did not fill up with new members as they have twelve members. But in Habsiguda area one member left as she was not able to repay the loan due to husband's death. Except these reasons beyond human control, there were no other reasons or expulsions of the members due to non-payment.

4.3 Economic Conditions of the Members

Economic conditions of the SHG members in all the three districts were observed. All the members in all the SHGs were having BPL cards. However, the physical examination of their dwellings, the purpose for which the loan amount is being utilized, indicates a different picture. Most of the members are having income through some economic activity. Only few are housewives. In Kapra mandal, the loan amount is spent for consumption purpose. Only one person reported to be doing some self-employment. Whereas, in Ghatkesar and Malkajigiri mandals, the group composition is mixed in nature. Some members are from low economic condition and some are having service with assured monthly income and in good position.

4.4 Recruitment of Office-Bearers

The selection of office-bearers, in each group in all the three districts that were covered generally, took place through consensus among the members in a meeting. The group members had chosen the first leader and second leader in the presence of VOA, who facilitated the formation of the group and conducted meetings during the initial stages of group formation. The group members had chosen those members as leaders, who had some educational qualification, so that they can maintain the records and deal with officers including bank personnel. It is observed that the educational qualification of the leaders is 12th standard.

4.5 Rotation of Office-Bearers

For proper functioning as well as the revitalization of leadership quality in a group, rotation of office-bearers is desirable. This is because if the same people continue in office for a long time, there may not be an opportunity for others to learn the activities and will not develop confidence to handle monitory matters. One of the functions of the SHGs is *Developing and encouraging the decision making capacity of members*. Hence, it is essential to make office-bearers by rotation.

In the study groups, it was observed that rotation of office-bearers is not a regular phenomenon. The first leader and second leaders have been continuing in their position since its inception. Since the rules have been changed, now all the groups have reported that they have changed their leaders. Most of the members are not coming forward to become leaders because they cannot devote more time and attend meetings and they are not literate to handle group activities. The members mentioned satisfaction with the work of their leaders

5 Functioning of the Groups

5.1 Meetings

Group meeting is a very essential aspect of SHGs as providing a forum for members for discussing their social and economic problems and to provide a platform for member for exchange of idea are functions of SHGs. For this purpose, it is important for group members to hold regular meetings to share information, make plans, solve problems, take decisions, etc.

All the members attend meeting regularly as the groups mostly were formed out of self-motivation and to address their need. Usually, if a member does not come in time, other members go to her house and call her to the meeting. In Habsiduda, some groups have imposed Rs. 2/- as fine for not attending the meeting. But in Kapra and Ghatkesar, it was reported that all the members attend the meeting regularly.

Generally, the group meetings were held in the evenings of every 8th day of the month, so that the members could attend after completing their day's work. The venue for the meetings was either the house any member or school playground or temple courtyard. In Vompuguda village, they meet in any members house, while in Venkatapuram and Swarnapuri the groups meet in temple courtyard. But in Habsiguda the members of all the groups complained that they do not have any place to meet. So they sit on the road and conduct the meeting which is not going to serve the functions of SHGs. Since they are sitting on the road, they cannot sit leisurely and discuss other social issues. The frequency of the meetings is only once in a month when the members bring their savings + loan instalment. Research studies indicate that groups, which have regular meetings, have lesser rate of absenteeism among their members, a lower tendency to default (Gonzalez-Vega 1998; Hulme and Mosley 1996) and are more likely to sustain overtime.

It has been found that the members actively participate in the meetings and the cases of default are nil in Kapra and Ghatkesar. However, in Uppal, some groups are facing the problem of not attending the meeting and default. It is observed that apart from Office bearers, the other members also participate actively, and the relationship is cordial and there are no serious differences among the members. They also help the members to put pressure on those members who tend to delay the repayment and discourage the defaulters.

5.2 *Topics for Discussion in the Meetings*

When questioned about the topics for discussion in the meeting, the members informed that they discuss issues relating to collection of savings, collection and distribution of loans, dealing with defaulters, issues related to applying for loans and issues to be raised by the group members nominated for the federation meetings.

The groups in the three districts that were surveyed have a set of lending norms and practices relating to internal loans from own savings and, linkage loans from banks decided by mutual consent. These rules and practices are related to the conditions for providing loans to members from internal savings, purposes for which the loans will be extended to the members, the number of instalments through which the members are supposed to repay the loans, rates of interest to be charged for the loans sanctioned for different purposes, mode of repayment of loans (both internal as well as linkage loan) and the measures to be adopted in case of default of loan, etc.

Almost all groups more or less have common rules and procedures, there is a difference in the rates of interest to be charged on the loans given on the group savings and penalty to be imposed on the defaulters.

5.3 *Savings and Borrowing*

Thrift and saving is one of the five ‘P’s on SHGs functions, and mobilization of a small amount of saving is one of the important objectives of the functioning of the SHG. Credit needs of rural women are fulfilled totally through SHG. SHGs enhance equality of status of women as participants, decision-makers and beneficiaries in the democratic, economic, social and cultural spheres of life (Gurumurthy 2000). At the time of organizing the group, generally, all the members in the group decide the amount of contribution to be given by each member per month. The frequency of group savings in all the SHGs is monthly and it is fixed. Each group has fixed a particular date and time for the group meeting and each member has to bring her contribution to the meeting.

The saving per month per person is fixed initially at Rs. 50 but later it has been increased to Rs. 100/- in all the 25 groups that were interacted with. The average amount of accumulated saving with the bank per group and per member observed to be Rs. 24,000 in Ghatkesar, Rs. 12,000/- in Uppal and Rs. 4800/- in Kapra mandals, respectively, with wide variation across the groups.

The internal savings of groups has been utilized by groups to provide loan to their members to meet a variety of urgent needs of members. All the groups have provided loan to their members from internal savings. And when more than one person needs the loan, it is divided between by convincing the members. The average amount of interest rates charged by groups on the internal savings is Rs. 2/- which is lower than the market rate. The SHGs model with bank lending to groups of poor women without collateral has become an accepted part of rural finance. Over a half a million SHGs have been linked to banks over the years (Anupam 2008). With regard to linkage of SHGs with formal credit institutions, it is learnt that all the 25 groups have linkage with bank. These groups have received three loans. After depositing monthly savings for 6 months, the groups received first loan of Rs. 50,000/-. After timely repayment, they received second loan of Rs. 1,000,000/- and then a third loan of Rs. 300,000/-. Bank provides loan to groups for starting petty business, purchase of agricultural inputs or for other purposes. Some groups received loans from Gram Sabha under Srinidhi project for the purchase of animals such as cow/buffalo, goats, etc.

The objective of SHGs is to empower women. The economic empowerment means that women are now capable of earning some money to contribute to the family kitty (Nagnur et al. 2014). It is widely felt that access to credit with lower rate of interest will reduce rural indebtedness and members will use their loan amount for productive activity but it was observed that the members utilized more than 90% of their share of the loan for health, children's education and other reasons. Only few used their loans as investment to start small business like opening of Tiffin centre, bidi making, cloth shop, tailoring shop, etc. The information during the discussion revealed that apart from the linkage loans members still take loans from moneylenders, gold loan, etc. to meet their needs.

But the repayment is as per the norm and there are no defaulters due to monitoring and pressure exerted by members on individual members to prevent default of loan in almost all groups that were interviewed. If anyone does not pay on the day the instalment is to be paid, they charge a fine of Rs. 100/-. In case, where a member is out of station or in difficult situation, then showing the group solidarity the rest of the members contribute and pay her instalment also and later take money from her. This attitude is all due to SHG movement. However, in Habsigudu SHGs, there are some wilful defaulters and because of them the banks stopped sanctioning loans to SHGs in their area.

During the discussion, all the members raised the issue of pavala vaddi (interest Subsidy). In 2004, the then government of undivided Andhra Pradesh decided to give loans to SHGs on pavala vaddi, i.e. 0.25% interest per month. This interest incentive was paid in 6 months to all the SHG members who have an on-time repayment track record. And some SHGs received this incentive also. But now none of them is getting this incentive and the government has not issued any clarification on this issue. So the SHG members are feeling that the banks (and in some cases the group leaders) are cheating them and charging higher rate of interest while the government is providing loan at 0.25% rate.

5.4 Awareness Regarding the Functioning of the Groups

For proper maintenance of records, and other activities that are taken up by the group, the members should be aware of the functions of SHGs. To ensure transparency in decision-making, maintenance of records, better awareness among the members regarding the rules and regulations is essential. During the group discussion, members were asked if they are aware of the various procedures and ability to handle bank transactions. Although all members said that they have full knowledge but the confidence level indicates that all of them are not aware and are mostly dependent on the VOA for maintenance of accounts and in some groups hardly one or two members have some knowledge about maintenance of records.

Though a few training camps were organized at the SHG federation level in the study areas, still the groups are dependent on the VOAs for maintaining the accounts properly. For the purpose, each group pays Rs. 100/-per month to VOA.

5.5 Bookkeeping and Accounting Practices Followed by Groups

All the 25 groups that were interacted are maintaining five-sets of records. These are attendance register, savings register, cashbook loan register, other accounts register and the minutes of meetings register. All these registers are kept in the custody of one office-bearer or with VOA. In all the groups, the first and second leaders are educated; hence, the records are maintained as per the directions received from VOA.

Some training facilities have been provided by the promoters of the SHGs, such as the block office, or federation of SHGs and NGO groups. The office-bearers have received training related to candle making, fishery, and other types of activities for a short period of time. It is learnt that now the leaders are teaching how to do bank transactions to other members by taking members to the bank in rotation. This initiative ensures women's empowerment as they have total control over their organizations in terms of financial and managerial matters (Kapur 2001).

5.6 *Performance of the Groups*

The success or failure of any group depends on the performance of the group members. SHG approach is felt as the best strategy for women empowerment. For continuity of any group, the performance is essential. When all the members were questioned about their opinion regarding the performance of their group, they said that they are satisfied with the performance of their group and they have no complaints. None of the groups are facing internal problems as they are homogenous socially and more or less economically also. Further, they formed groups to help each other voluntarily, motivated by observing other groups.

Box-1: Success Story from the study area

Case-1

Maheshwari aged 30, lives in Ghatkesar Mandal Swarnapuri colony/village. They have their own house. It is a joint family. Maheshwari have three children (girls) who are studying in primary school. As it was a joint family, husbands' income is not sufficient to meet the family requirements. And she cannot go out to earn for the family. Motivated by her neighbour, Maheswari joined the SHG group. She received Rs. 10,000/- loan from group savings and Rs. 10,000/- from "Srinidhi" earlier *Velugu* programme and started *saris* business in her house. She herself runs the business. The extra income is helping the family to meet children's school fee, family medical expenditure and other daily expenditure. She feels a sense of achievement and empowered.

Case-2

Jyoti aged 23 years, recently shifted to Vampuguda village. She came to know about SHG groups in the neighbourhood and formed her own group. She is 12th pass and learnt all the rules from her friends who are in the other groups. When the VO was not cooperating to get bank loan, she herself met the bank officials and got loan sanctioned for her group. With the loan amount she got, she started *bidi* making business. From *bidi* making she earns about Rs. 2000/- per month. As the leader of the group, she was not willing to pay money as commission to VOA for writing accounts and for help in bank transactions. She is managing everything on her own and is very confident about her group's stability.

Case-3

Lakshmi age 40, lives in Swarnapuri colony/village. She lives in a rented house and her husband is a casual worker. She joined SHG group getting motivated by her neighbour. She availed loan from Sreenidhi and SHG podupu. With that amount she started mobile Tiffin centre. Now she has extra income to meet the family needs. She earns about Rs. 200/- per day. She feels joining SHG made her financially strong.

The success stories in the box above indicate the fulfilment of SHGs objectives of empowering individual member economically. Most of the SHGs are concentrating on enabling their members in availing of loan for productive purpose and gain economic prosperity through loan/credit. But in the state of Gujarat the functioning of SHGs went beyond finances and addressing the other objectives such as encouraging community togetherness through sharing of information and ideas; supporting group members in resolving personal problems and also assist community in recognizing major problems and help in resolving them.

Two women Damini Vaishnav and Vasanti Kevadia of Savar Kundla Taluk in Amreli in rural districts of Gujarat have created presidents indicating that SHGs means not only credit and thrift but also growing together. These two women were engaged in manufacturing embroidery products and handicrafts articles and participated in the exhibition held at Mumbai and Ahmedabad where they sold goods worth Rs. 270,000. NABARD helped them in participating in the exhibition. To increase their turnover and with an intension to outsource their requirements, these two women (Damini and Vasanti) started a social engineering movement by engaging 2000 women from 20 to 25 neighbouring villages. Presently, Vasanti made her house as training centre to train women to form more SHGs, while Damini is engaged in creating 10 SHGs to include 200 women. Looking at this president, a number of SHGs are suddenly springing up leading to a new wave of self-reliance in the state (as reported by Himanshu Bhayani in business standard February 14, 2013).

Looking at the increase in the number of SHGs in Kavida and Kundla, the National Bank for Agriculture and Rural Development (NABARD) has started associating with the SHGs in other towns namely Bagasara, Savar Kundla, Khambha and Lathi-Lilya-Damnagar, in the Amreli district and is also taking initiatives to promote the same.

Traditionally, Bagasara was known for its imitation jewellery and embroidery work, but now it is turning fast into an SHG centre. The town now has 100 SHGs and voluntary organizations which are engaged in making consumer goods like, processed foods, beauty products, textiles, decorative articles and cleaning products. 'The 1350 women member strong SHGs manufacture these items and are also sell them by door-to-door marketing'. Total savings of all the groups in Bagasara alone amounts to Rs. 20 lakh. This type of participation is the real motive of SHGs, which helps members growing together.

The women SHGs in the Gir region of Gujarat went beyond microfinance to fight social taboos about widows to help them lead a better life and showed the collective power women to the society. A group of women from Kodinar block came together in 1999 to form an SHG with the objective of encourageing women to get into the habit of saving. Like any other SHG the savings of the members were pooled together and used for lending to members themselves and also for bank loans. But a call for help from a young widow, changed it into a platform to fight superstitions and meaningless social practices and ensure social equity and justice. In Gir region, widows are to observe perpetual mourning and are compelled to wear black dresses and are not allowed to participate in auspicious ceremonies. The Sorath Mahila Vikas Mandali (SMVM) put aside the caste divide which is inherent in the community and focused on social equity and justice for women by helping Rasilaben a young widow of 24 years, who lost her husband in a road accident. The mandali presented her with a colourful saree, bangles, nose ring and bindi which are strictly prohibited for a widow.

In 2011, they started the widow recognition programme, through which they started an awareness programme among the villagers in respect of the rights of widows and as to how they should be treated with due respect, dignity and equality. The task was not easy as the community was not willing to change their attitude towards this social customs and the mandali was levied with allegations. In spite of accusations the mandali continued their efforts through rallies, community meetings, awareness camps and house visits. With an undeterred effort for 4 long years, finally the mandali could make 500 widows lead a normal life with the acceptance and support of communities across 68 villages (as reported by Palak Gosai, in Village Square, 16th September, 2017).

5.7 Problems and Concerns of the Groups

It was informed that members in different groups solved the disputes among themselves through mutual discussion and convincing each other in group meetings. Members in certain groups faced problems in getting bank loans due to lack of knowledge with respect to submission of documents. The Village Organization Assistants (VOA) reluctance to assist these groups was cause sited for the problem. As per the SERP guidelines, the VOAs function was to facilitate loans to all needy and eligible members of SHGs from banks, Srinidhi and from various sources and projects for livelihoods and other purposes. Further, the guideline says that VOA shall not collect any charges for extending bank loan and Srinidhi loans except as per guidelines issued by VO based on resolution of executive Committee of VO. The VOA is paid Rs. 5000/- per month as honorarium. Contrary to these guidelines each and every member of the SHG pays Rs. 10/- every month for the payment of VO. Further, they have to pay 10% of the loan sanctioned to VO. And each SHG has to pay Rs. 100/- to VO for writing accounts. These payments are creating additional burden on the economically weaker members.

6 Conclusion

SHGs and various microfiancé schemes are helping women to raise their level and contribute to the economy (Sharma 2017). It has been observed that SHGs have been successful in making the poor especially women to inculcate the habit of thrift. All the SHG groups in the study area are following Panchasutras and have maintained the minimum number of members as they felt that small group is manageable for interaction among the members, and feasible for financial management of the SHG. Majority of the members regularly attend meetings and participate in the meetings where the decisions are taken. All the SHGs that were contacted, reported of having bank accounts and have recently changed their leaders as the rules have been modified. All the SHGs have become members of SHG federation.

It has been observed that the interaction and discussions in the meetings are cordial, and there are no serious problems with the functioning of the groups. As a result, most groups have been functioning well and the members could solve the problems through discussions and understanding among themselves. It was also found that the groups are effectively enforcing the adherence to rules of groups and timely repayment of loans was high in all the groups. Almost all the groups received revolving fund and one or more loans from the internal saving at low rates of interest and utilized the same for social and medical purposes. Similarly, all the groups received more than two loans from banks which only few utilized for investment purpose. Repayment of loans was satisfactory due to group solidarity and peer pressure exerted by members. Most of the members are aware of banking procedures.

However, certain shortcomings are observed. The CRPs are conducting basic training programmes but most of the SHG members are not attending such training programmes. Those who have received the training are not using for any productive activity. The SHGs do not have dedicated bookkeepers and only the leaders who have some education background are aware of bookkeeping and record management procedures. The major concern of the members was interest subsidy on bank loans. The government introduced interest subsidy on timely repayment of bank loan and then stopped extending this facility without giving any notification. This has resulted in developing a suspicion that the VO is taking higher interest on the loans in collusion with bank employees. Hardly one-fourths of the members have some knowledge about the maintenance of accounts and bookkeeping, because of their low level of literacy and lack of adequate training facilities. As a result, the group members have to depend on their office-bearers; and majority of the groups have to take the help of knowledgeable persons outside the group to maintain the accounts and other required registers. For writing the accounts, they have to pay Rs. 100/- every month. So practically every member, apart from the mandatory saving of Rs. 100/- need to pay an extra of Rs.40/- (Rs. 10/- for VOA + Rs. 10/- for Grama Sangham for expenses + Rs. 10/- for Mandal Mahila Samakhya and Rs. 10/- for writing accounts).

The purpose of SHGs bank linkage was to remove middleman squeezing the needy credit seeker. But what was observed is since the VOA facilitates in documentation for obtaining loan and explains procedures she needs to be paid commission by the group after receiving the loan. Failing which she will not help them or give information related to loans. The SHG members expressed their helplessness and in fact requested the researcher not to reveal their groups' name or their area name. This is a major concern and a possible solution is bank officials organizing monthly meeting with SHG members and advise them about the loans and the documentation that needs to be done. With this, the poor can save the commission money.

One of the objectives of the SHGs is to develop together. Studies found micro-entrepreneurship has had a positive effect on women's self-confidence, economic empowerment, improved standard of living and sense of achievement. However, what was observed in the study was SHG members are investing loans in individual income generating activity. None of the group members are willing to come forward for starting group activity and collective growth. The loans taken are utilized for investing in the family business or for children's education or marriages, etc. So, the empowerment or sense of achievement is still far off. The SHGs need the guidance of NGOs to initiate income generating activities for collective development. Further, the bank officials also should play a proactive role by counselling and guiding the women in selecting and executing profitable income generating activities (Manimekalai 2004). To ensure that the SHGs start a common economic activity, a possible solution can be after giving three major loans to the group a restriction indicating that unless the group starts a common activity next major loan will not be sanctioned. Otherwise, it will continue as women kitty group.

Another problem that all the groups are encountering is lack of space for meetings. Since some groups meet in members house or on the road, they do not have the privacy to discuss the social problems, because they have to vacate the place as early as possible. Hence, they hurriedly finish the financial transactions and leave. The functioning of SHGs has been viewed only from an economic perspective till date (Anant Kumar 2006). If a place is demarcated for meetings, the group members will spend some time together and can discuss matters which are non-financial in nature and can gain strength from each other to deal with other problems. For example, the FGDs were conducted in the nearby school compound which made all the members speak-out without any hesitation. Some such arrangement should be made to make SHGs achieve the intended goals.

Some local initiatives from NGOs are successful. SHGs are very much in need in Telangana to achieve the desired objectives just like the way Damini Vaishnav and Vasanti Kevadia of Savar Kundla Taluk in Amreli district, Gujarat did in by providing work to 2000 women in the neighbouring villages; and the social moment of SMVM of Giri region in Gujarat, transformed itself into a platform to get rid of meaningless stigmas and ensure social equity and justice to widowed women.

References

Anant Kumar. (2006). Self Help Groups. Women's health and empowerment-global thinking and contextual issues. *Jharkhand Journal of Development and Management studies, 4*(3), 2061–2079 (XISS, Ranchi, September).

Anupam, K. (2008). Indian microfinance-An avenue towards human capital development. *Management Account, 43*(11), 827–834.

Gonzalez-Vega, C. (1998). Do financial Institutions have a role in assisting the poor? In M. Kimenyi, R. Wieland, & J. D. von Pishke (Eds.), *Strategic issues in microfinance*. Aldershot, UK: Ashgate Publishing.

Gurumurthy, T. R. (2000). *SHGs empower Rural Women* (pp. 36–38). Kurukshetra, February.

Himanshu, B. (2013), *SHGs help rural Gujarat to wealth*. Business Standard, Ahmadabad, February 14. http://www.business-standard.com/article/sme/shgs=help-rural-gujarat-to-wealth-106120101112_1.html. Accessed on February 14, 2018.

Hulme, D., & Mosely, P. (1996). *Finance against poverty* (Vols. 1 & 2), London: Routledge.

Kapur, P. (2001). *Empowering the Indian Women*. Publication Division, Ministry of Information and Broadcasting, Government of India.

Khalil, O. (2000). *Microfinance institutions: Effective weapon in the war against rural poverty*. www.muslimedia.com.

Manimekalai, K. (2004). *Economic empowerment of Women through Self-Help Groups* (pp. 15–18). Third Concept, February.

Nagnur, S., Rayanagoudar, R., Chandavani, V., & Pawar, V. (2014). Self help group strategy to empower Rural Women. *International Journal of Home Science Extension and Communication Management, 1*(2), 63–67.

Palak, G. (2017). *How one women-run SHG helped 500 widows across 68 villages in Less than 4 years*. Village square, September 16. https://www.thebetterindia.com/115637/women-shg-gir-stand-for-dignity-of-widows. Accessed on March 20, 2018.

Raja Reddy, K., & Reddy, C. S. (2012). *Self help Groups in India-a study on quality and sustainability*. Enable Publication, December 2012.

Self Help Groups (SHGs) in India; Brief paper, Ethiopian delegation, New Delhi, 2014.

SGSY Programme and Self Help Groups in Churachandpur District; Shodhganga.inflibnet.ac.in/bitstream/10603/169450/8/08_chapter2.Pdf. Accessed on March 28, 2018. https://www.aajeevika.gov.in/sites/default/files/resources/NRLM-Mission-document.

Sharma, N. (2017). Economic empowerment of rural women and self Help groups in Punjab: A literature survey. *EPRA International Journal of Economic and Business Review, 5*(6), 93–100.

Status of Micro Finance in India 2015–16, NABARD.

The Bharat Microfinance Report 2015, Sa-Dhan and NABARD.

Gender Digital Divide in India: Impacting Women's Participation in the Labour Market

Sharmistha Sinha

1 Introduction

Digital technology and globalization has brought in a sea change in the landscape of work. Access to work has increased, consumer behaviour and demands have diversified, flows of data and information have increased, smart services are extending, supply chain management is dealt by smart systems, nature of supply service employment—operators and actors in the wider digital ecosystem have changed. Non-localized businesses, expanding platform economies, Industry 4.0 and Industrial Internet of Things (IIOT) are emerging in both developed and developing economies. Many goods and services today, as demonstrated by the 'app economy', are entirely virtual and pass through the internet, often on palmtop at fingertip. Be it education, or trade or medical services, or cloud computing services, machine-to-machine communication, in every sphere exchanges through digital medium have increased. The number of internet users has more than tripled in a decade—from 1 billion in 2005 to 4.05 billion at the end of 2017, implying an increased connectivity globally (Internet World Stats 2018). Artisans, entrepreneurs, app developers, freelancers and small businesses are participating directly on digital platforms reaching an enormous global customer base. 360 million take part in cross-border e-commerce (McKinsey Global Institute 2016). Scope and velocity of trade and services have increased significantly, thus supporting the economic growth and share of exports. Digital payment systems and digital ID systems provide better access to public and private services and subsidies, reducing leakages and delays and help promoting inclusive growth.

In India, there had been significant strides in digital outreach to every corner of the country. Mobile penetration is increasing rapidly, digital transactions, Jandhan-Aadhaar-Mobile (JAM) trinity, online public services and e-commerce,

S. Sinha (✉)
National Institute of Labour Economics Research and Development, Delhi, India
e-mail: sinha.sharmistha@gmail.com

NILERD, *Reflecting on India's Development*,
https://doi.org/10.1007/978-981-13-1414-8_14

platform economies are spreading wide. Total number of wireless telephone subscribers, in 2016, have crossed the 1 billion mark (it reached 1186 million as in June 2017), of which rural subscribers comprise 42% (TRAI 2018a); teledensity, reaching to as much as 249.91 in cities like Delhi. Number of smartphone users in India is estimated to reach 530 million by 2018. Total Internet subscribers have increased to 445.96 million as in 2017, with rural areas comprising 29% (TRAI 2018b). This digitization push is likely to have a multiplying force with far-reaching positive implications for the society. The Indian economy has rebound to accelerate faster to a higher growth trajectory. A recent study by McKinsey Global Institute (2014) shows that the adoption of key technologies across sectors spurred by the Digital India initiative could help boost India's GDP additionally by $550-billion to $1-trillion annually by 2025.

At this outset, when the economy and the labour market is going digital, women's participation in the economy is not improving. Gap between women and men on economic participation is wide with India ranking as low as 139th among 144 countries and scoring persistently low in terms of Economic Participation and Opportunity (according to the World Economic Forum 2017). In India, labour force participation rate among women is only 27% as against 75% among men (Labour Bureau 2016). Therefore, there are some disparities which are hindering women to benefit from the transformational gains of the changing digital economy.

Studies Jiang and Luh (2017) and Antonio and Tuffley (2014) show that women in the developing world have significantly lower technology participation rates than men, which is primarily because of the gendered socio-cultural perception. The studies, however, reflect that as and when women participate in the global digital society, benefits accrue at household level as well as to the economy at large. Globally, there persist gender inequalities in terms of economic participation, control and ownership of productive assets, occupational segregation, etc. In this scenario, lack of free access to use of and benefit from ICTs can have a negative impact amplifying the gender divide across different social and economic groups.

The present paper explores the scope for women's economic participation and empowerment in this digital era in the Indian context. The country is in a threshold when it is poised to grow at a higher rate, a structural change is emerging in the labour market with more and more women moving out of agriculture, increasing participation of females in education, several initiatives being taken to drive digital technology, and therefore, it is important that we look at the gender digital divide in India to understand whether an equitable information society is emerging or gender inequality is exacerbating. The paper studies the divide in terms of disparity in access, usage and the factors responsible for the gap and those that impede women's economic empowerment and benefit from the digital dividends. Finally, it attempts to suggest a set of policies so that women become a part of and gain from the 'Smart' labour market.

2 Digital Divide: Access and Beyond

Connectivity and access are increasing, but still more than half of the world's population—3.9 billion people—are offline (ITU 2016) and, therefore, bereft of the benefits from the many opportunities that the digital revolution offers for empowerment and development. Emerging economies are adopting technology rapidly, but Internet penetration rates, that is, the percentage of workers in a country using the new technology and the diffusion is low in the emerging and transition economies (40%) as compared to developed countries (81%) (Key ICT indicators 2005–2016, ITU 2017). In terms of M2M penetration rates, as per the ITU data, it is highest in countries which are highly industrialized and advanced economies (ITU Facts and Figures 2016). Therefore, technological sophistication, connectivity and access are increasing; but there exist high inequality, with the premium mainly accruing to the highly skilled and advantageous section of the population. Further, the purpose of using it differs; the more educated, wealthier section make greater use of advanced services, like e-commerce and online financial and government services, automation and data exchange in manufacturing technologies, connecting systems and services that goes beyond machine-to-machine (M2M) communications; than those with lower levels of education and income, who use the Internet predominantly for communication and entertainment purposes; thus, the digital divide actually transcends the divide of access and connectivity and operates at many levels.

There is, therefore, 'Access divide', which is the disparity between individuals and groups that do or do not have access to technologies. And then there is 'multi-dimensional' digital divide which reflects more the interrelationships of technology with race, gender, culture and social constructs, which in turn affects the use of digital technology.

3 Digital Gender Gap—Exclusion in the Digital Era

Digitally, 12% fewer women than men benefit from Internet access worldwide, rising to 16% in developing countries and 33% in least developed countries (ITU 2017[1]). In 2017, the regional gender gap was largest in Africa (25%) and negative in the Americas (−2%) (Fig. 1).

The opportunities for empowerment created by digital economy are broad, from access to education, health services to more economic opportunities (both wage labour and entrepreneurship), improving social status, autonomy and participatory decision-making, financial empowerment, combating violence, leveraging data, digital media consumption, etc. If the gap is not closed, the potential opportunities for

[1]ITU is the United Nations specialized agency for information and communication technologies. The data is adopted from ITU Facts and Figures 2016, available at https://www.itu.int/en/ITU-D/Statistics/Documents/facts/ICTFactsFigures2017.pdf. Accessed on 20 February 2018.

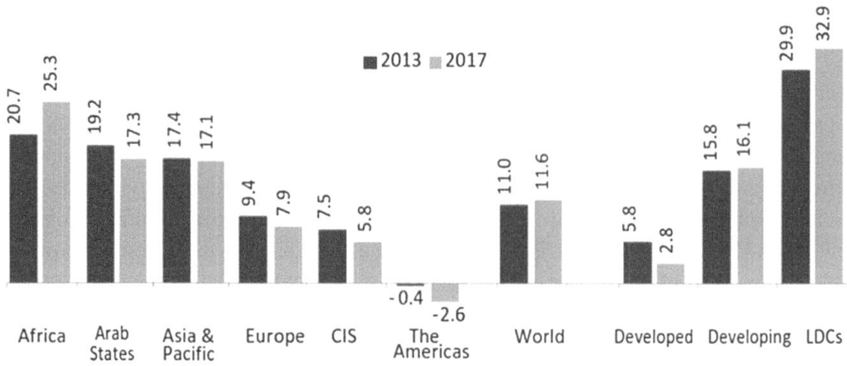

Fig. 1 Internet user gender gap (%), 2013 and 2017. *Note* Estimates: gender gap represents the difference between the Internet user penetration rates for males and females relative to the Internet user penetration rate for males, expressed as a percentage. CIS refers to commonwealth of independent states. *Source* ICT facts and figures 2017 available at https://www.itu.int/en/ITU-D/Statistics/Documents/facts/ICTFactsFigures2017.pdf accessed on 27/07/2018

empowerment would be missed by women and newer inequalities will arise or the existing ones will widen. The 12th Annual Internet Governance Forum, 2016, convened by the United Nations broached for approaches to provide internet access to all members of the society and close the digital divide that is exacerbating inequalities (UNDP 2016). Without affordable and universal access to ICTs and broadband connectivity, it would not be possible to support the development efforts in line with the sustainable development goals and minimize the trade-offs among goals.

Closing gender digital divide would not only require achieving Goal 9 or Goal 5 (to achieve gender equality and empower all women and girls), but addressing inequality (Goal 10), decent employment opportunities (Goal 8), education (Goal 4), regulations and governance (Goal 16), climate change (Goal 13), etc., thus needing coordination for implementation.

Ensuring digital access alone will not lead to empowerment—be it digital or economic or social. There are other analog components, like education, skilling, income, asset holding, age, occupation, sector at which women work, patriarchal mindset, unpaid work burden and different other social barriers that shore up the disparity. It should be looked through the lens of intersectionality, which integrates diversity, with special attention to gender-related issues of subgroups (e.g. rural women, girls, women in refugee camps).

4 India in the Digital Era

The Digital India initiative is one of the biggest reforms brought in by the Government of India to ensure that public services reach the citizens. The JAM trinity is an initiative to ensure direct transfer of subsidies to intended beneficiaries and thus elimination of intermediaries and leakages, through linking the Jan Dhan scheme (financial inclusion scheme), Aadhaar numbers (unique identity number) and mobile numbers of individuals.

It has benefitted immensely the direct beneficiaries of government policies and programmes, like Direct Benefit Transfer (DBT) of wages of MGNREGA, DBT of different scholarships, etc. This has reduced the economic and social dependence, increased decision-making and enhanced action; therefore, it paved a way for breaking the beads of traditional gendered norms forcefully laid upon women.

With increasing digital connectivity and related initiatives, there is impact on financial empowerment also, albeit indirectly. The State Bank of India, the largest bank in India, using a large random sample of Jan Dhan and Mudra accounts opened by it between August 2014 and March 2016, found that there had been an enabling traction across Jan Dhan, Aadhaar and Mudra loans, and that women have increased and better access to credit (Ghose and Ghosh 2016). In states with high women literacy, of which 25% are below the age group of 45 years, there were more inward remittances, and concomitant cash withdrawals as well.

However, there are still challenges to overcome in ensuring that all are included in an increasingly connected and Internet-enabled world.

4.1 Disparity in Access

4.1.1 Gender Gaps

High gender disparities are prevalent in the society that limits women's ownership and usage of mobile phones and Internet. With a population of over 1.3 billion and a gender gap in ownership of 36%, India has an estimated 114 million fewer women than men owning a mobile phone, as estimated by GSMA[2] (2015). They are more likely to borrow phones from friends and family than own their own device. Men are 25% more likely to own a SIM card than women. Mobile Internet users were 389 million till December 2016 (IAMAI and IMRB 2016) with men dominating the Internet user base forming about 71% of the total user base, and women forming 29%. Usage among men has been growing at 50% as against 46% for women. In urban India, however, there is more parity, with the ratio of men and women Internet users being 62:38. GSMA, Telenor-BCG (2015) in their respective reports, also reveal similar statistics concurring that women and senior citizens form a significant part of the unconnected population in the country. Even among Internet users, there is a stark gender difference in usage pattern, highest being in case of e-commerce (Fig. 2).

[2]A global association of mobile operators.

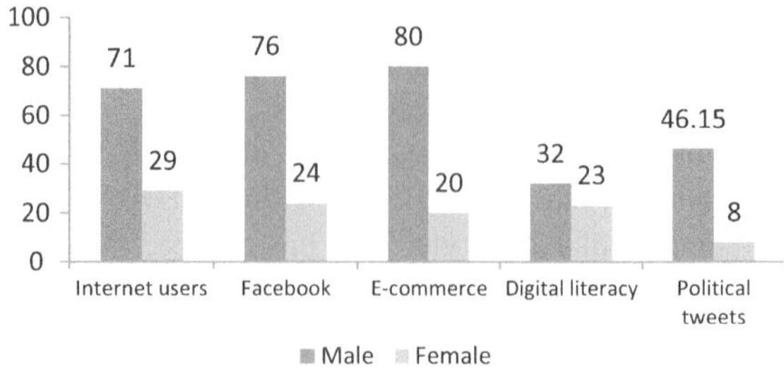

Fig. 2 Digital gender divide in India (%) *Source* Jain (2016)

The following section reflects upon how women contribute to and benefit from the emerging 'Smart' labour market in India.

5 Women in the Digital Economy

i. *Employment in IT-BPM Sector*

The IT-BPM sector is a crucial growth catalyst for the Indian economy. Employment in IT, wired, wireless communication-related sectors in India is about 3.83 million, of which males comprise 3.35 million and women only 0.4 million (i.e. only 10%) (NSS 2011–12). In this sector, the high employment generating sub-sectors are computer programming, consultancy and related activities, wired telecommunications activities and retail sale of information and communications equipment in specialized stores. Share of females in these sub-sectors account to be 17.5, 5.7 and 4.7%, respectively. Whereas in sub-sectors like data processing, hosting and related activities, web portals and wholesale of computers and computer peripheral equipments, share of women range about 21–22%, but sadly, total employment in these sectors is itself lesser as against the first-mentioned sub-sectors (Fig. 3).

ii. *Confluence of Digital Technology and Labour—Initiatives to Empower Women*

The reach and scale of Rural Distribution Network (RUDI), a women-led agricultural cooperative operated by SEWA, has increased dramatically in recent years, with the introduction of a unique mobile management information system (MIS), called RUDI Sandesha Vyavhar (RSV or RUDI information exchange) in 2012. The members 'RUDIbens', procure raw agricultural produce from marginal farmers at market prices, add value to that stock by cleaning and processing it before packaging and sell it at affordable prices through a network of over 3000 RUDIbens. Prior to the technology, RUDIbens had to visit processing centres in person or send via intermediaries, which often resulted in delay or loss. Now, using the RSV digital technology, they are being able to capture sales and place orders for additional stock via SMS using their simple feature phones. Now, RUDI reaches over 11 million households annually with its high-quality, affordable, brand RUDI

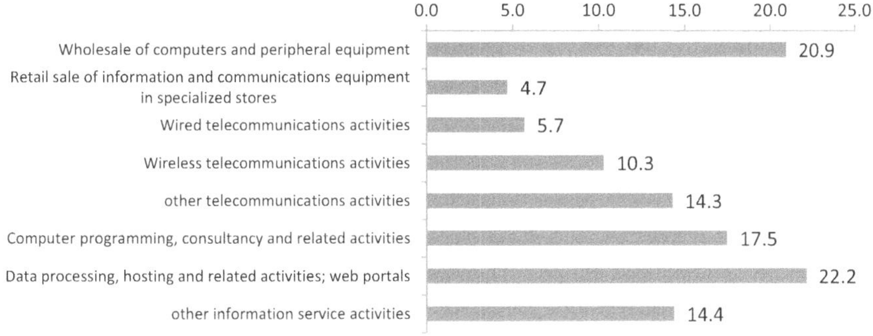

Fig. 3 Share of females among total in ICT, wired, wireless communication-related sectors *Source* NSS 2011–12, GOI

products. Income of the members have increased, and they can now generate simple reports on their handsets and can use data and communicate much easily and faster than ever before. Most important the informal supply chain management has become much more formalized. The application is being rolled out to RUDIbens through various marketing and training activities, which also offer additional support with capacity building and long-term enterprise development (Cherie Blair Foundation 2016a, b).

Such confluence of technology and labour is empowering women entrepreneurs across the world. 'Business Women' is an innovative service providing 100,000 women across Tanzania, Nigeria and Indonesia with business tips and training via their mobile phones. The service, availed mainly by women own account workers, micro-entrepreneurs in the retail sector has empowered women entrepreneurs to feel more confident, to gain access to information, improved distribution channels; through the web app they can now tap into valuable existing networks and attract and retain customers more. Similarly, a partnership initiative of First Bank Nigeria, YTF and the Blair Foundation for Women provided training on mobile banking products and agency business, to over 2400 women entrepreneurs in Nigeria providing the opportunity to become agents in the retail network of First Bank Nigeria. Large number of women has now become active Firstmonie banking agents, who in turn provide those living in rural and underserved areas with branchless banking and mobile financial services. The FANIKISHA initiative promotes women entrepreneurs in the informal small and micro-enterprises in Kenya by enhancing their business skills and financing (UNDP 2012).

iii. *Women in the Mobile Value Chains*

As mobile penetration is expanding rapidly, markets are emerging in mobile value chains (MVC).[3] Opportunities are opening for women entrepreneurs to gain a great

[3]'Value chain', here, specifically refers to retail networks of the Mobile Network Operators, i.e. the channels through which MNOs get their products into the hands of end consumers.

deal in the mobile sales business in India. In different initiatives, like Sanchar Shakti programme, Shakti Vani, etc. in different states in India, many women are trained by Mobile Network Operators (MNOs) (Vodafone, Unilever, Uninor) to act as retailers within their own communities. It is estimated that 30% of sales agents at the end of the MVC are women (Cherie Blair Foundation 2011), often in small family-owned stores. Women are seen as having specific advantages as sales agents; they are good 'networkers' particularly in rural areas, they have patience and they are better at explaining products and interacting with customers, they can reach out to women consumers. Therefore, different MNOs make use of their women's network as distribution channels. Participating women are trained in sales, basic business administration and IT skills. Then, they are given a loan for the purchase of their first stock of scratch cards and begin operating as an independent business.[4]

Women engaged in the MVCs, no doubt, have gained in terms of increased income, more knowledge, self-confidence, improved social status, etc., but also a large number of women cannot leverage the benefits and become entrepreneurs, not because of their inefficiency or lack of access, but because of societal reasons like lack of family support, social stigma, security issues (as sales agents need to travel to remote places), etc. Also, be it mobile vendors or owners of retail outlets, women are at the lower end at lower paid roles, operating at a very small scale at small margins. The factors behind this can largely be attributed to cultural stereotype of gender roles within the family and in larger society, limited education and the lack of productive assets such as capital available to women. With respect to retail outlets, very few are owned by women. They work mostly as family helpers, the business/contract mainly owned by male members. Women are benefiting from advances of digital economy, but lag behind men. Interestingly, from MNO's perspective, their business have gained extensive market penetration, particularly rural market, women buyers have increased, sales efficiency has increased and certainly, there is more brand publicity, all at a much lower cost. Therefore, returns on this investment are very high. The rate at which access to market for the MNOs increases, access to and rise in income for the women increases at a lower pace. The benefits for women remain the lowest in the value chain.

iv. *E-retail: Artisan Economy*

Organized e-retailers like Craftsvilla, Jaypore, iTokri, etc. have changed the market of the artisans from remotest corners of the country. These e-retailers provide an interface to significant number of artisans across India to sell handicrafts, jewellery, tribal artefacts and ethnic products and provide them opportunity to venture into business. Also, the artisans have gained more awareness and access to more government schemes and programmes. More common online platforms are being

---

[4]Similar initiatives are seen in other countries also. Hapinoy Stores in Philippines, M-Pesa Women's Empowerment Initiative, Technoserve, Tigo and Vodacome initiative in Tanzania, A-Johara in Qatar and Ruma in Indonesia are some of the examples. However, at every country, women are at the lower end of the value chains.

created. These are, however, limited success stories and there are large number of small-scale and budding craft enterprises within the craftmark member base and also artisans that face incorrect pricing, wrong product developments, poor quality and poor supply chain management (AIACA 2013). In such cases, women face the brunt more, as they are disproportionately more in these sectors, not just as paid workers but also unpaid workers. The e-retail artisan sector is restricted to very few sectors and catering to very few people. The e-commerce in India, in general, needs to diversify and expand more to be more inclusive. As per CRISIL report, the online marketplace holds a mere 18% while online ticketing has 65% market share in the 400 billion e-commerce market in India.

v. *Initiatives to Improve Education, Health Care, Information*

There are several initiatives which may not directly empower women economically, but bring in a wind of change by educating them and enabling them to address various other issues like education, health care, information, etc. Initiatives like 'Mahila Shakti' and 'My Health, My Voice' use mobile to impart education at a very basic level and helping pregnant women get access to their rightful free governmental health facilities. The 'Hello Sakhi' initiative is helping the victims of domestic violence through mobile phones, and helping them with legal assistance, counselling and rehabilitation support. It has become their closest friend by helping over 11,000 women across 940 villages in Gujarat so far. In the rural Tilonia district of Rajasthan, a mobile phone and a community radio are platforms for rural women to get knowledge, share their views and ideas on various issues, thus empowering them to become change agents. Besides, Mobile One, e-FIR, different sub-projects under e-Kranti, iClik (Instant Complaint login Internet Kiosk) centres, Utility IDs, etc. provide services that help women.

6 What Leads to the Disparity? Challenges in and Outside the Labour Market

i. **Lack of Education and Skills**

In the face of rapidly changing technology and the nature of work, there is a dramatic shift in skill requirements, demanding ability to work with data, analysis, managing inventories digitally, presentation, basically, using technology in jobs at all levels. Without even the basic knowledge of reading or writing, there will not be any meaningful use of digital technology, even if there is access to it. Female literacy rate in India is only 65% as against 82% among men. Among the other social and religious groups, like for Muslims, SCs and STs, it is even lesser with 62, 56 and 49%, respectively. Therefore, even if women have access to technology, neither can the women read or write messages, nor, as in many cases, they know their phone numbers. According to GSMA (2018), 30% of women find reading/ writing difficulties to be the main barrier to mobile ownership.

It is observed that those with a secondary education or higher are considerably more likely to own a computer and access the Internet than those with less than a secondary degree (Pew Research Centre 2015). Only 18% of the women in India have secondary education or more (Census 2011). Along with education, Internet use is more common among people who have some English language ability. However, only 45% of children in Std. VIII could read simple sentences in English (ASER 2016). As it was observed in Fig. 1 that in America, a higher percentage of women than men are using the Internet, and these are also states that score highly on gender parity in tertiary education.

Being only mobile literate, but without formal education, does not suffice to succeed in this digital economy. Even though apps are developed for use by less educated, but in this information age it is also important to have critical and analytical skills to make sense of the vast amount of information available, make informed choices, and safeguard ones security and privacy.

In India, gender divide with regard to computer skills is also stark, with only 22.9% of the women knowing how to operate a computer, as against 32.3% men. In using the Internet to find necessary information, only 9.5% of females were able to do so, as compared to 17% for males. Gap in ability to able to send emails was even lesser, 8.7% as against 16% (Saha 2016).

Digital fluency, the extent to which people use digital technologies to become more knowledgeable, connected and effective, is a way to close the gender gap and level the playing field for women at work. However, in a survey of 31 countries, India scored the lowest in overall digital fluency for women scoring 12 points, with largest gaps between men and women (Accenture 2016). With higher rates of digital fluency among women, it is likely to have higher rates of gender equality in the workplace, higher education, more scope to search work, working from home or more flexible hours, etc. as is observed in nations like Sweden, Denmark, Norway, etc. which smoothens the way to participate in the economy.

To be able to gain skills and use effectively, access plays an important role. 77% of the bottom quintile of the households owns a mobile phone (Bhattacharya 2016). Even in underdeveloped rural areas, the share of households owning mobile phones is more than 75%. In metros, for towns it is 90%. However, in terms of access to Internet, only about a 25% of the households in metros have it. Access is low in other economic clusters, going down to only 3% in the underdeveloped rural areas. This indicates that digital connectivity is largely limited to verbal communications. High-value data services are accessed and used by only a few in the economy; therefore, it is natural that gains vide digital system would be skewed to advantage only a few. Further, within the household, gender equations decide the access and purpose of use of technology.

Lack of adequate and relevant technological skills, as also disparity in ownership, usage, using sophisticated tools, among women restricts their participation in the new economy, putting them at risk of missing out the opportunities and deepening the inequality. It also hampers their utilization of public welfare services.

ii. **Participation in the Labour Market**

Integration into the labour market also determines Internet usage and reaping benefits out of it. In India, the female labour force participation rate is very low and declining sharply over the years. Further, women have limited choices for employment across sectors, be it rural or urban areas. This sectoral segregation has been pervasive over time and exists even as women are moving out of agriculture. Within manufacturing and services, women are confined to few sectors like tobacco, textiles, apparel, retail trade, education, health and domestic services. To add to it, vulnerable employment which is an important indicator of job quality is very high among women. The quality characteristics of female employment in such sectors where women are more crowded reveals informality, no contracts, low pay and occupational segregation. In such a situation, even if there is access to digital technology, there is very little scope to leverage it for economic purpose (Fig. 4).

iii. **Unpaid Work Burden**

Domestic duties and care work, and the ideology of the marital household govern the entry to and withdrawal of women from the labour force to a large extent. And share of rural women engaged in domestic duties increased from 51.8% in 2005 to 59.7% in 2012, and 63% in urban areas, thus signifying burden of household activities, care work and non SNA/non-economic work. And the reason cited is mainly no other member to carry out the domestic duties. For basic facilities like water, only 52% of the households in India have access to household tap water connections (ICE 360). For the bottom quintile of the households, it is only 18%; remaining households have to either use handpumps or go out. And the data does not account for how far away the safe water is. Given the gendered structure of work within the household, it is mainly the female members who have to fetch the water.

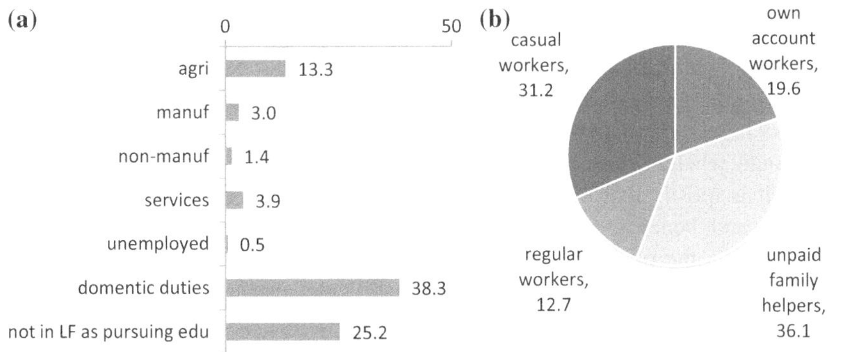

Fig. 4 **a** Distribution of female population, by economic sub-sectors, unemployed, not in labour force (%). **b** Distribution of the female workforce by status of employment *Source* Author's estimates from the National Sample Survey, 2011–12

OECD (2012) estimates reveal that in India, women spend 351.9 min per day on unpaid work while men spend only 51.8 min. This asymmetry and the time poverty that women faces is an important factor that prevents women from participating in the labour market, including in this newly advanced and expanded labour markets in which digital technology forms an integral part.

iv. **Challenges in the Working Sphere**

Even with growing e-commerce and access to digital technology in the economy, there are few core categories of challenges which are persistent and common across markets, industries and society at large that hinders women to expand and grow sustainably in the economy. And these are more often than not general obstacles that are rooted in the hegemonic gender system in the working sphere or otherwise, thus leading to an unequal footing between men and women, even in this digital era.

Difficulties in access to investment channels to fund growth; lack of ownership and control over productive assets; access to market information and relevant data for business-specific decisions; marketing; inadequate access to training and knowledge for business optimisation and growth; limited skills to use digital technology and leverage digital channels; lack of access to distribution channels and sales networks (both physical and digital); access to affordable insurance and language barriers are some factors that get into the way. Raising business visibility, access to marketplaces; access to information regarding market prices, competitors, customer demand, etc. are challenges for female entrepreneurs in both online and physical businesses. In case of online businesses, those dealing with material goods need warehousing. With lack of assets, stocks and inventories become a challenge restricting women to operate only at small scale. Lack of and access to digital knowledge poses difficulty to track consumer orders, locate products and resolve problems during shipment.

v. **Changing Work Structure**

The emerging 'platform economy' undoubtedly facilitate more flexible working arrangements, easing the way for many more women to enter the workforce. However, the very idea behind platform economies or gig economies is lowering down wages, while at the same time reducing the scope for collective bargaining or social dialogue. Here, workers themselves need to invest both capital and labour; even risks here are transferred from the business to the individual worker. There is also a doubt whether individuals engaged are to be considered employees or contractors. It is mostly that they are treated as contractors, thus avoiding any social protection and benefits, such as insurance or protection against workplace discrimination, by the platform economy.

The emerging 'crowdwork', 'work on demand', etc. also see platform economies linking workers to different assignments through online or apps; the work completed and delivered over the Internet to often anonymous purchasers in return for per-task payments. These types of works again fortify casualization and informalization of work, accentuate risk with no bargaining power and are very difficult to measure. Alike home-based work, this may also see increase in female participation because of both demand and supply-side factors. Given their household duties, restrictions on mobility, etc., women will take up the work, as they can then carry out both paid and unpaid work, and on the other hand, companies can do away with lower wages.

A significant share of women, mostly from marginalized and minority groups, works as domestic workers, in wellness sectors and alike. The emerging 'platform model' enables clients to hire their services merely through a call or online. However, their work structure remains the same, informal, no social security benefits, same working conditions and certainly no bargaining opportunities. It also exposes them to discrimination, as households can make their selection based on characteristics other than their skills, including age, gender, race, etc., given their details on the profile pages.

vi. **Automation**

With increased automation and advances in artificial intelligence, there would be new job creation, but there is also a huge risk of job dislocation, estimated to about 85% of Ethiopia, 77% in China and 69% in India (Frey and Rahbari 2016a, b). It is expected that job creation in the domestic textile and apparel sector, which is a high female employment generating sector in India, would be 2.9 million in the next 5 years as against target of 10 million, even though market size of the sector is expected to grow by 40% to $142 billion in the next years; the job deceleration being largely attributed to automation (E&Y 2016). Automation also implies that developing countries will no longer have the advantage of cheap labour, leading to premature de-industrialization.

In India, few women are in the manufacturing sector, concentrated in very few sub-sectors like textiles, apparel, etc. Women working in these sectors are already vulnerable, witnessing a job loss aftermath the global crisis. Now, exports have increased but stagnant for the last 3 years; therefore, new employment possibilities in these sectors are getting feeble. Now, if automation and artificial intelligence leads to job dislocation or bring in a radical change in it, requiring a very tech sophisticated skill set, women will face the brunt to a larger extent.

vii. **Income and Use of Technology**

Income is an important factor associated with internet use rates. For women in India, money provided by husband or general household budget is the main source to buy, or refill credit balance or paying monthly bill. In 2015, in India, only 21% of females bought from own money, as against, 90% in China, 71% in Mexico, 88% in Colombia and 81% in Kenya. In that case, women have limited choice and freedom in using the internet.

viii. **Companies' Perception**

Gender composition of customer base often plays an important role for a company to promote gender parity in the workforce, used mainly to tap into the female client base. Therefore, possibilities for women to participate in the economy depend not only on their talent but perception of companies and business needs.

ix. **Patriarchal Mindset**

One of the major factors restricting women to use the digital technology is the patriarchal mindset; there is still a certain section of the population that believes that mobile is an evil responsible for the violence and sexual abuse against women. Even in many states in India a ban is issued on women in using cell phones, referred as in Box 1.

Box 1: Ban on Women in Using Cell Phones: Instances from Different States in India

- In 2016, the panchayat (village-level governing body) in Basauli village in Uttar Pradesh has announced a complete ban on use of mobile phones or social media by unmarried girls, with hefty penalty and punishment clause in case of violation (Chauhani 2016). Similarly, a village council in Barmer, Rajasthan, many villages in Gujarat, Bihar and Haryana had banned women and girls from using or possessing mobile phones and more villages have joined the campaign, with an excuse that the devices distract them from their studies, 'debasing the social atmosphere'.
- In 2014, a khap panchayat (kangaroo court) and many other Panchayats in Uttar Pradesh had similarly banned mobile phones, jeans and other "western" items among young women in the village.
- A committee of the Karnataka Legislature has proposed a ban on mobile phones, citing that mobile is the reason behind kidnap and rape among school and college going girls.

This ban mostly applies to girls under the age of 18 and unmarried women.

Despite initiatives by the Government to connect each citizen under Digital India initiative and move towards more inclusive and comprehensive development of the country and its people, there is prevalent, rather thriving backlash against women's rights and gender equality in development in different parts of the country. The restrictions imposed or statements made regarding mobility of women or use of mobile phones to justify violence against women are sometimes by village-level governing bodies or government representatives. Such mindset blocks the very essence of inclusive development.

x. **Fear of Online Harassment**

One major factor associated with the Internet is fear, especially in context of trolling and cyber abuse. Even if there is access, women face more and a wider variety of online harassment and abuse. NCRB (2015) indicates that 'outraging modesty of women' ranks at the second position of motives behind cybercrimes, with increase in incidence, share in total and rise in ranking over the years.

7 Conclusion and Recommendations

The impact of digital revolution on female labour has been mixed. While there had been advances in women's economic empowerment, but because of the persisting socio-economic inequalities, the transformation remains far from desired. Sound policy frameworks need to be evolved not only to ensure universal and affordable access of technology and energy but increase the autonomy of women in the framework of new technology paradigm and equip them with the necessary education and skills to safely navigate the digital space.

Digital economy spreads with an implied promise that it increases labour productivity, thus leading to higher pay. However, globally, this does not seem to happen. Productivity has not grown at the rates expected, and the gains have not translated into higher wages for the most part. There is an overall decline in the labour income share of GDP (WDR 2016). This is coupled with high gender pay gap across the world. In India, gender wage disparity exceeds 30% with men earning more than women in similar jobs (International Labour Organization, Global wage report 2017). It is high even in those sectors where female participation is high. This reflects that there are some innate deformities in the structure itself leading to an exclusion of some from the opportunities that are getting created.

The downward movement of wage growth is not surprising though. With stiff competition for firms to provide cheap and innovative products and respond quickly to shifts in consumer needs and in the location of demand and more decentralization of business services, there is more flexible approach to production and commitments. To maximize profit and immediately respond to the changing need, more often than not, labour costs are driven down, cost of capital are shifted to the end worker itself and social protection and workers' rights are cut down upon.

With digital technology, employment patterns are getting just diversified in newer sectors, newer forms (platform, flexi, on demand, etc.). But that brings in increasing risks of job dislocation as well. It is very essential at this point to promote new dialogues for employment protection that avoids precarious forms of work, provides flexibility and freedom, brings forth best practices for regulating work structure and promotes some common standards. It is also crucial to see how relevant ILO conventions can be made applicable for this new form of workers. ILO's Private Employment Agencies Convention, 1997 (No. 181), acknowledges the role of private employment agencies on the labour market, and mandates countries that have ratified it to regulate and protect the rights of agency workers. It needs to be examined whether the mushrooming agencies are properly defined, whether they have proper registration or not, whether the existing legislations are comprehensive enough to cover this industry and whether the jobseekers, particularly migrants and other vulnerable groups are satisfied or not. It is now necessary to work out ways and means to ensure that regulations address the changing nature of work in India, including a gender perspective to cater to the needs of women workers which are often different from that of men.

The online platform economy is difficult to measure. There are some data at the individual firm level, but no comprehensive one is available; therefore, it is often difficult to measure the changing employment pattern by type of work, location, gender, etc. on the real-time basis.

It is observed that mobile operator-led initiatives are bringing more women into the MVC benefiting both participants and the MNOs involved, but women largely remain at the last end of the value chain. Gains for the MNOs are much higher at a lower cost. Many of these projects are partnership initiatives; therefore, there is more room and scope for dialogue to ensure that opportunities be created for women also rise to the higher levels of the value chain where margins are much higher, training opportunities better and working conditions safer. Except for some individual business case studies, no proper statistics are there on this subject. It is essential to collect data to look at both MNOs' services and performance of the retail agents to understand the skill gaps.

Mobile and Internet, in today's world, is just not a device to talk or chat, it is a tool for business, opportunities for online jobs, information about different skill development opportunities, online education, information about scholarships, insurance, digital transactions, mobile banking, etc. There are designated Mobile Apps for different public and private services. But if the social inequalities and stereotypes persist, the services would translate less than envisioned.

Leveraging the benefits of digital payments needs equality in access and usage of Internet, bank accounts, service development, capacity development, information and gender-sensitive and enabling environment.

The gender order in the society, where unpaid care mainly bestows upon women, interacts with the paid labour market too. In a scenario, where there is lack of basic facilities like piped water, drinking water, toilet facilities and providing child care, elderly care, all are largely entrusted to women, and gender gaps in the labour market would be slow to close. Online gender-based abuses and violence are looming large, not just in India but globally. We should not see it only from a protectionist framework, but also from a human rights framework, balancing all her rights without restricting her freedom.

Therefore, gender-based digital gap and socio-economic empowerment are interrelated. Limited ICT access and use adversely affect the chances of women to integrate into the labour market, while, in turn, the exclusion of many women from the economy tends to entrench the gap in ICT use. Gender divide in access and use of digital technology basically mirrors the inequities in paid and unpaid work persisting in the physical world. Therefore, unless women are socio-economically at the equal footing as men, it is unlikely that women can leverage the opportunities, be it trade or manufacturing or financial services, created by digital transformation.

References

Accenture. (2016). Getting to equal how digital is helping close the gender gap at work. https://www.accenture.com/t20160303T014010__w__/in-en/_acnmedia/PDF-9/Accenture-IWD-2016-Research-Getting-To-Equal.pdf#zoom=50. Accessed March 1, 2018.

AIACA. (2013). Annual report 2012–13, All India artisans and craftworkers welfare association. Available at http://www.aiacaonline.org/sites/default/files/Annual-Report-1-10-2013.pdf.

AISHE. (different years). All India survey on higher education report (different years from 2010–11 to 2016–17), Ministry of Human Resource Development, Government of India.

Antonio, A., & Tuffley, D. (2014). The gender digital divide in developing countries. *Future Internet, 6*(4), 673–687, October, 2014.

ASER. (2016). Annual Status of Education Report, Pratham.

Bhattacharya, P. (2016). 88% of households in India have a mobile phone, December 6, 2016. Available at file: C:/Users/new/Downloads/mint-article4.pdf.

Chauhani, A. (2016). Panchayat bans mobile phones among girls, Times of India, February 20, 2016. Available at http://timesofindia.indiatimes.com/city/agra/Panchayat-bans-mobile-phones-among-girls/articleshow/51060339.cms.

Cherie Blair Foundation. (2011). Women entrepreneurs in mobile retail channels: Empowering women, driving growth, TNS RMS and Cherie Bair Foundation. Available at http://www.cherieblairfoundation.org/wp-content/uploads/2012/07/Women-Entrepreneurs-in-Mobile-Retail-Channels.pdf.

Cherie Blair Foundation. (2016a). Supply chain management solutions in India. Available at http://www.cherieblairfoundation.org/supply-chain-management-solutions-in-india/.

Cherie Blair Foundation. (2016b). Mobile financial services for women in Nigeria, Cherie Blair Foundation for women. Available at http://www.cherieblairfoundation.org/mobile-financial-services-for-women-in-nigeria/.

Ernst and Young. (2016). *Textile industry as a vehicle of job creation for inclusive growth*. India: Texprocil.

Frey, C. B., & Rahbari, E. (2016a). Do labor-saving technologies spell the death of jobs in the developing world? World Bank. Available at https://www.brookings.edu/wp-content/uploads/2016/07/Global_20160720_Blum_FreyRahbari.pdf.

Frey, C. B., & Rahbari, E. (2016b). Technology at work: How the digital revolution is reshaping the global workforce, March 25, http://voxeu.org/article/how-digital-revolution-reshaping-global-workforce.

Ghose, K., & Ghosh, S. K. (2016). Empowering women through JAM, The Indian Express, July 21, 2016.

GSMA. (2015). Bridging the gender gap: Mobile access and usage in low and middle-income countries.

GSMA. (2018). The Mobile Gender Gap Report 2018.

IAMAI-IMRB. (2016). Mobile internet in India 2016, Internet and Mobile Association of India.

International Labour Organization. (2017). Global wage report 2017.

International Telecommunication Union. (2016). ICT facts and figures 2016, United Nations Development Group. Available at https://www.itu.int/en/ITU-D/Statistics/Documents/facts/ICTFactsFigures2016.pdf.

International Telecommunication Union. (2017). ICT facts and figures 2017, United Nations Development Group. Available at https://www.itu.int/en/ITU-D/Statistics/Documents/facts/ICTFactsFigures2017.pdf.

Internet World Stats. (2018). https://www.internetworldstats.com/stats.htm. Accessed February 28, 2018.

Jain, M. (2016). India's internet population is exploding but women are not logging in. Available at https://scroll.in/article/816892/indias-internet-population-is-exploding-but-women-are-not-logging-inia.

Jiang, W. J., & Luh, L. H. (2017). Gender digital divide in a patriarchal society: What can we learn from Blinder-Oaxaca decomposition? *Quality & Quantity: International Journal of Methodology, 51*(6), 2555–2576.

Labour Bureau. (2016). Report on fifth annual employment - unemployment survey 2015–16. Ministry of Labour and Employment.

McKinsey Global Institute. (2014). Global flows in a digital age: How trade, finance, people, and data connect the world economy, April. McKinsey and Company.

McKinsey Global Institute. (2016). Digital globalization: The new era of global flows, March. McKinsey and Company.

NCRB. (2015). Crime in India 2015 statistics. National crime records bureau. Ministry of Home Affairs. Government of India.

NSS. (2011–12). Unit level data from the employment-unemployment survey under national sample survey, Ministry of Statistics and Programme Implementation, Government of India.

OECD. (2012). Time spent in paid and unpaid work, July 27, 2018. Available at https://stats.oecd.org/index.aspx?queryid=54757.

Pew Research Centre. (2015). Internet seen as positive influence on education but negative on morality in emerging and developing nations, Pew Research Centre Studies, March 19, 2015. Available at http://www.pewglobal.org/files/2015/03/Pew-Research-Center-Technology-Report-FINAL-March-19-20151.pdf.

Saha, D. (2016). India's digital inequality: How far behind we really are in taking the internet to the masses, The News Minute, May 7, 2016. Available at http://www.thenewsminute.com/article/indias-digital-inequality-how-far-behind-we-really-are-taking-internet-masses-42837.

Telecom Regulatory Authority of India. (2018a). TRAI Press Release, Number 48/2018, April, New Delhi. Available at http://trai.gov.in/sites/default/files/PRTSDEng24042018.pdf. Accessed on May 7, 2018.

Telecom Regulatory Authority of India. (2018b). TRAI Press Release, Number 50/2018, May, New Delhi. Available at http://trai.gov.in/sites/default/files/PRNo.50Eng04052018.pdf. Accessed on May 7, 2018.

Telenor-BCG. (2015). The unconnected senior citizens of Asia. Available at https://www.telenor.com/media/articles/2015/the-unconnected-senior-citizens-of-asia/.

UNDP. (2012). Promoting women in business and investment—Fanikisha initiative. http://www.ke.undp.org/content/kenya/en/home/operations/projects/inclusiveeconomicgrowth/promoting-women-business-investment.html.

UNDP. (2016). Urgency in closing the digital divide voiced at conclusion of Internet governance forum. http://www.un.org/sustainabledevelopment/blog/2016/12/urgency-in-closing-the-digital-divide-voiced-at-conclusion-of-internet-governance-forum/.

WDR. (2016). World development report 2016: Digital dividends. World Bank.

World Economic Forum. (2017). The global gender gap report 2017, Geneva.

Sanitation Programmes in India: An Evaluation Study with Special Reference to Health and Growth

Ruby Dhar, Anita Kakkar and Chaitali Roy

1 Introduction

Most developing countries do not consider hygiene and sanitation as a priority issue, despite it being a major cause of death and diseases. Poor sanitation adversely affects the quality of life and has negative socio-economic consequences. India shares a heavy burden of world's sanitation problem. Open defaecation is a serious problem in India as more than 30% of its population still defaecates in the open. Even worse, where the toilets are built, their usage has not sustained over a period of time.

The paper attempts to assess the sanitation situation in India, with a focus on rural sanitation, by looking at importance of sanitation, India's standing in global sanitation assessment, traces the history of India's sanitation programmes, looks at the expenditure pattern of better and poor performing states, examines the relationship of sanitation with socio-economic indicators and discusses the challenges impacting the achievement of sanitation targets.

For this purpose, the paper has been divided into seven sections. Section 2 presents the importance of sanitation to development; Section. 3 looks at India's global standing; Section. 4 discusses the evolution of sanitation programmes in India. Section 5 focuses on the current situation of rural sanitation in different states of the country and looks at the better performing and poor performing states in terms of plan outlay, expenditure, construction and usage of toilets. Section 6 assesses relationship

R. Dhar (✉) · A. Kakkar · C. Roy
NILERD, Sector A-7, Institutional Area, Narela, Delhi, India
e-mail: ruby.dhar@nic.in

A. Kakkar
e-mail: anitakakkar2004@yahoo.co.in

C. Roy
e-mail: drchaitali_pal@yahoo.co.in

NILERD, *Reflecting on India's Development*,
https://doi.org/10.1007/978-981-13-1414-8_15

between sanitation and few socio-economic indicators. Section 7 presents the challenges impacting achievement of sanitation targets. Section 8 summarizes the paper.

The data for the paper is taken from a number of secondary sources, i.e. research studies, reports presented by government, international organizations and NGOs.

2 Sanitation and Development

> 50% of the health burden of malnutrition was estimated to be attributable to environment and in particular to poor water, sanitation, and hygiene.
>
> Preventing Disease through Healthy Environments, WHO Report, 2006, pp. 44.

Water and sanitation are not only fundamental to human development and well-being but also critical to the achievement of other development objectives such as adequate nutrition, gender equality, education and eradication of poverty.

Recognizing the importance of sanitation as a matter of development priority, United Nations declared 1981–90 as the International Water and Sanitation Decade (IWSD). United Nations General Assembly in 2010 recognized access to safe water and sanitation as a human right.

But why is sanitation important?

Drinking water and proper sanitation are important indicators of health, hygiene and safe environment. Individual health and hygiene is largely dependent on adequate availability of drinking water and proper sanitation. There is, therefore, a direct relationship between water, sanitation and health. Consumption of unsafe drinking water, improper disposal of human excreta, improper environmental sanitation and lack of personal hygiene have been major causes of many diseases in developing countries.

Many development economists have pointed out that early-life health (Currie and Vogl 2012) and exposure to infectious disease (Cutler et al. 2010) are important factors shaping adult human capital and economic productivity. Sanitation is one of the characteristics of a person's physical environment that is most important for health and human capital development. Poor sanitation is widely considered as a major obstacle to well-being in many parts of the world. An estimated 844 million people lack basic drinking water service and 892 million people worldwide still practice open defecation (UNICEF and WHO 2017).

Coffey et al. (2016) in their paper 'Sanitation, Disease Externalities, and Anemia evidence from Nepal' argue that anaemia which impairs physical and cognitive development in children and reduces human capital accumulation can be prevented through proper sanitation.

Poor sanitation is responsible for one of the heaviest existing disease burdens worldwide. The diseases associated with poor sanitation and unsafe water account for about 10% of the global burden of disease (Prüss-Üstün et al. 2008). Diseases associated with poor sanitation are diarrhoeal diseases, acute respiratory infections, undernutrition and other tropical diseases such as helminth and schistosomiasis infections (Mara et al. 2010; Chadwick 1842; Fewtrell et al. 2005). Open defecation spreads bacterial, viral and parasitic infections, including diarrhoea, polio, cholera and hookworm, and is an important cause of child stunting (Spears 2013; Chambers and Von Medeazza 2013; Coffey et al. 2013; Ghosh et al. 2014) and infant death (Hathi et al., forthcoming).

Diarrhoeal diseases are the most common sanitation-related diseases. Globally, about 1.7 million people die every year from diarrhoeal diseases, and 90% of them are children under 5 years, mostly in developing countries. Eighty-eight percent of cases of diarrhoeal diseases worldwide are attributable to unsafe water, inadequate sanitation and poor hygiene (Mathers et al. 2006; World Health Organization 2009).

Some 842,000 people in low- and middle-income countries die because of inadequate water, sanitation and hygiene each year, representing 58% of total diarrhoeal deaths. Poor sanitation is believed to be the main cause in some 280,000 of these deaths (WHO 2017).

Spears (2012) found a link between sanitation coverage and height. According to him, 54% of the cross-country variation in the height of under 3-year-old children was due to sanitation coverage alone. Because poor sanitation has been linked to infant mortality, child stunting (Cutler and Miller 2005; Headey 2015) and other health outcomes (Nandi et al. 2016), a better understanding of the causes of open defecation and the prospects for its decline are priorities for the research and policy.

Chambers (2010) advocates that most of the infections caused by poor sanitation can be avoided by bringing about behavioural changes. A paper by Shandra and Shandra (2011) demonstrated that higher levels of access to an improved water source and an improved sanitation facility are associated with lower levels of child mortality within Sub-Saharan African nations.

Poor sanitation was shown to be a cause of a wide range of adverse impacts on population health, as well as national economies. The magnitude of economic losses associated with poor sanitation in developing countries has been substantial. The economic losses of 2% of the total GDP in four countries (Cambodia, Indonesia, the Philippines and Vietnam) represent only the impacts of poor sanitation on five areas: health, water resources, environment, tourism and other welfare concerns. This figure would have been much greater if other impacts, such as suffering from disease, aesthetics and user preference, time loss from seeking private places to urinate (especially women), losses from marine fisheries and the losses to wildlife from polluted water resources, an unclean environment, etc. (World Bank 2008a) had been included. The Economics of Sanitation Initiative was launched in 2007 with a WSP study from East Asia, which found that the economic costs of poor sanitation and hygiene amounted to over US$9.2 billion a year (2005 prices) in Cambodia, Indonesia, Lao PDR, the Philippines and Vietnam. The groundbreaking study was the first of its kind to attribute dollar amounts to a country's losses from poor sanitation.

Sanitation also has socio-economic equity implications. Vulnerable groups (the poor, children, women, the disabled and the elderly) have suffered the most from the economic impacts of poor sanitation (Hutton et al. 2008; Wright 1997; UNICEF 1999).

In fact, diseases associated with poor sanitation have been closely correlated with poverty and infancy, and alone, account for about 10% of the global burden of disease.

The lack of improved sanitation largely contributes to the fact that a child dies every two and a half minute from preventable diarrhoeal diseases. It also impacts the vulnerable populations such as persons with disabilities and women, who are more exposed to sexual violence. Lack of private toilets in schools is a major reason why girls do not continue their education once they enter puberty. Poor sanitation and water supply also result in economic losses estimated at $260 billion annually in developing countries (End open defecation, UN).

A paper by Isunju et al. (2011) highlighted a lack of recognition of actual drivers for sanitation improvements and the complexities in the provision of sanitation services in the context of urban slums with a mix of tenants and landlords.

Open defaecation perpetuates a vicious cycle of disease and poverty. The countries where open defaection is most widespread have the highest number of deaths of children aged under 5 years as well as the highest levels of malnutrition and poverty, and big disparities of wealth (media centre–factsheets).

3 Sanitation: India's Global Standing

Efforts have been made at both international and national levels to provide access to safe drinking water and improved sanitation facilities to the people especially those in poor and developing countries. The Millennium Development Goals (MDGs) envisaged a better world by reducing to half the proportion of the population without safe drinking water and basic sanitation by 2015. However, by the end of MDGs deadline over 90% of the world's population had access to improved sources of drinking water but was not able to meet the sanitation target.

> I am moved by the fact that a child dies every 2 and a half minutes from diseases linked to open defecation. Those are silent deaths – not reported on in the media, not the subject of public debate. Let's not remain silent any longer.
>
> UN Deputy Secretary-General, Jan Eliasson (May 2014)

SDG's target number 6 seeks 'to ensure availability and sustainable management of water and sanitation for all' and aims by 2030 'to achieve access to adequate and equitable sanitation and hygiene for all and end open defecation, paying special attention to the needs of women and girls and those in vulnerable situations'.

According to WHO/UNICEF Joint Monitoring Report 2017, 12% of the world's population still defecates in the open with wide variation among rural (24%) and urban areas (2%). In India, 40% of people practice open defecation with 56% in rural areas and 7% in urban areas. About 90 countries have made very slow progress towards achieving basic sanitation and are likely to miss the target of universal coverage by 2030.

Out of 4.5 billion people who do not have safely managed sanitation, as many as 2.3 billion still do not have basic sanitation services, which includes 600 million people who share a toilet with other households and 892 million people—mostly in rural areas—who defecate in the open.

Majority of the world's open defecators live in South Asia with India accounting for about 93 percent of them. Afghanistan, Bangladesh, Bhutan, Maldives, Nepal, Pakistan and Sri Lanka have much smaller numbers of people without toilets. Open defecation is mostly a rural practice in India, Nepal and Pakistan, and few of the poorest rural households have a toilet (Fig. 1).

Open defecation is still a major problem globally, though some countries and regions have made remarkable progress. Ethiopia has achieved the largest decrease in the proportion of the population practicing open defecation (as reflected in Table 1).

The table reveals the achievement of few selected countries in sanitation for the period from 2000 to 2015 along with HDI value, HDI rank and gross national income per capita for year 2015.

The table reflects that there is no direct relationship between human development index value, HDI rank and gross national income with achievements in sanitation efforts of countries. Countries with lower development index than India have been able to achieve ODF status or have much lower OD rates than India. Ethiopia which has about one-third of gross national income than India has been able to reduce OD from 80% to 27% and rural OD from 90% to 32%; a feat India has not yet been able to achieve.

Bangladesh achieved open defecation-free status in 2015 despite having lower HDI rank and gross national income than China and India which had 3% and 56% of people defecating in the open in 2015 (UNICEF and WHO 2017).

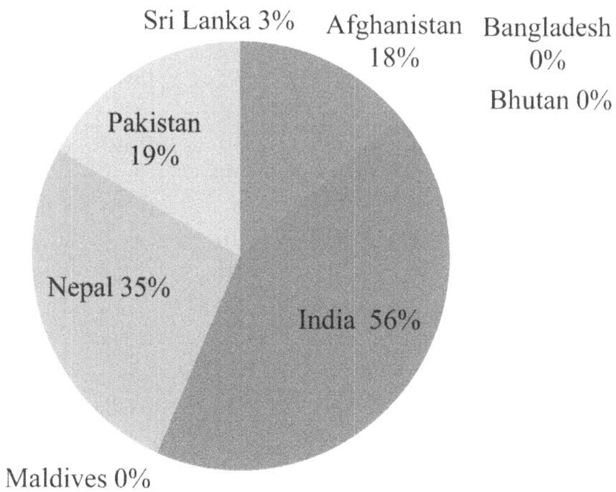

Fig. 1 Open Defecation Situation in Rural Areas of South Asian Countries. *Source* https://washdata.org/data accessed on January 8, 2018

Table 1 Open Defecation in Selected Countries and Human Development Index Values

	Open defecation (National) in percentage				HDI value	HDI rank	GNI per capita (US $)
	2000	2005	2010	2015			
Afghanistan	26 (31) Shift (31) below 26	23 (28)	18 (23)	14 (18)	0.479	169	1871
Bangladesh	18 (22)	12 (15)	6 (8)	0 (0)	0.579	139	3341
Bhutan	11 (14)	7 (9)	3 (3)	0 (0)	0.607	132	7081
Botswana	21 (41)	18 (39)	18 (38)	17 (36)	0.698	108	14,663
Burkina Faso	71 (85)	64 (79)	56 (72)	48 (65)	0.402	185	1537
Cambodia	83 (92)	69 (78)	55 (64)	41 (51)	0.563	143	3095
Chad	71 (85)	70 (84)	69 (83)	68 (82)	0.396	186	1991
China	2 (4)	2 (3)	2 (3)	2 (3)	0.738	90	13,345
Ethiopia	80 (90)	62 (70)	44 (51)	27 (32)	0.448	174	1523
Ghana	22 (32)	21 (32)	20 (32)	19 (31)	0.579	139	3839
Haiti	38 (53)	30 (46)	24 (40)	19 (35)	0.493	163	1657
India	66 (82)	57 (73)	48 (64)	40 (56)	0.624	131	5663
Indonesia	32 (45)	25 (37)	19 (29)	12 (21)	0.689	113	10,053
Kenya	17 (20)	15 (19)	14 (17)	12 (15)	0.555	146	2881
Kiribati	49 (55)	43 (53)	37 (51)	35 (50)	0.588	137	2475
Lesotho	46 (54)	40 (50)	35 (45)	30 (40)	0.497	160	3319
Maldives	18 (24)	7 (11)	0 (0)	0 (0)	0.701	105	10,383
Mongolia	16 (35)	13 (34)	11 (32)	10 (31)	0.735	92	10,449
Mozambique	57 (70)	50 (63)	43 (55)	36 (47)	0.418	181	1098
Namibia	56 (75)	54 (75)	52 (76)	50 (76)	0.640	125	9770
Nepal	65 (71)	53 (59)	41 (47)	30 (35)	0.558	144	2337

(continued)

Table 1 (continued)

	Open defecation (National) in percentage				HDI value	HDI rank	GNI per capita (US $)
	2000	2005	2010	2015			
Niger	82 (93)	78 (90)	75 (88)	71 (85)	0.353	187	889
Nigeria	23 (29)	24 (32)	25 (34)	26 (36)	0.527	152	5443
Pakistan	41 (59)	31 (46)	21 (32)	12 (19)	0.550	147	5031
Sierra Leone	26 (38)	24 (34)	21 (31)	19 (27)	0.420	179	1529
Sri Lanka	0 (0)	3 (3)	3 (3)	3 (3)	0.766	73	10,383
Sudan	51 (64)	49 (62)	38 (50)	27 (38)	0.490	165	3846
Uganda	15 (17)	12 (14)	9 (10)	6 (7)	0.493	163	1670
Vietnam	18 (22)	13 (16)	8 (11)	4 (5)	0.683	115	5335
Zimbabwe	29 (42)	28 (41)	27 (40)	26 (39)	0.516	154	1588
World	20 (34)	18 (31)	15 (28)	12 (24)			

Note Figures in bracket represent open defecation in rural areas
Source https://washdata.org/data and http://www.hdr.undp.org/en/composite/HDI accessed on 20 January 2018

A look at the national and rural open defecation of medium human development category of countries with lower HDI rank (132–147 rank) than India (131 Rank) in Fig. 2 also shows that achievement in sanitation is not related to human development status of a country.

These figures on open defecation rates are indeed surprising. India despite rapid economic growth and improved literacy rate has not been able to achieve sanitation coverage as much as many countries where people are on average poorer, less educated and less likely to have access to an improved water source than people in rural India.

4 Sanitation Programmes in India

At independence, Indian government had an enormous task of bringing about socio-economic development as the population was poor, uneducated and lacked basic amenities.

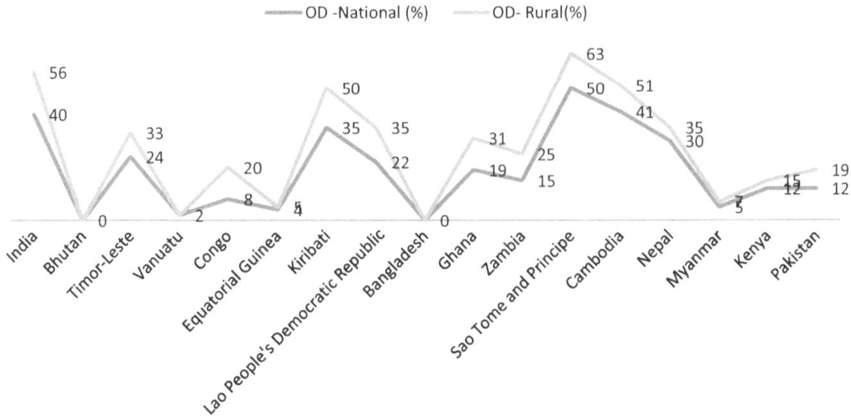

Fig. 2 National and Rural OD rates of countries with lower HDI rank than India under Medium Human Development Category. *Source* https://washdata.org/data and http://www.hdr.undp.org/en/composite/HDI accessed on January 20, 2018

Recognizing clean water and sanitation as important factors for health care, the First Five-Year Plan (1951–56) sanctioned a budget of Rs 140 crores towards these two basic necessities. The National Water Supply and Rural Sanitation Programme was launched with a focus to improve water supply in rural areas and sanitary practices. A special grant of Rs. 24 crores was provided to the states and 10,000 villages were identified for this purpose. In addition, 250 urban sanitation projects across 16 states were also undertaken. However, by the end of 1956, only 100 villages and 32 urban sanitation projects were successfully implemented.

The Second Five-Year Plan (1956–1961) allocated Rs. 53 crores for urban water supply and sanitation, Rs. 28 crores for rural water supply and sanitation and a special grant of Rs. 10 crores for urban areas with municipal corporations. By the end of 1961, 1200 villages had sanitation facilities, an improvement from the results of the First Five-Year Plan, though still well short of the target of 10,000 villages (NDTV).

The focus of Third Five-Year Plan (1961–1966) and Fourth Five-Year Plan (1969–1973) was more on agriculture, industry and defence than water supply and sanitation. The sanitation programme suffered a setback during 60s and early 70s.

Sanitation returned as a policy priority with Minimum Needs Programme introduced in 1974 as a part of Fifth Five-Year Plan. The programme identified sanitation as a minimum need necessary for basic human life. Focusing on rural health as a target was set to achieve sustainable sanitation and drinking water supply for all by the year 2000.

However, despite an outlay of Rs. 170 crores from 1974 to 1979 for improving rural sanitation, rural sanitation coverage did not improve much because Minimum Needs Programme did not focus on sanitation as an issue in itself but clubbed it under health and no separate funds were allocated for toilets, spending on building and repairing of toilets.

According to Planning Commission's estimates, sanitation coverage remained as low as 2% in rural areas and 20% in urban areas by the end of 1980, though water supply had improved to 31% in rural areas, compared to 2.9% in 1971. By the end of 1970s, sanitation was still dismal in both rural and urban India.

Recognizing the importance of safe drinking water, sanitation and hygiene for health and development especially for developing countries which were plagued with numerous deaths due to lack of toilets and drinking water, the United Nations declared the 10-year period from 1981 to 1990 as International Drinking Water Supply and Sanitation Decade. The aim of the decade was to bring clean water and sanitation facilities to everyone by the end of 1990.

India in line with the UN declaration focused on sanitation as a priority and no longer as an extension of public health. The central government laid stress on eradication of open defecation and community participation in building toilets both through labour, finance and utilization of appropriate technology. States were asked to ensure supply of 40 litres of water per person per day, and conversion of dry latrines to low-cost sanitary latrines.

The first comprehensive national-level sanitation programme—Central Rural Sanitation Programme—was launched in 1986 by the Ministry of Rural Development with the objective of improving the quality of life of rural people and to provide privacy and dignity to women. Some of the salient features of the programme were as follows:

- Cost of construction of toilets was demarcated into three divisions: <1500, 1500–2000 and >2000.
- Financial assistance to BPL families for construction of Individual Household Toilets (IHHLs) for <1500 for which 60% cost was to be borne by central government, 20% by state government and remaining by the BPL family.
- Noting the importance of sanitary complexes for community spaces, an amount of up to Rs. 2 lakhs was provided for their construction.
- Schools were given financial assistance of up to Rs. 14,000 and anganwadis up to Rs. 3000 to build toilets.
- To address the issue of solid waste management in rural areas, costs of new SWM projects were to be borne by the centre, state and panchayat in the ratio of 60:20:20.
- Information, Education and Communications (IEC) activities that would impart the importance of sanitation in rural people and to bring out the behavioural change were to be arranged by centre, state and local bodies.

As a result of the adoption of the sanitation decade, along with the launch of the Central Rural Sanitation Program, the rural sanitation had improved to 9.5% and urban sanitation had improved to 63.9% by 1991 (Census 1991).

As per Planning Commission's estimates over 40 lakhs (4,337,609), toilets were constructed with a total expenditure of Rs. 757.62 crores between 1986 and 1997, but these achievements were much below the expected targets. Despite being a supply driven, highly subsidized scheme and with massive outlays, the programme led to a marginal increase in the rural sanitation coverage, with average annual increase of only 1%. It was found that many of the constructed toilets were not used due to lack of awareness, poor construction standards and issues related to maintenance cost. The concept of community sanitary complexes and school toilets also did not receive the desired response.

Due to the failure of CRSP, Total Sanitation Campaign (TSC) was launched as a demand-driven, community-led programme with major IEC inputs in 1999. The main features of TSC were mentioned as follows:

- Decentralized planning and implementation through village panchayats, focusing on demand-based toilet construction;
- Subsidy amount was increased to Rs. 3500 (Rs. 2200 was to be given by the central government, Rs. 1000 by the state government and Rs. 300 by the beneficiary);
- Continued focus on BPL households and a target of ending open defecation by 2017;
- More stress on community participation in construction of toilets;
- 15% of central funds for creating awareness on toilet usage with emphasis on IEC;
- The Nirmal Gram Puraskar was introduced in 2003, which rewarded ODF villages with cash awards.

Under the TSC, 2.4 crore toilets were built in a 12-year period, i.e. an average of 24 lakh toilets every year. An amount of about Rs. 10,000 crores was spent in 12 years which was not enough to achieve the target of eradication of open defaecation by 2017. The spending between states was uneven, resulting in some states doing well, while others lagged. While Sikkim and Goa were biggest per capita spenders, Bihar and Uttar Pradesh were the lowest. Up to 28,000 villages were awarded the Nirmal Gram Puraskar, till 2011.

By the end of 2011, rural sanitation coverage was 30.7% (up from 21.9% in 2001) and urban sanitation coverage was 81.4% (up from 73.7% in 2001).

Figure 3 shows India's achievement from 1991 to 2011 under CRSP and TCS. Though insufficient, the TSC did increase India's sanitation coverage, especially in rural areas as is evident from the figure.

In order to overcome the problems faced by TSC, the Twelfth Five-Year Plan (2012–17) adopted Nirmal Bharat Abhiyan with the focus on the following:

- Vulnerable sections of society, i.e. SC, ST, physically handicapped, women-headed households and small and marginal farmers;
- Removing distinction between APL and BPL families;
- Aimed to provide 100% access to toilets in rural households by 2022;
- The first programme to be converged with the Mahatma Gandhi National Rural Employment Guarantee Act (MGNREGA);

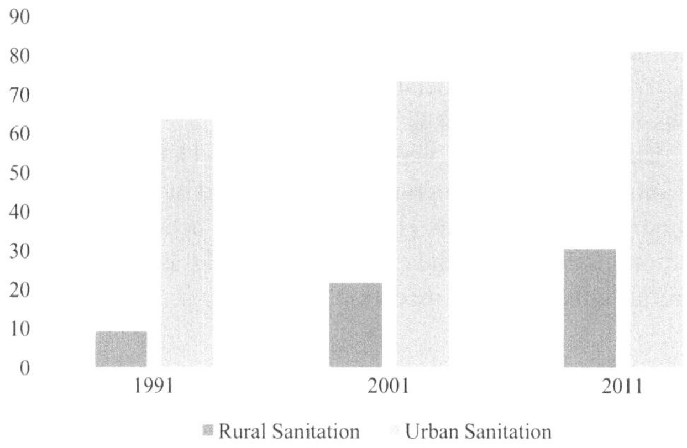

Fig. 3 Sanitation scenario in India. *Source* http://www.mdws.gov.in/sites/default/files/Total%20 Sanitation%20Campaign%20Sanitation%20for%20All%20-%202012.pdf accessed on 18 January 2018

- Under MGNREGA, sanitation-related works were included, allowing a beneficiary to earn up to Rs. 5400 while constructing a toilet or latrine;
- The government funding was also increased to Rs. 5500, bringing the total to Rs. 10,900 as the subsidy.

The NBA in its brief duration could not do much to change the sanitation scenario in India. A report by the Comptroller and Auditor General (CAG) (2015) said that the central government failed to utilize more than Rs. 3100 crores for building toilets under the NBA. More than nine states failed to utilize Rs. 212 crores each, resulting in their sanitation scenarios barely improving. Only 6% toilets were constructed in convergence with MGNREGA and Indira Awaas Yojana, thus resulting in major lags in improving the sanitation scenario.

In order to achieve Gandhian dream of having villages with total sanitation, the Prime Minister of India, Shri Narendra Modi, launched the Swachh Bharat Mission on 2 October 2014. The main aim of the scheme is to accelerate the efforts to achieve universal sanitation coverage and to put focus on sanitation. The salient features of the mission are as follows:

- The objectives of the mission were split under two ministries: Swachh Bharat Gramin, headed by the Ministry of Drinking Water and Sanitation, was responsible for rural India. Swachh Bharat Urban, under the Ministry of Urban Development, was responsible for implementing the programme across cities and towns.
- The mission aims to achieve a Swachh Bharat by 2019 along with scientific disposal of solid waste across the country, eradication of manual scavenging and creating awareness among people on sanitation.

- The estimated cost of the programme was pegged at Rs. 223,692 crores with 14,623 crores as centre's share and the rest to be borne by the states, private companies through Corporate Social Responsibility (CSR), Swachh Bharat cess and donations to Swachh Bharat Kosh.
- An amount of Rs. 2647 crores was spent between October 2014 and March 2015 by the union government on rural sanitation, and over 49 lakhs toilets were built in the first year in rural India. However, no such achievement was noted for urban sanitation. The figure stands at more than 614 lakhs toilets being constructed in rural India since the inception of SBM.

5 Achievements of States

In this section, we will look at the achievement of states during various sanitation programmes launched by the government. Then, we would focus on few selected better performing and poor performing states in terms of their sanitation coverage especially during the period 2014–18 and finally would assess if there is a relationship between a state's productivity, health, economic growth and its achievement in sanitation in next section.

As rural sanitation is a state's subject, it is for the state governments to allocate sufficient budget for construction and maintenance of toilets, provide adequate machinery for capacity building and IEC activities and collaborate with other institutions at national, regional, state, district and village level. Mobilization of resources, i.e. technological, financial and human, is a prerequisite for achieving results. Though most states had included TSC in their programmes, financial allocations for sanitation often were not adequate due to lack of priority attached to the programme. An analysis of the same is important because for a programme to be successful and achieve its targets, it is necessary for the state governments to give high priority to the programme in financial allocation. The second essential aspect is to give emphasis on capacity building and IEC activities.

Around 400,000 to 500,000 children below 5 years of age die due to diarrhoea annually in India. Young children bear a huge part of the burden of disease resulting from the lack of hygiene and sanitation. Consumption of contaminated drinking water, improper disposal of human excreta, lack of personal and food hygiene and improper disposal of solid and liquid waste have been the major causes of many diseases in India. High infant mortality rate and high levels of malnutrition are also attributed to poor sanitation (UNICEF—Improved water and sanitation to speed up the achievement of all eight MDGs). From the table given below, one finds that around 35% of India's rural population did not have access to sanitation facilities by July 2017 (Table 2).

It can also be seen from the table that there is wide disparity among states in achieving target of total sanitation in rural areas; some states have been able to achieve ODF status while others are still struggling to meet their targets. For this

Table 2 Percentage of Households with no Latrine Facilities in Rural India

State	2017[a]	2011	2001
A&N Islands	44.33	39.8	57.7
Andhra Pradesh	43.91	67.8	81.9
Arunachal Pradesh	17.11	47.3	52.7
Assam	26.45	40.5	40.4
Bihar	69.28	82.4	86.1
Chandigarh	0	12.0	31.5
Chhattisgarh	14.81	85.5	94.8
D&N Haveli	46.08	73.5	82.7
Daman & Diu	–	48.6	68.0
Goa	23.78	29.1	51.8
Gujarat	1.87	67.0	78.3
Haryana	0	43	71.3
Himachal Pradesh	0	33.4	72.3
Jammu and Kashmir	66.41	61.4	58.2
Jharkhand	44.12	92.4	93.4
Karnataka	32.90	71.6	82.6
Kerala	0.20	6.8	18.7
Lakshadweep	–	2.0	6.9
Madhya Pradesh	28.22	86.9	91.1
Maharashtra	17.02	62.0	81.8
Manipur	22.48	14.0	22.5
Meghalaya	13.92	46.2	59.9
Mizoram	25.12	15.4	20.3
Nagaland	18.82	30.8	35.4
NCT of Delhi	–	23.7	37.1
Odisha	58.45	85.9	91.1
Puducherry	52.07	61.0	78.6
Punjab	16.52	29.6	59.1
Rajasthan	20.91	80.4	85.4
Sikkim	0	15.9	40.6
Tamil Nadu	25.13	76.8	85.6
Tripura	29.29	18.5	22.1
Uttarakhand	0	45.9	68.4
UP	52.83	78.2	80.8
West Bengal	11.58	53.3	73.1
India	34.93	69.2	78.1

[a]State/UT-wise, percentage of rural households without access to toilets as on 17 July 2017 as per reply to unstarred question 845 of Lok Sabha

Source Census of India 2001 and 2011, and http://www.indiaenvironmentportal.org.in/files/file/Households%20without%20Toilet%20Facilities.pdf accessed on 30 January 2018

Table 3 States with Percentage of HHs with no Toilets

Sl. No.	Criteria (percentage of households with no toilets) (%)	States
1.	Less than 10	Chandigarh (0) Gujarat (1.87) Haryana (0) Himachal Pradesh (0) Kerala (0.20) Sikkim (0) Uttarakhand (0)
2.	10–20	Arunachal Pradesh (17.11) Chhattisgarh (14.81) Maharashtra (17.02) Meghalaya (13.92) Nagaland (18.82) Punjab (16.52) West Bengal (11.58)
3.	20–30	Assam (26.25) Madhya Pradesh (28.22) Manipur (22.48) Mizoram (25.12) Rajasthan (20.91) Tamil Nadu (25.13) Tripura (29.29)
4.	30–40	Karnataka (32.90)
5.	40–50	A&N Islands (44.33) Andhra Pradesh (43.91) D&N Haveli (46.08) Jharkhand (44.12)
6.	50–60	Odisha (58.45) Puducherry (52.07) UP (52.83)
7.	Above 60	Bihar (69.28) Jammu and Kashmir (66.41)

paper, we have categorized states according to number of households without toilet facilities in their rural areas as follows (Table 3).

For further analysis, we have divided states/UTs into two categories: better performing and poor performing. Six states/UTs are selected under each category.

5.1 *Better Achieving States and Poor Achieving States: A Comparison*

This section will look at better performing states (Arunachal Pradesh, Gujarat, Haryana, Kerala, Madhya Pradesh and West Bengal) and the poor performing states (Andhra Pradesh, Jammu and Kashmir, Bihar, Odisha, Puducherry and Uttar Pradesh) to assess why some of them were able to achieve sanitation results while others could not. Some of the factors that we have considered in this context would fall under broad areas of input (budget allocation), process (expenditure), output (construction of IHHLs) and outcome (usage of toilets).

a. Spending on Rural Sanitation

First, we will look at spending on rural sanitation in terms of total plan and total amount spent (Rs. in Lakhs) from 2001 to 2014 for the above-selected states/UTs. The rural sanitation scheme allocates funds for different sanitation activities in villages that include construction of toilets—for people in their houses and public toilets and institutions, money for improving awareness on need for toilets and creating a supply chain for manufacturing toilet-ware and waste management efforts (Table 4).

From the above table, one finds that states that have achieved better sanitation results have spent more than the states that have not performed so well. Among them, better performing states Haryana and Kerala have spent more than the plan outlay. Among the poor performing atates/UTs, Puducherry has spent only 13.8% of its plan outlay followed by Odisha with a spending of only 36.3% of the total plan amount followed by Bihar (43.5%).

Thus, better performance may be said to be related to the total spending by states. Uttar Pradesh is the only state among poor performers that has spent more than the planned outlay. However, despite huge funding, the state has not been able to achieve good results.

Table 4 Spending on Rural Sanitation from 2000 till 20 July 2014

	Total plan	Total amount spent	Total amount spent (%)
Better performing			
Arunachal Pradesh	6701	5268	78.6
Gujarat	70,232	59,831	85.2
Haryana	23,088	24,750	107.2
Kerala	22,190	24,071	108.5
Madhya Pradesh	170,289	169,965	99.8
West Bengal	174,148	149,511	85.9
Poor Performing			
Andhra Pradesh	178,188	126,911	71.2
Bihar	293,381	127,678	43.5
Jammu and Kashmir	40,599	21,125	52.0
Odisha	156,205	56,684	36.3
Puducherry	573	79	13.8
Uttar Pradesh	294,726	320,604	108.8

Source http://www.indiawaterportal.org/data-apps/#Money%20spent%7Cspending%20on%20rural%20sanitation accessed on 28 January 2018

b. Share of Centre, State and People

The Government of India, the state government and the rural households all contribute towards the various components of the sanitation scheme. While an initial share is planned, the money given depends on how much is actually spent. The general break up for the share of Government of India: state government: people has been 65:23:14 (indiawaterportal.org). Let us now look at the share of plan budget, money released and money spent by the selected states (Table 5).

The table shows that the states that have performed better have higher spending by people as compared to the states that have performed poorly except for Arunachal Pradesh and Madhya Pradesh but for these two states, the actual spending by centre (Arunachal Pradesh- 75.5% and Madhya Pradesh- 68.7%) is more than the planned spending. Bihar has the lowest people's contribution followed by Jammu and Kashmir, and these two states also show more than 60% HHs without toilets (Table 3). The findings reflect that the community mobilization is important for success of the programmes and that the people should be made equal partners in implementation of the sanitation programmes. One can also infer that in

Table 5 Money given versus money spent from 2001 till 20 July 2014

	Plan			Given			Spending		
	Centre	State	People	Centre	State	People	Centre	State	People
Better performing									
Arunachal Pradesh	69.6	23.3	7.1	67.6	28.8	3.5	75.5	20.7	3.8
Gujarat	62.5	24.7	12.7	60.2	25.1	14.7	60.8	24.4	14.8
Haryana	60.3	24.6	15.1	62.2	24.4	13.5	61.9	26.0	12.1
Kerala	53.5	25	21.5	51.8	20.1	28.1	52.3	21.5	26.2
Madhya Pradesh	66.4	24.7	8.9	70.6	19.9	9.5	68.7	23.8	7.4
West Bengal	64.2	25.2	10.6	55.7	20.5	23.8	54.4	19.5	26.1
Poor performing									
Andhra Pradesh	64.4	24.6	11	60.2	28.7	11.1	63.7	27.3	9.0
Bihar	67.4	24.3	8.3	70.6	26.6	2.7	70.9	25.9	3.2
Jammu and Kashmir	69.9	23.7	6.4	61.6	21.6	16.8	66.5	24.6	8.9
Odisha	66.9	24.2	8.9	67.6	24.8	7.5	65.4	24.8	9.8
Puducherry	84.1	–	15.9	100	–	–	100	–	–
Uttar Pradesh	65.2	24.4	10.4	55.9	33.7	10.4	56.8	34.2	9.0

Source http://www.indiawaterportal.org/data-apps/#Money%20spent%7CSpending%20on%20rural%20sanitation accessed on 28 January 2018

these states that have performed better, people were motivated for construction of toilets and also community mobilization was better as compared to states still lagging behind.

c. Expenditure versus total funds available

When we look at the total funds available with these states (opening balance, funds released and interest earned) from both centre and state and their expenditure in 2016–17 and 2017–18, the following picture emerges:

From Table 6, we find that Gujarat, Madhya Pradesh and West Bengal have spent more money from own resources in 2016–17 and 2017–18, while Arunachal Pradesh and Kerala have spent more resources in 2017–18. In FY 2017–18 till 16 February 2018, Madhya Pradesh had already spent nearly 17 times the funds available with it (including unapproved expenditure). Similarly, Bihar had spent 2.3 times more than the funds available, and Odisha and Andhra Pradesh have spent 1.7 times and 1.1 times more than the funds available with them, respectively. Madhya Pradesh despite having negative funds available in 2017–18 has spent around Rs. 42621.23 lakhs on sanitation. Increase in spending by states shows the priority accorded by government in making India Open Defecation Free.

The table also shows that once the states reach their targets, the centre's contribution has declined in the next financial year. Except in case of Odisha (where the state exceeded its central funding by more than 2.4 times in 2016–17), the centre's contribution has almost doubled for other poor performing states.

Table 7 gives the centre and state's expenditure on construction of IHHLs during 2016–17 and 2017–18.

Construction of IHHLs accounts for the largest share of total expenditure among all the states. In FY 2016–17, central expenditure was 100.72% while states contributed 101.13% of total expenditure on IHHL. In the year 2017–18 till 20 February 2018, the total expenditure incurred by centre and the states are 79.55% and 179.43%, respectively, for construction of IHHLs. Madhya Pradesh and West Bengal have spent more than the allotted funds on construction of toilets and that might be the reason for these states to achieve ODF status.

One finds that for 2017–18, Arunachal Pradesh, Madhya Pradesh and West Bengal have incurred large expenditure on IHHL construction. In case of Gujarat, Haryana and Kerala, negative fund's availability might be the reason for such low expenditure.

Interestingly, among the poor performing states also, the construction of IHHLs has been accorded high priority. Andhra Pradesh, Bihar and Odisha have spent more than the allotted funds on construction of IHHLs reflecting the priority they are giving to Swachh Bharat Mission—Gramin.

Funds for rural sanitation are provided primarily through Government of India (GOI). For Individual Household Latrines (IHHLs), states and beneficiaries are expected to contribute a share as well. GOI share for IHHLs is 60%, and the state share is 40% since FY 2015–16. For the North East states, Jammu and Kashmir and special category states, the GOI to state ratio is 90% to 10% and a condition that IEC should be at least 8% of the total expenditure.

Table 6 Funds and Expenditure of Selected States in 2016–17 and 2017–18

	Total funds		Expenditure approved		Expenditure unapproved		Percentage of expenditure	
	2016–17	2017–18	2016–17	2017–18	2016–17	2017–18	2016–17	2017–18
Better performing								
Arunachal Pradesh	7979.52 (4247.06)	15124.67 (306.88)	6493.78 (3938.94)	3020.10 (2264.57)	0.00	1426.74 (1200.04)	81.38 (92.75)	29.40 (112.8)
Gujarat	70439.09 (−10707.64)	33133.17 (−47084.62)	62631.09 (41565.09)	34371.95 (2360.97)	0.00	230.13 (156.43)	88.92 (0.0)	104.4 (0.0)
Haryana	7697.64 (5902.25)	4268.04 (3553)	3461.29 (2371.02)	3180.37 (2032.37)	0.0	22.32 (14.76)	44.97 (40.17)	75.04 (57.62)
Kerala	22526.91 (14070.26)	8784.23 (−1602.63)	13758.27 (9148.48)	783.19 (521.09)	0.0	4.05 (3.90)	61.07 (65.02)	8.96 (0.0)
Madhya Pradesh	105479.31 (1601.01)	127413.49 (−2530.88)	112124.28 (74138.14)	59697.91 (39686.73)		4403.46 (2934.50)	106.3 (4930.7)	50.31 (1684)
West Bengal	49333.97 (41185.93)	14751.05 (3587.45)	83808.41 (54185.05)	35809.18 (23322.95)		4321.90 (2648.13)	169.9 (131.6)	272.1 (729.4)
Poor Performing								
Andhra Pradesh	42820.58 (36974.13)	90383.66 (73963.22)	41516.96 (41724.16)	82916.92 (83450.03)	0.00	102.01 (108.57)	96.9 (112.8)	91.85 (112.9)
Bihar	17435.34 (14012.63)	32486.88 (4130.74)	14868.77 (9881.89)	11614.56 (7668.25)	0.0	2703.98 (1802.26)	85.28 (70.52)	44.07 (292.7)
Jammu and Kashmir	11350.67 (943.61)	20816.88 (1763.89)	5317.85 (779.92)	7594.57 (969.91)	0.0	501.73 (68.61)	46.85 (82.65)	38.89 (58.88)
Odisha	35757.72 (56687.59)	−7326.70 (12954.33)	86828.68 (57873.26)	30159.53 (20043.51)		2352.68 (1570.40)	242.8 (102.1)	0.00 (166.8)
Puducherry	1398.46 (663.12)	–	264.66	604.92 (299.18)	–	0.12	39.91 (0.0)	43.26 (0.0)
Uttar Pradesh	142269.01 (99071.15)	286403.35 (149778)	113239.68 (75238.12)	148795.90 (98932.36)		43735.98 (29240.36)	79.60 (75.94)	67.22 (85.58)

Figures in () reflect state data

Source http://sbm.gov.in/sbmReport/Report/Financial/SBM_StateReleaseAllocationincludingUnapproved.aspx (Format B2 (a1) accessed on February 16, 2018)

Table 7 Expenditure on Construction of Individual Household Latrines

	2016–17		2017–18	
State Name	Centre	State	Centre	State
Better performing				
Arunachal Pradesh	55.25	85.81	26.49	1111.82
Gujarat	86.77	−383.57	101.28	−47.98
Haryana	85.75	6.95	2.35	1.8
Kerala	59.71	63.59	0.85	−3.08
Madhya Pradesh	105.08	4585.55	48.46	−1626.76
West Bengal	164.64	128.01	260.6	698.16
Poor performing states				
Andhra Pradesh	96.14	112.4	91.58	115.26
Bihar	84.97	70.26	42.07	221.01
Jammu and Kashmir	44.73	71.78	38.06	53.36
Odisha	240.85	101.29	431.02	162.56
Puducherry	39.91	–	46.27	–
Uttar Pradesh	78.61	75.1	66.34	83.32
India	100.72	101.13	79.55	179.43

Source Calculation based on data available at http://sbm.gov.in/sbmReport/Report/Financial/ accessed on 20 February 2018

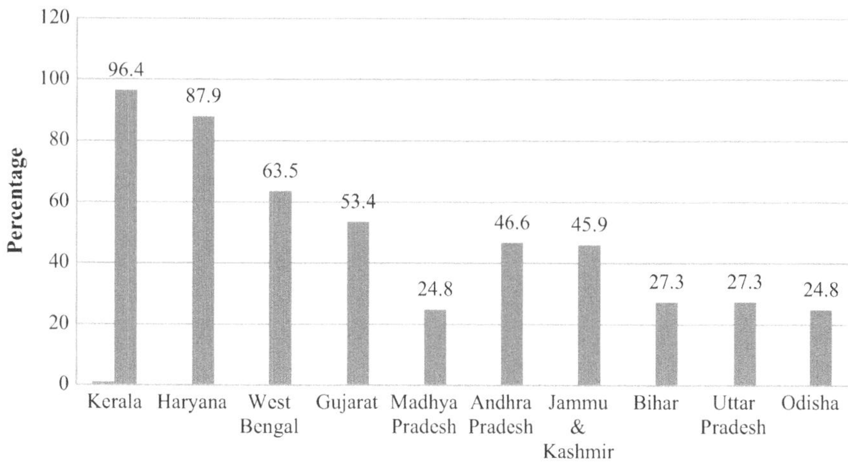

Fig. 4 Percentage of HHs having Access to Sanitary Toilets and using them in 2015. *Source* NSSO Survey 2015

A look at Swachh Survekshan—2016 shows that there is a wide disparity between the construction of IHHL and their actual usage. As per NSSO survey 2015, the usage of toilets in states is as follows (Fig. 4).

From the table, it is evident that construction of toilets does not ensure their usage as there are number of other factors that affect the choice of using the toilets or going for open defecation.

5.2 Achievements During 2014–18

With launch of Swachh Bharat Mission in 2014, the government is looking at achieving ODF status in rural areas by 2019. Achievements of the selected states viz-a-viz targets as per their annual implementation plan of corresponding years are shown in Table 8.

The data from Annual Implementation Plans of respective states reveal that the overall achievement of targets has been higher by states that have performed better when compared with states that have performed poorly in 2015–16 and 2016–17, a trend which was seen even during period prior to 2014. Gujarat has exceeded its targets in rural sanitation coverage and IHHL coverage in 2015–16, Kerala achieved its target in IHHL in 2016–17 and West Bengal exceeded it in 2016–17

Table 8 Usage of Toilets in Selected States

	Percentage of HHs having sanitary toilets	Percentage of people using HH/Community toilets (out of HHs having toilets)	Percentage of HHs having access to sanitary toilets and using them
Better performing			
Kerala	97.6	98.8	96.4
Haryana	90.2	97.4	87.9
West Bengal	65.1	97.5	63.5
Gujarat	55.5	96.2	53.4
Madhya Pradesh	27.5	90.1	24.8
Poor performing			
Andhra Pradesh	47.9	97.3	46.6
Jammu and Kashmir	47.4	96.9	45.9
Bihar	31.6	92.4	27.3
Uttar Pradesh	29.5	92.4	27.3
Odisha	26.3	94.2	24.8

Source http://swachhbharatmission.gov.in/sbmcms/writereaddata/images/pdf/report/Swachh-Survekshan-2016.pdf accessed on 15 February 2018

Table 9 Achievement versus Targets

	Rural sanitation coverage		IHHL total		Community sanitation complex	
	2015–16	2016–17	2015–16	2016–17	2015–16	2016–17
Better performing						
Arunachal Pradesh	63.68	73.65	60.77	47.89	22.67	13.38
Gujarat	179.22	100	125.72	100	–	–
Haryana	86	14.34	58.39	21.16	0	0
Kerala	97.3	34.7	27.02	100	35	5.5
Madhya Pradesh	37.5	53.4	48.33	66.63	0	145.18
West Bengal	74.12	20.56	84.29	121.18	34.31	53.38
Poor performing						
Andhra Pradesh	42.05	50.83	17.37	100	6.67	24
Bihar	46.42		8.16		0	
Jammu and Kashmir	38.58	42.72	40	20.11	76.89	23.75
Odisha	14	37	79	41	68	0
Puducherry	65	65.08	31.33	–	–	–
Uttar Pradesh	44.31	46.88	27.17	44.21	–	0.09

Source http://sbm.gov.in/sbmReport/Report/Monitoring/SBM_GetAIPDetails.aspx (Format I02) accessed on 15 February 2018

and Madhya Pradesh achieved 145.18% of its target in community sanitation complex in 2016–17. However, among poor performing states, we find that only Andhra Pradesh has been able to achieve its target in 2016–17 in the construction of IHHL. No other poor performing state has been able to achieve its target. Performance of Bihar, Odisha, Jammu and Kashmir and Uttar Pradesh has been dismal (Table 9).

A look at the ODF villages and household toilet coverage status clearly shows the discrepancy between better and poor performing states.

Table 10 and Fig. 5 clearly state that among the better performing states, all except Madhya Pradesh and West Bengal (who are also likely to achieve IHHL coverage by the end of this financial year) have achieved a total IHHL coverage and ODF village status while among the poor performing states except Andhra Pradesh all the other states have not even reached 60% coverage in IHHL status and 20% coverage in ODF status.

6 Relationship Between Sanitation and Socio-Economic Indicators

It has often been argued that better human development leads to healthier and educated labour force leading to higher productivity, and thus there seems to be a direct relationship between health of population and productivity. In order to see if

Table 10 ODF and IHHL coverage status of states

	ODF status			IHHL coverage		
	2015–16	2016–17	2017–18	2015–16	2016–17	2017–18
Better performing						
Arunachal Pradesh	2.95	23.55	100	60.27	83.68	100
Gujarat	18.18	82.08	100	62.97	93.67	100
Haryana	15.97	93.85	100	83.4	87.31	100
Kerala	0	100	100	95.84	99.99	100
Madhya Pradesh	3.69	31.45	42.13	47.69	67.13	88.64
West Bengal	18.53	47.72.	76.85	71.46	88.2	95.25
Poor performing						
Andhra Pradesh	1.84	16.64	42.8	53.62	64.72	86.69
Bihar	0.45	3.91	10.23	26.08	30.72	40.95
Jammu and Kashmir	0.28	1.57	6.94	28.42	33.92	50.84
Odisha	2.65	5.41	16.58	27.72	42.61	48.24
Puducherry	0	0	11.32	46	48.73	54.68
Uttar Pradesh	0.22	6.12	19.13	39.2	45.86	58.08

Source http://sbm.gov.in/sbmdashboard/ accessed on 17 February 2018

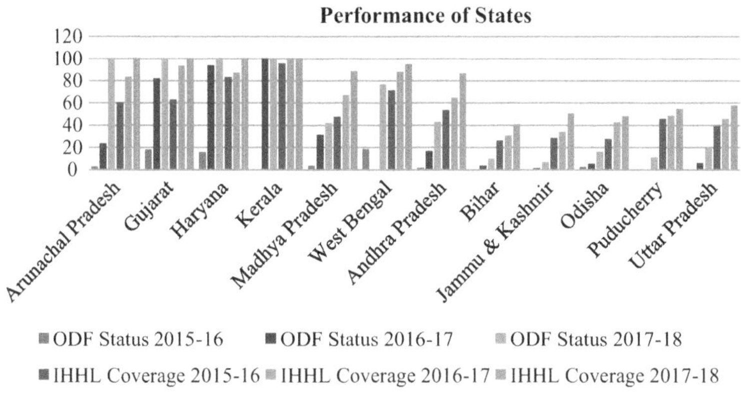

Fig. 5 Performance of states in ODF status and IHHL coverage. *Source* http://sbm.gov.in/sbmdashboard/ accessed on February 17, 2018

this argument holds true, let us look at the socio-economic indicators of the states like Per Capita Income (NSDP), GSDP, literacy rate, life expectancy, infant mortality rate, under-five mortality rate and poverty to determine if there is any correlation between these indicators and achievements of states in providing sanitation facilities. For the purpose of further analysis, the states are now grouped as percentage of households with toilet facilities.

Correlation has been calculated by taking into account the percentage of HHs having toilet facility in each state and other indicator listed in Table 11.

Table 12 shows that there is a moderate positive relationship between Per Capita Income (NSDP), literacy rate and life expectancy at birth with construction of toilets/latrines in HHs, i.e. states with higher number of HHs with toilets are likely to show higher per capita income, literacy rate and life expectancy. However, these economic indicators above are not solely responsible for construction of HH toilets and are not the cause of construction of toilets.

In case of health indicators, one finds a weak negative correlation between IMR and under-five mortality rate. Percentage of people below poverty line also has a weak relationship with number of HHs with toilets. Thus, one cannot clearly state that construction of toilets would automatically lead to lower IMR and under-five mortality rate or that poverty is the main reason for non-construction of HH toilets.

Planning Commission (2013) found that the people in the Nirmal Gram Panchayats enjoyed better quality of life by way of fewer incidences of diseases caused by improper hygiene and unsafe water supply, reduced medical expenses and increased time for earning. There has been a positive impact of the implementation of TSC on the level of income of the rural households.

Coffey et al. (2017) investigated the factors that are associated with latrine adoption in rural India between 2005 and 2012 using panel data, and found that economic status, education, demographic structure and investments in home improvement are only weakly associated with latrine adoption.

If we compare the socio-economic indicators with the usage pattern of states as discussed earlier, we find that states with higher access and usage are the states with higher per capita income, literacy rate, life expectancy and higher rate of IMR and under-five mortality rate. Thus, one can say that increasing the usage of sanitary toilets may result in increased productivity and lower IMR and under-five mortality rate.

7 Challenges Faced in Meeting Sanitation Goal

> Sanitation Coverage increased to 75.43% as on 01.01.2018. 284 Districts, 2586 Blocks, 1,32,038 GPs and 3,02,445 Villages have been declared Open Defecation Free (ODF) as on 01.01.2018. In addition, 9 States/UTs namely, Sikkim, Himachal Pradesh, Kerala, Uttarakhand, Haryana, Gujarat, Chandigarh, Arunachal Pradesh and Daman and Diu have also been declared ODF.
>
> Finance Minister in Budget Speech, 2018–19

The above statement of the Finance Minister points to the challenge the country faces in achieving ODF status by 2 October 2019, where only nine states/UTs have achieved ODF status out of 35 states/UTs despite rigorous efforts of the government.

Various studies point out to a multitude of factors that are responsible for non-responsiveness of people towards sanitation programmes of the government.

Table 11 States with percentage of HHs with Toilet Facility and other Socio-economic Indicators

Percentage of households with toilet facilities	Per Capita Income (NSDP) at current prices (Rs.) 2015–16	GSDP at current prices (Rs in crores) (2015–16)	Literacy Rate[a] (2017)	Life Expectancy[b] (2010–14)	Infant Mortality Rate[c] (2016)	Under-five Mortality[d] (2015–16)	Percentage of population below poverty line[e] 2011–12 (Based on MRP consumption)
More than 90%							
Chandigarh	242,386	30,304	86.43				21.81
Gujarat	138,023	994,316	79.31	68.7	30	43	16.63
Haryana	162,034	NA	76.64	68.6	33	41	11.16
Himachal Pradesh	124,500 (14–15)	NA	83.78	71.6	25	38	8.06
Kerala	155,516	588,337	93.91	74.9	10	7	7.05
Sikkim	227,465	16,637	82.20		16	32	8.19
Uttarakhand	151,219	184,091	79.63	71.1	38	47	11.26
80–90%							
Arunachal Pradesh	113,645	18,784	66.95		36	33	34.67
Chhattisgarh	84,767	260,776	71.04	64.8	39	64	33.74
Maharashtra	134,081 (14–15)	NA	82.91	71.6	19	29	17.35
Meghalaya	73,176	26,745	75.48		39	40	11.87
Nagaland	78,526 (14–15)	NA	80.11		12	37	18.88
Punjab	114,561 (14–15)	391,543	76.68	71.6	21	33	8.26
West Bengal		NA	77.08	70.2	25	32	19.98
70–80%							
Assam	60,952	224,234	73.18	63.9	44	56	31.98
Madhya Pradesh	62,334	543,975	70.63	64.7	47	65	31.65
Manipur	52,436 (14–15)	NA	79.85		11	26	36.89
Mizoram	85,659 (14–15)	NA	91.58		27	46	20.40

(continued)

Table 11 (continued)

Percentage of households with toilet facilities	Per Capita Income (NSDP) at current prices (Rs.) 2015–16	GSDP at current prices (Rs in crores) (2015–16)	Literacy Rate[a] (2017)	Life Expectancy[b] (2010–14)	Infant Mortality Rate[c] (2016)	Under-five Mortality[d] (2015–16)	Percentage of population below poverty line[e] 2011–12 (Based on MRP consumption)
Rajasthan	76,881 (14–15)	NA	67.06	67.7	41	51	14.71
Tamil Nadu	143,547	1,212,668	80.33	70.6	17	27	11.28
Tripura	71,666 (14–15)	NA	87.75		24	33	14.05
60–70%							
Karnataka	146,416	1,027,068	75.60	68.8	24	32	20.91
50–60%							
A&N Islands	121,954 (14–15)	NA	86.27			13	1.00
Andhra Pradesh	108,163	603,376	67.4	68.5	34	41	9.20
Jharkhand	62,816	241,955	67.63	68.6	29	54	36.96
40–50%							
Odisha	68,293	341,887	73.45	65.8	44	49	32.59
Puducherry	172,143	26,533	86.55			16	9.69
Uttar Pradesh	48,520	1,153,795	69.72	64.1	43	78	29.43
Below 40%							
Bihar	34,168	413,503	63.82	68.1	38	58	33.74
Jammu and Kashmir	72,958	118,387	68.74	72.6	24	38	10.35

Source https://rbidocs.rbi.org.in/rdocs/Publications/PDFs/13SDP_240617EE2A8970184542E895DCE89D75A02259.PDF and http://www.esopb.gov.in/Static/PDF/GSDP/Statewise-Data/StateWiseData.pdf accessed on 11 February, 2018

[a]http://www.pincodeindia.net/gdp-growth-rate.php accessed on 11 February, 2018

[b]http://www.censusindia.gov.in/Vital_Statistics/SRS_Life_Table/2.Analysis_2010-14.pdf accessed on 11 February, 2018

[c]http://niti.gov.in/content/infant-mortality-rate-imr-1000-live-births accessed on 11 February, 2018

[d]https://community.data.gov.in/tateut-wise-under-five-mortality-rate-during-2015-16/ accessed on 11 February, 2018

[e]https://www.rbi.org.in/scripts/PublicationsView.aspx?id=16603 accessed on 11 February, 2018 accessed on 11 February, 2018

Table 12 Correlation between percentages of HHs having toilets and other economic indicators

Variables	Percentage of HHs having toilets
Per Capita Income (NSDP) at Current prices	0.5662
Literacy rate	0.4633
Life expectancy	0.3287
Infant mortality rate	−0.3096
Under-five mortality	−0.2269
Percentage of population below poverty line	−0.2731

Source Author's Calculation

(a) Beliefs and values

Many studies show that despite the construction of toilets, all the people of the household do not use it and at least one member of the family defecates in the open. The reason for this is attributed to the traditional concept of 'Purity and Pollution' among Hindus. The assumption that economically sound households will build toilets and use them that does not work because of the centuries-old belief pattern.[1]

According to Nathoo (2015) in rural India, a strong cultural resistance to the buildup and disposal of excrement, and the view that going outdoors is more wholesome, is leading to rejection of the new latrines.'Emptying a pit in any other developing country… doesn't carry a social stigma in the same way as it does in India', says R.I.C.E's Sangita Vyas, referring to Hinduism's rigid caste system, which prescribes that dealing with human waste is the responsibility only of those at the very bottom of the social hierarchy.

Vijayaraghavan Chariar, a sanitation expert at Delhi's Indian Institute of Technology, stressed that defaecating outside has been the natural choice for centuries. He explained that some 'don't see a connection between open defaecation and poor health'. Therefore, it is not only a lack of proper facilities that is the problem but the cultural and social institutions of rural Indian populations regarding sanitation practices. According to Spears (2012), rural sanitation programmes have unfortunately paid little attention to the reasons why villagers reject affordable pit latrines. The government provides pit latrines without any thought to how they will be emptied, or what the social consequences will be, and the cost of socially acceptable toilets would be very high. A study by Coffey et al. (2017b) points out that widespread open defaecation in rural India is on account of beliefs, values and norms about purity, pollution, caste and untouchability that cause people to reject affordable latrines. Villagers' ideas about pollution, pit emptying and untouchability should be addressed to accelerate progress in sanitation and bring about social equality.

[1]For further details refer http://www.business-standard.com/article/economy-policy/building-toilets-not-enough-to-end-open-defecation-115032501279_1.html.

(b) Construction and monitoring

Another factor to consider is how to measure and monitor access to sanitation. If we consider that the ultimate goal of any sanitation programme is to end open defaecation, the measure and monitoring should focus not only on construction alone but also on the usage of toilets over a period of time. However, the access to improved sanitation is measured globally by considering a count of the number of toilets. This practice tells us about achievement of targets but does not reflect the actual usage, which is a true reflector of social and behavioural change. This overemphasis on output rather than outcome has been the biggest lacunae of the monitoring mechanism of sanitation campaigns.

An impact study by the World Bank's Water and Sanitation Programme in five states revealed that only 67% of the toilets even in NGP villages were being used, while this percentage fell to just 46% in non-NGP villages. (World Bank WSP 2008) World Bank (2008a), Water and Sanitation Programme (WSP) —Community-Led Total Sanitation in Rural Areas An Approach that Works , New Delhi.

A study, supported by UNICEF in 2008, revealed that in 56% of NGP Gram Panchayats, 70% families were still defaecating in the open and only 6 of the 162 NGPs had been able to sustain the NGP status.

In a study for the Ministry of Drinking Water and Sanitation, the Centre for Media Studies (2010) found that the key factors explaining the gap between access to and usage of sanitation facilities were poor quality of construction and unfinished toilets, a major reason for which was the very low incentive provided under the TSC.

According to Santosh Mehrotra et al. (2013), an important flaw in the programmes implemented in India is that there is no foolproof way of following up on implementation and lack of Community-led Collective Behaviour Change (CCBC) (also known as community-led total sanitation) or CLTS. He further states that states like Himachal Pradesh which adopted CLTS were able to achieve desirable results. He further argues that if we succeed in proper implementation of CLTS and India actually becomes ODF, then India's health and disease-related expenditure would reduce, which in turn will also lead to the better manpower and faster GDP growth.

NITI Aayog's Report of Sub-Group of Chief Ministers (2015) on Swachh Bharat Abhiyan states that 'the visible improvement in toilet coverage across Indian states is deeply undermined by the poor quality of operation and maintenance of these facilities'.

As per the All India Baseline Survey conducted by Ministry of Drinking Water and Sanitation in 2012–13, 1.39 crores of the total 7.41 crores household toilets in India were defunct or dysfunctional (Hindu 2016).

'Financial assistance provided under the previous Government programmes was inadequate and led to the improper construction of toilets, which slowly became dysfunctional', the NITI Aayog report states.

Even when toilets have been built, they are often not used. A survey in 2014 by the Research Institute for Compassionate Economics found that among the two-fifths of households with a working latrine, at least one family member preferred to defaecate outside. Toilets, often the only concrete structure in the house, are sometimes used to store firewood, grass, chickens, cow-dung cakes and food grains. They can also double as goat sheds or even shrines (Economist 2017).

(c) Overemphasis on subsidy

A baseline survey on water and sanitation conducted by the Indian Institute of Mass Communication (IIMC) in 1998 revealed that only 2% of the beneficiaries found subsidy to be a motivating factor for construction of toilets and around 55% of the people having private toilets were self-motivated. It also indicated that around 60% of the people were willing to pay for sanitation services in the rural areas of the country, thus explaining why subsidies did not help in achieving sanitation targets (Water Aid 2008a).

Vyas (2014) while comparing Nepal and India's achievement in sanitation found that in Nepal, the improvement in sanitation did not come about because the government started building toilets for people. In fact, in Nepal's Sanitation and Hygiene Master Plan, there is no provision for subsidizing toilet construction except for the ultra-poor. The incredible progress that the country has made suggests that the household financial resources are not part of the problem, even in such a poor country like Nepal.

Many scholars advocate that subsidies should not be individual based, but community based and behaviour change should precede subsidy.

Water Aid's report (2008b) Feeling the Pulse states that high subsidy has not really worked in the case of TSC: states such as Bihar and Chhattisgarh even with a high subsidy regime have the current coverage of IHHLs only at 22.17 and 32.63%, respectively. The report also points out that there is no uniform pattern of subsidy followed by states and the connection between subsidy and sanitation coverage is not strong.

(d) Lack of awareness and community mobilization

Another factor that affects the usage of toilets in rural India is lack of awareness among people about how to use, maintain and empty them.

Many studies have found that although Indian government is spending more money than governments of other countries in construction of toilets yet very often, people who receive government latrines do not use them for defaecation at all; they may repurpose the materials or use the latrine superstructure to bathe or wash clothes. Most people wrongly believe that government-provided soak pits will fill up in a matter of months, rather than years, and will require frequent emptying (Coffey et al. 2017a).

Linking service delivery processes and outcomes in rural sanitation: Findings from 56 districts in India finds that better performing districts under TSC focused on collective behaviour change to use toilets rather than practice open defecation while the poor performing districts focused on individual household toilet construction rather than the need for behaviour change to achieve ODF status.

In a report 'Beyond Sanitation- a story of ODF campaign in Jalna District of Maharashtra', CEO, Zilla Praishad Jalna, highlights the importance of community mobilization, transparency, social restriction, people's involvement through representatives, women empowerment and community leaders as harbingers of change. (Vinayak 2006)

Community-Led Total Sanitation (CLTS): Community-led total sanitation practices can ensure sanitation adoption among community as whole. The community as whole decides to adopt and practice sanitation to make a clean and hygienic environment that benefits everyone (Kar and Chambers 2008).
The following are the basic steps for this sanitation promoting practice: Pre-triggering (Selecting a Community); Triggering (Ignition movement); Post-Triggering (Action planning by the community); Follow-up (Scaling up and going beyond CLTS).
This technique of sanitation promotion practice has been used and promoted among countries like Bangladesh, India, Cambodia, Indonesia, Mongolia, Nepal, China and Pakistan in Asia; in Uganda, Zambia, Ethiopia, Tanzania, Kenya and Sierra Leone in Africa; in Bolivia in South America; in Yemen in the Middle East; and in other countries. It was started in 1999 and used for a long time. This sanitation promotion is still ongoing in some countries (Sharma and Biswas 2016).
'The best thing that one find in this sanitation promotion practice is the engagement of the local people and assisting them in understanding the need for sanitation and training them in using the locally available construction techniques for making toilets. They first of all lay stress on "triggering" which will surely help in gaining the support of the NGOs and other individual and organisations which are working in the field of sanitation and community development. This is evident from the case of Cambodia where government is supporting this campaign' (Kar and Chambers 2008).
Pali and Bikaner in Rajasthan, Nadia in West Bengal and Angul in Odisha have made use of CLTS by engaging the community especially Bal Samities which would whistle at people found defecating in the open as a result of social pressure people discontinued open defecation and in Bikaner the OD figure which were 29 percent in 2011 has changed to 82 percent in 2015.

Decade of the total sanitation campaign: Rapid assessment of processes and outcomes, WSP (2010) also highlights the importance of community mobilization. The report finds that the better performing states have used folk theatre, public meetings, documentary films, television spots, radio jingles, house-to-house visits and Participatory Rural Appraisal (PRA) methods for changing attitudes and behaviour of people. Water and Sanitation Programme (2010), A Decade of the Total Sanitation Campaign: Rapid Assessment of Processes and Outcomes.

Pali in Rajasthan has developed sanitation parks where there are models of affordable toilets that are available along with material needed and cost. People may choose the toilet as per their budget and need. The detailed descriptions of the material needed and the costs involved help visitors decide on a model suited to their need and budget, as also the soil and other conditions in the region.

As per country paper 'Towards Total Sanitation and Hygiene: A Challenge for India' presented at South Asian Conference on sanitation at Dhaka, Bangladesh on 21 to 23 October 2003 of Government of India (2003), the districts which reflected strong commitment to achieve results with a range of innovations, brought the leaders and managers closer to the people and used techniques that were participatory and inclusive were able to achieve better results. The paper highlights that some factors that have stood in the way of effective implementation of a rural sanitation programme include very low priority accorded to sanitation as a social and community issue. Inadequate emphasis on IEC and lack of infrastructure and systems to reach all rural households and inclination to promote a single model, i.e. twin-pit pour flush toilets (which are costly and therefore out of reach of many rural households), heavy reliance on subsidy, lack of motivation among implementers, technology support inconsistent with needs, insufficient involvement of NGOs, CBOs and the private sector, and importantly, scarcity of water. GOI, "Towards Total Sanitation and Hygiene: A Challenge for India" presented at South Asian Conference on Sanitation at Dhaka, Bangladesh on 21st to 23rd October 2003 https://mdws.gov.in/sites/default/files/CountryPaperonSanitationOct2003.pdf accessed on Febrary 22, 2018.

A cross-country evaluation study conducted by Outline India (2015), on behalf of Water Aid, to explore the reasons behind the remarkable performance of five states (Manipur, Sikkim, Meghalaya, Himachal Pradesh and Kerala) that had achieved strikingly good sanitation indices when compared to the national average found that 'Behaviour change' at the grass root level and community engagement in the process of change were the most effective strategies for the implementation of sanitation policies, across the five states.

Water Aid's (2006) report points out that mobilized communities and community leaders have made a great difference in inspiring other communities to act and achieve total sanitation in their villages. Widespread use of Community-Led Total Sanitation (CLTS) has been found to be instrumental in increasing sanitation coverage while weak civil society engagement led to low coverage and poor quality of sanitation facilities. WaterAid, (2006), "Total Sanitation in South Asia: the Challenges Ahead", London: WaterAid, Discussion Paper.

(e) Non-availability of verified data

An important issue pertains to non-availability of verified data on usage of these constructed toilets. The data that exists relates to construction of toilets that are verified and then entered in the information system. However, statewise comprehensive data on usage of toilets is not available. Absence of such data makes it difficult to know the sustainability of the behaviour change. Another problem with data is how to assess the impact of SBM as the programme, as the numbers are not exactly an indicator of the success of the Swacch Bharat Mission alone as it includes toilets constructed under several ongoing schemes such as the National Rural Employment Guarantee Act and the Indira Awas Yojna. Third, there is no data available on the impact of SBM on the disabled and how are they going to be integrated into the system.

(f) Capacity building
Another factor to look at is technology. Can we have same model for all states or do we consider geology, groundwater condition and social aspects of the region for choice of technology. States should also have requisite number of skilled manpower for construction and maintenance of toilets. The system of decentralized governance has not been able to address this issue in many states in an effective manner. Another important factor to be considered is the management of solid and liquid waste so that it does not pollute the soil and water and create health hazards. Efforts should be made to reuse water by adopting rainwater harvesting.

1. Women made inroads into male bastion, by donning the role of sanitation technicians in Gujarat. This has not only improved usage of toilets by women but has also empowered women as they are able to eke out a livelihood doing masonry work.
2. Sitamarhi District Administration (Bihar) in partnership with UNICEF started a unique initiative called Sokhta-Kranti that involves construction of soak pits in the region. The initiative saw the participation of the entire community and led to the construction of 2168 soak pits in schools, healthcare centres, police stations, etc.

8 Summing-up

India started its sanitation programmes in 1986 with CRSP—a nationwide sanitation programme for improving rural sanitation, demand-based Total Sanitation Programme in 1999 with emphasis on community participation and introducing rewards for open defecation-free villages, Nirmal Bharat Abhiyan in 2012 with increased subsidy, but these campaigns were not able to meet their targets and bring about significant change in sanitation scenario of the country. Some of the reasons for these were lack of political commitment as funds were allotted to states in the plan but were not timely released, lack of awareness among people, lack of community mobilization, issues related to maintenance, cost of construction, scarcity of water and technology-related issues.

Swachh Bharat Mission—Gramin, which was launched on 2 October 2014 is a flagship programme of present government and has unprecedented political support. The budget allocation for rural sanitation has increased considerably since 2014 and both centre and states are contributing significant amounts to the programme.

There is a strong relationship between sanitation and development. However, the emphasis of sanitation programme till SGM was more on creating awareness about the importance of construction of IHHL and not on its importance for public health.

India fares badly in global scenario and is responsible for major share of world's open defecation. It is the worst performing country in the South Asian region.

The central allocation towards rural sanitation programmes has been increasing over the years with substantial contribution by states. The states that have achieved ODF status have been consistent in their achievements. The amount paid by beneficiaries has been more than 65:23:14 in better performing states as compared to poor performing states. Under SBM-G, cost of construction of a toilet has been increased to Rs. 12,000 with centre paying 60% and states contributing 40% of the value.

From the analysis, we found that the better performing states have spent more than poor performing states. Under SBM-Gramin states that have been able to improve their performance have spent more than their approved budget, and many states like Madhya Pradesh, Maharashtra, Haryana, Uttarakhand, etc. have made remarkable progress in improving their HH sanitation coverage. Maximum budget has been spent on construction of IHHLs and very less amount on other components like IEC (which as per SBM guidelines should be about 8% of the total budget), sanitary complex expenditure, community incentives to Gram Panchayat (GP) and Solid Liquid Waste Management (SLWM) expenditure.

We found a moderate positive correlation between availability of toilets and per capita income, productivity and literacy rate and weak negative correlation between IMR, under-five mortality rate and poverty with availability of toilets.

The paper found beliefs and values, monitoring and evaluation, lack of awareness, community mobilization, overemphasis on subsidy, non-availability of verifiable data and capacity building at grassroot level as the main challenges that impact achievement of sanitation goals.

Initially, policymakers thought that the subsidy factor will enhance the demand for sanitation structure in rural India but it was proved wrong as sanitation facilities were created through social mobilization and behavioural changes brought by various awareness programme since late 80s. Thus, there is an urgent need to recognize that sanitation results cannot be achieved through increased sanctions or subsidies by government; Uttar Pradesh, Bihar and Odisha are good examples showing that increased expenditure may not result in target achievement.

The focus should be on community involvement for bringing about gradual change in perceptions and beliefs that would result in desired behaviour modification. Many states like Himachal Pradesh, Haryana and Madhya Pradesh have achieved success by using 'shame' and 'disgust' (especially by youth and children) to make people discontinue traditional practice of open defecation. However, one needs to be cautious in using this method as it may bring about temporary behaviour change.

Collaboration between all stakeholders needs to be encouraged: private sector, Gram panchayats, civil society and NGOs must work together.

To address the non-availability of data pertaining to sanitation, SBM has developed a national database with detailed information on latrine coverage down to the household level and a multistage verification process but it needs to collect time-series data to know the actual usage of toilets.

One has to recognize that there is no single fit sanitation system that can be adopted by all states; one needs to look at technical, environmental, financial, institutional, politico-legal and socio-cultural factors as per the local need of the community. It is necessary to empower rural people by involving them in decision-making regarding construction of the type of toilets.

By supporting non-coercive behaviour change, communication programmes, training and deploying field facilitators who can implement CLTS effectively, monitoring the use of toilets and hygiene behaviours, governments can help to make long-lasting change happen that is owned by communities.

And lastly, despite increased focus on sanitation in recent years, India does not have a clearly stated national policy on sanitation to act as a road map for the states, in the absence of which the states have depended on the guidelines of various programmes launched by the government from time to time.

References

Budget Briefs, SBM-G, GOI 2017–18 (vol. 9, issue 1).

Census of India. (2001). *Office of Registrar General and Census Commissioner of India.*

Census of India. (2011). *Office of Registrar General and Census Commissioner of India.*

Chadwick, E. (1842). *Report on an inquiry into the sanitary condition of the labouring population of Great Britain.* London: Her Majesty's Stationery Office.

Chambers, R. (2010). Faecal infections, undernutrition and sanitation‖. Retrieved from http://www.communityledtotalsanitation.org/resource/faecal-infections-undernutrition-and-sanitation , last accessed on 25 January, 2018.

Chambers, R., & VonMedeazza, G. (2013). Sanitation and stunting in India. *Economic & Political Weekly, 48*(25), 15.

Chariar, V. http://www.borgenmagazine.com/open-defecation-indias-health-hazard-poor/.

Coffey, D., Spears, D., & Vyas, S (2017). http://riceinstitute.org/research/switching-to-sanitation-understanding-latrineadoption-in-a-representative-panel-of-rural-indian-households/. Accessed on February 10, 2018.

Coffey, D., Deaton, A., Drèeze, J., Spears, D., & Tarozzi, A. (2013). Stunting among children: Facts and implications. *Economic & Political Weekly, 48*(34), 69.

Coffey, D., Geruso, M., & Spears, D. (2016). Sanitation, disease externalities, and anemia: Evidence from Nepal. *National Bureau of Economic Research, Working Paper 22940.* http://www.nber.org/papers/w22940.

Coffey, D., Gupta, A., Hathi, P., Spears, D., Srivastav, N., & Vyas, S. (2017a). Understanding open defecation in rural india untouchability, pollution, and latrine pits. *Economic & Political Weekly, III*(1), 59–66.

Coffey, D., Spears, D., & Vyas, S. (2017b). http://riceinstitute.org/research/switching-to-sanitation-understanding-latrine-adoption-in-a-representative-panel-of-rural-indian-households/.

Comptroller and Auditor General. (2015). http://www.mdws.gov.in/sites/default/files/12_fyp_vol_2_MDWS.pdf. Accessed February 10, 2018.

Currie, J., & Vogl, T. (2012). Early-life health and adult circumstance in developing countries. *National Bureau of Economic Research, Working Paper 18371*, Cambridge. http://www.nber.org/papers/w18371.

Cutler, D. M., Fung, W., Kremer, M., Singhal, M., & Vogl, T. (2010). Early life malaria exposure and adult outcomes: Evidence from malaria eradication in India. *American Economic Journal: Applied Economics, 2*(2), 196–202.

Cutler, D. M., & Miller, G. (2005). The role of public health improvements in health advances: The twentieth-century United States. *Demography, 42*(1), 1–22.

Economist. (2017). *Missing the mark*. https://www.economist.com/news/asia/21726756-building-lots-toilets-does-not-guarantee-they-will-be-used-indian-officials-are-humiliating. Accessed January 15, 2018.

Fewtrell, L., Kaufmann, R. B., Kay, D., Enanoria, W., Haller, L., & Colford, J. M., et al. (2005). Sanitation, and hygiene interventions to reduce diarrhoea in less developed countries: A systematic review and meta-analysis. *The Lancet Infectious Diseases, 5*(1), 42–52 (PubMed).

Ghosh, A., Gupta, A., & Spears, D. (2014). Are children in West Bengal shorter than children in Bangladesh. *Economic & Political Weekly, 48*.

Hathi, P. et al. (forthcoming). Place and child health: The interaction of population density and sanitation in developing countries. *Demography*.

Headey, D. D. (2015). The nutritional impacts of sanitation at scale: Ethiopia, 2000–2011. *Working paper, IFPRI*.

Hindu. (2016). http://www.thehindu.com/data/What-numbers-tell-us-about-Open-Defecation-in-India/article15422326.ece on February 4, 2018.

Hutton, G., Rodriguez, U. E., Napitupulu, L., Thang, P., & Kov, P. (2008). *Economic impacts of sanitation in Southeast Asia*. Jakarta: World Bank.

Indian Institute Of Mass Communication. (1998). *Water and sanitation a baseline survey*. On Behalf of Rajiv Gandhi National Drinking Water Mission. http://www.mdws.gov.in/sites/default/files/IIMC_Report.pdf. Accessed January 25, 2018.

Isunju, J. B., Schwartz, K., Schouten, M. A., Johnson, W. P., & van Dijk, M. P. (2011). Socio-economic aspects of improved sanitation in slums: A review. *Public Health, I25*, 368–376. https://www.researchgate.net/publication/281093499_Isunju_et_al_2011.

Kar, K., & Chambers, R. (2008). *Handbook on community-led total sanitation*. Brighton, BN1 9RE, UK.: Institute of Development Studies at the University of Sussex.

Mara, D., Lane, J., Scott, B., & Trouba, D. (2010). Sanitation and health. *PLoS Med, 7*(11), e1000363. https://doi.org/10.1371/journal.pmed.1000363.

Mathers, C. D., Lopez, A. D., & Murray, C. J. L. (2006). The burden of disease and mortality by condition: Data, methods, and results for 2001. In: A. D. M. C. Lopez, M. Ezzati, D. T. Jamison, & C. J. L. Murray (Eds.), *Global burden of disease and risk factor* (pp. 45–240). New York: Oxford University Press (PubMed).

Media Centre- Factsheets. http://www.who.int/mediacentre/factsheets/fs392/en/. Accessed January 27, 2018.

Mehrotra S., & Ghosh, D. (2013). *Addressing the world's worst sanitation problem: a programme re-design to use not just build toilets*. IAMR Occasional Paper No. 2/2013.

Nandi, A., Megiddo, I., Ashok, A., Verma, A., & Laxminarayan, R. (2016). Reduced burden of childhood diarrheal diseases through increased access to water and sanitation in India: A modeling analysis. *Social Science & Medicine*.

Nathoo, L. (2015). http://www.independent.co.uk/news/world/asia/india-rejects-the-toilet-how-government-sanitation-drives-have-failed-to-sway-those-who-believe-10466041.html. Accessed January 30, 2018.

NDTV. http://swachhindia.ndtv.com/india70-two-decades-and-the-five-year-plans-which-focused-on-sanitation-10604/. Accessed January 20, 2018.

NITI Aayog. (2015). Report of the Sub-Group of Chief Ministers on Rationalisation of Centrally Sponsored Schemes, August 2013.

Outline India. (2015). http://www.dnaindia.com/analysis/column-the-invisible-thought-partner-for-a-swachh-bharat-2111087. Accessed February 1, 2018.

Planning Commission. (2013). *Evaluation study on total sanitation campaign*. Programme Evaluation Organisation.

Prüss-Üstün, A., Bos, R., Gore, F., & Bartram, J. (2008). *Safer water, better health: Costs, benefits and sustainability of interventions to protect and promote health*. Geneva: World Health Organization.

Shandra, C. L., & Shandra, J. M. (2011). *World Bank structural adjustment, water, and sanitation: A cross-national analysis of child mortality in Sub-Saharan Africa*. Bruce London.
Sharma, S. N., & Biswas, A. (2016). Best practices for ensuring total sanitation. *International Journal of Research (IJR)*. https://internationaljournalofresearch.com/2016/09/16/best-practices-for-ensuring-total-sanitation/?\. Accessed April 10, 2018.
Spears, D. (2012). Policy lessons from implementing India's total sanitation campaign. *India Policy Forum–2012–13*, http://testnew.ncaer.org/image/userfiles/file/IPF-Volumes/Volume%209/2_Dean%20Spears.pdf.
Spears, D. (2013). How much international variation in child height can sanitation explain? *World Bank Policy Research Working Paper 6351*.
Twelfth Five Year Plan. (2012–2017). Rural drinking water and sanitation. *Economic Sectors Volume II*. Planning Commission, Government of India.
UN. End Open Defecation. http://www.un.org/millenniumgoals/endopendefecation.shtml. Accessed February 9, 2018.
UNICEF. (1999). *Sanitation and hygiene: A right for every child*, New York.
UNICEF, & WHO. (2017). *Progress on sanitation and drinking-water-2017 update*, Geneva.
Vinayak, N. (2006). *Beyond sanitation' 2006–07*. Pune: Yashvant Rao Chavan Academy of Development Administration.
Vyas, S. (2014). http://www.business-standard.com/article/opinion/sangita-vyas-most-rural-indians-can-afford-a-toilet-but-don-t-want-one-114061001295_1.html. Accessed February 1, 2018.
WaterAid. (2008a). *Feeling the pulse: A study of the total sanitation campaign in five states*.
WaterAid. (2008b). *Tackling the silent killer: The case for sanitation*. New Delhi.
World Bank, Water and Sanitation Program. (2007). *An approach that works: Community led total sanitation in rural areas*. New Delhi: Water and Sanitation Program.
World Bank, Water and Sanitation Program. (2008). *Linking service delivery processes and outcomes in rural sanitation: Findings from 56 districts in India*.
World Bank. (2008a). *Economic impacts of sanitation in Cambodia: A five-country study conducted in Cambodia, Indonesia, Lao PDR, the Philippines, and Vietnam under the economics of sanitation initiative*. Water and sanitation program research report, Jakarta.
WHO. (2017). http://www.who.int/mediacentre/factsheets/fs392/en/.
World Health Organization. (2009). *Global health risks: Mortality and burden of disease attributable to selected major risks*, Geneva.
Wright, A. M. (1997). *Toward a strategic sanitation approach: Improving the sustainability of urban sanitation in developing countries*, UNDP-World Bank.
World Bank, Water and Sanitation Programme_India_TSC_Report_Vol 1_Press.

Websites Accessed between January 10—February 20, 2018

http://www.wsp.org/content/economic-impacts-sanitation.
http://www.unicefrosa-progressreport.org/opendefecation.html.
http://unicef.in/Story/798/Improved-water-and-sanitation-to-speed-up-the-achievement-of-all-eight-MDGs.
http://sbm.gov.in/sbmreport/Report/Physical/SBM_TargetVsAchievement.aspx.
http://www.indiabudget.gov.in/ub2018-19/impbud/impbud.pdf.
http://indiaenvironmentportal.org.in/files/file/Swachhta_%20Status_Report2016.pdf.
http://swachhbharatmission.gov.in/sbmcms/writereaddata/images/pdf/report/Swachh-Survekshan-2016.pdf.
http://www.dnaindia.com/analysis/column-the-invisible-thought-partner-for-a-swachh-bharat-2111087.
http://www.indiaenvironmentportal.org.in/files/file/Linking-Service-Delivery-Processes-Outcomes-Rural-Sanitation-Findings-Districts-India.pdf. Accessed on January 22, 2018.
http://www.borgenmagazine.com/open-defecation-indias-health-hazard-poor/.

https://rbidocs.rbi.org.in/rdocs/Publications/PDFs/13SDP_240617EE2A8970184542E895DCE89D75A02259.PDF.

http://www.esopb.gov.in/Static/PDF/GSDP/Statewise-Data/StateWiseData.pdf.

http://www.pincodeindia.net/gdp-growth-rate.php. Accessed on February 11, 2018.

http://www.censusindia.gov.in/Vital_Statistics/SRS_Life_Table/2.Analysis_2010-14.pdf.

http://niti.gov.in/content/infant-mortality-rate-imr-1000-live-births. Accessed on February 11, 2018.

https://community.data.gov.in/tateut-wise-under-five-mortality-rate-during-2015-16/.

https://www.rbi.org.in/scripts/PublicationsView.aspx?id=16603.

http://sbm.gov.in/sbmdashboard/. Accessed on February 17, 2018.

http://sbm.gov.in/sbmReport/Report/Monitoring/SBM_GetAIPDetails.aspx. (Format I02) Accessed on February 15, 2018.

http://swachhbharatmission.gov.in/sbmcms/writereaddata/images/pdf/report/Swachh-Survekshan-2016.pdf.

http://sbm.gov.in/sbmReport/Report/Financial/.

http://sbm.gov.in/sbmReport/Report/Financial/SBM_StateReleaseAllocationincludingUnapproved.aspx.

http://sbm.gov.in/sbmreport/Report/Physical/SBM_TargetVsAchievement.aspx.

http://www.indiawaterportal.org/data-apps/#Money%20spent%7CSpending%20on%20rural%20sanitation.

http://tsc.gov.in/tsc/Report/Financial/RptFinancialProgressStatewiseDistrictwise.aspx%3Fid%3DHome, http://data.gov.in/dataset/nirmal-bharat-abhiyan-district-wise-financial-progress-date.

http://www.indiaenvironmentportal.org.in/files/file/Households%20without%20Toilet%20Facilities.pdf.

http://unicef.in/Story/798/Improved-water-and-sanitation-to-speed-up-the-achievement-of-all-eight-MDGs.

http://www.mdws.gov.in/sites/default/files/12_fyp_vol_2_MDWS.pdf.

http://swachhindia.ndtv.com/india70-indias-first-nationwide-sanitation-programme-in-1986-focused-on-improving-rural-sanitation-10640/.

https://washdata.org/data and http://www.hdr.undp.org/en/composite/HDI.

http://www.unicefrosa-progressreport.org/opendefecation.html.

http://www.wsp.org/content/economic-impacts-sanitation.

https://economics.mit.edu/files/10743.

Exploring the Reasons for Non-utilization of Family Planning and Reproductive Health Services in Kanpur Nagar District of Uttar Pradesh

Richa Sharma

1 Introduction

Right to health is a basic human right and flows from the right to life. Article 3 of the Universal Declaration of Human Rights, 1948 which India also ratified, states in unambiguous terms that every person has the right to life. Specific mention of the right to health has been made in Article 25 of the Declaration which states that every person has a right to a standard of living adequate for the health and well-being of himself and of his family. This includes food, medical care and right to security in the event of sickness. The Declaration also states that motherhood and childhood are entitled to special care and assistance. The Indian Constitution, though does not specifically mentions right to health as a fundamental right it does, however, under Article 47, a Directive Principle of State Policy, lay down that '*the State shall regard the raising of the level of nutrition and the standard of living of its people and the improvement of public health as among its primary duties*……'. Other Directive Principles of State Policy speak of the duty of the State to provide for maternity relief, and to make effective provision for the right to public assistance in case of sickness.

It is proven beyond doubt that '*Health*' is a highly valued goal and a key indicator measuring the quality of life of the people of the country. For the growth and development of the nation state, it is important for the human resource to be healthy enough to contribute to such growth and development of the nation. Thus, health is recognized as a key component and a vital indicator of the nation's human capital. Rightly so the Alma Ata Declaration in 1978 to which India also is a signatory, brought back health at the centre stage of human development by reaffirming health as a fundamental right and indicated the goals, the principles and the framework for attaining health.

R. Sharma (✉)
National Institute of Labour Economics Research and Development, Delhi, India
e-mail: richasharmanilerd@gmail.com

NILERD, *Reflecting on India's Development*,
https://doi.org/10.1007/978-981-13-1414-8_16

India's development experience in areas including Family Welfare and public health demonstrates that political will, leadership, action and mobilization, drive success. Therefore, India launched the National Family Planning Programme in 1951 with the objective of '*reducing the birth rate to the extent necessary to stabilize the population at a level consistent with the requirement of the National economy'.* With the aim to achieve goals of population stabilization, the Government of India from time to time reviewed its policies, adopted its strategies and its activities. But in spite of the family planning programme, being in existence for nearly 68 years, the population stabilization still remains a distant dream as the prime objective under the National Population Policy (2000) of achieving total fertility rate of 2.1 by the year 2010 is still elusive.

If it is to list the reasons why despite best of the efforts and elaborate family welfare programmes and huge governmental spending, India's progress in controlling its runaway population has been limited besides low levels of achievement on range of reproductive, health care and family planning indices, may broadly be classified into

- Lack of universal access to basic healthcare facilities even today.
- High infant and child mortality rates in high population growth states.
- Low literacy rates, especially female literacy.
- Persistence of high levels of rural and urban poverty.
- Inadequate awareness of options to meet the unmet needs for reproductive and family planning services.

In India, there are wide disparities between rural and urban areas in infrastructure facilities and social services. The rural–urban distribution of population, therefore, becomes important in terms of availability and accessibility of healthcare facilities and qualified healthcare providers. Secondary and tertiary health care, in particular, tend to congregate in urban areas. Even urban slums in urban areas, a characteristic feature of India cities where majority of the city population lives, are considered to have much better access to healthcare facilities than rural areas. The problem of access is particularly difficult in the case of small villages and scattered settlements in remote backward, tribal and hilly areas.

Since the launch of healthcare programmes in India, the focus was primarily on increasing the reach and access of healthcare services among the rural population. Little or no attention was paid to urban healthcare services. Population in urban areas was just 11.4% in 1901 which increased to 28.53% in 2001 to 31.16% in 2011. According to an estimate (RGI 2006), the urban population from its current level is estimated to increase to 43.2 crores by 2021. It is further estimated that slum population in urban areas in India will grow at double the rate of urban population during the next few decades. Ever increasing urban population and the sheer absence of the urban healthcare policies and programmes had not only put tremendous pressure on the healthcare services which already are in bad shape but has also led to tremendous increase in the slum settlements with very poor reach and access to basic healthcare facilities and other basic minimum for a healthy life.

The National Rural Health Mission programmes launched in 2005 saw a paradigm shift in the implementation of the family welfare programmes in India. The focus under NRHM shifted family welfare to health. NRHM being a centrally sponsored scheme had a pre-agreed funds sharing pattern between centre and states. Range of conditional cash transfer schemes were devised and implemented in order to increase the utilization of reproductive and child health services at health institution under the supervision of trained medical practitioner. This saw marked shift from home to institutional deliveries. The health indicator such as anaemia among pregnant women resulting in low birth weight babies still needs lot of attention. As the NRHM evolved, it was felt that the focus largely still remained at improving the reach and access of healthcare services in rural areas. Urban counterparts were totally left out. Thus, in 2013 realizing this felt need of providing basic healthcare services to the urban residents the National Urban Health Mission (NUHM) programmes were launched in May 2013 to try and bridge the very poor reach and access to basic healthcare facilities in urban slum settlements. Urban PHCs were built right within the identified slum areas providing basic preventive and curative healthcare services within slums.

Apart from the availability/access constraints, there are some deep-rooted cultural practices and mindset that restricts people from seeking institutionalized healthcare services in times of need. Benson (2000) elaborated seven concepts for physicians to tackle the culture of poverty syndrome among care seekers. It is this culture of poverty syndrome evident among Indian population that leads to non-compliance on range of healthcare services that is provided to them. Be its consumption of 100 plus IFA tablets during pregnancy, or initiation of breastfeeding within one hour of delivery or seeking healthcare services from local available quacks instead of visiting healthcare facility for proper treatment and check-ups, etc.

2 Literature Review

Generally speaking, government healthcare providers are crowded and have longer waiting time in India, the reason, why even the poor people rush to private health care providers if someone falls sick in the household. The other problem with the government health facility is that they are built on land that is free and provided by the local administration. Often availability of such land use to be away from the main habitation leading to longer travel time to cover such long distances to reach the health facility. If these two factors are discounted, the government healthcare providers are far better than the private healthcare provider. The 2012 study published in PLOS Medicine by Basu et al. (2012) which evaluated the performance of public and private healthcare systems in low- and middle-income countries concluded that they did not find any evidence to support that the private sector healthcare provider is more efficient, accountable or medically effective than the public healthcare provider. However, it was mentioned that public healthcare provider lacks timeliness and hospitality towards patients. Indian Public Health Care System is unparalleled in the world providing almost free preventive and curative healthcare services to its population.

It is important to explore the reasons of non-use of contraception and other reproductive care services by the end users as it helps informed decision-making leading to better policy intervention. Recent studies exploring the reasons for such non-use of services are limited for the want of quality data. Retrospective demographic and health surveys have their limited scope within which they are conducted, and it is often entirely missing or left out to explore detailed reasons for non-use of family planning and other government healthcare services. In 2007, the study published by Guttmacher Institute looked into the factors responsible for contraceptive use and non-use in United States leading to unintended pregnancy. The finding from the study suggested government to asses the method specific use difficulties and regular counselling of women regarding method choice. Khader et al. (2006) in their study published in 2006 focusing IUCD discontinuation rate, causes and its determinants among Jordanian women visiting UNRWA health centres suggest the desire to conceive as the prime reason for IUCD discontinuation. The study suggested better counselling and case selection for better IUCD retention rates. T. Ping in his 1995 study focusing four countries north of China studied the IUD discontinuation pattern and its correlates after the initiation of provincial family planning regulations and the family planning target responsibility system. The findings from the study suggest that the pattern of discontinuation was contingent on individual demographic profile such as parity of women and other institutional variables. Women with one child were more likely to discontinue IUD compared to those with two or more children. The push for sterilization by the government and sterilization being preferred choice among higher parity women is also contributing factor for IUD discontinuation. Andrade and Orchard (1987) reported that the pain and blood loss due to IUD during the first month is an issue in developing countries where anaemia among women is already very high and blood loss due to IUD compounds of the problem. Da Silva et al. (1987) using 148 users as their study subject in Brazil reported excessive bleeding as prime reason for IUD removal. Toivonen et al. (1987) in 1987 reported similar findings of increased bleeding and pain. They also reported spontaneous ejection of IUD due to poor placement and unsuitability by the uterus. They also reported a tendency to develop venereal disease as a contraindication for IUD use. Hubacher et al. (2009) in their 2006 study on IUD hypothesized that increased uterine bleeding and pain leads to IUD removal and they studied 1947 prospective first time IUD users for a period of 1 year. The study reported more menstrual pain among those with IUD than without IUD. However, mixed effect regression approach applied to several groups showed decreased menstrual pain and bleeding over time. They reported older women being better off than younger women in managing side effects. However, inter-menstrual spotting tended to get worse over time among IUD users as the reasons for removal. In their study, they found nulliparous women reporting increased levels of side effects, compared to parous women. Pastermack et al. in 2012 explored if the bleeding and cramping was the reason for IUD removal more among adolescents than adult women. They concluded that adolescents were not more likely to remove IUD compared to adults. Kolding and Majeed (2013) study also reported prolonged bleeding and pain as the most common reasons for early removal of intrauterine device.

To prevent anaemia during pregnancy, 100+ IFA tablets are issued to women attending antenatal care clinics as the consumption of IFA not only reduces maternal morbidity but reduced the chance of premature birth. In spite of huge benefits of 100 plus IFA consumption during pregnancy, the NFHS-4 data shows only 30.3% of the women in India having consumed all the IFA tablets issued to them. This percentage in Uttar Pradesh as per NFHS-4 (2015–16) was just 12.9%. The percentage was mere 6.0% in 2005–06 (NFHS-3). Not consuming all of the IFA is the prime reason for low birth weight babies leading to premature deaths and high neonatal burden in Uttar Pradesh. Pal et al. in their 2013 study focusing rural India suggested poor compliance on the IFA tablets received and suggested more training of frontline health workers for compliance. Sarada and Thilak (2016) in their evaluation on Weekly Iron Folic Acid Supplementation (WIFS) programme for adolescent in rural schools of Kannur in Kerala cited parent's resistance/they feeling healthy as the prime reason for non-consumption of issued WIFS tablets. Besides, it was also cited that they developed stomach pain hence did not consumed. Gautam et al. (2005) study on IFA cited poor compliance and women citing 'forgot to take tablets' as the main reasons for non-consumption. The study also suggested evolving better operational strategies to increase IFA intake among pregnant women. Ogbuanu et al. (2009) study looked into variations in the self-reported reasons for not breastfeeding race/ethnicity and other selected maternal and hospital support characteristics. According to the study, 38% of Arkansas mothers did not initiate breastfeeding as envisaged in 'Healthy People 2010' breastfeeding objectives of United States. Individual reasons were cited by mothers who never breastfed their child. The study recommended targeting subgroups of population such as Black Hispanics, etc. for improved rates of Breastfeeding. India has nearly universal breastfeeding policy and adherence is good. To support and achieve universal breastfeeding goal apart from governmental efforts, donor-supported programmes such as infant and child feeding programme are also taken up from time to time. The current study using the USAID Kanpur 2006 reproductive and child health survey looks into the reasons for not using public health facility when sick by place of residence. The study also analyzes the reasons for not using contraception, discontinuation of IUCD, reasons for not breastfeeding besides reasons for not consuming full set of IFA tablets during pregnancy and differentials by place of residence, if any.

Uttar Pradesh being the largest state in India in terms of Population and Kanpur Nagar district being an important industrial city of Uttar Pradesh the district was natural choice for being the study subject. It has a population of 4,524,324 of which 67% live in urban areas. It is estimated that about 30% of Kanpur urban population lives in slums. The population density in the Kanpur district is 1449 persons per square km. According to Census 2011, the overall sex ratio is 852 females per 1000 males, and child sex ratio (0–6 years) is 870, are lower than the Uttar Pradesh state averages (sex ratio—908 and child sex ratio—899).

3 Objectives

- To study the differences in the levels of the reasons of non-use of reproductive and family planning services by place of residence, and
- To study the differentials in the reasons of non-use of family planning services according to place of residence using multinomial logistic regression.

4 Survey Design, Sample Size and Methodology

Simple percentage distribution was used to study the relative influence of the reasons of not wanting to use government health facility, reasons for never wanting to use contraception, reasons for not consuming IFA tablets and place of delivery in Kanpur Nagar district by place of residence. To study the differentials by place of residence, multinomial logistic regression analysis was also carried out.

Kanpur Nagar reproductive and child health survey was designed to provide estimates for key parameters at the district level, also disaggregated by rural, urban slum and urban non-slum place of residence. Totally, 5000 households were selected, comprising 2000 households from rural areas and 1500 households each from urban slum and urban non-slum areas. A two-stage sampling procedure was adopted. In the first stage, 80 villages (Primary Sampling Units—PSUs) were selected using the probability proportional to size (PPS) methodology. In case of small villages having less than 50 households, link villages were selected and villages having more than 300 households were segmented, and two segments were selected for household listing and interviews. All the households in the selected village were listed and grouped into households having a child below 3 years (stratum 1) and those not having a child below 3 years (stratum 2). In the second stage, 25 households (15 from stratum 1 and 10 households from stratum 2) were selected using circular systematic sampling with a random start. The households selected were then administered the survey questionnaire. In urban areas, a three-stage sampling procedure was adopted. In the first stage, 250 Census Enumeration Blocks (CEBs) were selected using a simple random sampling technique. In the second stage, all 250 CEBs were classified as slum and non-slum after spot verification, and 75 CEBs each from the slum and non-slum strata were selected. All the households in the CEBs selected in the second stage were listed, and grouped into households having a child below 3 years (stratum 1) and those not having a child below 3 years (stratum 2). In the final stage, 20 households (12 households from stratum 1 and 8 households from stratum 2) were selected using circular systematic sampling with a random start. These households in urban areas were then administered the survey questionnaire. Interviews were completed in 4781 households, with an overall completed household response rate of 95.6%. The completed household response rate from rural areas was 96.6, urban non-slum areas had a response rate of 95.2, and in urban slums the response rate was 94.8%. From the 4781 households covered, 5329 currently married women age 15–49 years (eligible women) were identified. Interviews were successfully conducted for 4806 eligible women, with overall completed eligible women (EW) response rate of 90.2. The completed eligible women (EW) response rate was highest in rural areas (93.5%) and lowest in urban non-slum areas (86.8%).

5 Findings

Looking at the utilization pattern of family planning and reproductive health services among urban rich and urban poor in Uttar Pradesh intervention strategies could be prioritized for better programme outcomes. Using the USAID Reproductive Health Survey (UP-RHS) of 2006 the data was analysed to look into the Family Planning and Reproductive Health services utilization pattern among urban poor and urban rich within the urban areas to have a broad overall picture of the prevailing gaps in the utilization pattern before looking into the reasons of non-use of such services in Kanpur Nagar district. While the use of any modern contraceptives was 52% among urban rich, only 24% urban poor used such methods of contraception. The unmet demand for family planning in Uttar Pradesh in 2006 among urban poor was much higher (35%) compared to urban rich (19%). Ninety-eight percent of the urban rich utilized any ANC services during pregnancy, while only 75% of the urban poor did so. Fifty-two percent of the urban rich made 4 + ANC visits, while only 20% of the urban poor made such visits to hospital during pregnancy. The compliance on 100+ Iron and Folic Acid tablet consumption was much better (64%), while only 19% consumed all the 100+ IFA tablets among urban poor. Two doses of Tetanus Toxid injections were received by 91% of the of the Urban rich, while only 44% of the urban non-poor received two doses of the TT injections during pregnancy. These findings clearly indicate wide health utilization gaps within urban areas of Uttar Pradesh justifying the need for focused urban health intervention which rightly came so in the year 2013 in the form of National Urban Health Mission (NUHM) by the Ministry of Health and Family Welfare (MOHFW), Government of India.

Table 1 presents the reasons for not using government health facility for household members, i.e. children, male and female in times of sickness. For the treatment of children, the most cited reasons for non-utilization were the poor quality of care provided by government health facilities (56.5%), non-availability of a nearby facility (49.8%) and waiting time being too long (28%) at the government

Table 1 Reasons for not utilizing government health facilities for children, females and male

Reasons	Urban			Rural	All areas
	Non-slum	Slum	Total		
Children					
No nearby facility	45.9	55.4	49.0	51.4	49.8
Timing not convenient	9.8	8.1	9.2	7.7	8.8
Health personal often absent	11.2	8.9	10.5	15.1	11.9
Waiting time too long	32.6	30.3	31.8	19.5	28.0
Poor quality of care	61.8	52.2	58.6	51.6	56.5
Do not know the place	3.5	6.2	4.4	3.7	4.2
Other	12.1	10.1	11.5	16.2	12.9
Number of households	1667	827	2494	1133	3627
Females					
No nearby facility	45.7	55.6	48.9	52.4	50.0
Timing not convenient	9.4	7.8	8.9	7.6	8.5
Health personal often absent	11.3	8.8	10.5	15.0	11.9
Waiting time too long	33.5	29.4	32.2	18.6	28.0
Poor quality of care	60.8	51.7	57.9	51.6	55.9
Do not know the place	3.1	6.5	4.2	3.6	4.0
Other	12.3	10.1	11.6	15.6	12.8
Number of households	1894	892	2787	1244	4030
Males					
No nearby facility	45.7	54.5	48.6	52.1	49.7
Timing not convenient	9.4	8.4	9.1	7.6	8.6
Health personal often absent	11.0	8.6	10.3	15.1	11.7
Waiting time too long	32.6	29.6	31.6	18.7	27.6
Poor quality of care	61.1	52.1	58.2	51.2	56.0
Do not know the place	2.9	6.0	3.9	3.7	3.8
Other	12.8	10.4	12.0	15.9	13.2
Number of households	1897	904	2801	1252	4053

Percent distribution of households not utilizing government health facilities by reasons for not utilizing them, Kanpur Nagar, 2006

health facility. Across the place of residence (urban non-slum, slum and rural), these were most important reasons cited by the household members while not seeking treatment of sick children at government health facility. Regarding the treatment for females and males too, the most cited reasons for not using the government health facility were poor quality of care, non-availability of nearby government facilities and waiting time being too long at the health facility. Urban areas have little longer waiting time at government facilities which are obvious due to overcrowding at these facilities.

Responses were also coded on the average distance that household inmates travel to seek delivery care services both for private and government providers and are presented in Table 2. Higher percentages (49%) of households reported nearest health facility being a government health facility for delivery, while 44% cited private health facility and 7% reported NGO sector health facility as nearby health facility for delivery care. The government-run facility being near the home was reported by 73% of the rural households, while only 38% in urban households said so. Urban households both non-slum and slum areas reported having private sector hospital (53%) as nearby health facility for delivery care service. The mean distance to the nearest health facility providing delivery care service is 8 km (Table 3). A wide urban–rural difference in mean distance to healthcare facility is observed. In rural areas, nearby delivery care health facility is at 19 km distance, while in urban areas it is just 3 km. NGO run hospitals are concentrated in urban areas as one have to travel 2 km to get delivery care at such facility compared to 19 km in rural areas. Private hospitals are also at a distance of 2–3 km for delivery care services compared to rural counterparts who have to travel in-between 7 and 25 km to seek delivery care at private hospitals. However, since the launch of ambulatory services through 108 and 102 ambulances under National Health Rural Mission (NrHM 2005–12) programmes, the distance to hospitals has been taken care of as these ambulances are available round the clock to the rural as well as urban population.

Table 4 presents the reason for not consuming all the IFA tablets the pregnant women received during their antenatal check-ups. Thirty-nine percent of the women reported feeling sick as the prime reason they did not consume all of the IFA tablet/syrup received. Higher proportion of women (41%) in urban non-slum areas reportedly felt sick compared to slum residents (37.2%). In rural areas, 39% women did not consume all of the IFA tablet/syrup received as they felt sick. Forty-three percent cited reasons other than those listed as standard reasons for not consuming

Table 2 Nearest health facility providing delivery care services

Health facility	Urban			Rural	All areas
	Non-slum	Slum	Total		
Public medical sector					
Govt./municipal hospital	32.4	31.6	32.2	10.2	25.0
Govt. dispensary	0.3	0.0	0.2	0.2	0.2
UHC/UHP/UFWC	1.9	4.3	2.6	1.9	2.4
CHC/PHC/FP centre	0.8	0.9	0.8	60.2	20.1
Other govt. health facility	2.0	1.2	1.7	0.2	1.2
NGO sector	10.3	8.2	9.6	0.6	6.7
Private medical sector					
Pvt. hospital	50.3	52.9	51.1	25.7	42.8
Other pvt. health facility	2.0	0.9	1.6	1.1	1.5
Total percent	100.0	100.0	100.0	100.0	100.0
Number of households	2224	1006	3230	1551	4781

Percent distribution of households by type of nearest health facility providing delivery care services, Kanpur Nagar, 2006

Table 3 Mean distance to the nearest health facility providing delivery care services

Health facility	Urban			Rural	All areas
	Non-slum	Slum	Total		
Public medical sector					
Govt./municipal hospital	2.91	3.33	3.04	22.88	5.66
Other govt. health facility	5.54	4.65	5.22	18.31	16.30
NGO sector	2.31	2.17	2.28	18.63	2.74
Private medical sector					
Pvt. hospital	2.28	1.98	2.19	17.26	5.12
Other pvt. health facility	3.25	3.67	3.32	25.22	8.41
Any govt. facility	3.27	3.55	3.36	18.95	10.86
Any pvt. facility	2.32	2.01	2.32	17.58	5.23
Any facility	2.67	2.61	2.65	18.58	7.82

Mean distance to the nearest health facility providing delivery care services by type of facility, Kanpur Nagar, 2006

Table 4 Reasons for not consuming all IFA tablet/syrup received by selected characteristics

Characteristics	Reasons for not consuming all IFA tablet/syrup received[a]							Number of mothers[b]
	Don't need them all	Consti pation	Pain in abdomen	Stomach upset or diarrhoea	Feeling sick	Black stools	Others	
Age (in years)								
15–19	10.8	18.1	8.2	2.6	27.0	2.1	53.9	17
20–24	14.9	2.6	4.8	5.6	40.1	0.0	45.8	88
25–34	16.6	10.4	6.7	6.2	39.9	0.7	38.1	69
35–49	14.4	10.5	11.0	7.7	40.7	0.0	38.7	12
Parity								
1	16.2	5.8	5.2	6.3	34.2	0.0	48.9	59
2	16.5	5.0	5.9	4.6	46.9	0.7	38.8	52
3	8.1	5.9	8.6	6.8	41.4	0.0	46.9	28
4+	16.5	13.0	6.4	5.4	34.3	1.0	38.9	48
Place of residence								
Urban non-slum	15.4	7.0	2.8	7.6	40.8	0.0	41.3	43
Urban slum	12.6	6.0	7.9	1.7	37.2	0.8	48.5	43
Urban	14.0	6.5	5.4	4.6	39.0	0.4	44.9	86
Rural	16.1	8.2	6.9	6.6	38.7	0.5	41.8	101
Religion								
Hindu	15.7	7.9	6.2	6.6	40.4	0.3	40.8	153
Muslim	12.6	5.4	6.5	1.3	32.4	1.1	53.7	33
Other	0.0	0.0	0.0	0.0	0.0	0.0	100.0	0

(continued)

Table 4 (continued)

Characteristics	Reasons for not consuming all IFA tablet/syrup received[a]							Number of mothers[b]
	Don't need them all	Consti pation	Pain in abdomen	Stomach upset or diarrhoea	Feeling sick	Black stools	Others	
Caste/tribe								
Scheduled caste/tribe	17.3	10.8	8.8	6.8	34.0	0.6	41.4	58
Other backward caste	12.8	7.3	7.1	5.7	43.5	0.6	41.6	79
Other	16.4	3.6	1.6	4.3	37.1	0.0	48.2	49
Education								
Illiterate	16.6	6.9	6.3	3.5	32.5	0.5	45.5	69
Literate, <8th grade	15.0	3.5	9.2	4.0	40.8	0.0	45.9	35
8–11th grade	12.6	8.5	5.5	7.7	43.0	0.8	41.7	59
12+ grade	18.9	12.2	2.7	8.9	42.2	0.0	39.7	22
Other (informal)	0.0	10.8	10.8	15.7	73.5	0.0	0.0	2
SLI quintiles								
Q1	13.3	9.6	9.6	5.2	33.5	0.0	38.3	37
Q2	17.0	4.5	4.5	5.9	40.9	0.0	44.1	49
Q3	11.5	6.9	6.9	3.5	40.4	2.0	42.0	42
Q4	15.2	5.0	5.0	4.1	36.0	0.0	53.9	38
Q5	21.8	4.8	4.8	13.4	45.7	0.0	33.1	20
Total	15.1	7.4	6.2	5.7	38.8	0.4	43.3	187

Percentage of mothers who received IFA tablet/syrup and not consumed all of them by reasons for not consuming, according to selected characteristics, Kanpur Nagar, 2006

[a]Total percent may not add to 100.0 because of multiple responses

[b]Mothers who gave birth to a child during last 2 years preceding the survey and received IFA tablet/syrup

all of IFA/syrup issued to them. Fifteen percent said they do not need them all. Within urban areas, higher proportion of non-slum residents (15.4%) than slum residents (12.6%) reported they do not need all the IFA tablets issued. In rural areas, 16.1% of the respondents reported they do not need all the IFA tablets issued to them. Stomach upset or diarrhoea was reported by 5.7% of the respondents, as the reason for not consuming all of IFA tablet/syrup. In urban areas, 7.6% of the non-slum and 1.7% of the slum respondents reported stomach upset or diarrhoea for not consuming all of IFA. In rural areas, 6.6% of the respondents reported stomach upset or diarrhoea as the reason for not consuming all the received IFA tablets. Higher proportion (46%) of women belonging to Q5 quintile reported feeling sick as the reason for not consuming all the 100+ IFA tablets issued to them during pregnancy.

Table 5 Current use of contraceptives

Method	Urban			Rural	All areas
	Non-slum	Slum	Total		
Oral pills	4.7	4.3	4.6	2.7	3.9
Condom	17.8	16.2	17.3	10.9	15.2
IUCD/copper-T	3.3	2.6	3.1	1.4	2.5
Injection	0.3	0.5	0.3	0.1	0.2
Female sterilization	17.8	14.7	16.8	13.4	15.7
Male sterilization	0.1	0.1	0.1	0.3	0.2
Rhythm/periodic abstinence	7.9	7.7	7.8	12.1	9.3
Withdrawal	3.2	2.2	2.9	5.0	3.6
Other	0.0	0.3	0.1	0.4	0.2
Not using any method	45.0	51.3	47.0	53.8	49.3
Total percent	100.0	100.0	100.0	100.0	100.0
Any modern method	44.0	38.5	42.2	28.7	37.7
Any modern spacing method	26.1	23.6	25.3	15.0	21.8
Any method	55.0	48.7	53.0	46.2	50.7
Number of women	2178	1031	3209	1597	4806

Percentage distribution of currently married women by current use of contraceptives by method, according to place of residence, Kanpur Nagar, 2006

Table 5 provides the current use of contraception by currently married women by modern method used. This data relates to 2006 and since then there has been increase in the level of current use of modern contraceptive the women. NFHS4 data fact sheet for Kanpur Nagar district which relates year 2015–16 put modern method use at 40%. This is slightly higher than USAID reproductive and child health survey of 2006 which puts modern method use at 38%. Now the question is has the use of modern contraceptive increased just 2% in over ten years? It may probably be so for the fact that the family planning programme is on the back burner since the launch of national rural health mission programmes. This calls for renewed focus of the government to bring family planning programme at the core of all the health-related programmes. The demographic theory says 60% of the contraceptive prevalence rate is needed to reach the goal of total fertility rate of 2.1 or a replacement fertility rate. The use of traditional methods is reported around 19% as per NFHS 4 2015–16 data, which is very high in case of Kanpur Nagar and the effective protection that these traditional methods provide in preventing unwanted pregnancies is very low.

Table 6 provides the reasons for non-use of contraception among those who never used contraceptives. Twenty-six percent said they wanted more children so never used contraception. This was followed by menopause/hysterectomy (17%), sub-fecund/in-fecund (7%), post-partum/breastfeeding and infrequent sex

Table 6 Reasons for never use of contraceptives

Reason	Urban			Rural	All areas
	Non-Slum	Slum	Total		
Husband away	0.7	2.5	1.3	2.6	1.8
Not having sex	0.4	0.0	0.2	0.2	0.2
Infrequent sex	5.1	5.4	5.2	4.5	4.9
Menopausal/hysterectomy	14.9	21.2	17.1	15.8	16.6
Sub-fecund/in-fecund	9.4	6.6	8.4	4.1	6.8
Post-partum/breastfeeding	4.2	4.1	4.2	5.3	4.6
Wants more children	26.0	26.5	26.2	26.3	26.2
Opposed to family planning	0.8	0.1	0.6	0.2	0.4
Husband opposed	4.2	3.7	4.0	4.1	4.0
Other people opposed	0.1	0.3	0.2	1.3	0.6
Against religion	1.2	1.6	1.3	1.1	1.2
Knows no method	0.0	0.3	0.1	0.2	0.2
Knows no source	0.0	0.0	0.0	0.4	0.1
Health concerns	4.0	4.4	4.2	3.0	3.7
Worry about side effects	0.1	1.9	0.7	1.5	1.0
Hard to get method	0.0	0.4	0.1	0.6	0.3
Costs too much	0.0	0.1	0.0	0.0	0.0
Inconvenient	0.0	0.1	0.0	0.2	0.1
Afraid of sterilization	0.0	0.1	0.0	0.9	0.3
Do not like existing methods	1.5	2.6	1.9	2.7	2.2
Other	27.0	17.1	23.5	24.6	23.9
Do not know	0.6	0.9	0.7	0.6	0.7
Total percent	100.0	100.0	100.0	100.0	100.0
Number of women	703	382	1085	638	1724

Percent distribution of never users of contraceptives by reasons for non-use, according to place of residence, Kanpur Nagar, 2006

Note Total may not add to 100.0% because of multiple responses

(5% each), husband opposed or have health concerns (4% each), husband away or do not like existing method (2% each). Table 6 also provides the rural–urban differentials. Not much difference by place of residence categories was observed for the reason wanting to have more children so never used contraceptives which hovered around 26% across urban non-slum, slum and rural areas.

The percentage of slum women citing menopause/hysterectomy as the reason for non-use of contraception was 21%, while 15% said so among those residing in the non-slum areas. Menopause/hysterectomy as the reason for non-use of contraception was cited by 16% of the rural women. Infrequent sex was cited as the reason by 5% of women across place of residence category. Twenty-four percent cited other reasons other than listed as the reason for never use of contraception with 27% saying so in non-slum areas, 17.1% in slum areas and 25% in rural areas.

Table 7 presents the percentage distribution of the lapsed user's of modern contraception especially oral pills, condoms and IUCDs for the reasons of discontinuation. We discuss the reasons for discontinuation of IUCDs mainly as the government time and again launches new types of IUCDs providing protection for longer duration. In the entire sample, only 195 respondents could be traced who discontinued IUCD and provided the reasons for discontinuation of IUCD/Copper-T with 149 from urban areas and 46 from rural areas. Within urban areas, 114 respondents of IUCD/Copper-T discontinuation were from non-slum areas, while 35 were from slum areas. Among those who discontinued IUCD/Copper-T, 40.0% gave reason that it created health problems in them. The percentages in rural areas among those discontinued due to health problems were lower (34.0%) compared to urban areas (41.2%). Within urban areas, 44.2% of the non-slum women said so, while this percentage in slums was 32%. Around 23.1% of the women in Kanpur Nagar discontinued IUCD/Copper-T because they wanted to have a child with higher percentages in rural areas (29%) compared to urban counterparts (2%). Within urban areas, 22% of the non-slum women and 20% of the slum residents discontinued as they wanted more children. Twenty percent of the women respondents said they discontinued IUCD/Copper-T as it created menstrual problems, while higher percentages said so in rural areas (23%) compared to urban areas (19%). Condoms were primarily discontinued as the respondents across place of residence wanted more children, while the oral pills were discontinued as they created health-related problems.

Table 8 presents the percent distribution of children age 0–35 months by reasons for never breastfeeding or stopped breastfeeding, according to place of residence. Twenty-nine percent of the respondents in Kanpur Nagar said they became pregnant so have stopped breastfeeding or never breastfed with higher percentages of women in rural areas (40%) saying so compared to urban (23%) women. Within urban areas, 27% of the slum women and 20% of the non-slum women said so. Twenty-five percent of the women said they got insufficient milk to feed the child, the reason they discontinued breastfeeding with 18% in rural areas and 30% in urban areas saying so. Within urban areas, 31% of the non-slum women and 27% of the slum women cited getting insufficient milk as the reason for discontinuing breastfeeding. Among other reasons for discontinuing breastfeeding or never breastfeeding child includes child refused breast milk (10%) or the respondent was ill or too weak to breastfeed (9.0%), and another 19% said they child was of weaning age so they discontinued breastfeeding. Refusal of breast milk by child was cited more by non-slum (13.0%) compared to slum (8.3%) and rural residents (7.5%).

Table 9 presents the multinomial logit regression estimates for the reasons of contraceptive non-use by place of residence after controlling for respondents current age, religion, caste, respondents education, and husbands educational levels. The 'rural' place of residence category is used as a base category. The standard interpretation of the multinomial logit regression is that for a unit change in the predictor variable, the logit of outcome rural category is expected to change by its respective parameter estimate given the other predictors in the model are held constant.

Table 7 Reasons for discontinuation

Reasons	Urban			Rural	All areas
	Non-Slum	Slum	Total		
Oral pills					
Method failed/got pregnant	7.3	6.6	7.0	10.4	8.0
Lack of sexual satisfaction	0.0	0.4	0.2	0.0	0.1
Created menstrual problem	8.5	7.9	8.3	16.6	10.6
Created health problem	41.3	61.6	49.4	50.8	49.8
Inconvenient to use method	2.5	1.7	2.2	0.0	1.6
Hard to get method	2.7	0.3	1.7	1.1	1.5
Put on weight	2.6	3.7	3.1	0.0	2.2
Did not like the method	4.4	1.4	3.2	2.6	3.0
Wanted to have a child	25.0	14.6	20.9	19.7	20.5
Wanted to replace dead child	0.0	0.0	0.0	0.3	0.1
Lack of privacy	0.0	0.0	0.0	0.0	0.0
Husband away	1.1	3.3	1.9	0.0	1.4
Costs too much	6.0	0.0	3.6	0.0	2.6
Other	8.6	5.5	7.4	6.2	7.0
Number of women	150	99	248	97	346
Condom					
Method failed/got pregnant	10.0	15.7	11.7	11.6	11.7
Lack of sexual satisfaction	14.3	18.0	15.4	5.9	12.3
Created menstrual problem	0.0	1.4	0.4	3.2	1.3
Created health problem	9.7	10.6	10.0	8.9	9.6
Inconvenient to use method	4.3	3.0	3.9	5.4	4.4
Hard to get method	0.8	2.4	1.3	5.2	2.6
Did not like the method	14.1	6.9	12.0	14.5	12.8
Wanted to have a child	44.0	35.6	41.5	38.5	40.5
Wanted to replace dead child	0.0	0.4	0.1	0.3	0.2
Lack of privacy	0.3	0.3	0.3	3.2	1.2
Husband away	1.7	0.5	1.3	3.0	1.9
Costs too much	1.9	0.4	1.5	1.3	1.4
Other	6.9	6.1	6.7	4.3	5.9
Number of women	207	87	294	144	439
IUCD/copper-T					
Method failed/got pregnant	0.5	0.0	0.4	1.7	0.7
Created menstrual problem	19.1	17.8	18.8	23.1	19.8
Created health problem	44.2	31.8	41.2	34.0	39.5
Inconvenient to use method	0.0	1.8	0.4	0.9	0.5
Put on weight	2.6	6.2	3.4	0.0	2.6
Did not like the method	0.0	1.2	0.3	3.6	1.1
Wanted to have a child	21.9	20.2	21.5	28.6	23.1

(continued)

Table 7 (continued)

Reasons	Urban			Rural	All areas
	Non-Slum	Slum	Total		
Lack of privacy	0.0	0.0	0.0	1.0	0.2
Husband away	0.5	0.0	0.4	0.0	0.3
Costs too much	2.3	1.2	2.0	0.0	1.5
Other	16.6	25.4	18.7	9.1	16.4
Number of women	114	35	149	46	195

Percentage of lapsed users of modern spacing methods by reasons for discontinuation, according to method and place of residence, Kanpur Nagar, 2006
Note Total may not add to 100.0% because of multiple responses

Table 8 Reasons for not breastfeeding by place of residence

Reasons	Urban			Rural	All areas
	Non-slum	Slum	Total		
Mother ill/weak	11.9	6.9	9.9	8.2	9.2
Nipple/feeding problem	0.5	0.9	0.7	0.4	0.6
Mother not at home	0.7	0.2	0.5	0.4	0.5
Mother working	1.2	0.3	0.8	0.4	0.7
Became pregnant	20.4	26.8	23.0	39.7	29.3
Starting using contraception	0.0	0.2	0.1	0.0	0.1
Child ill/weak	1.0	1.6	1.3	1.7	1.4
Insufficient milk	31.3	26.9	29.5	18.3	25.2
Child refused	12.5	8.3	10.8	7.5	9.5
Weaning age	17.3	20.9	18.8	18.8	18.8
Other	3.2	6.9	4.7	4.7	4.7
Total percent	100.0	100.0	100.0	100.0	100.0
Number of children	372	262	634	385	1019

Percent distribution of children age 0–35 months by reasons for never breastfeeding or stopped breastfeeding, according to place of residence, Kanpur Nagar, 2006

Therefore in Table 9 the coefficient 0.024 is the multinomial logit estimate comparing those respondents who cited menopausal/hysterectomy as the reason for non-use of contraception compared to those who cited reasons as husband away/not having sex/infrequent sex for urban non-slum place of residence to rural place of residence given the other variable such as respondents current age, religion, caste, respondents education and husbands educational levels are held constant. The multinomial logit for menopausal/hysterectomy as the reason for non-use of contraception relative to those whose husband is away/or not having sex/or had infrequent sex is 0.024 unit higher for urban non-slum residents relative to rural

Table 9 Multinomial logit regression estimates for reasons of non-use of contraception by place of residence

Multinomial logistic regression	Number of obs = 1744			
	LR chi2 (36) = 380.14			
	Prob > chi2 = 000			
Log likelihood = −1659.8797	Pseudo R2 = 0.1027			
	Coef.	**Std. Err.**	**Z**	**P > z**
Urban non-slum residence				
Husband away/not having sex/Infrequent sex (ref)				
Menopause/hysterectomy	0.024	0.36	0.07	0.948
Sub-fecund/in-fecund/post-partum breastfeeding	1.177	0.33	3.48	000***
Want more children	0.861	0.32	2.63	0.009**
Opposed to family planning/husband opposed/other people opposed/against religion	0.865	0.37	2.31	0.021*
Knows no method/knows no source/health concerns/worry about side effects/hard to get method/costs too much/inconvenient/afraid of sterilization/don't like existing methods	0.418	0.36	1.15	0.250
Others/don't know	0.930	0.31	2.95	0.003**
Urban slum residence				
Husband away/not having sex/Infrequent sex (ref)				
Menopause/hysterectomy	0.112	0.29	0.38	0.701
Sub-fecund/in-fecund/post-partum breastfeeding	−0.140	0.28	−0.48	0.628
Want more children	0.036	0.26	0.14	0.891
Opposed to family planning/husband opposed/other people opposed/against religion	−0.384	0.32	−1.18	0.239
Knows no method/knows no source/health concerns/worry about side effects/hard to get method/costs too much/inconvenient/afraid of sterilization/don't like existing methods	0.166	0.28	0.59	0.555
Others/do not know	−0.241	0.26	−0.93	0.354

Place of residence = rural is the base outcome

The predictors controlled in the model includes respondents current age, religion, caste, respondents education and husbands education

***significant at 000 level of significance

**significant at <0.01 level of significance

*significant at <0.05 level of significance

residents given all other predictor variable in the model as constant. However, this was not statistically significant. Similarly, the multinomial logit for respondents citing reason for contraceptive non-use as being sub-fecund/in-fecund/or going through post-partum breastfeeding relative to those whose husband is away/or not having sex/or had infrequent sex is 1.17 unit higher for urban non-slum residents relative to rural residents, given all other predictor variable in the model as constant. Respondents citing reason of contraceptive non-use as wanting to have more children compared to whose husband is away/or did not have sex/or had infrequent sex for them the multinomial logit estimate is 0.86 unit higher for urban non-slum resident compared to rural residents and is statistically significant at one percent level of significance, given all other predictor variable in the model as constant. Respondents citing reason that they are opposed to family planning/husband opposed/other people opposed/or its against religion relative to those whose husband is away/or not having sex/or had infrequent sex for them the multinomial logit estimate is 0.87 unit higher for urban non-slum resident compared to rural residents and is statistically significant at 5% level of significance, given all other predictor variable in the model as constant. The multinomial logit for respondents citing reasons other than listed for not using contraception relative to those whose husband is away/or not having sex/or had infrequent sex for them the multinomial logit estimate is 0.93 unit higher for urban non-slum resident compared to rural residents and is statistically significant at one percent level of significance, given all other predictor variable in the model as constant. There were no significant differences by reasons of non-use of contraceptive among urban slum residents relative to rural residents.

The multinomial logit regression for reasons of non-use for other reproductive health indicator was not taken up due to less number of overall cases.

6 Discussion and Conclusion

As the distance to public health facility is much higher for those living in slums and rural areas, it is something that government have to look into before constructing the new public health facility in any given area. Under the National Urban Health Mission programme of Ministry of Health and Family Welfare, Government of India, rightly so envisaged constructing the Urban Primary Health Care centre's right within the slum communities. Since the launch of NUHM programme in 2013, efforts are on to make more and more urban PHC established and made operational. However, the pace of making urban PHC functional in the districts of Uttar Pradesh needs seeding up in order to reduce poor individuals out of pocket spending on health. More counselling should be provided to non-users of contraceptive methods. Currently, in Uttar Pradesh PPIUCD programme is run with the support of JHEPIGO with the prime focus of increasing the PPIUCD numbers, such programmes should pay more attention in addressing the users concerns and fears through its inbuilt counselling component. Anaemia among pregnant women is a big challenge and realizing the health implications of blood anaemia among pregnant women the National Nutritional Anaemia Prophylaxis Programme (NNAPP) was initiated in 1970. However, even after lapse of 47 odd years, the compliance on 100+ IFA tablets consumption in Uttar Pradesh is very poor. As per NFHS4 data, it is just 12.9%. The current government intervention at the moment is geared towards addressing supply-side bottlenecks while it is high time to evolve strategies that ensure compliance on intake of IFA tablets issued.

7 Policy Recommendation

As the Government of India through Ministry of Health and Family Welfare under its Janani Suraksha Yojana (JSY) scheme is providing cash incentives to pregnant mother for delivering at government health facility and under the Janani Shishu Suraksha Karyakram (JSSK) scheme is providing free transport, check-up, diagnostic and dietary services to the pregnant mothers at the government health facility, it is opportune time to link the cash incentives to be provided only if the pregnant women complied and consumed the issued 100+ IFA tablets. The blood tests are done routinely during antenatal visits of all pregnant women visiting for check-ups as diagnostics tests are free under JSSK scheme, the anaemia levels can be verified through the regular haemogram/haemoglobin test during antenatal visits to health facility. By evolving such mechanism, Government may to some extent will not only be able to check anaemia among pregnant women but also address neonatal deaths. Anaemic women usually deliver low birth weight babies resulting in premature deaths. This may not be difficult implementing as through Mother and Child Tracking System (MCTS) portal each pregnancy is already being micro-managed for services due to the pregnant women. As of now, the governmental response in tackling anaemia during pregnancy is to issue 100+ IFA tablets and syrups, whether or not there was compliance in consuming these tablets is left solely to the pregnant women. To increase uptake of IUCD more counselling especially to address fears relating to health concerns among users is needed.

8 Scope for Future Research

Medical scientist should look into addressing the health concerns of the pregnant mothers for uptake of IFA tablets during pregnancy. Efforts should also be made by the medical fraternity in addressing the IUCD discontinuation rate much of that is as use of IUCD causes health-related problems among pregnant mothers. Retrospective population surveys have their limited ability in providing answers to many of the expert opinions/comments none the less they address large proportion of such comments.

Acknowledgement and Limitation Author would like to place of record their sincere gratitude to Dr. G. Narayana formerly Country Director, Futures Group International India limited for the use of dataset. As the study focuses primarily on the reasons of not using the reproductive and child healthcare services, which is largely a social construct, it is presumed that not much would have changed. USAID survey of 2006 stands out as it was only of its kind which also elicited responses on the reasons for non-use by place of residence (non-slum, slum and rural areas). NFHS-4 data will be used to build this analysis as that being the more recent data available at the district level.

References

Andrade, A. T., & Orchard, E. P. (1987). Quantitative studies on menstrual blood loss in IUD users. *Contraception, 36,* 129–144.

Basu, S., Andrews, J., Kishore, S., Panjabi, R., & Stuckler, D. (2012). Comparative performance of private and public healthcare systems in low-and middle-income countries: A systematic review. *PLoS Medicine, 9*(6), e1001244.

Benson, D. S. (2000). Providing health care to human beings trapped in the poverty culture. *Physician Executive., 26*(2), 28–32.

Da Silva, P. A., Martelly, J. U., Gauza, J. E., & Barbosa, L. C. (1987). Evaluation of the IUD: Causes for removal. *Jornal Brasiliero Ginecologia., 97*(5), 211–213.

Gautam, V. P., Bansal, Y., Taneja, D. K., & Ingle, G. K. (2005). A study on compliance to iron folic acid therapy and its effects on anemia during pregnancy. *India Journal of Preventive and Social Medicine, 3 4,* 102–107.

Hubacher, D., Pai-Lien, C., & ParkSide, S. (2009). Eeffects from the copper IUD: Do they decrease over time? *Contraception, 79*(5), 356–362. https://doi.org/10.1016/j.contraception.2008.11.012.

Khader, Y. S., Qaderi, S. E., & Khader, A. M. (2006). Intrauterine contraceptive device discontinuation among Jordanian women: Rate, causes, and determinants. *Journal of Family Planning Reproductive Health Care, 32*(3), 161–164. https://doi.org/10.1783/147118906777888279.

Kolding, L., & Galib Majeed, H. (2013). Reasons for removal of intrauterine devices among women in general practice. *Ugeskrift for Laeger, 175,* 884–886.

National Family Health Survey 1998-99 (NFHS-2)

National Family Health Survey 2006 (NFHS-3)

National Family Health Survey 2017 (NFHS-4)

National Population Policy. (2000). Planning Commission, Government of India.

Ogbuanu, C. A., Probst, J., Laditka, S. B., Liu, J., Baek, J. D., & Glover, S. (2009). Reasons why women do not initiate breastfeeding: A southeastern state study. *Women Health Issues, 19*(4), 268–278. https://doi.org/10.1016/j.whi.2009.03.005.

Pal, P. P., Sharma, S., Sarkar, T. K., & Mitra, P. (2013). Iron and folic acid consumption by the ante-natal mothers in a rural area of India in 2010. *International Journal of Preventive Medicine, 4*(10), 1213–1216.

Pasternack., Tucker, K., Lovato, C., Espey, E., Ogburn, T., Leeman, L., et al. (2012). Reasons for intrauterine device removal: A comparison of adults and adolescents. *Contraception, 83*(3), 319.

Ping, T. (1995). IUD discontinuation pattern and correlates in four countries in north China. *Studies in Family Planning, 26*, 169–179.
RGI. (2006). *Registrar General & Census Commissioner*. India Ministry of Home Affairs, Government of India.
Sarada, A. K., & Thilak, S. A. (2016). Evaluation of weekly iron and folic acid supplementation programme for adolescents in rural schools of Kannur, North Kerala India: A cross-sectional study. *International Journal of Medical Science and Public Health, 5*, 2259–2263.
Toivonen, J., & Luukkainen, T. (1987). Contraceptive coils and their problems. *Duodecim, 103*(9), 546–551.

The manufacturer's authorised representative in the EU is Springer Nature Customer Service Centre GmbH, Europaplatz 3, 69115 Heidelberg, Germany. If you have any concerns regarding our products, please contact ProductSafety@springernature.com

Printed and bound by CPI Group (UK) Ltd, Croydon, CR0 4YY
01/10/2026
02225861-0017